Belief, Action, and Rationality over Time

Action theorists and formal epistemologists often pursue parallel inquiries regarding rationality, with the former focused on practical rationality, and the latter focused on theoretical rationality. In both fields, there is currently a strong interest in exploring rationality in relation to time. The exploration raises questions about the rationality of certain patterns over time. For example, it raises questions about the rational permissibility of certain patterns of intention; similarly, it raises questions about the rational permissibility of certain patterns of belief. While the action-theoretic and epistemic questions raised are closely related, advances in one field are not always processed by the other. This volume brings together contributions by scholars in action theory and formal epistemology working on questions regarding rationality and time so that researchers in these overlapping fields can profit from each other's insights.

This book was originally published as a special issue of the *Canadian Journal of Philosophy*.

Chrisoula Andreou is Professor of Philosophy at the University of Utah, USA.

Sergio Tenenbaum is Professor of Philosophy at the University of Toronto, Canada.

Previous titles published from the *Canadian Journal of Philosophy*:

New Essays on Thomas Reid
Edited by Patrick Rysiew

New Essays on the Nature of Propositions
Edited by David Hunter and Gurpreet Rattan

Belief, Action, and Rationality over Time
Edited by Chrisoula Andreou and Sergio Tenenbaum

Belief, Action, and Rationality over Time

Edited by
**Chrisoula Andreou and
Sergio Tenenbaum**

LONDON AND NEW YORK

First published 2017
by Routledge
2 Park Square, Milton Park, Abingdon, Oxon, OX14 4RN, UK

and by Routledge
711 Third Avenue, New York, NY 10017, USA

Routledge is an imprint of the Taylor & Francis Group, an informa business

© 2017 Canadian Journal of Philosophy

All rights reserved. No part of this book may be reprinted or reproduced or utilised in any form or by any electronic, mechanical, or other means, now known or hereafter invented, including photocopying and recording, or in any information storage or retrieval system, without permission in writing from the publishers.

Trademark notice: Product or corporate names may be trademarks or registered trademarks, and are used only for identification and explanation without intent to infringe.

British Library Cataloguing in Publication Data
A catalogue record for this book is available from the British Library

ISBN 13: 978-1-138-21496-5

Typeset in Myriad Pro
by RefineCatch Limited, Bungay, Suffolk

Publisher's Note
The publisher accepts responsibility for any inconsistencies that may have arisen during the conversion of this book from journal articles to book chapters, namely the possible inclusion of journal terminology.

Disclaimer
Every effort has been made to contact copyright holders for their permission to reprint material in this book. The publishers would be grateful to hear from any copyright holder who is not here acknowledged and will undertake to rectify any errors or omissions in future editions of this book.

Contents

Citation Information	vii
Notes on Contributors	xi
Foreword *Chrisoula Andreou and Sergio Tenenbaum*	1
1. The real puzzle of the self-torturer: uncovering a new dimension of instrumental rationality *Chrisoula Andreou*	2
2. Rationality with respect to people, places, and times *Larry S. Temkin*	16
3. Action as a form of temporal unity: on Anscombe's *Intention* *Douglas Lavin*	49
4. Synchronic requirements and diachronic permissions *John Broome*	70
5. The courage of conviction *Sarah K. Paul*	87
6. Continuing on *Michael G. Titelbaum*	110
7. Memory, belief and time *Brian Weatherson*	132
8. A defense of objectivism about evidential support *Brian Hedden*	156
9. Don't stop believing *Jennifer Rose Carr*	184
10. Understanding Conditionalization *Christopher J. G. Meacham*	207
11. Risk, rationality and expected utility theory *Richard Pettigrew*	238

CONTENTS

12. Costs of abandoning the Sure-Thing Principle   267
    Rachael Briggs

13. Revisiting Risk and Rationality: a reply to Pettigrew and Briggs   281
    Lara Buchak

    Index   303

Citation Information

The chapters in this book were originally published in the *Canadian Journal of Philosophy*, volume 45, issues 5–6 (October–December 2015). When citing this material, please use the original page numbering for each article, as follows:

Foreword
Foreword
Chrisoula Andreou and Sergio Tenenbaum
Canadian Journal of Philosophy, volume 45, issues 5–6 (October–December 2015) pp. 561

Chapter 1
The real puzzle of the self-torturer: uncovering a new dimension of instrumental rationality
Chrisoula Andreou
Canadian Journal of Philosophy, volume 45, issues 5–6 (October–December 2015) pp. 562–575

Chapter 2
Rationality with respect to people, places, and times
Larry S. Temkin
Canadian Journal of Philosophy, volume 45, issues 5–6 (October–December 2015) pp. 576–608

Chapter 3
Action as a form of temporal unity: on Anscombe's Intention
Douglas Lavin
Canadian Journal of Philosophy, volume 45, issues 5–6 (October–December 2015) pp. 609–629

Chapter 4
Synchronic requirements and diachronic permissions
John Broome
Canadian Journal of Philosophy, volume 45, issues 5–6 (October–December 2015) pp. 630–646

Chapter 5
The courage of conviction
Sarah K. Paul

Chapter 6
Continuing on
Michael G. Titelbaum

Chapter 7
Memory, belief and time
Brian Weatherson

Chapter 8
A defense of objectivism about evidential support
Brian Hedden

Chapter 9
Don't stop believing
Jennifer Rose Carr

Chapter 10
Understanding Conditionalization
Christopher J. G. Meacham

Chapter 11
Risk, rationality and expected utility theory
Richard Pettigrew

Chapter 12
Costs of abandoning the Sure-Thing Principle
Rachael Briggs

Chapter 13
Revisiting Risk and Rationality: a reply to Pettigrew and Briggs
Lara Buchak
Canadian Journal of Philosophy, volume 45, issues 5–6 (October–December 2015) pp. 841–862

For any permission-related enquiries please visit:
http://www.tandfonline.com/page/help/permissions

Notes on Contributors

Chrisoula Andreou is Professor of Philosophy at the University of Utah, USA.

Rachael Briggs is Professor of Philosophy at Stanford University, USA.

John Broome is Emeritus White's Professor of Moral Philosophy at the University of Oxford, UK, and Adjunct Professor of Philosophy at the Australian National University, Canberra, Australia.

Lara Buchak is Associate Professor of Philosophy at UC Berkeley, USA.

Jennifer Rose Carr is Assistant Professor of Philosophy at the University of California, San Diego, USA.

Brian Hedden is Lecturer in Philosophy at the University of Sydney, Australia.

Douglas Lavin is Reader in Philosophy at University College London, UK.

Christopher J. G. Meacham is Associate Professor of Philosophy at the University of Massachusetts, Amherst, USA.

Sarah K. Paul is Associate Professor in the Department of Philosophy at the University of Wisconsin-Madison, USA.

Richard Pettigrew is Professor of Philosophy at the University of Bristol, UK.

Larry S. Temkin is Distinguished Professor and Chair of the Department of Philosophy at Rutgers University, USA.

Sergio Tenenbaum is Professor of Philosophy at the University of Toronto, Canada.

Michael G. Titelbaum is Associate Professor in the Department of Philosophy at the University of Wisconsin-Madison, USA.

Brian Weatherson is Marshall M. Weinberg Professor of Philosophy at the University of Michigan, Ann Arbor, USA, and Professorial Fellow and Arché, University of St Andrews, UK.

Foreword

The bulk of the contributions in this volume were presented at a conference on *Belief, Action, and Rationality over Time* hosted by the University of Wisconsin-Madison, and sponsored by the *Canadian Journal of Philosophy*, the UW-Madison Philosophy Department, and a gift from Rodney J. Blackman. The aim of the conference, which was organized by Sarah Paul, Michael Titelbaum, Chrisoula Andreou, and Sergio Tenenbaum, was to stimulate discussion among action theorists and epistemologists interested in overlapping debates concerning belief, action, rationality, and time. This volume brings together ten new articles and an author-meets-critics section, all geared toward advancing these debates.

Chrisoula Andreou and Sergio Tenenbaum

The real puzzle of the self-torturer: uncovering a new dimension of instrumental rationality

Chrisoula Andreou

Department of Philosophy, University of Utah, Salt Lake City, UT, USA

ABSTRACT
The puzzle of the self-torturer raises intriguing questions concerning rationality, cyclic preferences, and resoluteness. Interestingly, what makes the case puzzling has not been clearly pinpointed. The puzzle, it seems, is that a series of rational choices foreseeably leads the self-torturer to an option that serves his preferences worse than the one with which he started. But this is a very misleading way of casting the puzzle. I pinpoint the real puzzle of the self-torturer and, in the process, reveal a neglected but crucial dimension of instrumental rationality.

1. Introduction

Warren Quinn's puzzle of the self-torturer raises intriguing questions concerning rationality, cyclic preferences, and resoluteness. The case of the self-torturer is supposed to illustrate that cyclic preferences can be rational and to suggest that, in cases where they are, rationality calls for some form of resoluteness. Criticisms of the case have largely focused on resisting the idea that the case of the self-torturer is a case of rational cyclic preferences.[1] My sense is that the responses to these criticisms by defenders of the puzzle are compelling and that the puzzle really does challenge some traditional assumptions about (instrumental) rationality.[2] But I also think that what makes the puzzle of the self-torturer puzzling has not been properly identified. The puzzle, it seems, is that a series of rational choices foreseeably leads the self-torturer to an option that serves his preferences worse than the one with which he started. But this is a very misleading way of casting the puzzle raised by the case of the self-torturer. My aim in this paper is to identify the real puzzle of the self-torturer and, in the process, reveal a neglected but crucial dimension of instrumental rationality. I will show that the subjective responses that instrumental rationality is responsive and accountable to are not just the agent's preferences, where preferences can be understood as *relational* appraisal responses, in a sense that will be discussed below. Our subjective responses include appraisals that do not qualify as relational in the relevant sense – appraisals associated with a rational requirement that can, in theory and in practice, justify an agent's sometimes purposely acting against his preference(s) regarding the options among which he must currently choose.[3]

2. Quinn's puzzle of the self-torturer and his proposed resolution

Quinn describes the situation of the self-torturer as follows:

> Suppose there is a medical device that enables doctors to apply electric current to the body in [extremely tiny] increments.... The device has 1001 settings: 0 (off) and 1 ... 1000. Suppose someone (call him the self-torturer) agrees to have the device, in some conveniently portable form, attached to him in return for the following conditions: The device is initially set at 0. At the start of each week he is allowed a period of free experimentation in which he may try out and compare different settings, after which the dial is returned to its previous position. At any other time, he has only two options – to stay put or to advance the dial one setting. But he may advance only one step each week, and he may *never* retreat. *At each advance he gets $10,000.*
>
> [T]he self-torturer cannot feel any difference in comfort between adjacent settings [or at least he cannot, with any confidence, determine whether he has moved up a setting just by the way he feels]...[but] there *are* noticeable differences in comfort between settings that are sufficiently far apart. Indeed, if he keeps advancing, he can see that he will eventually reach settings that will be so painful that he would then gladly relinquish his fortune and return to 0. (1993a, 198) [4]

Given the circumstances, the self-torturer finds himself with the following preferences: for every pair of settings n and n + 1, he prefers (the situation at) n + 1 over n; but he also prefers 0 to 1000. His preferences over the settings thus form a loop (as in Figure 1) and are, in this sense, cyclic.

According to Quinn, although it is tempting to dismiss the self-torturer's cyclic preferences as irrational, the preferences seem 'perfectly natural and appropriate given his circumstances';[5] and, given these preferences (and the

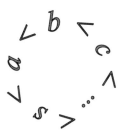

Figure 1. Read 'x < y' as 'y is preferred to x', and 'x < y < z' as 'x < y & y < z'.

possibility that the self-torturer might be stuck with them), the self-torturer has 'a real problem of rational choice: How to take reasonable advantage of what the device offers him without ending up the worse for it' (200).

In Quinn's view, it is clear that the self-torturer needs to pick an acceptable stopping point and then resolutely stick to his plan. But this approach is not supported by the prevailing theory of instrumental rationality, which prohibits an agent from 'forgo[ing] something that he would in fact prefer to get, all things considered' (205). Given that, for any setting n between 0 and 999, the self-torturer prefers to stop at setting n + 1 than to stop at setting n, and given that, when the self-torturer is at setting n, stopping at setting n + 1 is still an available option (in the sense that, were the self-torturer to decide that he should stop at setting n + 1 he could), stopping at setting n, is according to the prevailing theory of instrumental rationality, impermissible. Quinn thus rejects the prevailing theory of instrumental rationality in favor of a theory that requires some resoluteness. At the heart of the theory is

> the principle that a reasonable strategy that correctly anticipated all later facts (including facts about preferences) still binds. On such a theory of rationality some contexts of choice fall under the authority of past decisions....In these contexts... [a]n agent is not rationally permitted to change course even if doing so would better serve his preferences. (207)

Presented somewhat more formally, Quinn's reasoning in favor of resoluteness can be captured as follows:

P1: The self-torturer's cyclic preferences are rationally permissible.

P2: If the self-torturer's cyclic preferences are rationally permissible and rationality does not involve resoluteness, then rationally-governed choice will lead the self-torturer to an alternative that is worse than the alternative he began with (even if there are no unanticipated developments).

P3: Rationally-governed choice will not lead one to an alternative that is worse than the alternative one began with (at least if there are no unanticipated developments).

C: Rationality involves resoluteness.

3. A complication

As Quinn anticipated, many have had qualms about P1. But even if Quinn is right about P1 and the theorists who oppose P1 are, as Quinn suggests, making things 'too easy on [themselves]' and 'too hard on the self-torturer' (199), Quinn's reasoning seems problematic.

Notice first that, as Quinn makes explicit, his concern is with instrumental rationality. Moreover, putting aside complications he sees as irrelevant in relation to the puzzle of the self-torturer, he does not question, but instead endorses, the prevailing assumption that instrumental rationality 'is and ought to be the slave of the agent's preferences' (209).[6] But, in that case, it seems like 'worse' in

P3 must, for the sake of consistency, be interpreted as 'worse in terms of serving the agent's preferences.'[7] This, however, puts P3 in tension with Quinn's endorsement of resoluteness, since, as Quinn understands resoluteness, it sometimes requires an agent to choose an alternative that serves his preferences worse than another available alternative. And if it is sometimes permissible to end up with an alternative that serves one's preferences worse than another available alternative, why would it not be permissible to end up with an alternative that serves one's preferences worse than the alternative with which one started? Relatedly, if it is rationally permissible to make a series of choices that leads one to an alternative that is worse than another alternative that one could have opted for, why would it matter whether the other alternative is the alternative one began with, an alternative that was available after one took some further steps, or an alternative that would be available if one continued to proceed?

Consider, by way of illustration, the following case: Suppose, to borrow an example from (Andreou 2015a), one has access to five cups of tea. '[T]he leftmost tea (tea1) is very hot but not very flavorful, and the rest are such that each is more flavorful but not quite as hot as the one just to the left of it; tea5, on the far right, is very flavorful but also lukewarm' (1).[8] Suppose further that 'one's preferences over the cups of tea (taking into account both temperature and flavor) are cyclic, with tea2 preferred to tea1, tea3 preferred to tea2, tea4 preferred to tea3, tea5 preferred to tea4, but tea1 preferred to tea5' (1–2). Suppose also that these cyclic preferences are rationally permissible. Now assume that one does not possess any of the teas and that (as per Quinn's suggestion that, given rationally permissible cyclic preferences, it is rationally permissible to make a series of choices that leads one to an alternative that serves ones preferences worse than another alternative that one could have opted for) selecting teaN is rationally permissible even though teaN serves one's preferences worse than teaM. Why should the permissibility of selecting teaN change if, instead of it being the case that one never previously possessed any of the teas, the scenario is such that one was initially given teaM? In both scenarios, one selects teaN even though teaM is available. Why should the fact that one was initially given teaM change the permissibility of ending up with teaN?

My point, in short, is that, as soon as it is granted that, in cases like the case of the self-torturer, one is rationally permitted, indeed rationally required, to stick with an option even though it serves one's preferences worse than another available alternative, then it seems ad hoc to insist that rationality does not permit a series of choices that leads one to an option that serves one's preferences worse than the alternative one began with.[9]

4. The real puzzle of the self-torturer

What shall we say, then, about the case of the self-torturer? Well, if we grant, as I will, that it is rationally permissible for the self-torturer to end up with an alternative that serves his preferences worse than some other alternative he could have opted for, then, given my reasoning in the previous section, we cannot just assume that rationality prohibits the self-torturer from making a series of choices that leads to an alternative that serves his preferences worse than the alternative he began with.[10] But then we've lost our apparent reason for thinking there is something irrational about the self-torturer's proceeding at each point and thus going to 1000.[11] And this is puzzling, since, intuitively, there is something irrational about the self-torturer's proceeding at each point and thus going to 1000. I turn now to identifying where the irrationality in this scenario lies. (As will become apparent, one can identify where the irrationality in this scenario lies, without pinpointing or even supposing that there is a specific setting at which the self-torturer rationally should stop. There may instead be a fuzzily bounded range of rationally acceptable stopping points, with no clear first rationally unacceptable stopping point. I say more concerning the presumed vagueness in the self-torturer's situation below.)

In a nutshell, the irrationality in the self-torturer's proceeding at each point and thus going to 1000 lies not in the fact that the self-torturer ends up with an alternative that serves his preferences worse than the one he started with, but in the fact that (though unimpaired by any lack of information about his situation) the self-torturer ends up with a terrible alternative when non-terrible alternatives are available. Now to explain.

My explanation relies on a distinction that is drawn from David Papineau's work on color perception – the distinction is between 'categorical responses' and 'relational responses.' I begin with a review of the relevant points, which borrows freely from my discussion of the distinction, and a variation on it, in my previous work.[12]

In 'Can We Really See a Million Colours?' Papineau (2015) argues that 'our conscious colour experience is the joint product of two different kinds of perceptual state' (277): via one state, we have *categorical* color responses, wherein we experience a surface as of a certain color, say cN, where cN is among the finite set of distinct conscious visual color experiences {c1, c2, c3, …cS} the perceiver can have; via the other state, we have *relational* color responses, wherein we experience adjacent color samples as either the same or as in some way different from one another.[13] As Papineau explains, his position has interesting implications concerning the interpretation of color discrimination data. Consider, for example, the view that 'human beings are capable of well over a million different conscious visual responses to coloured surfaces' (274). This view is based on (1) evidence that, when comparing pairs of color samples, humans can consciously register color differences between more than a million different samples, and (2) the assumption that 'our consciously registering a *difference in colour* must derive from our first having *one* colour response to the left-hand side surface, and *another* colour response to the right-hand [side] surface, and thence registering that there is a difference' (274). But if, as Papineau argues, 'the detection of colour differences between adjacent surfaces does not [always] derive from prior [independent] responses to each surface, there is no need to posit a million such responses to account for the discrimination data' (275). For there is then room for the visual system to issue 'a relational judgement that two adjacent samples ... *differ* even in cases where the two surfaces produce [the *same* conscious visual experience, and so] the *same* categorical colour response [when viewed each on its own]' (278); moreover, there is, as Papineau makes clear, room for the possibility that one's conscious visual experience when viewing one pair of color samples, say, sample 23 next to sample 24, can be the same as one's conscious visual experience when viewing a different pair of samples, say sample 27 next to sample 28.

As Papineau emphasizes, it is 'entirely consistent' with his view that categorical color responses can vary from person to person (276). Whereas I might have the same conscious visual experience when I view color sample 2 (by itself) and when I view color sample 3 (by itself), you might have a different conscious visual experiences when you view color sample 2 (by itself) than you have when you view color sample 3 (by itself). There is certainly room for

> variations in culture, training, and natural endowment [to] make a significant difference to the repertoire of [categorical] colour responses available to different individuals. Maybe some individuals are ... only capable of a few dozen such responses, while others—painters or interior decorators, say—are capable of many hundreds. (276)

Whether Papineau's position concerning color perception is correct is not something we can or need to take up here. What is important for my purposes is that Papineau's distinction between categorical responses and relational responses, or rather the related distinction between *categorical appraisal responses* and *relational appraisal responses*, can be used to illuminate the nature of instrumental rationality and the puzzle of the self-torturer. Notice first that in appraising an alternative, I might respond *categorically* with something like 'X is terrible' or I might respond *relationally* with something like 'X is worse than Y.' The first sort of response is *categorical* in the sense that it indicates the appraisal category that I see X as falling in. The second sort of response provides no such category information. To appraise X as worse than Y leaves completely open the question of what category I place X in on the spectrum from, say, terrible to fantastic. It indicates only how I appraise X and Y in relation to each other.[14]

Note that, in the sense of interest here, to say that a response is a *categorical* appraisal response is not to say that it is or purports to be objective. My appraisal of the taste of vegemite as terrible counts as a categorical appraisal response even though my appraisal is, I grant, thoroughly subjective. Note also that, in the sense of interest here, to say that a response is a *categorical* appraisal response is not to say that there were no comparisons or contrasts in play when the response occurred. I might find a piece of chocolate terrible-tasting because I am used to very high-end chocolate. Still, 'this chocolate tastes terrible' says something about where I place (the taste of) this chocolate on the spectrum from, say, terrible to fantastic (and so about whether my culinary experience is positive, negative, or neutral); the judgment 'this chocolate tastes worse than the chocolate I had yesterday' does not, in itself, provide any such information.

As in the color case, once one distinguishes between categorical and relational responses, there is room for scenarios such as the following: K is capable of both categorical responses and relational responses with respect to appraisals of a particular type in a particular domain or over a particular set of options; the number of distinct categorical responses K has along the most refined spectrum of categorical responses available to her for appraisals of the relevant type in the relevant domain or over the relevant options is finite; and, even when K uses the most refined spectrum of categorical responses available to her for appraisals of the relevant type in the relevant domain or over the relevant options, K sometimes has relational responses that prompt her to discriminate between alternatives that she has the same categorical response to when she considers each on its own. To take a concrete case, there is room for scenarios such as the following: K is capable of categorical and relational responses concerning the goodness (to K) of various samples of chocolate; the set {terrible, very bad, bad, fair, good, great, fantastic} figures as the most refined spectrum of K's categorical appraisal responses concerning the goodness (to K) of various samples of chocolate; in considering two chocolate samples, say A and B, K has the same categorical appraisal response when she considers each on its own, and yet she also has a relational response of the form 'A is worse than B.' As Papineau emphasizes, there is no guarantee that our categorical responses and our relational responses will prompt the same discriminations.[15]

Note that to say that the number of distinct categorical appraisal responses an agent has in a particular domain or over a particular set of options is finite is not to say that every alternative the agent considers will fall squarely into one appraisal category or another. The possibility of vagueness, understood as involving fuzzy boundaries, is by no means ruled out. Quinn casts the puzzle of the self-torturer as involving vagueness, and I will not here question the phenomenon or its role in generating the puzzle and supporting the possibility of rationally cyclic preferences.[16] My aim, recall, is to argue that, even if it is true that, given the self-torturer's situation, the self-torturer's subjective appraisals, as Quinn describes them, are rationally permissible, we need to rethink the puzzle of the self-torturer and the challenge it raises for the conception of instrumental rationality according to which an instrumentally rational agent always chooses in accordance with her preference(s) regarding the options among which she must currently choose.

It is important for my purposes that an agent with cyclic preferences (such as the self-torturer) can be led, over a *series* of steps guided by his preferences, from a certain option to one that is determinately in a lower (appraisal) category. Notice, however, that, given the possibility of vagueness, there is no need to suppose that, at some point along the way, the agent must have a preference that prompts him to swap his current option for one that is determinately in a lower category. For, roughly put, given fuzzy boundaries, the transition, over a *series* of steps, from a certain option to one that is determinately in a lower category can occur without there being any single step in the agent's preference loop that takes him from his current option to one that is determinately in a lower category; it can thus occur without there being, at some point along the way, a preference favoring an option that is determinately in a lower category.

My discussion so far suggests that, if an agent's preferences are cyclic, one should not expect to find a thoroughly tidy relation between the agent's categorical responses to the alternatives she faces and the agent's relational responses to the alternatives she faces; or at least this is so if (i) her relational responses are understood as capturing her (pairwise) preferences between the available alternatives, and (ii) the categorical responses that are relevant in the case at hand, even if they are complicated by vagueness, involve categories that can be arranged from lowest to highest (as with the categories *terrible, very bad, bad, fair, good, great, fantastic*). However, it might be claimed that if an agent's preferences over a set of options are cyclic, then the only categorical responses she can have to the options will be such that the relevant categories cannot be arranged from lowest to highest, but instead form a loop. The case of the self-torturer speaks against this view. Although the self-torturer's preferences over his options are cyclic, the self-torturer can and does have categorical responses like 'that would be a terrible result' and 'that would be a fantastic result'; and he does *not* see the spectrum from *terrible* to *fantastic* as forming a loop so that talk of higher and lower appraisal categories is out of place – to the contrary, it is precisely because talk of higher and lower appraisal categories seems perfectly in order in the case of the self-torturer that it is plausible to suggest that the self-torturer should not end up with options in some of the available categories. (More on this below.) If the case of the self-torturer were such that talk of higher and lower appraisal categories were out of place, it is far from clear that we could substantiate the claim that some of the options in the case ought to be avoided. It is the combination of cyclic preferences and non-cyclic categories that makes the case particularly interesting.

It might be suggested that, insofar as the categories associated with a set of categorical responses can be arranged from lowest to highest, we can say that the agent has preferences over the categories, and that *these* preferences are not cyclic. For example, in the case of the self-torturer, we can say that the self-torturer has preferences over the categories in the spectrum from *terrible* to *fantastic*, and that *these* preferences are not cyclic. I will not here delve into this suggestion. I want only to emphasize that it in no way undermines the idea that the self-torturer's pairwise preferences between the options he actually faces are cyclic. Moreover, it does not support the idea that *all* of the self-torturer's subjective appraisal responses are preferences (understood as subjective *relational* appraisal responses). To say that the self-torturer prefers the category *fantastic* to the category *terrible* is to say that the self-torturer prefers options to which he has the subjective categorical appraisal response 'this is fantastic' over options to which he has the subjective categorical appraisal response 'this is terrible'; subjective *categorical* appraisal responses (and the valences they convey) remain in play.

Now consider the following proposal, which is related to P3 (in my reconstruction of Quinn's reasoning).

P3*: Rationally-governed choice will not lead one to an alternative that is (determinately) in a lower appraisal category than another available alternative (at least if there are no unanticipated developments and the set of appraisal categories is finite).

Notice that P3* applies only when talk of higher and lower categories is in order, and so only when the categories in play do not form a loop.

P3* is, I think, quite plausible and it can accommodate the idea that it is rationally impermissible for the self-torturer to end up at 1000 without dismissing the self-torturer's cyclic preferences as rationally impermissible.[17] Some might see P3* as going further out on a limb than necessary relative to the case of the self-torturer, and favor instead the following more modest proposal:

P3': Rationally-governed choice will not lead one to a terrible alternative when an alternative that is (determinately) in a higher appraisal category is available.[18]

I should thus note that, while I will focus on P3*, the gist of my reasoning below holds even if P3* is replaced with P3' (and P2* in the argument below is altered accordingly).

Insofar as rational cyclic preferences are possible, P3* implies that instrumental rationality does not always endorse following one's preferences regarding the options among which one must currently choose, even if these preferences are rationally permissible. (Note that P3* is consistent with the possibility that rationality allows the agent to use her discretion in terms of deciding where exactly to deviate from her preferences, so long as the result conforms to P3*.) Preferences are relational responses. If the self-torturer had nothing but the relational responses that Quinn describes and these responses were rationally permissible, then there would be no way to show that it is irrational for the self-torturer to end up at 1000. But his subjective appraisal responses also include appraisal responses of the form 'alternative X is terrible,' and instrumental rationality is also accountable to these responses. From here, we can get to an internally consistent argument that fits with the spirit of Quinn's resolution of the puzzle of the self-torturer, though Quinn himself failed to properly identify the problem or its resolution:

P1: The self-torturer's cyclic preferences are rationally permissible.

P2*: If the self-torturer's cyclic preferences are rationally permissible and rationality invariably requires one to act on one's preferences/relational appraisal responses regarding the options among which one must currently choose, then rationally-governed choice will lead the self-torturer to an alternative that is in a lower appraisal category than another available alternative (even if there are no unanticipated developments).

P3*: Rationally-governed choice will not lead one to an alternative that is in a lower appraisal category than another available alternative (at least if there are no unanticipated developments and the set of appraisal categories is finite).

C*: Rationality does not invariably require one to act on one's preferences/relational appraisal responses regarding the options among which one must currently choose.

In the case of the self-torturer, the agent's categorical appraisal responses are such that some alternatives count as *terrible* and some do not – indeed, some may count as *good*, *great*, or even *fantastic*. As such, it is not rationally permissible for the self-torturer to end up with a terrible alternative. Notice that it need not be that, in all cases of cyclic preferences, the agent's categorical appraisal responses to the available alternatives fall in different categories. Since relational responses can prompt discriminations that are not prompted by the agent's categorical responses, it may be that an agent's relational responses to a set of alternatives reflect cyclic preferences even though her categorical responses place them all in the same category, say *fair*. Recall the tea case, wherein the leftmost tea (tea1) is very hot but not very flavorful, and the rest are such that each is more flavorful but not quite as hot as the one just to the left of it; tea5, on the far right, is very flavorful but also lukewarm. It may be that the agent's preferences over the teas are cyclic, even though she counts all the teas as *fair*. If so, and if the cyclic preferences are rationally permissible, then we can see why it can be rationally permissible for her to end up with any of the teas, and why it doesn't matter which one she started with. Given that the agent's preferences over the teas are rationally cyclic, instrumental rationality cannot forbid the agent from ending up with a tea that is dispreferred to another available tea; it can require that the agent not end up with a tea that falls in a lower category than another available tea, but when all the teas fall in the same category, this doesn't occur no matter which tea she ends up with.

Notice that my reasoning leaves room for the possibility that, when an agent's preferences over a set of options are not cyclic, rationality may, in that case, require that the agent act on her relational responses/preferences regarding the options among which she must currently choose, even if she has the *same* categorical response to all the options. As such, it does not follow from my reasoning that an agent need only attend to her categorical appraisal responses.

5. Conclusion: the moral regarding instrumental rationality

The traditional conception of instrumental rationality combines the idea that instrumental rationality is grounded in our subjective appraisal responses with the assumption that our preferences, understood as relational appraisal responses, exhaust our subjective appraisal responses; but, in addition to our relational appraisal responses, we have subjective categorical appraisal responses. It is precisely when the latter responses are in play that it can be irrational to end up with some alternatives but not others even if one's preferences are rationally cyclic. Without categorical appraisal responses, any alternative in a preference loop would be just as rationally permissible as any other. With categorical appraisal responses, this need not be so. Relatedly, for some alternatives, ending up with that alternative can be rationally impermissible regardless of whether or not the alternative serves the agent's preferences worse than the one that the agent started with or whether or not the agent ended up there as a result of deviating from a prior plan; it can be impermissible because it is in a lower appraisal category than another alternative that the agent could have opted for. The moral, in short, is that, the subjective responses that instrumental rationality is responsive and accountable to are not just the agent's preferences. Our subjective responses also include appraisals that do not qualify as relational in the relevant sense – appraisals associated with a rational requirement (P3*) that can, in theory and in practice, justify an agent's sometimes purposely acting against his preference(s) regarding the options among which he must currently choose.

Notes

1. See, for example, (Voorhoeve and Binmore 2006) and (Arntzenius and McCarthy 1997).
2. For a recent discussion and defense of the puzzle, see (Tenenbaum and Raffman 2012).
3. As will become apparent, the justification can hold even if, as in the case of the self-torturer, there is no threat of the agent ending up with the alternative he started with minus repeated transaction costs. Otherwise put, the justification can hold even if the scenario is such that, once an alternative is passed up, it cannot be regained for a price, and so the problem at issue is not the problem of the agent being 'money-pumped.' For the original presentation of 'the money pump argument,' see (Davidson, McKinsey, and Suppes, 1955). For my critique of the view that the money pump argument establishes that cyclic preferences are irrational, see (Andreou 2007). There, I argue that what the money pump argument shows is that an agent should not always follow his preferences regarding the options among which he must currently choose, even if these preferences are basic and the agent finds that he is stuck with them even after he is fully informed. But because the problem at issue in the case of the self-torturer is not the problem of being money-pumped, we need a different justification for why the self-torturer should not always follow his preference(s) regarding the options among which he must currently choose.
4. Quinn himself does not add the qualification 'or at least he cannot, with any confidence, determine whether he has moved up a setting just by the way he feels,' but--for reasons that I will not get into, because they are complicated and tangential given my purposes in this paper--I think the qualification is helpful.
5. If the self-torturer's preferences are in order, then the case of the self-torturer qualifies as a 'spectrum case' supporting the intransitivity of '___ is rationally preferred to ___.' For extensive discussion of spectrum cases and intransitivity, see (Temkin 2012).
6. In 'Putting Rationality in its Place,' Quinn suggests that instrumental rationality is 'mere cleverness' and not a 'real virtue' of practical rationality if one's practical reasoning is not constrained by good ends (1993b, 234).

7. Interestingly, Quinn, at one point, maintains that 'better than... is transitive' (199). But, if 'better than' is understood as (something like) 'better in terms of serving the agent's preferences,' it is not clear that Quinn is entitled to maintain that 'better than' is transitive while also maintaining that the self-torturer's preferences are genuinely and rationally cyclic. And if 'better than' is not understood in terms of the agent's preferences, it is not clear that Quinn is entitled to assume that the relation is relevant to instrumental rationality, given his endorsement of the prevailing assumption that instrumental rationality 'is and ought to be the slave of the agent's preferences' (209). My aim of 'uncovering a new dimension of instrumental rationality' in this paper may ultimately be of help here, but the issue is complicated and so I am working it out in a separate manuscript on the 'better than' relation (in progress).
8. The Online First version of the article, which is the version currently available, is not officially paginated, but I have added page numbers for convenience.
9. In 'Intransitive Preferences, Vagueness, and the Structure of Procrastination,' Duncan MacIntosh argues that 'if the self-torturer really has intransitive preferences... he rationally should proceed to the maximum level' (2010, 73). Relatedly, he claims that, for an agent with intransitive preferences,

    > each position he could have been in is such that if he does not move to a different position, he is pair-wise worse off. So, he would have been irrational to stay where he was. In moving, he has not made himself any worse off than he was before. (76)

    I disagree with MacIntosh's reasoning, but my concerns about Quinn's take on the puzzle of the self-torturer have been influenced by MacIntosh's thought-provoking challenges concerning the assumed irrationality of the self-torturer's proceeding to 1000.
10. Quinn's suggestion that it is rationally permissible for the self-torturer to end up with an alternative that serves his preferences worse than some other alternative he could have opted for is, of course, controversial. Although defending the suggestion is beyond the scope of this paper, I here accept it as plausible enough to be worth taking on board, at least for the sake of argument.
11. Keep in mind that, since that the self-torturer's preferences are cyclic, we cannot say that his going to 1000 appears far lower in his ranking of his options (and is in this sense much less preferred) than the option of stopping at 0.
12. The discussion I am borrowing from in the next several paragraphs appears in (Andreou 2015b); there Papineau's distinction is used to illuminate the notion of parity.
13. Raffman (1994) raises this possibility and uses the distinction to argue that two color patches that are seen as belonging to different categories when judged singly can be seen as belonging to the same category when judged pairwise. This is in turn used to 'explain, in an *intuitively* compelling way, how a difference in kind can obtain between the endpoints (among others) of an effectively continuous series' and thus resolve the paradox in sorites cases (43). Quinn's puzzle incorporates the assumption that, whatever the explanation, a difference in kind can obtain between the endpoints of an effectively continuous series. (More specifically, Quinn assumes that someone can go from no pain to excruciating pain via a series of unnoticeable or barely noticeable differences.) I will make the same assumption without committing to any particular explanation (though I do find Raffman's explanation plausible).

14. Note that, although in the case of the self-torturer, the focus is on the consequences of the available alternatives, there is nothing in the idea of an appraisal response that requires that appraisal responses to potential actions be consequence-oriented; relatedly, there is, for all I say here, room for appraising an action as terrible even if it does not have terrible consequences.
15. I say a great deal more about this and consider potential objections in (Andreou 2015b).
16. For some forceful argumentation suggesting that vagueness is not crucial for supporting the possibility of rationally cyclic preferences, see (Temkin, 2012, chapter 9).
17. Relatedly, P3* figures as a plausible initial response to the worry, raised by Temkin (1996), that, given the pervasiveness of intransitivity, there may be 'no rational basis for choosing between virtually any alternatives' (209). But Temkin seems more open to the possibility of rational dilemmas than Quinn, and so Temkin may not see P3* as supporting C*, but may instead cast P3* as ensuring, in coordination with the negation of C* (and assuming that one's preferences are rational), that we are in a rational bind. As indicated above, I have accepted, at least for the sake of argument, Quinn's view that it is rationally permissible for the self-torturer to end up with an alternative that serves his preferences worse than some other alternative he could have opted for.
18. Thanks to Sarah Stroud for pointing out that I could make do with this more modest proposal.

Acknowledgments

My thanks for helpful comments from Donald Bruckner, Matthew Frise, Preston Greene, Elijah Millgram, Michael Morreau, Doug Portmore, Theron Pummer, Andrew Reisner, Jonah Schupbach, Jacob Stegenga, Sarah Stroud, Christine Tappolet, Larry Temkin, Sergio Tenenbaum, Mariam Thalos, Ralph Wedgwood, Mike White, participants of the University of Wisconsin-Madison workshop for this special issue on *Belief, Action, and Rationality over Time*, participants at the 2015 work-in-progress workshop at the Philosophy Institute at the University of Saarlandes, students in my PHIL 4010 and PHIL 7500 courses, two anonymous referees, and audience members at my presentations at CRE at the University of Montreal, at the 2015 Pacific Division APA meeting, and at the 2014 Society for Applied Philosophy meeting. Thanks also to Arif Ahmed, Doug Portmore, and Sergio Tenenbaum for thought-provoking discussion (via PEA Soup) on interpreting Quinn's position. Finally, I am grateful to the College of Humanities at the University of Utah for a travel grant supporting my presentation of the ideas in this paper.

References

Andreou, Chrisoula. 2015a. "Cashing out the Money-pump Argument." *Philosophical Studies* doi:10.1007/s11098-015-0555-5.

Andreou, Chrisoula. 2015b. "Parity, Comparability, and Choice." *Journal of Philosophy* 112: 5–22.

Andreou, Chrisoula. 2007. "There Are Preferences and Then There Are Preferences." In *Economics and the Mind*, edited by Barbara Montero and Mark D. White, 115–126. London: Routledge.

Arntzenius, Frank, and David McCarthy. 1997. "Self Torture and Group Beneficence." *Erkenntnis* 47: 129–144.

Davidson, Donald, J. McKinsey, and Patrick Suppes. 1955. "Outlines of a Formal Theory of Value." *Philosophy of Science* 22: 140–160.

MacIntosh, Duncan. 2010. "Intransitive Preferences, Vagueness, and the Structure of Procrastination." In *The Thief of Time: Philosophical Essay on Procrastination*, edited by Chrisoula Andreou and Mark D. White, 68–86. New York: Oxford University Press.

Papineau, David. 2015. "Can We Really See a Million Colours?" In *Phenomenal Qualities*, edited by Paul Coates and Sam Coleman, 274–297. New York: Oxford University Press.

Quinn, Warren. 1993a. "The Puzzle of the Self-Torturer", In *Morality and Action*, edited by Philippa Foot. 198–209, Cambridge: Cambridge University Press.

Quinn, Warren. 1993b. "Putting Rationality in Its Place". In *Morality and Action*, edited by Philippa Foot. 228–255, Cambridge: Cambridge University Press.

Raffman, Diana. 1994. "Vagueness without Paradox." *The Philosophical Review* 103: 41–47.

Temkin, Larry S. 2012. *Rethinking the Good*. Oxford: Oxford University Press.

Temkin, Larry S. 1996. "A Continuum Argument for Intransitivity." *Philosophy & Public Affairs* 25: 175–210.

Tenenbaum, Sergio, and Diana Raffman. 2012. "Vague Projects and the Puzzle of the Self-torturer." *Ethics* 123: 86–112.

Voorhoeve, Alex, and Ken Binmore. 2006. "Transitivity, the Sorites Paradox, and Similarity-based Decision-making." *Erkenntnis* 64: 101–114.

Rationality with respect to people, places, and times

Larry S. Temkin

Department of Philosophy, Rutgers University, New Brunswick, NJ, USA

ABSTRACT
There is a rich tradition within game theory, decision theory, economics, and philosophy correlating practical rationality with impartiality, and spatial and temporal neutrality. I argue that in some cases we should give priority to people over both times and places, and to times over places. I also show how three plausible dominance principles regarding people, places, and times conflict, so that we cannot accept all three. However, I argue that there are some cases where we should give priority to times over people, suggesting that there is impersonal value to the distribution of high quality life over different times.

1. Introduction

Many believe that, regarding rationality, there are important respects in which we should treat people, places, and times the same. I think this is correct. On the other hand, many of the same people also believe that, regarding rationality, there are important respects in which we should treat people, places, and times differently. I think this, too, is correct. This raises the obvious question of under what circumstances, and in what respects, we should, or should not, treat people, places, and times the same. This is, I believe, an extremely important, but underexplored, question which raises a host of rich, complex, and thorny issues. In this article, I will begin the difficult task of addressing this question.

The aim of this article is not to *settle* the question of how we should think about people, places, and times for the purposes of practical reasoning. Far from it. Such a task lies well beyond the scope of a single article. Instead, I wish to explore a number of issues pertinent to this topic. I cannot emphasize enough the *preliminary* nature of my exploration. I am acutely aware that many of my arguments and examples are merely suggestive, rather than conclusive; that not everyone will share my intuitions about the examples I give; that some who share my intuitions will offer deflationary accounts as to why such intuitions are not to be trusted; that some will draw different conclusions than I do regarding what the examples and our intuitions about them suggest; and that some of my arguments and examples are open to serious worries or objections that I cannot adequately deal with here. In addition, my article makes no attempt to be complete, or to offer an even-handed treatment of the issues.

In Section 2, I'll offer just a few of the many considerations that might be offered in support of the view that in certain respects, we should treat persons, places, and times the same in our practical deliberations. In Sections 3–5, the bulk of the article, I will offer considerations – some of them obscure and many of them controversial – in support of the view that often we may, and sometimes must, treat people, places, and times differently in our practical deliberations. In Section 6, I'll note a number of related issues that still need to be addressed. Despite all these hedges and qualifications, I hope to convince the reader that the issues raised in this article are interesting and important, and that they require much more attention than they have heretofore been given.

One final caveat. Many of the examples presented in this article involve moral considerations, many of which are axiological in nature. But I hope it is clear that they have implications for the domain of non-moral practical reasoning, as well as the domain of practical reasoning for which moral considerations are pertinent.

2. Stage setting

The view that there are important respects in which we should treat people, places, and times the same for the purposes of practical reasoning is supported by an ingenious argument of Parfit's (1984, Part Two). Parfit contrasted three different positions, each with a different structure: a *present-aim theory*, which someone like Williams (1981a, 1981b, 1985) might adopt; a *self-interest theory*, which has been a dominant conception of individual rationality since the early Greeks (Plato, *The Republic*); and a *neutralist theory*, favored by classical utilitarians like Mill (*Utilitarianism*) and Sidgwick (1907). Parfit offered an intriguing strategic metaphor, suggesting that the self-interest theory occupied an indefensible 'no man's land' between the other two positions. Parfit noted that the present-aim theory is a 'pure' theory, *relativizing* the reasons one has to a particular person, place, and time.[1] On such a view, for the purposes of practical deliberation, only an agent's *own* interests matter, and only those that the agent has *here* and *now*, at the time and place where the practical deliberation is occurring. Likewise, neutralist theories are 'pure', in that, for the purposes of practical deliberation, they treat *all* people, places, and times *neutrally*, giving equal weight to the interests of all people at all places and all times.[2] By contrast, the self-interest theory is a 'hybrid' theory, it *relativizes* with respect to *people*, telling each person that she only needs to give weight to *her* interests, but it is *neutral* with respect to *space* and *time*, holding that a person should give *equal* weight to *each* moment of her life, no matter where, or when, it occurs.

Parfit suggested that the self-interest theory's hybrid position may be unstable and indefensible. In particular, he claimed that the strongest arguments that the self-interest theory might muster in opposition to the present-aim theory, against relativizing with respect to place and time, might analogously tell against relativizing with respect to individuals, and so may carry one *from* the present-aim theory, *beyond* the self-interest theory, and all the way *to* the neutralist position. Likewise, Parfit suggested, the strongest arguments that the self-interest theory might muster in opposition to the neutralist position, against being neutral with respect to *people*, might analogously tell against being neutral with respect to place and time, and so may carry one *from* the neutralist position, *beyond* the self-interest theory, and all the way *to* the present-aim theory.

Thus, Parfit suggested, there are powerful reasons for any theory of practical reasoning to be 'pure,' and to treat people, places, and times alike: either we should be *relative* with respect to all three, or we should be *neutral* with respect to all three, but what we should *not* do is to treat people, places, and times *differently* insofar as we believe that reasons are either relative or neutral.

Many theorists accept the view that we should treat people, places, and times the same, and that in fact we should be *neutral* between them. This is the view of many consequentialists, including all of the classical utilitarians.

The view that rationality requires us to be *neutral* with respect to time was expressed nicely by Henry Sidgwick, when he wrote that:

> 'Hereafter *as such* is to be regarded neither less nor more than Now.' ... the mere difference of priority and posteriority in time is not a reasonable ground for having more regard ... [for] one moment ... [over] that of another ... 'a smaller present good is not to preferred to a greater future good' (allowing for differences of certainty). (1907, Book III, 381)

Similar claims might be made with respect to people and places. Thus, echoing Sidgwick, one might hold, regarding persons, that:

> Me *as such* is to be regarded neither less nor more than You. The mere difference of who is who – that I am I, and you are you – is not *itself* a reasonable ground for having more regard for one of us over the other. Hence, a smaller good for one person is not to be preferred to a greater for another (merely in virtue of the fact that each person is the person that he or she is).

Likewise, one might hold, regarding space, that:

> Here *as such* is to be regarded neither less nor more than There. The mere difference of nearness or distance in space is not a reasonable ground for having more regard for one location over that of another. Hence, a smaller nearer good is not to be preferred to a greater further good.

Now, as an egalitarian, who also believes in certain agent-relative duties and permissions, I have never been attracted to the sort of 'pure' neutralist position of classical utilitarianism, whose sole focus is on *how much* utility obtains, without regard to how it is *produced* or *distributed* by, and across, different people, places, and times. Still, there is a powerful attraction to the kind of reasoning expressed by Parfit and Sidgwick, in support of the views that in *some* important respects, we should treat people, places, and times the same, and be *neutral* with respect to all three. Unfortunately, here, as elsewhere, the devil is in the details and, sadly, an adequate account of the details has not yet been given. More to the point, whatever kernel of truth there may be to the sort of views expressed by Parfit and Sidgwick, I believe that there is good reason to reject any blanket suggestion that we should treat people, places, and times the same, or be neutral between them, beyond the standard agent-relative objections that have been mustered against such positions.[3] While I cannot fully defend my view here, in the remainder of this article, I shall present a few of the considerations that underlie my thinking about this matter. As we will see, the question of whether we should treat people, places, and times the same goes well beyond the issue of whether reasons should be neutral with respect to each, relative with respect to each, or neutral with respect to some but relative with respect to others.

3. Some musings about space and time, and worries about treating them the same

It may seem *obvious* that we should treat space and time the same. However, I'm not so sure about this, especially if it is supposed to be an a priori *truth* that holds regardless of the metaphysics of space and time. Suppose, for example, that we lived in a universe that extended infinitely in all directions, spatially, and infinitely towards the past and future, temporally. Suppose, further, that time's passage is not an illusion, and that time is 'directional,' such that the past is receding at a constant rate from the steadily changing present, even as the future is steadily moving at the same constant rate towards the present.[4] *Perhaps* such a view is incoherent, or metaphysically impossible, but if not, must we treat space and time the same for the purposes of practical deliberations?

Consider the following thought experiment. Suppose I learn that our civilization will live in our galaxy another 1000 years, and then die out. I also learn that in a distant galaxy, another civilization will exist for the same 1000 years, and then die out. I then learn that this is also the case in some third and fourth distant galaxies. I find this all quite interesting. It is somewhat *pleasing* to me to learn that there are, in fact, advanced civilizations living in galaxies far away.

Next, suppose I also learn that beyond the fourth galaxy, there is nothing but cold, empty, space. This, too, I find interesting. However, I must confess that learning that fact bothers me some, but not very much. Indeed, if events beyond the fourth galaxy were about to unfold which would make those distant reaches inhospitable to all life forms in perpetuity, I wouldn't think it especially important for us to make significant sacrifices, if we could, to prevent that from happening.

Suppose, on the other hand, I vary the story. As before, I learn that civilization in our galaxy will die out in 1000 years, but I learn that after ours dies out, another civilization will arise and persist for 1000 years in a second galaxy. I also learn that this will happen again, a third and fourth time. But after that, I learn, there will be *nothing* but cold, empty, space, *forever*. For some reason, *that* knowledge would bother me a *lot*. Indeed, if events were about to unfold which would make the universe uninhabitable for any life forms 4000 years from now, unless we made significant sacrifices to prevent that from happening, I would feel quite *strongly* that we should do so, and I would feel that way even if I knew that *our* civilization was going to die out in 1000 years, and that the distant future civilizations would do nothing to further *our* particular hopes, projects, or ideals.[5]

Here is a variation of the example. Suppose that I am living in a world where the only sentient beings are human, where our civilization will have persisted for a total of 10,000 years before dying out, and where there are 10 billion people alive during each period where our civilization exists, each of whom is at a high level, h. I believe that no other civilizations exist elsewhere in space, and that no other civilizations existed before ours, or will exist after ours. I then learn that I am mistaken in one of two ways. Either I am mistaken about there being no other civilizations in space, and in fact there are 10,000 other planets that will be populated by 10 billion beings also at level h during the same time period that our planet is populated, but I am right that no other civilizations will exist in the universe prior to, or after, our civilization; or, alternatively, I am mistaken that no other civilizations exist during another time period, and in fact that are 10,000 other civilizations of 10 billion beings, each of whom is living at level h in a distinct non-overlapping 10,000 year time period of its own, but I am right that there are no other civilizations living elsewhere in space during the time period where our civilization persists. Here, I believe it would be much better if I were mistaken in the second way than the first. And that is because I believe it would be much better for there to be 100,010,000 years where different groups of 10 billion sentient beings are living at a high level, than for there to be only 10,000 years where the universe is occupied by sentient beings with high-level lives, even if, during those 10,000 years, there would not merely be 10 billion people alive, but 100,010 billion people alive.

Note, in both cases, there would be the same sum total of utility. Indeed, in both cases, the *very same* people might exist at the *very same* levels of well-being. Still, I believe that the alternative where the many people with high levels of well-being are dispersed throughout time, so that there are lots of cases of high-quality lives stretched over many eons, is better than the alternative where the many people with high levels of well-being are dispersed throughout space, so that there are lots of cases of high-quality lives stretched over many miles, or acres.

Let us add another variation to the example. Suppose that I was mistaken in both respects. The reality is that our civilization is at the end of a long line of 10,001 contemporaneously populated planets, like ours, extending deep into space along a single ray from the center of our planet, and, in addition, it is the last of 10,001 non-overlapping civilizations, also like ours, extending deep into the past for roughly 100,000,000 years. I then learn that long ago, an infallible predictor set matters in motion that would determine how the universe would unfold, depending on the actions of the members of our planet.

If we took certain steps, A, which would lower the quality of our lives by 20%, then, in fact, there would be an additional 10,000 contemporaneous civilizations extending deep into space along another ray from the center of our planet, each of whose members would be at level h. If we didn't do A, then there would be no other planets elsewhere in space populated by sentient beings during our civilization's existence, other than the 10,000 contemporaneously populated planets about which I already know. In addition, I learn that if we took certain other steps, B, that would also lower the quality of our lives by 20%, but, in that case, there would be an additional 10,000 non-overlapping civilizations, like ours, each of whose members would be at level h, extending forward in time for a total of another 100,000,000 years after our civilization dies out. If we don't do B, the universe will remain utterly devoid of all sentient life once our civilization, and the other 10,000 contemporaneous civilizations, come to an end.

Faced with the knowledge of these alternatives, I think it would be important that our civilization took steps B, to ensure that high-level sentient life persisted in the universe for another 100,000,000 years, and that it would almost certainly be wrong of us not to do so. I think it would be much less important for our civilization to take steps A, to ensure that there be even *more* high-level civilizations living in space at the same time as ours, *in addition* to the 10,000 other such civilizations that will *already* be existing elsewhere in space during that time. Moreover, I think it would probably not be wrong of our civilization to fail to do A.

My own view about this case is that the universe might well go *best* if we did *both* A and B, go second best if we did B but not A, go third best if we did A but not B, and would go worst if we failed to do either A or B. Hence, I am *not* denying that, other things equal, it might be important to populate different regions of space with high-quality lives. But the key point, for my present purposes, is that I think we should treat time and space *differently*, in this context. Specifically, I believe that, in certain cases at least, we should give *greater* priority to filling differing periods of *time* with quality life, than to filling different locations in *space* with quality life.[6]

Is it crucial to this example that the different periods of time to be filled come *after* our civilization will die out? Not to my mind. I would feel similarly about the greater importance of doing B, rather than A, if as a result of our doing B, which would lower the quality of our lives by 20%, there would be an additional

10,000 non-overlapping civilizations, like ours, each of whose members would be at level *h*, extending *backward* in time for a total of *another* 100,000,000 years *before* the 100,000,000 years of civilization that preceded our civilization's existence. Thus, my thought is not merely that it is more important for high-quality life to be dispersed into the *future*, rather than to be dispersed across *space*, but rather that, more generally, it is more important for high-quality life to be dispersed across *time* rather than across *space*.[7]

Here is another example. As before, suppose, that our civilization consisted of 10 billion people, all at the high level of *h*, and that altogether our civilization would last 10,000 years, before dying out. I then learn that we were the first sentient beings to exist in the universe, and that no other sentient beings will exist for another 7,000,000,000,000,000,000,000,000,000 (7 octillion) years, after which there will be one more sentient civilization, like ours, with 10 billion people that will last for 10,000 years, before the universe grows cold, forever. I would, of course, feel incredibly lucky to know that we were one of only two sentient civilizations that would ever exist in the whole duration of the universe. But I would also feel that the overall goodness of the universe was a *pittance* compared to what it might have been. I would think it a great cosmic tragedy that the vast majority of time periods in the universe were utterly devoid of high-quality sentient life. Correspondingly, if our civilization could somehow find a way to ensure that high-quality sentient life would continue for the seven *octillion* years after our civilization dies out, I believe there would be *powerful* reason for us to do so, and I believe this even if it would require *substantial* sacrifice on the part of our civilization to bring about the better outcome.

Consider, next, the following. If one travels by plane from one end of the US to the other, and gazes out one's window, one may be struck by the fact that outside of a few major metropolitan areas, much of the US consists of vast unpopulated tracts of land. The same is true for Canada, Australia, Russia, and much of Africa, Asia, South America, and Northern Europe. Iceland is almost devoid of people; Greenland, the Artic, and Antarctica even more so. Moreover, 71% of the Earth's surface is water. When I think about these facts, I *don't* think that it is a great cosmic tragedy that the vast majority of spatial locations, right here on Earth, are utterly devoid of high-quality sentient life. Should I?

Nor do I believe that my reaction here is solely due to the assumption that if all those spaces were filled with sentient life, none of it would be of high quality. Even assuming that *everyone* who would live on the Earth would have a high-quality life, I don't see a compelling reason to increase the size of the Earth's human population from 7 billion to, say, 100 billion or more, even if we could.

Or let us turn our gaze inward, for a moment. It is estimated that 1% of every atom is composed of protons, neutrons, and electrons, and that the other 99% is empty space.[8] And it is estimated that the average human adult has 7,000,000,000,000,000,000,000,000,000 (7 octillion) atoms in his or her body. There are over 7 billion humans on the Earth. Given all this, should we regard it as a great cosmic waste that the *vast majority* of spatial locations within each human body is devoid of high-quality sentient life? Would our world, or the universe, be much better if within each atom of each human being (not to mention all the other atoms on Earth!), there were subatomic sentient beings possessing high-quality lives? If, contrary to fact, our civilization could somehow find a way to create subatomic sentient beings with a high quality of life, would there be powerful reason for us to fill each of the 7 octillion atoms of each 'average' adult human, as well as all of the other innumerable atoms of the rest of the 7 billion members of the human population, as long as when doing so our own quality of life remained the same? Would there be powerful reason to bring about such an outcome, even if doing so required a *substantial* sacrifice on the part of our civilization?

Suffice it to say, when I think about *all* the locations of space on Earth devoid of sentient beings with high-quality lives, I'm not moved in anything like the way I am when I think of vast regions of time that are devoid of such beings. In sum, in general, I think it important that many *times* be filled with flourishing beings, but not nearly as important that many *spaces* be filled with flourishing beings.[9] Perhaps I'm mistaken about all this, of course. But, for now, at least, I see no compelling reason to abandon my views about this matter.

I have been focusing on cases involving the high-quality lives of sentient beings. Unsurprisingly, my judgment would flip regarding the relevant importance of filling time vs. space if the lives in question were miserable – well below the level at which life ceases to be worth living.

Suppose, for example, that there are two ways in which the universe might unfold. In one, there are 10 billion planets, each populated with 10 billion people, each of whom lives for 100 years, and all of whom are suffering unrelenting agony. In the other, there are 10 billion planets each populated with 10 billion people, each of whom lives for 100 years, and all of whom are suffering unrelenting agony. Assume that the very same people exist in each universe, and that no one else exists, other than the 100,000,000,000,000,000,000 people in sheer agony. From the *subjective* standpoint of each individual, it won't matter which universe exists. And from the standpoint of total disutility, each universe will be identical. Suppose, however, that in the first alternative, each person lives *simultaneously*, while in the second alternative, each planet is populated during a different time period. In that case, I think the second alternative is *worse* than the first. I think a universe where there is *vast* suffering, but where the suffering only lasts for 100 years, is much better than a universe where there is the same *total* amount of vast suffering, yet there are great numbers of people in great agony not merely for 100 years, but for 1000 trillion years. So, in my judgment, it is bad if many *spaces* are filled with agonizing lives that are worth *not* living, but it is *worse* if many *times* are filled with agonizing lives that are worth *not* living. Thus, the relative importance of filling times, or spaces, with sentient beings, depends on whether the value of those being's lives are worth living, or worth *not* living.[10]

Let me turn, next, to a different point. Suppose that God were deciding to populate an infinite number of planets, and time periods of 100 years each, with sentient beings whose lives were *miserable*. Her plan is to have 10 billion miserable beings living on planet one billion and one, during time period one billion and one, 10 billion *different* miserable beings living on planet one billion and two, during time period one billion and two, 10 billion *different* miserable beings living on planet one billion and three, during time period one billion and three, and so on, for all of eternity. Just before doing so, God decides that She will create the *very same* miserable beings as She was originally intending to, and that each of them will live during the *very same* time periods as She was originally intending for them, but that She will *shift* which particular *planets* they occupy, so that *each* person's *place* in space would be different.

Specifically, suppose that God decides to put the people who *would* have occupied planet one billion and one on planet one, instead, the people who *would* have occupied planet one billion and two on planet two, instead, the people who *would* have occupied planet one billion and three on planet three, instead, and so on. One might, if one likes, imagine that each of an infinite number of planets are spaced an equal distance apart, say *k* miles, along an infinite, straight, Euclidean line, so that God's choice involves placing each person on the planet She originally intended for them, or, instead, shifting each person *k* billion miles in the same direction along the line of planets to a different planet. To my mind, the difference between these two prospects has *no* moral significance. As between *these* options, where everything is the same except for *where* in *space* the infinite people lived, I would be *utterly* indifferent.

Suppose next, however, that God decides that She will create the *very* same miserable beings and place them on the *very* same planets as She was originally intending to, but that She will shift *when* they live. Specifically, suppose that God decides to put the people who *would* have occupied time period one billion and one in time period one, instead – where, we are assuming, time period one begins one billion years *earlier* than time period one billion and one – that She decides to put the people who would have occupied time period one billion and two in time period two, instead, the people who would have occupied time period one billion and three in time period three, instead, and so on. I find the difference between *these* two prospects to be morally significant. Notwithstanding the so-called 'fact' of infinity that tell us that, over the course of time, there will be just *as much* miserable existence in each of the two alternatives, I believe there is reason to favor God's original plan, over Her revised plan, in which miserable existence will begin one *billion* years *earlier*, and then continue, unabated, afterwards.

If you aren't convinced by the previous example, consider a variation that would directly affect you. Suppose that God tells you that She is planning to send you to Hell, where you will suffer unbearable pain. She then tells you that once you are sent to Hell you will remain there forever, but that She is willing to give you some choice as to *when* your agony begins. You can either start immediately, or you can start sometime later; however, if you choose to start later, God will put you in a state of suspended animation between now and when you start, so that you will experience nothing between now and when you begin your torments in Hell. Dismayed, you begin asking how long you can delay it. A week? Sure. A Month? No problem. What about a year? A decade? A century? God is happy to go along with any of those choices. You decide to be bolder. You ask if you can delay by a *million* years. She agrees that that, too, is possible. You decide to be bolder still. Having recently learned how big an octillion is, you ask God if you could delay your entry to Hell by an octillion number of years. At this point, you have tried even God's (infinite!) patience, and She replies that yes, indeed, you can delay your entry by that much, but no longer!

At this point, what would you decide? Would you reason that since you won't be gaining anything positive by delaying, and will be spending an eternity in Hell once you're there, it doesn't matter *when* you start, since at the end of time, as it were, you will have spent *just as much* total time in Hell? Or would you choose to enter a state of suspended animation, and delay your entry as long as possible, taking the option of entering Hell in an octillion years? I know what I would choose, for myself, or anyone else that I dearly loved. I would choose the *latest possible* entry date that God permitted, and I believe that it would be perfectly rational for me to do so, and *irrational* for me *not* to do so![11]

Suppose, next, that God tells you that she is planning to send you to Hell immediately. She further informs you that Hell consists of an infinite number of planets spaced an equal distance apart, say k miles, along an infinite, straight, Euclidean line, each of which is labeled by an integer. As it happens, she is planning to place you on planet 1, where you will remain for one year, after which you will be on planet 2 for a year, then planet 3 for a year, and so on, for all of eternity. However, if you want, you have the option of entering Hell on any of the other planets located along the infinite straight line, where you will remain for one year, after which you will be moved to the next highest numbered planet where you will again remain for a year, and this pattern will continue for all of eternity. You immediately ask if any of the planets are less torturous than the others. She assures you that they are not. They are all equally torturous. At that point, would you bother to shift your entry point into Hell to a different planet at a different location in space? Would you try to bargain with God to please let you move your entry point from planet 1 to planet 2, planet 100, planet 1 million, or planet 1 octillion? I see no reason why one would. If, in fact, Hell's planets are all equally bad, it seems clear that there would be *no* rational basis for preferring to be in one particular location in space rather than any other.

I realize that these past two cases involve infinity, and that our intuitions about such cases are notoriously problematic. Nevertheless, I don't think my views about these cases are implausible, and they suggest a further asymmetry about space and time for the purposes of practical reasoning. In some infinite cases, at least, merely shifting the *spatial* locations of sentient beings will be morally irrelevant, whereas shifting the *temporal* locations of sentient beings may be significant.[12]

4. Dominance principles with respect to people, places, and time

Parfit's argument against the Self-Interest Theory suggests that rationality requires that we treat persons, places, and times the same in certain key respects, and, in particular, that if we should be neutral with respect to one, we should also be neutral with respect to the others. Reasoning along similar lines, it might seem natural to assume that *if* we accept a dominance principle with respect to *one* of these categories, then we should *also* accept a similar dominance principle with respect to the other categories. Consider, for example, the following three dominance principles regarding utility.

Spatial Dominance Principle: for any two alternative outcomes, A and B, if A and B involve the same regions of space, and A is better than B regarding utility in *every* region of space, then A is better than B regarding utility.

Temporal Dominance Principle: for any two alternative outcomes, A and B, if A and B involve the same regions of time, and A is better than B regarding utility in *every* time period, then A is better than B regarding utility.

Personal Dominance Principle: for any two alternative outcomes, A and B, if A and B involve the same people, and A is better than B regarding utility for *every* person who will ever live, then A is better than B regarding utility.

Intuitively, many would find each of the preceding dominance principles plausible. Moreover, as indicated, influenced by reasoning of the sort appealed to by Parfit, many might assume that if one of the dominance principles is true, then the others must also be true. But this assumption is clearly false. To see this, consider Diagram 1.[13]

T1, S1 P_1 Good Life (*GL*); P_2, P_3 Bad Life (*BL*)   T1, S1 P_1 Bad Life (*BL*); P_2, P_3 Good Life (*GL*)

T2, S2 P_{1-3} GL; P_{4-9} BL   T2, S2 P_{1-3} BL; P_{4-9} GL

T3, S3 P_{1-9} GL; P_{10-27} BL   T3, S3 P_{1-9} BL; P_{10-27} GL

T4, S4 P_{1-27} GL; P_{28-81} BL   T4, S4 P_{1-27} BL; P_{28-81} GL

⋮   ⋮

⋮   ⋮

⋮   ⋮

O_1 O_2

Diagram 1.

O_1 is one possible outcome. In that outcome, there is one person, P_1, living in time period one, and spatial region one, who has a *good* life, well *above* the level at which life ceases to be worth living, but there are *twice* as many other people, P_2 and P_3, who have *bad* lives, well *below* the level at which life ceases to be worth living. In time period two, P_1 through P_3 have moved to spatial region two, where they all enjoy good lives, but unfortunately, in that time period, and at that location, twice as many other people, P_4 through P_9, have come into existence, and their lives are as bad as P_2 and P_3's lives were during T_1. In time period three, P_1 through P_9 have all moved to spatial region three, where they all enjoy good lives, but unfortunately in that time and location, twice as many other people, P_{10} through P_{27}, have come into existence, and their lives are as bad as P_2 and P_3's lives were during T_1. Outcome One continues to unfold, in this ever-expanding manner, forever, with each time period lasting for one day, and each person living for 100 years total, before dying. Here, and below, we assume that the positive value of each good moment is the same, the negative value of each bad moment is the same, and that the two values sum to zero, so that a life containing an equal number of moments of good and bad life will have a net value of zero, a life containing more moments of good life than bad life will have a positive net value, and a life containing more moments of bad life than good life will have a negative net value.

Outcome Two contains the *very same people* as Outcome One, P_1, P_2, P_3, etc., and is analogous to, though the reverse of, Outcome One. Specifically, in Outcome Two, there is one person, P_1, living in time period one, and spatial region one, who has a *bad* life, well *below* the level at which life ceases to be worth living, but there are *twice* as many other people, P_2 and P_3, who have *good* lives, well *above* the level at which life ceases to be worth living. In time period two, P_1 through P_3 have moved to spatial region two, where they all suffer bad lives, but fortunately, in that time period, and at that location, twice as many other people, P_4 through P_9, have come into existence, and their lives are as good as P_2 and P_3's lives were during T_1. In time period three, P_1 through P_9 have all moved to spatial region three, where they all suffer bad lives, but, once again, fortunately in that time and location, twice as many other people, P_{10} through P_{27}, have come into existence, and their lives are as good as P_2 and P_3's lives were during T_1. As before, Outcome Two continues to unfold, in this ever-expanding manner, forever, with each time period lasting for one day, and each person living for 100 years total, before dying.

Given our assumption that each moment of good life would balance equally against a moment of bad life, and the further moral assumption that in this example, there is no reason to favor one person over that of any other, how do Outcomes One and Two compare regarding utility?

On an *Impersonal Neutralist View*, of the sort favored by classical utilitarians, O_1 and O_2 might be judged as *equally good*. After all, if one is indifferent to *where* in space, time, or lives goods or bads are located, and *only* pays attention to *how much total* good and bad exists in the world, then one may judge that O_1 and O_2 are equally good, since, in each outcome, there would be an infinite number of good days, and an infinite number of bad days lived, and in each case the orders of infinity of the number of good and bad days would be the same.

Alternatively, if one compares the two outcomes place by place, or moment by moment, Outcome Two would be clearly *better* than Outcome One, in accordance with the Spatial and Temporal Dominance Principles. This is because for *every* spatial region, S_n, and *every* temporal region, T_n, there will be twice as many people with good lives as with bad lives in Outcome Two, while there will twice as many people with bad lives as with good lives in Outcome One.

So, should we conclude that, regarding utility, Outcomes One and Two are *equally good*, in accordance with the Impersonal Neutralist View, or that Outcome Two is *better than* Outcome One, in accordance with the dominance principles with respect to space and time? I find such judgments *very* hard to believe. After all, in O_1, each person has exactly *one* bad day, and the *rest of his or her 100 year life* is good. In O_2, on the other hand, each person has exactly *one* good day, and *the rest of his or her 100 year life* is bad. I know which of these outcomes I would want to obtain for myself, a loved one, or anyone else who was not pure evil!

O_1 is a world where *everyone* has lives that are very good *every single day but one*. O_2 is a world where *everyone* has lives that are very bad *every single day but one*. Clearly, *every* member of O_1 has a life which is, on balance, *well* worth living, whereas *every* member of O_2 has a life which is, on balance, *well* worth *not* living. Given all this, I firmly believe that Outcome One is *better* than Outcome Two, in accordance with the Personal Dominance Principle regarding utility.

In this example, we can accept the dominance principle regarding *people*, or we can accept the dominance principles regarding *space* and *time*, but we *cannot* do both! Here we have a *proof* that, unless we reject *all three* dominance principles, in some cases, at least, we *should* not, and *cannot*, treat space and time the same way as we treat people. So, *should* we reject all three dominance principles, in favor, perhaps, of the Impersonal Neutralist View? I don't see why. At least in the sort of case that we have been considering, the Personal Dominance Principle seems clearly true![14,15]

The preceding argument suggests that, for certain cases, at least, we should give priority to distributions of well-being across people over distributions of well-being across time. And earlier, I suggested being more concerned about distributions of well-being throughout time, than throughout space. The priority rankings of people over both time and space, and time over space, for some cases, at least, might be further buttressed by considering Diagram 2.

In Diagram 2, O_1 and O_2 are outcomes with an infinite number of people, P_i or Q_j, with each person, located at a particular location in space, S_k, and a particular location in time, T_l, at a level corresponding to one of the integers. So, for example, in Outcome One, person P_0 is at level 0, at temporal location 0

T_{-4}, T_{-3}, T_{-2}, T_{-1}, T_0, T_1, T_2, T_3, T_4, ...

S_{-4}, S_{-3}, S_{-2}, S_{-1}, S_0, S_1, S_2, S_3, S_4, ...

.... P_{-4}-4, P_{-3}-3, P_{-2}-2, P_{-1}-1, $P_0$0, $P_1$1, $P_2$2, $P_3$3, $P_4$4, ...

O_1

.... T_{-3}, T_{-2}, T_{-1}, T_0, T_1, T_2, T_3, T_4, T_5, ...

.... S_{-5}, S_{-4}, S_{-3}, S_{-2}, S_{-1}, S_0, S_1, S_2, S_3, ...

.... Q_{-4}-4, Q_{-3}-3, Q_{-2}-2, Q_{-1}-1, $Q_0$0, $Q_1$1, $Q_2$2, $Q_3$3, $Q_4$4, ...

O_2

Diagram 2.

and spatial location 0, while in Outcome Two, person Q_{-4} is at level −4, at temporal location −3 and spatial location −5. For the purposes of this example, I am assuming that the metaphysics of space and time allow for the identification of the same spatial and temporal locations across different possible outcomes, so that for each k and l, S_k corresponds to the very same location in space in each outcome, and T_l corresponds to the very same location in time in each outcome. If such an assumption is coherent, then Diagram 2 illustrates that, for some cases, at least, the Spatial and Temporal Dominance Principles are incompatible with each other. Thus, for such cases, we can reject both, but we can't accept both. This is because, in Diagram 2, Outcome One is *better* than Outcome Two at every point in *time*, but it is *worse* than Outcome Two at every point in *space*.

Now assume, temporarily, that the populations of the two outcomes are wholly distinct. In that case, I can see why someone might claim that each outcome is *equally* good, since each involves an infinite number of people, such that for each integer, there is exactly one person whose level of well-being is accurately represented by that integer. In that case, one would be rejecting *both* the Spatial and Temporal Dominance Principles. But my own judgment, in this case, is that we should *accept* the judgment yielded by the *Temporal* Dominance Principle, and *reject* the judgment yielded by the *Spatial* Dominance Principle. That is, in this case, I would judge Outcome One as better than Outcome Two, since it is better at each moment in time, and, to my mind, there is neither a compelling reason to ignore this consideration, nor a countervailing reason outweighing it.

But, of course, as the previous discussion makes plain, I believe that there *could* be such a reason. In particular, if the *same* people would exist in each outcome, and they would *each* be better off in one of the outcomes than the other, then, in accordance with the *Personal* Dominance Principle, I would regard the outcome in which they were all better off as better than the other outcome, regarding utility, regardless of how the two outcomes compared in accordance with either the Spatial or Temporal Dominance Principles.

5. Avoiding cases involving infinity

Some people will worry about some of my examples because they involve appeals to infinity about which our intuitions are notoriously unreliable. For those who have such worries, let me make several comments.

First, I believe that one must distinguish between different kinds of examples involving infinity. Some rely on moves that are clearly dubious, for example, when one 'reorders' the different members of an infinite sequence, say, by 'moving forward or backwards' certain members of the sequence, but not others, in order to shift our intuitions about the overall value of the infinite sequence, either when considered by itself, or in comparison with some other sequence. I fully *agree* that any intuitions that we might have about such 'reordered' infinite sequences are not to be trusted, but I note that *none* of my appeals to infinity involve such dubious moves. Indeed, I believe there is nothing 'tricky,' artificial, or dubious about the infinite sequences that I have considered in this article, that provides good reason to doubt our intuitions or judgments about them. To the contrary, although I cannot pursue this further, here, I believe that there are good reasons to accept our judgments about the various examples I have invoked involving infinity.

Second, I remind the reader that not all of my arguments involved appeals to our intuitions about infinite cases. Many of my arguments focused on finite cases.

Third, while I find some of my cases involving infinity particularly compelling – which is why I employ them – I believe that my main conclusions *could* have been argued for without appealing to such examples. In particular, I believe that there are a host of strong reasons, that don't appeal to infinity, to worry about any 'pure' neutralist position requiring us to be strictly neutral between any 'locations' of people, places, or times at which utility might obtain. I also believe that there are some finite cases where we should reject the rankings generated by the Spatial and Temporal Dominance Principles. In support of these claims, I offer the following observations.

First, consider the widely held view that the *shape* of a life matters, so that a life that begins poorly, but steadily improves, and ends well, would be better than a life that begins well, but steadily declines, and ends poorly, *even if* the two lives contained the same *total* amount of well-being. Clearly, this view is not strictly neutral as to *when*, in a life, well-being occurs.

But notice, most people holding this view regard space and time differently in this respect. They *don't* believe, for example, that if someone was at level 100 for the first 20 years of his life, at level 400 for the next 20 years, at level 700 for the next 20 years, and at level 1000 for his final 20 years, that the *overall* quality of his life would vary depending on *where*, in space, he lived *during* those different periods. Such a life would be *equally* good if the person lived in *one* place all his life, or in *different* places. Indeed, as long as the levels for each period weren't affected, he could move to any combination of different *places*, *in any order*, without affecting the overall quality of his life. So, this is a non-infinite example where many believe that space and time should be treated differently, as the ordering of well-being in *time* seems *relevant* for the overall quality of a life, in a way that the ordering of well-being in *space* does not.

Next, consider three principles that I presented in my book, *Rethinking the Good*:

> *The Second Standard View – Trade-offs between Quality and Number Are Sometimes Undesirable Even When Vast Numbers Are at Stake*: If the quality of one kind of benefit is 'sufficiently' low, and the quality of another kind of benefit is 'sufficiently' high, then an outcome in which a relatively small number of people received the higher quality benefit would be better than one in which virtually any number of people received the lower quality benefit. (Temkin 2012, 32)

> *The Disperse Additional Burdens View*: in general, if additional burdens are dispersed among different people, it is better for a given total burden to be dispersed among a vastly larger number of people so that the additional burden any single person has to bear within her life is 'relatively small,' than for a smaller total to fall on just a few, such that their additional burden is substantial. (Temkin 2012, 67–68)

> *The Consolidate Additional Benefits View*: in general, if additional benefits are dispersed among different people, it is better for a given total benefit to be consolidated among a few people, such that each person's additional benefit is substantial, than for a larger total benefit to be dispersed among a vastly larger number of people, so that the additional benefit any single person receives within her life is 'relatively small.' (Temkin 2012, 68)

I don't have time to repeat my arguments for these principles here, but in my book, I noted that most people, including many consequentialists, accept such principles. Such principles reflect an *anti-additive-aggregationist* approach, which opposes the simple additive-aggregationist approach of classical utilitarianism. For most people, we don't simply care about *how much* utility obtains in a given outcome, we *also* care about how that utility is *distributed* throughout the outcome, and that means that most people are *not* strictly neutral, as classical utilitarianism requires, as to *where* utility is located, with respect to people, places, and times.

Moreover, importantly, our concern about how utility is distributed does *not* merely reflect our concern for *other* distributive principles, such as equality or justice. It reflects our judgment about what is relevant to making one outcome *better* than another, *even regarding utility*. Thus, there is room for judging that though one outcome has *more* utility than another, it is still *worse* regarding utility. And this is because, for many, *one* fundamental concern is about the way in which different amounts and distributions of utility *affect people*, for better or worse, and this, I believe, reflects a *person-affecting* view, and not simply an impersonal neutralist position.

The anti-additive-aggregationist principles have wide appeal, both within, and between, lives. For example, they help explain why many find Parfit's Repugnant Conclusion repugnant (Parfit 1984, 381–390; Temkin 2012, 34–35, 37, 41–42, 324–328). Even if there is more *total utility* in Z than in A, Z's utility is dispersed across *many* lives, so that each person's life is *barely worth living*, whereas A's utility is consolidated among far fewer lives, so that each person's life is *well worth living*. Here, our ranking of A as better than Z reflects the wide person-affecting view that focuses on how the people in the two outcomes fare, and rests on the anti-additive-aggregationist position that lots of tiny benefits spread across innumerable masses don't *add up, normatively*, in the way that they would need to to make Z better than A.[16]

Similar results apply within lives, where most people judge a long life that includes two years of *excruciating* torture and fifteen mosquito bites per month, as *worse* than a long life that contains *no* torture but *sixteen* mosquito bites per month, even as they acknowledge that if the life were long *enough*, the *total* amount of disutility would be greater in the latter life than the former. Here, too, our anti-additive-aggregationist principles tell us that the discomfort of one extra mosquito bite per month doesn't *add up, normatively*, in the way that it would need to to outweigh two years of excruciating torture. Here, too, we are not merely concerned with the *total* amount of disutility in a life, and utterly neutral as to where, when, and to whom (in this context, which person stage) it obtains; rather, we are concerned about how the disutility is *distributed* throughout the life, and how the *person* is *affected*, for better or worse, by that distribution. The plain fact is that some distributions of vast amounts of total disutility can be benign, while some distributions of much smaller amounts of total disutility can be disastrous.

So, bearing all this in mind, return to the example depicted in Diagram 1, but this time, imagine that the outcomes don't extend infinitely, but 'only' for a billion years. How do the two outcomes compare in that case? I believe, in accordance with the spirit of the Disperse Additional Burdens and Consolidate Additional Benefits Views, that O_1 would still be *better* than O_2, even though there is twice as *much* badness in O_1 as in O_2, and twice as *much* goodness in O_2 as in O_1.

How could that be? Well, by now, the answer is familiar. The question, for me, isn't merely about how much *total* goodness and badness exists, but about how the *people* are *affected* for better or worse, by the distribution of whatever goodness and badness there is. In O_1, there will be many people with good lives for every day but one, for 100 years, many with good lives for every day but one, for 99 years and 364 days, many with good lives for every day but one, for 99 years and 363 days, many with good lives for every day but one, for 99 years and 362 days, and so on. To be sure, on the *last* day of O_1's existence, there will be a *vast* number of people who live only one day, whose lives, for that day, will be very bad. But still, the badness for them only lasts a *single day*, and I don't believe that that badness *adds up, normatively*, across the lives of the many who will live *only one day*, in the way that it would need to outweigh the *really good lives* that would have been lived for *many* years by *many* others.

In O_2, on the other hand, there will be many people with bad lives for every day but one, for 100 years, many with bad lives for every day but one, for 99 years and 364 days, many with bad lives for every day but one, for 99 years and 363 days, many with bad lives for every day but one, for 99 years and 362 days, and so on. To be sure, on the *last* day of O_2's existence, there will be a *vast* number who live only one day, whose lives, for that day, will be very good. But still, the goodness for them only lasts a *single day*, and here, as before, I don't believe that that goodness *adds up, normatively*, across the lives of the many who live only *one* day, in the way that it would need to tooutweigh the *really bad lives* that would have been lived for *many* years by *many* others.

In sum, looking at how all the different *people* are *affected* for better or worse in each outcome, and taking account of the anti-additive-aggregationist principles that I find compelling in cases like this, as well in many other cases, including the Repugnant Conclusion, I would judge that, *even regarding utility*, Outcome One is *better* than Outcome Two. Of course, in making this judgment, I am not denying the obvious truth that Outcome Two has *more* utility than Outcome One. Of course it does! Rather, I am reflecting the appeal of person-affecting views, that pay attention not merely to *how much* utility there is in any outcome, but to how the *people* are *affected*, for better or worse, by the distribution of however much utility there is.

If my judgment about this case is correct, and I realize that not everyone will agree with me about this, then we have reason to reject the Spatial and Temporal Dominance Principles *even in finite cases*. After all, as before, Outcome Two is better than Outcome One at *every* location in space and time. At first blush, this is a somewhat surprising result. However, on reflection, I believe it is the right one.

6. The Limbo Man, the Capped Model, and other unresolved issues

In discussing the badness of death, Kamm (1993, 19, 49–55) introduces several variations of a case she calls the *Limbo Man*. Kamm suggests that the *finality* of death, its *permanence*, the *extinction* of our lives may play a special role in our explaining some of the attitudes toward death that are almost universally shared. Kamm suggests that the recognition that once our lives are over, they are over *forever*, opens the possibility that there might be reason to be concerned about when our lives begin, as well as when our lives end.

Kamm suggests, for example, that if the universe spanned a given period of time, and we were going to live our one and only life for 70 years sometime within that span, then even if one assumed that the conscious experiences of our life would be *exactly* the same on either scenario, and that all the (non-location-in-time-related) *goods* of life that we would possess would be *exactly* the same on either scenario, there might still be reason to want our 70-year life to obtain towards the *end* of the universe rather than towards the beginning.

Kamm suggests that there might be at least two related reasons for this. First, as long as we have not yet existed, the *potential* for our existing will still be there, and one might believe that there is value in such potential. Second, one might believe that it is better for us, or our lives – though *not* due to any impact on our states of consciousness or the goods that we possess during our lives – if the time during which we will never again exist is as short as possible, so that our extinction comes as late as possible. On this view, the badness of *never existing again* is distinct from, and has special significance, relative to the mere badness of *not* existing, which, of course, will also be true of us at each moment *before* we come to exist.

For Kamm, then, if someone had a choice of living a normal lifespan, filled with a given set of experiences and goods of life, or a chance of starting that life for a period of time, going into limbo for an extended period of time, and then finishing off the remainder of one's life many centuries or more later, there could be reason to do the latter, even if it were *no better* in terms of one's set of experiences and (non-time-related) goods of life. As indicated, for Kamm, this is because there might be something good about both preserving, as long as possible, the possibility of a period of one's future existence, and minimizing, as much as possible, the period during which it is true that you will *never exist again*.

In many respects, Kamm's discussion is orthogonal to my own. She is concerned about the badness of death, and the asymmetry between our attitudes towards *death*, and the period during which we won't exist that comes *after* it, and our attitudes towards *birth*, and the period during which we won't exist that comes *before* it. I am focused on civilizations, containing large populations, and my concern is not with the prospect of any given civilization coming to an *end*, but with the possibility of there being large periods of time devoid of *any civilizations at all* whose members possess high-quality lives. But though Kamm's concerns are different than mine, they have a bearing on mine in several respects.

First, I have pointed out an asymmetry in my thinking about space and time. I note that the ubiquitous fear of death that has been almost universally held throughout the history of humanity, and which has inspired so much art and literature, is a *time*-related attitude. It is *not* a *space*-related attitude. Kamm's discussion takes as its starting point the commonplace that the vast majority of humans fear their own death. For many, the prospect that there will be an eternity of time after they die during which they *will never exist again* is *terrifying*. Many can't bear to even contemplate that prospect, and many others simply refuse to accept it. Indeed, throughout human history, religions have arisen to help people confront their earthly deaths, holding out the promise of eternal life.

Nothing akin to this holds regarding the many different *spaces* beyond ours that we will *never, ever, occupy*! Looking out into space, we might feel tiny and insignificant. We might even find ourselves deeply *disappointed* that we never get to explore that great unknown. But we don't look into space with utter *terror* at the realization that *we* will never be *there*. We have no trouble contemplating, or accepting the fact, that there may be an infinity of spaces, beyond all those that we will ever occupy. And no religions have arisen to help us cope with that reality!

Kamm's Limbo Man lives for a period, puts himself in limbo, then lives out the duration of his life at a much later period of time. In doing this, he gains nothing in terms of his experiences or the (non-time-related) goods of life, but he succeeds in significantly delaying the day when it will be true that he will no longer ever exist again. Kamm thinks that there could be reason to be this kind of Limbo Man. But Kamm doesn't consider a Limbo Man who lives in different locations, puts himself in limbo, then lives out the duration of his life at a place much further away in space than the place he was when he went into limbo. This is, I believe, no accident.

If Kamm is right, there can be rational significance to *when* we live in time, connected to the desirability of both the potential that we shall one day exist in the future, and the delay of the time after which we shall never exist again. But there seems to be no analogous rational significance to *where* in space we live. Assuming that our experiences and (non-space-related) goods would be the same, the potential of our coming to exist at one point in space seems no more valuable than the potential of our coming to exist at any other point in space, far away from the first. Nor does there seem to be any rational reason to want to start our lives at one point in space, and finish them at another, merely so as to reduce the amount of space outside the first point that will never be occupied by us.

In sum, I suggest that Kamm's discussion of our attitudes towards death – attitudes which are decidedly time related but not space related – implicitly support my contention that there is reason to treat space and time differently for the purposes of practical reasoning. However, Kamm's discussion is of interest to me not merely for that reason, but because it raises a host of interesting questions about individual lives that might be similarly raised about large groups of lives.

In this article, I have contended that it is more important that large gaps in time be filled with many high-quality lives, than that large gaps in space be filled with high-quality lives. But even if that is so, there are a host of other, Kamm-like questions that might be raised. For example, suppose that there will only be one super-large civilization in the whole of the universe's existence, and that the very same people will exist in that civilization and all have lives of the very same high quality of existence, no matter when in time that they existed. If there would be, say, a *quintillion* (1,000,000,000,000,000,000) people, each of whom lived for 100 years with a high quality of life, would it matter if they lived later, rather than earlier, in the life of the universe? For example, if the life of the universe, and time itself, had a beginning and an end, and all of the people were going to be alive during the same 10,000-year period, would it be better if they all lived in the middle rather than the beginning, but better still if they all lived at the end?

Similarly, even if I am right that, in general, it would be good if the different 'empty' periods of time were 'filled' with high-quality lives, that still leaves many possibilities open. For example, suppose that we thought that 100 billion people were enough to 'fill' any given 10,000-year period of time. Then, on my view, it would be better if the quintillion people were spread out in time, so that there were 1000 *distinct* 10,000-year periods, each filled with 100 billion people. Still, that leaves it open whether we think it matters *how* those different periods were dispersed throughout the life of the universe.

Retaining our previous assumption that the universe, and time, had a beginning and an end, one might think that it doesn't matter. Or one might think, perhaps influenced by Kamm, that it would be best if the different periods were all bunched together, so that there was a steady run of high-quality life for 10 million years coming at the *very end* of time. Perhaps one might think that it was important that high-quality life span the entire life of the universe, but that all this required is that the very *first* 10,000-year period be populated with lots of high-quality life, and that the very *last* 10,000-year period be populated with lots of high-quality life, but that beyond that it wouldn't matter how the different 10,000-year periods of high-quality life were distributed through time, as long as they remained non-overlapping. Alternatively, perhaps one might think it best to distribute the different periods of high-quality life throughout time, so as to minimize the length of any period of time during which there would be no high-quality life![17]

These questions are not intended to be exhaustive, but merely indicative of the wide range of issues that need to be considered once one acknowledges that, *ceteris paribus*, it is good if 'empty' periods of time be 'filled' with high-quality lives. And, of course, similarly issues will arise if one believes that there is some reason to 'fill' empty locations in space with high-quality lives, even if one grants that such reasons are less weighty than the analogous ones pertinent to time. Moreover, we may or may not have the same view of these issues, depending on whether or not we think that time and space are finite or infinite.

I mention these issues, only to leave them aside. They are a reminder – as if any were needed! – of the very preliminary nature of this work.

In *Rethinking the Good*, I introduced a position I called the *Capped Model of Moral Ideals* (Temkin 2012, 328–350). On a Capped Model, in certain contexts of comparison, there may be an upper limit on how good a given outcome may be regarding any particular ideal and, similarly, an upper limit on how good an outcome can be, all things considered. I acknowledged that the Capped Model faced a host of serious objections, and that there were a large number of unresolved questions regarding it. Even so, I argued that we needed something like the Capped Model in order to capture the anti-additive-aggregationist views that underlie certain of the judgments that most people hold about how different outcomes compare. Thus, for example, in the Repugnant Conclusion, most people believe, in accordance with a Capped Model, that no matter *how many people* there may be in an outcome where everyone who exists have lives that are barely worth living, the *value* of the well-being in that outcome will never rise to the point that it outweighs the *value* of the well-being in an alternative outcome where 10 billion people exist, all of whom have extremely high-quality lives. And likewise, most people believe that the all things considered value of the former outcome will never exceed that of the latter.

I cannot repeat, here, my lengthy discussion of the Capped Model in *Rethinking the Good*. But I note that much of this article is implicitly reflecting different views as to how best to develop the Capped Model. For example, I am suggesting that we should not have a single cap for how good an outcome may be regarding well-being over the course of time, but rather that we must have separate caps for each 'substantial' period of time. Regarding space, however, I am tempted to the view that a single cap that covers all of space at any given time period might be appropriate. On the other hand, if we do have different caps for different regions of space, perhaps the levels of those caps will be lower than the levels of the caps for time, or perhaps the levels of the caps for space may vary depending on how full other spatial regions already are.

Many of the unresolved issues in this paper are connected with unresolved issues regarding the Capped Model. Correspondingly, thinking further about what to say about the kinds of cases presented in this article may help illuminate how we should think about the Capped Model. By the same token, in the Rawlsian spirit of reflective equilibrium (Rawls 1971),[18] thinking further about how best to understand and interpret the Capped Model may help inform our judgments – sometimes confirming and sometimes leading us to revise our intuitions – about the sorts of cases this article considers.

Unfortunately, I cannot explore the Capped Model here. But let me point out just one way in which thinking more about the Capped Model might help illuminate our thinking about the kinds of issues this article raises. Regarding well-being, I believe that for each time period, we will need a different cap – a different upper limit – on how good an outcome can be regarding well-being, that will largely be a function of the (well-being) level of the best-off people in that outcome, and the number of people at that level. So, for example, for any given time period, the upper level of how good an outcome can be, regarding well-being, when everyone has a life that is barely worth living will be much lower than the upper level of how good an outcome can be, regarding well-being, when everyone has a life that is well worth living. More generally, I believe that the higher quality lives a population possesses, the higher cap there may be on how good an outcome can be regarding well-being.

Let us suppose that if people have a very high quality of life, k, the upper level on how good an outcome can be when everyone in a given time period has lives of quality k, is n. Let us further suppose that if people have a very high quality of life, $k + x$ where x is a positive number, the upper level on how good an outcome can be when everyone in a given time period has lives of quality $k + x$, is $n + y$. If x is a relatively small, we can assume that the difference between n and $n + y$ won't be too significant. Next, suppose that a population of 10 billion people is sufficiently great, that if 10 billion people are all at level k, the value of that outcome will be *very close* to the upper limit for that outcome, namely n. And likewise, suppose that a population of 10 billion people is sufficiently great, that if 10 billion people are all at level $k + x$, the value of that outcome will be *very close* to the upper limit for that outcome, namely $n + y$.

By hypothesis, it will then be the case that the value of the outcome in which 10 billion people are at level $k + x$, will be greater than the value of the outcome in which 10 billion people are at level k, but not *much* greater. By the same token, given the nature of the Capped Model, since, by hypothesis, a population of 10 billion is enough to get a population *very near* the upper limit for how good that outcome can be regarding well-being (depending on the levels of those 10 billion people), it follows that if 20 billion people were at level $k + x$, during the very same time period, rather than only 10 billion people, that would improve the overall value of the outcome regarding well-being *slightly*, but *only* slightly. And the same is true, of course, if 20 billion people were at level k, during the very same time period, rather than only 10 billion people. That, too, would improve the overall value of the outcome regarding well-being *slightly*, but *only* slightly. Since, by hypothesis, we have assumed that the overall value of $n + y$ is not much higher than the overall value of n, it follows that having 20 billion people at level $k + x$, during any given time period, will be not much higher than having 20 billion people at level k, during any given time period.

Now suppose that the only people living in the universe would be the 20 billion people at level k. But that they could either all live during the same time period, in which case the total value of well-being in that outcome would be very close to n, or there could be 10 billion people living in each of two distinct time periods, each living at level k. In *that* case, there would be two distinct time periods during which the value of the well-being would be nearly n. Even if one is not a simple additive aggregationist for determining the value of an outcome – as one won't be if one adopts a Capped Model – it seems, given the considerations of this article, that there might be strong reason to attach significantly greater value to the outcome in which the 20 billion people were spread out over two distinct time periods, than to the outcome in which all 20 billion people lived during the same time period.

If this reasoning is all correct, then we might believe that there is strong reason to attach greater value to the outcome in which 20 billion people are all at level k, but spread out over two distinct time periods, than to the outcome in which all 20 billion people are at level $k + x$, but they all live during the *same* time period. But notice, we might suppose that it would be the *very same people* in the two different outcomes. In that case, we would be valuing one outcome more highly than another, because of how the well-being in that outcome is distributed *temporally*, even though the presumably better outcome would be *worse* for everyone who ever lived! This is because, in the supposedly better outcome, everyone would be at level k, while in the supposedly worse outcome, everyone would be better off, at the slightly higher level $k + x$.

I have argued at length, elsewhere, that there are a host of *impersonal* ideals – ideals that have value beyond the extent to which they are good or bad *for people* (Temkin 1993a, 1993b, 2000, 2003a, 2003b, 2003c). Such ideals open up the distinct possibility that one outcome could be *worse* than another, even though there is *no one for whom* it *is* worse and, similarly, that one outcome could be *better* than another, even though there is *no one for whom* it *is* better. Clearly, if the way in which an outcome's well-being is distributed in time or space can be relevant to our assessment of the overall value of that outcome, beyond the extent to which it affects the quality of lives (the experiences and non-time-related and non-space-related goods) of the sentient beings in that outcome, then the relevant temporal and spatial factors are *impersonal* in nature. This is an important but, on reflection, not surprising result.

Earlier in this article, I considered some examples that led me to conclude that, for *certain cases and contexts*, I favor people over times, and times over space. At the time, the reader may have been puzzled as to why I qualified my remarks in the way that I did. The preceding explains why. While there are some cases where I clearly favor how well-being is distributed across people, over how well-being is distributed across time, in some cases, such as the one I have just discussed, my judgment goes the other way. Here, as elsewhere, morality is enormously complex, and there are few, if any, simple principles that hold uniformly, and without exception or qualification, across all cases.

7. Conclusion

There is a rich tradition among game theorists, decision theorists, economists, and many philosophers, to identify rationality with the sort of impartial, neutralist, perspective commonly associated with classical utilitarianism, but with the acknowledgment that we need a wider conception of the good than classical utilitarianism endorses, and that we might need to allow for special agent-relative duties and permissions in assessing the rationality of people's beliefs, cares, and actions. On such a view, there is an important respect in which we should treat people, places, and times, the same, and be neutral with respect to all three.

I agree that there are important respects in which rationality *does* require us to treat people, places, and times the same, and to be neutral with respect to all three. But it is far from self-evident to what the substantive content of this position amounts. In this article, I have argued that there are certain cases and contexts where we ought, rationally, to treat space and time differently. I have further contended that there are certain cases and contexts where we ought, rationally, to treat people differently than space and time. I have argued that in some cases and contexts, we should give priority to people over both times and places, and to times over places. However, I have also suggested that in some cases and contexts, we should give priority to time over people.

I believe that the considerations presented in this article are plausible, so far as they go. Even so, as I have noted throughout, this article is very much a preliminary work. Accordingly, much more work needs to be done to properly assess what rationality requires of us in our treatment of people, places, and times, whether with respect to our beliefs, our cares, or our actions.

Notes

1. Throughout this article, I sometimes speak in terms of *place*, and sometimes speak in terms of *space*, depending on which sounds better linguistically in the particular context of usage. But I am using these terms interchangeably, understanding any particular place to correspond to a spatial location.
2. For the sake of simplicity, I follow Parfit (1984) in my presentation, by putting my discussion in terms of being neutral with respect to different 'people.' However, in this context, the scope of the word 'people' needn't refer only, or to all, *human* beings; it might refer to all *rational* beings or, as it does for many, to all *sentient* beings.
3. To be clear, and fair to Parfit, nothing in Parfit's argument against the self-interest theory commits him to denying this claim. To the contrary, Parfit could, and would, accept that there are *numerous* respects in which we should treat persons, places, and times differently, and he could, in fact, accept many of the claims and arguments that I shall be making in the following sections. The point is just that while Parfit has illuminated an important truth, not to be lost sight of, that in *certain respects* we should treat persons, places, and times the same, I hope to illuminate a different, but compatible, important truth, *also* not to be lost sight of, that in certain *other* respects, we should, and must, treat persons, places, and

times differently. In addition, I hope to illustrate some of the sometimes surprising respects in which this is so.

I might add that while Parfit could accept most, and perhaps all, of what follows, Sidgwick, perhaps, could not. This depends on whether or not one interprets Sidgwick to be a mental state theorist, who believes that the only sources of intrinsic value and disvalue are positive and negative conscious states, respectively. That view, combined with Sidgwick's additive-aggregationist maximizing approach, which assesses the value of an outcome solely as a simple additive function of the individual instances of intrinsic value and disvalue which obtain in that outcome, implies that one must be strictly neutral between people, places, and times, for the purposes of moral reasoning. Such a view is incompatible with most of the claims that I make in the following sections.

However, it is worth noting that it is not the maximizing structure of consequentialism, per se, that is incompatible with much of what follows, but rather the maximizing structure of consequentialism when it is combined with a particular conception of intrinsic value like that of the mental state theory (Here, I focus on the part of Sidgwick's view according to which there was always *sufficient reason*, and hence it was always practically rational, to act morally. In fact, as Parfit (2011, 6–7, 130–149) has pointed out, Sidgwick (1907) accepted the dualism of practical reasoning, according to which there was *also* always *sufficient reason*, and hence it was also always practically rational, to act self-interestedly.).

I am grateful to Shelly Kagan (personal communication, October 2, 2015) for suggesting that I consider the theoretical underpinnings that might lead some people to think that we should, in fact, be strictly neutral between persons, places, and times for the purposes of practical reasoning. What the preceding discussion reveals is that the positions I shall argue for in the following sections are incompatible with mental state versions of maximizing consequentialism, or other theories of that ilk.

4. I realize that some of these assumptions will be controversial on certain interpretations of modern physics. For example, some believe that one cannot meaningfully distinguish between space and time, as the universe is composed of (inseparable) space/time points. Likewise, some believe that space and time had a beginning, perhaps at the moment of the Big Bang, and likewise, that space and time may have an end, depending on how much matter there is in the universe, and whether the Universe will eventually collapse on itself and everything, including space and time, will come to an end at a single point of singularity. In addition, some believe that time's passage is an illusion, and others, appealing to Einstein's theory of special relativity, will insist that the direction of time is relative to one's point of reference.

Still, there are a number of distinguished philosophers of science, metaphysicians, and physicists who would accept that the assumptions I am making are compatible with our best scientific views of the universe, and it is hard to deny that the assumptions I am making *might* have been true of our universe or some other universe (I am grateful to my colleague, the philosopher of physics Barry Loewer, who confirmed in an email on 16 October 2015, that the philosopher of physics, Tim Maudlin, 'thinks that time has an intrinsic direction, and he is willing to say that "time passes," and that some 'metaphysicians think that time "moves" in a more robust and non-metaphorical sense ... [including] Dean Zimmerman ... CD Broad, Michael Tooley, [and] Tim Williamson.' Loewer also noted that 'two physicists that are in the "time really moves" camp are Lee Smolin and George Ellis.').

So, one way of interpreting the following arguments is that they may give us pause for treating space and time the same even on our best current scientific understanding of the universe, and would give us reason for treating space and time differently in any universe where something like a Newtonian conception of space and time was true. Accordingly, we should be wary of any a priori arguments in support of the claim that rationality requires that we treat space and time the same for the purposes of practical reasoning.

5. Scheffler (2013) has argued that having descendants who will help realize some of our deepest hopes, projects, or ideals helps to give our lives value and meaning that they otherwise would lack. Scheffler's views are entirely compatible with my own, and I am happy to accept them. But they point to *other* reasons why one might be more concerned about the future than about what happens elsewhere in space than those I am trying to illuminate here. As my example makes plain, I believe that even if the future civilizations were unrelated to our own, and would do *nothing* to further *our* particular hopes, projects, and ideals, I *still* believe that there would be strong reason to ensure that such civilizations would exist if they would have high-quality lives. In addition, I believe that such reasons would be stronger than any we would have to ensure, were it possible, that such civilizations obtain elsewhere in space contemporaneous with our own.

Similarly, Jeff McMahan (personal communication, October 2, 2015) suggested a variety of considerations that might lead us, in general, to give greater weight to there being high-quality sentient lives existing in the future, than to there being high-quality sentient lives existing elsewhere in space. According to McMahan, these might include views we have about the importance of the preservation of value, views about the importance of progress, and views about the importance of greater diversity of experiences. My response to McMahan is threefold.

First, as with what I said about Scheffler's view, I don't regard my position as incompatible with McMahan's. Depending on the details of the case, there could be more than one reason for valuing the existence of *future* civilizations over the existence of contemporaneous civilizations elsewhere in space. But second, in my examples, I wasn't, in fact, assuming that there was greater diversity of experiences over time than across space, nor was I assuming that there would be *progress* between our current civilization and the future, unrelated, civilizations. Thus, my views about such cases weren't, in fact, turning on such factors. Moreover, importantly, I note that the notions of *preservation* of value, and *progress*, have a temporal dimension built in to them, but not a spatial dimension. So, McMahan's suggestions regarding those factors would, if correct, not be a *rival* to my own, but rather a further elucidation of some of the *reasons* why we should treat space and time differently for the purposes of practical reasoning.

Finally, Jonathan Weisberg (Q&A, *Belief, Action, and Rationality Over Time* Workshop, University of Wisconsin-Madison, September 6, 2015) suggested that our intuitions about such cases might reflect the psychological phenomenon of our 'not wanting the story to end'; perhaps traceable to our early childhood when our parents read us bedtime stories and we didn't want the story to end, since when it did, our parents would leave, and we would be left alone in the scary dark! It is always difficult to *prove* that such a deflationary account plays *no* role in our intuitions about such cases, but when I think hard about such cases,

I don't believe that the best, or main, explanation of my intuitions about them lies in the sort of deflationary account that Weisberg suggests.

This is further supported by cases that I will consider later, where I have similar views about the greater importance of filling *past* temporal regions, or *gaps* between present and future temporal regions, relative to the importance of filling other contemporaneous spatial regions, or 'empty' gaps between different regions of space that are occupied by high-quality sentient lives. In such cases, it appears that our propensity to 'not want the story to end' would have no explanatory role to play as to why we have the intuitions we do.

6. Thoma (2015) notes that there are two different possible ways of 'filling' space with sentient life, and wonders which one I have in mind. On one, we add new sentient beings to locations in space that were previously empty. On the other, we make previously existing sentient beings *larger*, so that they occupy more space, including some previously unoccupied space.

   I had the former notion in mind, but Thoma's observation points to another issue that may have a bearing on how we should regard space and time for the purposes of practical reasoning. It is clear that my thoughts occupy time – each thought begins at one point in time, ends at another, and spans a given time period. It is much less clear that my thoughts exist in space.

   As has long been observed, unlike physical objects that clearly do exist in space, thoughts lack extension, shape, or mass. To be sure, I think of my thought as occurring 'within my head,' and my head is a material substance that occupies a given region of space; but does my thought occupy the region of space from ear to ear and from chin to scalp? That sounds odd, and not quite right. Does the thought 'I am hungry' occupy *more* space, as one grows from toddler, to teenager, to adult? That doesn't seem right, either. Similarly, if I were given extraordinary growth hormones, so that I ballooned up to the size of a planet, I don't think that my thought 'I am hungry' would then be planet-sized, occupying the vast spatial region that my body would then occupy.

   If this is right, then we see another way that we have to treat space and time differently, for the purposes of practical reasoning. Regarding contiguous future *temporal* regions, we could result in a net gain in the total amount of time that was filled with high-quality sentient life in either of two ways; either we could 'fill' it with new sentient beings who would have high-quality lives, or we could, in principle, 'fill' it by extending our own lifespans. But regarding contiguous *spatial* regions, it seems that we could result in a net gain in the total amount of space that was filled with high-quality sentient life in only one way, by 'filling' it with new sentient beings who would have high-quality lives. Were we to 'fill' such contiguous spaces either by moving into them, or by making ourselves larger, it seems that either way there would be no net gain in how much high quality sentient life obtained in the spatial regions in question.

   Finally, this discussion makes plain that when I talk of 'high quality sentient life,' I am referring to the well-being of sentient beings that is related to *consciousness*. It also suggests that talk of 'filling' a region of space with high-quality sentient life is metaphorical, in a way that talk of 'filling' a temporal region with high-quality sentient life need not be. I am grateful to Thoma's observation and query for leading me to consider and clarify my view of these matters.

7. Thoma (2015, 10) questions whether I can legitimately conclude from my examples that 'filling space is less important than filling time.' Thoma contends that such a conclusion is indefensible in the absence of a conversion scale that would tell us what length of time is equivalent to what area in space. But Thoma

is skeptical whether such a conversion scale is even intelligible. What would it mean, Thoma wonders, to contend that one acre was equivalent to a given amount of time?

Thoma raises an interesting question. But I'm not sure how much I should be troubled by it. The question *isn't* whether, for example, a galaxy in space is equal to 100 billion years of time. Rather, the question concerns the extent, if any, to which adding billions and billions of high-quality lives to an otherwise 'empty' galaxy (one devoid of sentient life) would significantly improve the outcome, if there were *already* billions and billions of high-quality lives being lived *elsewhere* in the universe *at the same time*; vs. the extent, if any, to which adding billions and billions of high quality lives to an otherwise 'empty' 100 billion years would significantly improve the outcome if it is true that there *have been* or *will be* billions and billions of high-quality lives lived *at different times* (perhaps, to keep the situations analogous, at the very same locations to which the 'extra' lives would be added).

I don't believe that we need an answer to the former question – Thoma's question – in order to answer the latter questions – which are mine. And I believe that the answers that we get to the latter questions, and others like them, support my claim that 'it is more important for high quality life to be dispersed across time rather than across space' – at least if that claim is charitably, and properly, interpreted.

Consider someone who claims that freedom is non-instrumentally valuable; that is, valuable *itself*, beyond the extent to which it promotes other valuable ideals. Suppose that person also believes that pleasure is non-instrumentally valuable, and so believes that eating ice cream is valuable, at least for her, in virtue of the pleasure that it gives her. Echoing Thoma, one might wonder whether there is a conversion scale between the value of freedom and the value of pleasure. What would it mean, one might wonder, to contend that eating a gallon of ice cream was equivalent to a given amount of freedom? Yet, admitting that the question is interesting, and even that it raises a host of deep and important issues, I still think it could be perfectly intelligible, and even true, to assert that freedom was more valuable than eating ice cream!

Note, if we don't believe that the value of freedom is *lexically prior* to the value of pleasure – and I don't, as, setting health issues aside, I would *gladly* trade a tiny infringement on my freedom, for a lifetime of ice cream indulgence! – we may need to say a bit more to convey exactly what we have in mind in saying that freedom is more valuable than eating ice cream. But I trust that this could be done. For example, we might just mean that a lifetime devoid of ice cream eating would be better than a lifetime devoid of freedom. But the point is that we might be able to perceive the truth of such a claim, even in the absence of having a conversion scale of the sort to which Thoma is referring.

Similarly, I might not have a conversion scale between areas and times, and yet I might be correct in claiming that 'it is more important for high quality life to be dispersed across time rather than across space.' The content of my claim can be derived from the examples I presented in support of it, though admittedly, perhaps only imprecisely. That content is, I believe, intelligible and defensible, and does not require that filling 'empty' times with high-quality life has *lexical priority* over filling 'empty' spaces.

There is, of course, much more that could be said in response to Thoma's worry, but, given my space constraints, I hope to have said enough for this article's purposes.

8. Indeed, by some standards of measuring how much of each atom is 'occupied' by material entities, an atom is 99.9999999999999% empty space. See, http://physics.stackexchange.com/questions/39143/percentage-of-water-that-is-void-or-empty-space.

9. Shelly Kagan (personal communication, October 2, 2015) wonders how far I would push the idea of the importance of filling empty times with high-quality sentient life. Suppose, for example, that there was a planet teeming with high-quality life, such that for 12 hours each day everyone was awake, and experiencing high levels of consciousness, but that for another 12 hours each day, everyone fell into a deep, dreamless, sleep, utterly devoid of conscious experiences. Would I think it a 'great tragedy' that there was so much 'empty' time over the course of each year? Would the world be better if half of the people had their sleep cycles shifted, so that at every moment, there were always large numbers of people experiencing high levels of consciousness? What if there were only five minutes each day, or five seconds each day, where everyone was completely unconscious? Would the outcome really be better, even in *such* cases, if people's sleep cycles were shifted so as to fill *every* available period of time with high levels of consciousness? Kagan finds this hard to believe.

    I confess that I am tempted to the view that, if possible, it *would* always be better, other things equal, to fill *any* empty period of time, no matter how short, with many instances of high levels of consciousness; though, obviously, the shorter the period is, the less important it would be. But I'm not committed to this view. What I *am* committed to is the thought that it is bad if there are significantly lengthy periods of time – leaving it open for now whether we understand that to be on the scale of a decade, century, millennium, or eon – which are utterly devoid of high-quality life. It is better, I think, if there are large numbers of high levels of consciousness obtaining within, and spread throughout, each such period. But whether it is important that there be *no gaps at all* of high-level consciousness *within* each period, or exactly how small such gaps would have to be for them to be unobjectionable, are questions about which I have no firm views or commitments.

10. This example is a variation of an infinite one suggested to me by Jeff McMahan (after my lecture at the Oxford Moral Theory Seminar, May 18, 2015) in defense of the view in question. McMahan noted that he thought that a universe where, for all of eternity, there were billions of people in extreme agony, and no one else existed, would be worse than a universe involving an infinite number of planets, each populated by billions of people in extreme agony, and no one else existed, if, in the latter case, all of the universe's agony obtained within a single short period, such as 30 or 100 years. I agree.

    Frances Kamm (personal communication, October 2, 2015) indicated that she might value a universe where lots of conscious life existed for all of eternity, over a universe where an infinite amount of conscious life existed for only 30 or 100 years, even if all of the conscious life was suffering greatly. But when pressed, it became clear that Kamm only thought this on the assumption that, all things considered, there was value to the existence of conscious life, *even if* that life involved unrelenting suffering. McMahan and I were assuming differently in making our claims. But if we agreed with Kamm, then our cases would be similar to my initial cases, where the argument purported to show that it was more important to fill time than space with conscious beings if, all things considered, the lives of those conscious beings were valuable.

11. There are at least two reasons one might think this rational. First, following Nagel (1986), one might believe that there are different perspectives on the world that one might rationally take, each of which reflects its own reality. In particular, one can take a (more or less) 'objective perspective,' which reflects the world as it is, from the 'outside,' as it were. In addition, one can take a (more or less) 'subjective perspective,' which reflects the world as it is, from the 'inside,' as it were. Even if one grants that from a certain objective perspective, there would be nothing to choose between the two alternatives, it seems undeniable that considering the *lived life* as it would be *experienced from the inside*, there would be every reason to delay the timing of one's entrance into Hell as long as possible! On Nagel's view, both perspectives reflect reality, and both are sources of genuine reasons to believe, care, or act. A fortiori, on Nagel's view, it would be perfectly rational to delay one's entry into Hell.

    Second, one might grant that there are various perspectives and theories which would regard the life with the delayed entrance into Hell and the life where one enters Hell immediately as *equally bad*. But surely there are *some* perspectives and theories that would regard the life with the delayed entry into Hell as *better* than the life that begins in Hell immediately, while there would appear to be *no* perspectives or theories that would rank the life that begins in Hell immediately as *better* than the life with the delayed entry into Hell.

    Accordingly, even if we attach *most* credence in the theories that regard both lives as equally good, as long as we attach *some* credence in the theories that regard the delayed entry life as best, and *no* credence in the theories that regard the immediate entry life as best, then from the standpoint of *practical rationality*, we have everything to gain and nothing to lose by following the theories that favor the delayed life. This follows from simple dominance-type reasoning, since if, in fact, a theory that regards the two theories as equally good is true, then we won't be any *worse off* if we pick the delayed entry life, while if, in fact, a theory that regards the delayed life as best is true, we will be better off if we follow it, and worse off if we don't! A powerful argument in support of the *practical rationality* of choosing in accordance with the line of reasoning suggested is presented and defended in Ross (2006). Ross's argument is discussed and employed at numerous points in Temkin (2012, 35–36, 40–41, 125–127, 171–173, 261–262, 443–445).

12. Note, our previous discussion would support a similar, though possibly weaker, conclusion for finite cases. If it is more important to fill temporal locations that are devoid of high-quality sentient life than spatial locations that are devoid of such life, it would be more important to shift the *temporal* locations of some people in an overcrowded world to some point in the future that would otherwise be devoid of high-quality life (say, via suspended animation, if that were possible), than it would be to merely shift the *spatial* location of the people in question by sending them to another planet that would otherwise be devoid of such life (say, via teletransportation, if that were possible). For further discussion of this position, see Section 6.

13. The following case is my own, but it was sparked by an example I first heard from John Broome, many years ago, which he called 'Expanding Heaven and Expanding Hell.' Broome credited his example to Cain (1995). Although my views about this topic were arrived at independently, other philosophers have developed similar arguments in order to make similar points. See, for example, Vallentyne (1993), Cain (1995), Lauwers (1997), Vallentyne and Kagan (1997), Machina (2000), Lauwers and Vallentyne (2004), Bostrom (2011), and Campbell (2015).

Interestingly, while Cain (1995) uses an example similar to mine to arrive at the same conclusion that I do regarding the relative status of Personal and Temporal Dominance Principles for certain cases and contexts, Campbell (2015) produces a series of ingenious examples in order to show that, depending on one's theory of personal identity, there will be other cases where the relative status of Personal and Temporal Dominance Principles would be the reverse of what Cain and I argue for. I don't happen to favor the reductionist view of personal identity that would lead to Campbell's results, but many do, and for those who do, Campbell's arguments are quite compelling.

14. As recognized in note 13, Campbell (2015) has shown that, depending on one's view of personal identity, there may be cases where the judgment yielded by the Personal Dominance Principle seems false. Moreover, in Section 6, I will present other cases where the Personal Dominance Principle seems false, that don't depend on one's views about personal identity. Thus, on reflection, I believe that the Personal Dominance Principle needs to be revised, or limited in scope, and the same is true of the other dominance principles.

15. For reasons of the sort adduced in note 11, assuming that we give *some* credence to thinking that the Personal Dominance Principle applies in such a case, then for the purposes of practical reasoning, we should choose *as if* that is the correct theory, even if in fact we give more credence, and even much more, to the Impersonal Neutralist View. This is because, for Pareto-like reasons, in *this* kind of case, we have everything to gain and nothing to lose by following the recommendation of the Personal Dominance Principle. See Ross (2006), and Temkin (2012, 35–36, 40–41, 125–127, 171–173, 261–262, 443–445.

16. My use of the terms 'narrow person-affecting view' and 'wide person-affecting view' vary in certain important respects from Parfit's use of those terms, but in ways that need not concern us here. See Parfit (1984, 393–401; Temkin 416–45).

17. I am grateful to Frances Kamm (personal communication, October 2, 2015), for leading me to see that there were a slew of issues of this sort that ultimately need to be considered and resolved.

18. The methodological approach of seeking 'reflective equilibrium,' famously championed by Rawls, was, as Rawls himself acknowledges, previously employed by Sidgwick (1907).

References

Bostrom, Nick. 2011. "Infinite Ethics." *Analysis and Metaphysics* 10: 9–59.
Cain, James. 1995. "Infinite Utility." *Australasian Journal of Philosophy* 73: 401–404.
Campbell, Tim. 2015. "Personal Ontology and Bioethics." PhD diss., Rutgers University.
Kamm, Frances. 1993. *Morality, Mortality Vol I: Death and Whom to Save from It*. New York: Oxford University Press.
Lauwers, Luc. 1997. "Infinite Utility: Insisting on Strong Monotonicity." *Australasian Journal of Philosophy* 75: 222–233.
Lauwers, Luc, and Peter Vallentyne. 2004. "Infinite Utilitarianism: More is Always Better." *Economics and Philosophy* 20 (2): 307–330.
Machina, Mark. 2000. "Barrett and Arntzenius's Infinite Decision Puzzle." *Theory and Decision* 49 (3): 291–295.
Nagel, Thomas. 1986. *The View from Nowhere*. New York, NY: Oxford University Press.
Parfit, Derek. 1984. *Reasons and Persons*. Oxford: Oxford University Press.
Parfit, Derek. 2011. *On What Matters*. 1 vol. Oxford: Oxford University Press.
Rawls, John. 1971. *A Theory of Justice*. Cambridge, MA: Harvard University Press.
Ross, Jacob. 2006. "Rejecting Ethical Deflationism." *Ethics* 116: 742–768.
Scheffler, Samuel. 2013. *Death and the Afterlife*. New York: Oxford University Press.
Sidgwick, Henry. 1907. *The Method of Ethics*. 7th ed. London: Macmillan.
Temkin, Larry. 1993a. *Inequality*. New York: Oxford University Press.
Temkin, Larry. 1993b. "Harmful Goods, Harmless Bads." In *Value, Welfare, and Morality*, edited by R. G. Frey and Christopher Morris, 290–324. Cambridge: Cambridge University Press.
Temkin, Larry. 2000. "Equality, Priority, and the Levelling down Objection." In *The Ideal of Equality*, edited by Matthew Clayton and Andrew Williams, 126–161. London: Macmillan.
Temkin, Larry. 2003a. "Equality, Priority or What?" *Economics and Philosophy* 19: 61–87.
Temkin, Larry. 2003b. "Egalitarianism Defended." *Ethics* 113: 764–782.
Temkin, Larry. 2003c. "Personal Versus Impersonal Principles: Reconsidering the Slogan." *Theoria* 69: 20–30.
Temkin, Larry. 2012. *Rethinking the GoodMoral Ideals and the Nature of Practical Reasoning*. New York: Oxford University Press.
Thoma, Johanna. 2015. "Larry Temkin: Rationality with Respect to People, Places and Times." Paper presented at the Belief, Action, and Rationality over Time Workshop, University of Wisconsin-Madison, Madison, WI, September 6.
Vallentyne, Peter. 1993. "Utilitarianism and Infinite Utility." *Australasian Journal of Philosophy* 71: 212–217.
Vallentyne, Peter, and Shelly Kagan. 1997. "Infinite Value and Finitely Additive Value Theory." *The Journal of Philosophy* 94 (1): 5–26.
Williams, Bernard. 1981a. "Persons, Character and Morality." Chap. 1 in *Moral Luck*. Cambridge: Cambridge University Press.
Williams, Bernard. 1981b. "Internal and External Reasons." Chap. 8 in *Moral Luck*. Cambridge: Cambridge University Press.
Williams, Bernard. 1985. *Ethics and the Limits of Philosophy*. Cambridge, MA: Harvard University Press.

Action as a form of temporal unity: on Anscombe's *Intention*

Douglas Lavin

Philosophy Department, University College London, Gower Street, London, UK

ABSTRACT
The aim of this paper is to display an alternative to the familiar decompositional approach in action theory, one that resists the demand for an explanation of action in non-agential terms, while not simply treating the notion of intentional agency as an unexplained primitive. On this Anscombean alternative, action is not a worldly event with certain psychological causes, but a distinctive form of material process, one that is not simply caused by an exercise of reason but is itself a productive exercise of reason. I argue that to comprehend the proposed alternative requires an account of the temporality of events in general. An event does not simply have a position in time, but is itself temporally structured. With the inner temporality of events in view, the Anscombean conception of action as a specifically self-conscious form of temporal unity is made available for critical reflection.

Introduction

You will agree that Pynchon's third *Proverb for Paranoids* is equally suited to philosophers: 'If they can get you asking the wrong questions they don't have to worry about the answers.' I begin by contrasting two familiar ways of motivating and framing the problem of action: the *standard (decompositional) approach* through Wittgenstein's question 'What is left over?' and *Anscombe's approach* through a sense of the question 'Why?' These ways of entering into philosophical reflection are correlated with distinct and opposed conceptions of intentional bodily action: on the one hand, as a compound of metaphysically independent inner psychical and outer material elements joined by a generic bond of causality, and, on the other, as an essentially self-conscious and rational form of material process. These approaches are also correlated with a number of salient, though infrequently discussed, differences of emphasis, diets of example, habits of expression and strategies of argument. The contrasting features typically figure as part of the pre-theoretical background. In holding them up against an alternative, my hope is that such features will lose the appearance of innocence and inevitability. Still I believe that the decompositional project, not Anscombe's has been the primary beneficiary of a false appearance of inevitability, and I think that once this appearance is dissolved, the attractions of the Anscombean alternative will come into view. In what follows, I try to show that reflection on the temporal structure of movement in general and action in particular is the crucial first step. Only by proceeding in this way can we understand what it could mean to say that action is a form of temporal unity.

Wittgensteinian arithmetic

Mere movements

Wittgensteinian arithmetic is the standard point of departure in contemporary action theory:

> Let us not forget this: when 'I raise my arm,' my arm goes up. And the problem arises: What is left over if I subtract the fact that my arm goes up from the fact that I raise my arm? (1963, §621)

This matters because the question itself forces a definite shape on subsequent reflection. It presupposes that an account of what it is to do something intentionally – what it comes to that, say, I raised my arm – will be a description of a compound of metaphysically distinct explanatory factors.

When I raise my arm, my arm rises; when I move a matchbox, the matchbox moves. 'Raise' and 'move,' like 'open,' 'close,' 'cool,' 'break,' 'burn,' 'sink' and 'melt,' are members of a class of English verbs with transitive and intransitive uses where the following holds:

(Movement) $X A_{transitive}$-ed Y only if $Y A_{intransitive}$-ed.

My arm's rising and the matchbox's moving are physical events, elements of the observable world of matter in motion. Of course, one's arm might rise or a matchbox might move even if one does not raise the one or move the other – maybe it's just the wind. It will seem to some that in such a case, we have a movement which may be 'exactly the same' as the movement in an intentional action (Searle 1983, 89).[1] A presupposition of Wittgensteinian arithmetic is that an account of the nature of action begins with a not-intrinsically-intentional movement (my arm's rising$_{intransitive}$, the matchbox's moving$_{intransitive}$), and through the addition of further distinct factors to the equation, comes to characterize what amounts to intentional action (I raised my arm, I moved the matchbox). On this view, action consists of a not-intrinsically-intentional happening, a 'mere happening,' occurring in a context where certain further facts obtain. The basic task for the philosophical investigation of action is now set: to arrive at a specification of these further facts. The central questions of action theory then concern how to specify the something else (beliefs, desires, intentions, policies, acts of will, the agent herself, others?), and how to characterize the sort of relation (event-causal, agent-causal, triggering, structuring, sustaining, others?) joining this to 'what merely happens' when someone does something intentionally.

Whatever the disputes about how to execute this task properly, those taking it up share two further, intertwined assumptions, one about causality, the other about thought. Taken together, these constitute the framework of the *decompositional approach* to the theory of action.

Causality as a factor in the equation

When I raise my arm, but not simply when my arm rises, and when I move the matchbox, but not simply when the matchbox moves, it is natural to speak of me as generating, authoring, producing, or bringing about something, as making something happen. This is a harmless way of marking the causal character of concepts used in ordinary thought and talk of action. It is equally harmless to mark this by speaking explicitly of 'cause': If I moved the matchbox, I caused the matchbox to move; If I raised my arm, I caused my arm to rise. Indeed, the following holds of any member of the class of verbs with transitive and intransitive forms:

(Causality) $X A_{transitive\text{-}}ed\ Y$ only if X caused Y to $A_{intransitive}$.

The schema makes plain that causality, in some sense, is central to agency and its exercise in action (Hornsby 1980). But on the decompositional conception, it reveals more than this: it identifies a further distinct factor that can be added to the Wittgensteinian equation. According to the decompositional theorist, doing something intentionally (I raised my arm, I moved the matchbox) *is* a mere happening (my arm's rising, the matchbox's moving) *caused* by some factor x, so that solving for this x would be tantamount to laying bare the metaphysical structure of action.

This step is non-trivial, not a mere restatement of the innocuous verbal implication captured by (Causality). To see this, consider first a parallel verbal implication: I painted the door red only if I colored the door red; and likewise I stained (lacquered, dyed, glazed …) the door red only if I colored the door red. Obviously, we do not articulate a distinct factor in the analysis of intentional action by displaying this common element of 'coloring.' This is not only because the 'verbs of coloring' are such a limited class, but because 'I colored the door red' is itself simply another ordinary action description. It raises exactly the same questions as the more determinate reports of action (I painted …, I laquered …). Admittedly, the class of transitive causative verbs is more abstract and wide-ranging than the class of coloring verbs. Should this raise hopes that

(Causality) is a significant step in the decompositional analysis of action? After all, if 'cause Y to A-$_{intransitive}$' is itself just the verb phrase in an ordinary action description, the implication licensed by (Causality) would not reveal the causal element in everyday practical thought to be a distinct factor that might figure in a non-trivial analysis of action. Why think it is otherwise?

The decompositional theorist's interpretation relies on a further transformation. If I caused the matchbox to move, I caused the matchbox's moving; If I caused my arm to rise, I caused my arm's rising. We can state this generally as

(Event Nominalization) X caused Y to A$_{intransitive}$ just when X caused Y's A-ing$_{intransitive}$.

This principle allows transposition of subject-verb statements (X caused Y to A) into a grammatically relational form (X caused Y's A-ing). Here the causality involved in action takes on the appearance of a relation joining particulars, and thus as belonging to the same category as 'is as large as' and 'hates.' The decompositional approach characteristically takes appearances at face value: it presupposes that the causal element introduced by the transitive verbs employed in ordinary representation of action is a *real relation* between distinct, fully determinate particulars – some factor x and a mere happening.[2] The relation here is itself *generic*: the principles that transform 'I moved the matchbox' into 'I caused the matchbox's moving' also transform 'the sun warmed the stone' into 'the sun caused the stone's warming.' And the causal element involved in intentional action description appears to be the same as the causal element involved in descriptions of what happens that are not intentional. And again the decompositional theorist characteristically takes appearances at face value: the causality involved in action is, he assumes, just an instance of causality we encounter elsewhere, perhaps everywhere else, in nature.

We thus arrive at the problem of action as the decompositional theorist conceives it: what differentiates the specifically rational case is neither what happens (movement) nor how that derives from something else (causality). It must then be what it derives from, the cause. In this way, the discipline of action theory becomes focused on the question of the distinctive source of what merely happens.

Mind and action

This brings us to an assumption about the role of mind in action characteristic of the decompositional approach. Again, our starting point is a truism. When I do something intentionally or with reason, I do not do it unwittingly, but knowingly in execution of an aim. We use certain forms of emphasis to mark this (*I* did it, I *myself*). We speak explicitly of the person or rational agent as the source and guide of what happens. And we speak of the mind (I've got a mind to …) and certain determinations of mind (This is my will …) in this role: in action I give the world a piece of my mind, I impose my will on the world. This is unruly language.

We domesticate it a bit by replacing talk of mind and will with a certain range of psychological judgments: When I raise my arm, I want (intend, try, aim) to raise it. Quite generally, where *X*'s *A*-ing is an intentional action:

(Mind) $X\ A_{transitive}$-ed Y only if X wanted (intended, aimed) to $A_{transitive}\ Y$.

Where (Causality) explicitly registers a causal element in everyday talk of action, (Mind) explicitly registers an element of thought: an action is a kind of happening that bears a certain relation to the subject's own thought. One does not need to be a decompositional theorist to recognize something sound in this observation: anyone who understands what action is should admit it. But again, the decompositional theorist characteristically adopts a certain non-trivial interpretation of the point. He first observes that the following is possible: someone intends (wants, aims, etc.) to raise his arm, even though his arm does not go up – maybe he has had a change of mind, maybe he is prevented, maybe once upon a time William James has secretly etherized his arm upon a table, in which case nothing at all happens. And this observation appears to confirm what his interpretation of the other elements involved in the constitution of action already implies: that the psychological factor involved in intentional action is analytically distinguishable from the elements of movement and causality. The latter elements – the rising of an arm or the moving of a matchbook, and the causal relation in virtue of which these events are connected to something mental – are not themselves intrinsically mind-involving. The arm-rising is of a kind that could occur whether or not it is caused by an intention, and the causal relation to the arm-rising, too, is not a special kind of causal nexus, say, a connection partly constituted by intention, but a generic causality that also binds, say, the sun to a stone, fire to smoke, or a dog to its bone. And by the same token, the existence of the psychological element involved in action does not by itself imply the existence of any outward movement or change. Whatever might tend to follow in its wake, the condition of mind involved in intentionally doing something is entirely complete in its existence even when it remains utterly without effect: it is, in this respect, like a wish or a daydream, a 'purely interior' thing.

Thus we can say that, on the decompositional view, the operation of mind through which what happens (typically a bodily movement) is an expression of intelligence and will is not itself an act of making something happen. It is rather a merely interior state or event which contributes to the constitution of an act of making something happen only when it stands in a not-intrinsically-intention-governed causal relation to a not-intrinsically-intention-governed movement or happening. If we take Wittgenstein's question to set the topic for action theory, this way of looking at things seems nearly inevitable. What could an understanding of the nature of action be if not a description of when a manifold of elements, none of which severally presuppose the notion of someone's making something happen intentionally, constitute someone's making something happen intentionally?

Anscombe's 'enquiries into the question "why?"'

Anscombe's *intention* contains the seeds of a wholly other, non-decompositional approach to understanding action, an approach grounded in a different sort of inquiry, prompted by a different sort of demand. When our outlook is shaped by the decompositional approach, Anscombe's question, the task it sets, and the answer it delivers can be difficult to recognize.

Familiar ways of placing *Intention* on the action theoretical map read it, in effect, as addressing the kinds of questions that arise within the decompositional framework. Think, for example, of the tendency to read Anscombe's opening remarks on three ways we use the word 'intention' as showing that the expression applies both to minds (inner mental states) and movements (outer worldly happenings), with a view to then raising familiar, decompositionally oriented questions about their interrelations, but then subsequently developing unfamiliar answers, which give explanatory priority to an outer, merely behavioral element.[3] But is Anscombe' intention to characterize distinct mental and worldly elements and the relations between them? This is a bad fit with, for example, her later remark that 'to a certain extent the three divisions of the subject made in §1, are simply equivalent' (2000, §23).[4] Or think instead of the tendency to treat her dismissive remarks about an appeal to the concept 'cause' in an account of action as displaying allegiance to an alternative candidate for the real relation joining thought and movement when someone does something for a reason.[5] But is Anscombe's Intention to deny the causal character of action explanation? This is a bad fit with the fact that her inquiry culminates with the thought that intentional action just is the content of a specifically practical form of knowledge–knowledge that is 'the cause of what it understands' (§48).[6] Although I understand the impetus to read Anscombe through this lens, it plainly does not square with the central narrative of her text.[7] At several points, she expresses opposition to the entire decompositional approach: it is a mistake, she says in §47, to begin with the idea of a prior and independently constituted domain of material events and then to go looking for a difference within this; 'we do not add anything' to what happens, she says in §19, in describing someone's doing something as intentional.

It might appear that to reject the enterprise of decomposition is simply to give up on the project of explaining what action is. And yet, Anscombe also opposes those who would take 'doing something intentionally' to be a conceptual or metaphysical primitive.[8] Now, as everyone knows, Anscombe defines the concept of intentional action in terms of 'a certain sense of the question "Why?"': action is what 'gives application' to this question; it is such as to figure in a certain form of account (§5). What exactly is the relevant sense of 'Why?' It is, she says, the sense that asks for a 'reason for acting,' but she then rejects this characterization on the ground that it is unilluminating. We do not elucidate the concept of action by locating it within an interdefinable circle of concepts. If we are to explain the very idea of doing something intentionally in terms of the applicability of the question 'Why?', Anscombe says, we must isolate the relevant sense of the question in terms that do not presuppose an understanding of the concept of intentional action. The Anscombean approaches the topic of action through this question 'Why?' The task it sets is to isolate the relevant sense in accord with this methodological constraint.

In proceeding under this constraint, while at the very same time eschewing the project of decomposition, Anscombe shows, I think, that she aims to lay hold of a form of thought or mode of predication that gives rise to the whole circle of concepts. Near the end of *Intention*, she says quite specifically that 'the term "intentional" has reference to a form of description of events' (§47). Her idea seems to be that the concept 'intentional' is a formal category, perhaps as the Fregean notions of 'object' and 'concept' are. These are concepts that characterize what fall under them in terms of their suitability to figure in a certain distinctive form of thought: an 'object' is whatever can be designated by the subject-term of an elementary Fregean proposition of the form '*a* is *F*' and a 'concept' is whatever can be designated by the predicate of such a proposition. Similarly, on the Anscombean approach, 'intentional' is to be understood through reflection on a certain form of bringing something under a concept, specifically through the articulation of a distinct species of event predication or, as I say below, *kinēsis* (movement) ascription.

One respect in which Anscombe's approach contrasts with the decompositional approach comes out in this characterization of the concept 'intentional' as grounded in a special '*form* of description of events.' The characterization suggests that event description – the description of worldly happenings unfolding over time – takes several distinct forms, and that we make progress in philosophical understanding by differentiating them.[9] By contrast, the decompositional theorist is committed to showing apparently diverse forms of event description – transitive descriptions of intentional actions, and intransitive descriptions of events that carry no implication of agency – to be of a single basic form. On his view, the only form of description of worldly happening we must recognize in the analysis of action carries no implication of intentional agency: intransitive, not-intrinsically-intentional descriptions of mere (bodily) movements. Understanding intentional action does not require recognizing another, irreducibly different form of event description for an analysis: events describable as intentional actions turn out just to consist in intransitive, not-intrinsically-intentional (bodily) movements with certain specific causes. Thus the project of the decompositional theorist is precisely not to understand action by specifying its distinctive form of event description; his project is rather to identify a single, homogeneous class of event descriptions common to intentional actions and non-intentional happenings, and then to specify further features that events describable in this way must exhibit when someone has done something intentionally.[10]

Another contrast between Anscombe's approach and the decompositional approach comes out in details of the 'scene of action' launching her inquiry. Recall that the decompositional approach begins here: someone *has done* something (I moved the matchbox, I raised my arm). The crucial first step in raising the problem of action is to *eliminate* the point of view of the agent from the description of what takes place (The matchbox moved, My arm rose), here conceived as fully determinate particulars (the matchbox's moving, my arm's going up). At the outset, our attention is focused on what is already there and not anybody's doing. The subsequent investigation is chiefly an attempt to make our way back. Anscombe's approach begins elsewhere: someone observes another *in the midst of doing* something (I see that she is walking upstairs). And then, in a crucial step in framing the task for action theory, the observer addresses an explanatory question to the observed (I ask her 'Why are you walking upstairs?'), thereby entering *the point of view of the self-conscious subject*. At the outset, our attention is focused on the standpoint of the agent looking ahead – the view from within, on what is not yet done (Why am I walking upstairs, you ask? I am walking upstairs because …). Anscombe's subsequent investigation is essentially an interrogation of this practical self-consciousness. The approach presupposes that knowledge of the nature of agency, of the efficacy of will, is internal to it. Here the task for the philosophy of action is not to substitute knowledge for ignorance, but to make explicit what must, in some sense, already be known simply in being an agent.

In taking the Anscombean approach, we must not ever leave *either* the point of view of the self-conscious subject, *or* the sphere of description of material events. It is difficult to see what she might have in mind, exactly what this approach is meant to involve and where it could lead. To get this into view, I think we must attend to certain features of ordinary thought and talk of events: not to the features at the center of Davidson's 'The Logical Form of Action Sentences,' (e.g. adverbial modification and nominalization transcription), but rather to temporal features and their interpretation. Event description is characteristically of what 'takes time' and 'comes to completion' – a temporally bounded whole with distinct phases. Against this background, we begin to see what it might be for action theory to have the task of elucidating a distinct form of event description, or as I will often say a distinct form of event. This, it will emerge, is the task of articulating a unity of part and whole – more specifically, a distinct *form of unity* of a developing process and its phases, one that captures the aspects of 'causality' and 'mind' that must be part of any illuminating treatment of the progress of the deed.

The internal temporality of movement

To display this temporal structure properly, we must focus on the representation of movement in complete thoughts.[11] Consider the following:

(1) Jones was walking across the street.
(2) Jones walked across the street.

The subject (Jones), predicate (walk across the street), and tense (past) are common features of these thoughts. And yet they are not the same: that Jones was walking across the street does not entail that Jones walked across the street. The propositions differ in aspect. What the proposition with imperfective aspect (1) represents as in-progress, the correlated proposition with perfective aspect (2) represents as completed. 'Walk across the street' can also enter into thought bearing the present tense:

(3) Jones is walking across the street.

The subject (Jones), predicate (walk across the street), and aspect (imperfective) are common to it and (1). But they are not the same: that Jones was walking across the street does not entail that Jones is walking across the street. They differ only in tense: what (3) casts in the present tense (1) casts in the past. And, now, what of the other past tense thought, the past-perfective (2)? What contrasts with it simply in bearing the present tense? Answer: nothing. Perfective aspect is logically incompatible with present tense meaning.[12] There are, then, two possibilities for predicating 'walk across the street' in the past tense, but only a single possibility in the present. Put into a metaphysical register, the point is this: 'walk across the street' has two ways of 'being past' (being in progress and being complete), yet only one way of 'being present' (being in progress).

The distinction of aspect (as well as the corresponding metaphysical contrast between being underway and being complete) has nothing especially to do with 'walking across the street,' or quite generally, with concepts deployed in action. The predicative materials in, say, 'The sun is setting,' 'The cherry tree is blooming,' 'The robin is flying to its nest,' and 'Jones is baking a cake' admit the contrast of aspect which is captured in this abstract table of judgments:

(Kinēsis 1)

	Past	Present
Imperfective	S was φ-ing	S is φ-ing
Perfective	S φ-ed	

I am drawing on a tradition reaching back to Aristotle whose abstract category of *kinēsis* (movement) is specified in these aspectual terms. A predicate expresses a *kinēsis* when it generates the contrast of aspect, that is when it can enter into propositions of the distinct forms represented in (Kinēsis 1).[13]

'Jones walked across the street' and 'Jones is walking across the street' are not simply independent propositions: they have the same subject and predicate. And, no one should deny that the difference is, in some sense, temporal: (2) is past while (3) is present. The question is, how should we understand this temporal difference if not as the sum of a difference in tense, available prior to and independent of the contrast of aspect, plus an additional difference of aspect? Our three propositions come as a package, and we grasp the distinctive temporality of movement through reflection on the relations among them.[14] I want to make two points in this connection. First, walking across the street, flying to a nest, and movement generally, *take time*. The contrast of aspect specifies a duration internal to movement: S φ-ed only if S was φ-ing but had not yet φ-ed. At the heart of the perfective is the idea of *progress come to completion*. Second, walking across the street, flying to a nest, and movement generally, can be *interrupted*. The contrast of aspect specifies an end or limit internal to movement: S is φ-ing only if S has not yet φ-ed but looks forward to having φ-ed. At the heart of the imperfective is the idea of *completion not yet attained*. But in what sense does, say, 'Jones is walking across the street' involve the description of the here and now in the light of completion? Not by incorporating the actual future into the description of current events. Being in progress is compatible with never finishing: S is φ-ing does not entail S will have φ-ed. Still, the concept deployed in imperfective judgment (walk across the street) specifies a terminus or limit (being across the street), a point beyond which progressive truth cannot continue. Only this stopping point is internal to the description of the proceedings: it specifies what is to be, even if not what will be in fact. When things don't turn out (bus accident half-way across), we say that things were interrupted, that something interfered. And these expressions, like progressive truth itself, presuppose the presence of a real tendency toward (and not just an idle hope of) completion (Boyle and Lavin 2010, sec. 4).

I have said that action, indeed, *kinēsis* (movement) quite generally, takes time and tends toward completion. When a movement is underway and so not yet complete, it is incomplete by degree (just getting going, about half-way done, almost there). This is a presupposition of the thought that a *kinēsis* is quick, slow, or some speed: when something is underway, there is a rate at which it is approaching completion. Typically, as X is doing A through an interval, less and less still needs to be done. Things are coming along. What exactly does such progress consist in? It consists in a connection to *other* movements, themselves at various stages of completion. When something has begun, is in progress, and not yet complete (X is doing A), something else has already been done and other things are underway: the sun is setting: the sun went partially below the horizon, it is now sinking further below; the cat is stalking a bird: the cat crouched down, the cat is now slinking along; I am walking from Athens to Delphi: I walked from Athens to Thebes, now I am walking from Thebes to Delphi. It will be possible to link the process ascription 'X is doing A' with these others by saying 'in that,' and then mentioning other things that have already happened (a minute ago it did A^{**}), and further things that are happening (at the moment it's doing A^*):

(Kinēsis 2) S is φ-ing in that S ψ-ed and S is ω-ing.

As before, this is part of a depiction of the abstract category of movement and thus a structure that we find in any determinate form of movement (process or event).

The happenings here represented as phases, stages, or parts of an event might in other circumstances be a *mere heap*: it is not enough that the sun sank partly below the horizon, and is now sinking even further below, for it to be the case that the sun is setting – we might be in the Arctic Circle for summer holiday; walking from Athens to Thebes and then walking from Thebes to Delphi would not add up to a single event of walking from Athens to Delphi were I to get the idea of walking to Delphi only after I was already in Thebes. Not just any collection (*A*, *B*) or succession (*A* and then *B*) of events is a unity (*C*). But when such happenings (*A*, *B*) constitute the progress of a wider process (*C*), when they are lesser phases of some more inclusive going on, the whole is in the parts. Exactly this is marked by the fact that, at a certain resolution, what has gone on can be exactly the same (the sun went partly below the horizon, and is now moving upward), and yet in one case this is an interruption (a sunset spoiled by a giant, wayward asteroid colliding with earth), while in another case it is not (only the 'midnight sun' of the Arctic summer). A *kinēsis* (movement, process, event) is a principle of unity of temporal phases.

A form of description of events

Having noted these structural features of event and process description in general, we can return to clarifying the approach to understanding action implicit in Anscombe's claim that the term that 'intentional' relates to a 'form of description of events' (§47). A principal result of our consideration of the temporality of movement was this: where a process unfolds over time, there is some principle in virtue of which the phases of the process constitute a whole. Accordingly, there will be grounds for distinguishing different *forms of event* where there are distinguishable *forms of principle of unity* of parts in a whole. In particular, we would have grounds for recognizing intentional action as a distinctive form of event, if we had grounds for recognizing a distinctive type of unity that belongs specifically to intentional actions – a kind of unity we look for when we consider what happenings in a person's life are intentional actions, a unity whose presence is implied by event-or-process descriptions rightly characterized as 'intentional.' I want to suggest that Anscombe's investigation of action has given us grounds for recognizing such a distinctive form of unity, and that the perspicuous representation of it of it just is the substance of her account of action.

Anscombe's account famously begins by identifying of a special sense of the why-question and proceeds to describe a distinctive sort of order (the *A–D* order) that characteristically structures answers to it (2000, §26). I already noted that her account of the relevant why-question privileges the standpoint of the agent, inasmuch as this question is characteristically put *to the agent herself* at a moment *while she is acting*, and is supposed to be 'refused application' if an agent says, of some activity *A*-ing about which she is queried, 'I didn't know I was *A*-ing' (2000, §6?). This characterization of the why-question's addressee must be supplemented with a positive characterization of the kind of answer that it invites – the kind of answer it accepts as an explanation of a person's intentionally doing something. In the course of her discussion, it emerges that the special question 'Why are you A-ing?' admits of a variety of kinds of answers: the kinds I give when I say that I am tapping a spot on the wall 'for no particular reason,' kicked Jones 'out of anger' or 'because he killed my brother,' return five dollars to Smith 'because I promised,' massage my foot 'because I like to,' or seek to help another 'for its own sake.' Yet the characterization of one particular kind of answer is the heart of her account. This answer takes a teleological form: it cites a further objective pursued in A-ing, an aim spelled out by saying

    to do B.
    or
    I am doing B.

It is this specific kind of answer that shows the capacity for intentional action to be a power to realize concepts.[15]

Anscombe suggests that explanations of this type can and characteristically do come in chains or nested series, so that the kind of explanatory structure at issue is properly called an *order*. To take her well-known example of a man pumping poisoned water into a house cistern: he is moving his arm up and down (A), operating the pump (B), replenishing the house water supply (C), and poisoning the inhabitants (D). As Anscombe imagines them, such a list is not mere aggregate (A, B, C, D), or mere sequence of actions (A and then B, B and then ...), but elements of an explanatory order of means and ends. The end accounts for the means: it is the reason *why* the means are taken. (Why are you moving your arm up and down? I am operating the pump). The of the why-question displays our actions as an *order of ends*:

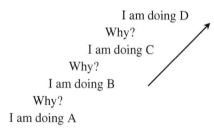

But equally, the means account for the end: the means are *how* the end is realized. (How are you poisoning the inhabitants? I'm replenishing ...) This how-question does not simply ask 'How is it happening?', but 'How are you doing it?' (§26). And the answer cites a further venture, one contributing to the realization an aim, a contribution spelled out by saying

    by means of doing C.
    or
    I am doing C.

Explanations of this type also come in chains or nested series, so that the structure at issue here is also an *order*. And the repeated application of the how-question eliciting such explanations displays our actions as an *order of means*

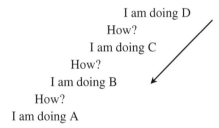

There is plainly a symmetry between purpose and efficacy: If *B*-ing is why I am *A*-ing, then *A*-ing is how I am *B*-ing; if *A*-ing is how I am *B*-ing, then *B*-ing is why I am *A*-ing. The order of means displayed by 'How?' is a mirror image of the order of ends displayed by 'Why?':

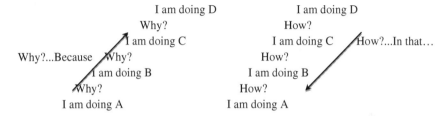

The means–end order is an explanatory order because it captures that for the sake of which things are done, and also, and equally, because it captures that by means of which things get done.

Taken together, these observations accomplish the very thing we said must be accomplished by an account of intentional action as a distinctive form of event: they characterize a specific kind of unity of parts or phases in a whole that is the principle governing our understanding of processes as actions. In the first place, they identify a specific kind of explanatory structure that unites the distinguishable parts or phases of an intentional action: these are characteristically bound together *teleologically*, in such a way that an overarching event-in-progress explains its lesser parts. We can display the relevant unity in explanations of the form

(Telic Explanation) S is ω-ing because S is φ-ing

where ω-ing is taken by the agent to be, and in the happy case is, a means conducive to, or a more specific activity constitutive of, φ-ing. Secondly, this ordering of means to ends is characteristically *self-conscious* in the following sense: the agent herself is aware of the elements that are ordered (for if she were not aware of them, the relevant why-question would not apply), and of the order in which they stand (for it is precisely this order that she is expected to articulate in response to Anscombe's question 'Why?'). Her awareness is not merely a passive cognizance of the means–end structure of her own activity. Where an instance of (Telic Explanation) is true, it is *because* she takes ω-ing to be a means of φ-ing, and has herself determined to φ, that she is ω-ing – and so on up to whatever overarching aim governs her present activity. This is agential awareness, an awareness that does not merely record but determines the order, and thus the progress, it comprehends. And so Anscombe calls the awareness articulated in response to her why-question 'practical knowledge,' knowledge that is 'the cause of what it understands.' Such knowledge, being inseparable from the order of events-in-progress that it governs, can be articulated by the subject in explanatory propositions with a first-person subject, as in

(Agential Awareness) I am doing *A* because I am doing *B*

where the relevant 'because' implies the subject's determination to do *A* in order to realize the wider aim of doing *B*.

My suggestion, in short, is that Anscombe's *A–D* order is an ordering of elements united in such a way as to satisfy (Telic Explanation) and (Agential Awareness), and that, if Anscombe is right, this form of unity is *essential* and *specific* to the form of event intentional action is. It is essential to the extent that the applicability of Anscombe's why-question genuinely characterizes the class of events that are actions; and it is specific inasmuch as the mode of order or unity brought out by this question belongs specially to just these events. I will not attempt to defend these claims here: to do so would be to argue for the adequacy of Anscombe's account of action. My concern in the present essay is to make clear what sort of account is on offer and to show how its availabilty depends on the availability of a certain conception of the temporality of action and practical thought.[16] For present purposes, the crucial point is that, in the proposed characterization of this form of unity of phases in an overarching process, we do not leave *either* the point of view of the agent *or* the description of material processes themselves. The elements of causality and mind that the decompositional approach represents as separable elements in an account of action, distinct from the characterization of the material process (what happens) that constitutes the action proper, appear in this story as structuring features of the relevant sort of material process itself: we are concerned with a kind of event or process whose principle of unity just is that the parts should come about *because* of the *subject's apprehension* of their contribution to a certain whole. If this characterization succeeds, we will have characterized an essentially self-conscious, self-constituting form of material progress, and thereby clarified what sort of thing an intentional action could be.

Examples, time, and causality

Having now seen how, from the outset, the Anscombean approach to understanding action builds in an orientation toward the standpoint of the agent, and toward the temporal structure of action as it appears from this internal, forward-looking standpoint, I want to note some telling contrasts with the decompositional approach. These contrasts emerge in the kinds of examples of action on which each typically focuses.

When Anscombe's argument requires her to give examples of intentional actions, the examples are, almost without exception, imagined in a certain characteristic way. In the first place, we are invited to think of an action *presently underway*, something the agent *is doing*, not yet something she *has done*. Secondly, the types of action Anscombe considers – crossing the road to look in a shop window, going upstairs to get one's camera, getting a Jersey cow, building a house, pumping poisoned water to fill a cistern and thereby poisoning the occupants of a house, etc. – are characteristically complex enterprises with discernible parts or phases, where the execution of a phase might itself take time, and might itself involve phases about which Anscombe's characteristic why-question could be raised. Finally, we are asked to imagine *the agent herself* being asked 'Why?' about the action underway – and asked in a mode that invites her to say what she knows *without observation* about the relevant happening.

With these features of Anscombe's examples in mind, if we consider typical examples of decompositional theorists, we will be struck by several contrasts. In the first place, the object of attention is typically a *completed* action (Jones buttered the toast, Shem kicked Shaun, the officer pushed the button that fired the missile that sank the Bismark), one whose real constitution from any parts belonging to it has already occurred and been settled once and for all, one that can be unproblematically referred to by a singular term denoting a concrete particular, a wholly determinate historical event (Jones's buttering the toast, The officer's sinking the Bismark). Secondly, the central focus of theoretical attention is characteristically on *brief or even quasi-instantaneous* actions in which there is *no discernible intentional structure* to speak of: such things as arm-raisings, button-pushings, and trigger-pullings. To be sure, decompositional theorists acknowledge the existence of complex, temporally extended actions (dancing a tango, directing a military campaign), but they characteristically seek to reduce such complex actions to coordinated sequences of 'basic actions' of which it is true that they are severally brief or quasi-instantaneous and lacking in discernible intentional structure. It is striking that the topic of 'basic action' – intentional doings that are supposed to be performed without the agent's intentionally doing anything else in order to do them – does not so much as appear in Anscombe's discussion, whereas it is the very foundation of the decompositional approach to action theory.

Finally, whereas Anscombe's question 'Why?' is characteristically posed to some 'you,' someone who would answer with a sentence beginning with 'I,' in the examples characteristic of the decompositional approach, we generally focus on agents who are specified *impersonally* (Jones, Smith, the officer). The preceding two features of the decompositional theorist's examples help to explain this shift away from the first-person standpoint. For, on the one hand, once an action is complete, the agent herself can no longer have a special practical knowledge of its structure: though she may retain a memory of the steps she took in performing it, her guiding role has come to an end, and her deed has now become a thing that has happened, a *fait accompli* whose larger aims and lesser elements she can only remember, not determine. And, on the other hand, where the actions in question are supposed to be basic actions, the agent can have no privileged knowledge of their composition from parts or phases even while her action is underway, for a basic action is by definition one the agent performs without intentionally doing anything else in order to perform it.

Thus the entire orientation of the decompositional approach points us away from the standpoint of the agent, and toward a consideration of actions as definite, achieved realities: realities in the life of some agent, to be sure, but considered in such a way that the practical point of view of this agent toward the relevant event does not come into the foreground, and the question of what binds the parts or phases of this event into a unity does not easily arise.

These contrasts between Anscombean and decompositional examples are evidently grounded in systematic differences between the two approaches. Given that Anscombe's approach seeks, not to understand action by decomposing it into various not-intrinsically-agency-involving parts, but to articulate the understanding of the nature of action implicit in the agent's forward-looking intentional operation, it is natural for Anscombe to focus on actions in progress, considered from the standpoint of the agent herself, with special attention to her understanding of the steps she must take to achieve her end. By contrast, given that the basic aim of the decompositional approach is to analyze action as a composite of a not-intrinsically-intentional bodily movement with some special precipitating cause, it is natural that decompositional theorists should focus on cases of action that seem to lend themselves to such analysis, and should seek to analyze other actions into sequences of these. Plainly, the actions that most readily lend themselves to decompositional analysis are those bodily movements that take relatively little time to perform and whose performance does not require any conscious consideration of means. For these are the actions that are most plausibly regarded as consisting of a not-intrinsically-intentional, quasi-automatic bodily movement causally triggered by some relevant intention (and perhaps monitored as it unfolds for conformity with this intention, so that perceived deviations can launch further movement-triggerings, etc.).

The decompositional theorist's focus on brief or quasi-instantaneous basic actions thus flows from the central commitment of his approach. Moreover, the emphasis on completed actions, and the tendency to describe these actions in impersonal terms, both serve to reinforce this approach, for both draw attention away from the agent's specific understanding of the structure of an action-in-progress. And it is precisely this agent-centered understanding of action that poses the most serious challenge to the decompositional approach.

Notes

1. Does the fact that S's being F implies S's being G, but that S can be G without being F, *entail* that it must be possible to decompose S's being F into S's being G and S's being H, where H is some nontrivial further condition, not identical to F itself? Answer is: No. For instance, S's being red implies S's being colored, and S can be colored without being red, but there is no prospect of analyzing what it is for S to be red into S's being colored plus some nontrivial further condition. Likewise with lots of cases: being a parent and being an ancestor, arguably; being a horse and being an animal, arguably; knowing something and believing something, arguably (Williamson 2000); perceiving something and having an experience of something, arguably (McDowell 1982). To infer that, if being G is a necessary but not sufficient condition for being F, there must be some nontrivial H which, when conjoined with G, constitutes a necessary and sufficient condition for being F, might be called the *fallacy of analysis*. For particular application to the analysis of action see (Ford 2011). This section develops an earlier treatment of the decompositional approach (Lavin 2013b).
2. Must we take these appearances seriously? At the very least, there is room for a different view. The verbs 'wore' in 'Jones wore a smile,' 'take' in 'Smith took a bath,' and 'perform' in 'I performed an act of moving the matchbox' do not express real relations even though the surface grammar of these sentences is relational. For further discussion, see Hyman's (2001) and Sellars (1991) on the logic of 'looks'.
3. Here is Michael Bratman: 'We use the notion of intention to characterize both people's actions and their minds ... A theory of intention must address both kinds of phenomena and explain how they are related. A natural approach, the one I will be taking here, is to begin with the state of intending to act ... Instead of beginning with the state of intending to act [some theorists] turn immediately to intention as it appears in action ... This is, for example, the strategy followed by Elizabeth Anscombe in her ground-breaking monograph, *Intention*' (1987, 5). Velleman (2007) approaches the text in a similar spirit.
4. The passage continues, 'That is to say, where the answers 'I am going to fetch my camera', 'I am fetching my camera' and 'in order to fetch my camera' are interchangeable as answers to the question 'Why?' asked when I go upstairs' (§23). She seems to be thinking that these are clearly all one notion and that we are confused about what that notion is.
5. Bratman again: 'It is standing in an appropriate relation to such [mental] states that makes an action intentional ... We can cite Anscombe, Goldman and ... Davidson as, among others, subscribers to this view ... Davidson and Goldman insist, while Anscombe emphatically denies, that the appropriate relation is in some sense a causal relation' (1987, 6).
6. In light of this, we do best to treat her early disparaging remarks (§5) as simply an insistence that we should not take the idea of causality for granted in our inquiry. And, in light of her final account, it would seem that this is because what is at issue in understanding 'intention' is laying hold of a certain distinctive *form* of causality (§48).
7. A number of recent essays are especially concerned to bring out just how utterly different Anscombe's account is from anything available within the decompositional framework, for example (Hursthouse 2000; Vogler 2001; Ford 2011; Hornsby 2011; Moran and Stone 2011; Stoutland 2011; Thompson 2011).
8. As I read it, the central aim of Anscombe's opening discussion of the three ways we speak of 'intention', as well as of a number of other early remarks, is to show

that an account is needed by inducing a condition of Augustinian perplexity. She says that when we are inclined to speak of different senses of a word which is not equivocal, we are 'in the dark' about the *kind* (not simply the content) of concept it represents. And yet, what could be more familiar – the phenomenon of intention is a pervasive and ineliminable part of human life. Moreover, unlike some other pervasive and ineliminable parts of human life, such as cell division, intentional action seems to be a process of which we necessarily have immediate and privileged knowledge. As Anscombe observes, if our concern were simply to determine on any particular occasion whether someone's saying 'I am going to such-and-such' is a prediction or an expression of intention, or if our concern were to determine, when someone is doing such-and-such, whether this is something she is doing intentionally, we could simply ask the subject. The subject who acts is in a special position to tell us what we want to know. And, as we will see, Anscombe's approach to the general theory of action presupposes this: it is essentially an interrogation of one who does things for reasons. The resulting account is merely the development of the self-consciousness of the agent.

9. A remark on *genus and species*: To define a certain Fs as 'members of genus G, with such-and-such specific differences' need not imply that we can explain what it is to be a G without appeal to an understanding of various concrete species of Gs. The genus might be, and often is, an *abstraction* from the species, rather than an independently intelligible kind-of-thing-to-be. Furthermore, if X and Y are species of a common genus G, and G's do A, it need not follow that there is any direct relation between what it is for an X to do A and what it is for a Y to do A. What it is 'to do A' might differ essentially from species to species, so that the generic notion of 'doing A' is a mere abstraction, not an independently intelligible way to do something.

10. This is not the place to enter into the details of the various ways one might work out a single, undifferentiated conception of the form of event talk. I have used formulations emphasizing the contrast of transitive and intransitive verbs to maintain contact with our earlier discussion of the decompositional theory. Still, to my mind, the account of event representation put in place by Davidson (1966) (which we all know has nothing especially to do with action) and worked out in terrific detail by Parsons (1990) is the most powerful framework within which to develop a decompositional theory of action. The central idea is that ordinary event talk – whether transitive or intransitive (The sun melted the wax, The wax melted), whether of something done intentionally or not (Jones turned on the light, Jones alerted the prowler) – is about a special class of concrete particulars, what Davidson calls 'events'. On this analysis, the sentences have the structure of existential quantification over this domain: 'For some event e, e is such that …'. In this framework, the commitment to the homogeneity of event description shows up most directly in this: the principle of individuation of events is prior to and independent of the truth of any descriptions of someone's having done something intentionally.

11. The temporality of events and actions will elude us, if we conduct our discussion using only the abstract nouns (e.g. 'event,' 'process,' 'happening,' 'behavior,' 'action') and event-denoting noun phrases (e.g. 'Jones' raising of his arm,' 'the matchbox's moving,' 'the movement of the matchbox') that are the stock-in-trade of much of action theory. The following discussion draws and improves on (Lavin 2013a, 2013b).

12. The claim is not that it is impossible to express a perfective thought in the grammatical present tense. The so-called reportative present does precisely

this (e.g. 'He shoots! He scores!'). The claim is that perfective thought (He shot. He scored.) cannot be analyzed as the past tense of a present tense thought (as of the form 'It was the case that p') because there is no present tense thought to do the relevant work (Galton 1984, 1–23).
13. Aristotle (2006), *Metaphysics* Theta 6, 1048b, 18–35. I was introduced to the philosophical importance of the topic of aspect by Thompson's (2008, ch.2) and also have been helped especially by Anscombe (1964), Galton (1984), Rödl (2012) and Waterlow (1982).
14. I am presupposing a certain take on this material. *First*, I am working with the idea that the aspectual contrast is a distinction among *ways* in which subject and predicate combine to form a complete thought. But if aspect is a form of predication, then it is not to be understood in terms of further material contents whether, say, implicit quantification over temporal intervals (Hamblin 1971), or as implicit quantification over particular events with certain primitive properties (Parsons 1990). *Second*, I am working with the idea that the metaphysical category of *kinesis* (event, process) is to be explained through the formal contrast of aspect. I develop and argue for these claims elsewhere (Haase and Lavin Forthcoming).
15. Anscombe asks, 'Would intentional actions still have the characteristic "intentional," if there were no such thing as ... further intention in acting?' (2000, §20). She answers: No. Her thought is that the very idea of a general capacity for intentional action contains the idea of a capacity to act on the basis of specifically instrumental thought, or again to act from a further intention or 'forward-looking motive'.
16. A first step in its defense would be to note (1) how the generic notion of a process proceeding toward some limit admits of a distinction between *non-telic* processes, in which parts or phases accumulate toward this limit but do not accumulate *because* they tend toward this limit, and *telic* processes, in which the accumulation does occur *because* it tends toward the relevant limit, and (2) how a further distinction can be drawn within the genus of telic processes between *non-self-conscious* telic processes in which the telic accumulation of parts or phases toward an end does not depend on any apprehension of the relation between parts and whole by the subject, and *self-conscious* telic processes in which a guiding apprehension of this relation by the subject is implied in the accumulation (Boyle and Lavin 2010).

Acknowledgements

I am particularly indebted to discussions with Matthew Boyle, Matthias Haase, Eric Marcus, Ram Neta, and Matthew Silverstein. I benefited as well from comments at Dartmouth and Oxford. I am grateful to the Alexander von Humboldt-Stiftung for generous financial support.

Funding

This work was supported by the Alexander von Humboldt-Stiftung.

References

Anscombe, G. E. M. 1964. "Before and After." *The Philosophical Review* 73 (1): 3–24.
Anscombe, G. E. M. 2000. *Intention*. Cambridge, MA: Harvard University Press.
Aristotle. 2006. *Metaphysics: Book Theta*. Translated by S. Makin. Oxford: Clarendon Press.
Boyle, Matthew, and Douglas Lavin. 2010. "Goodness and Desire." In *Desire, Practical Reason and the Good*, edited by Sergio Tenenbaum, 161–201. New York: Oxford University Press.
Bratman, Michael. 1987. *Intentions, Plans and Practical Reason*. Cambridge, MA: Harvard University Press.
Davidson, Donald. 1966. "The Logical Form of Action Sentences." In *The Logic of Decision and Action*, edited by Nicholas Rescher, 105–148. Pittsburgh, PA: University of Pittsburgh Press.
Ford, Anton. 2011. "Action and Generality." In *Essays on Anscombe's Intention*, edited by Anton Ford, Jennifer Hornsby, and Frederick Stoutland, 76–104. Cambridge, MA: Harvard University Press.
Galton, Antony. 1984. *The Logic of Aspect*. Oxford: Clarendon Press.
Haase, Matthias, and Douglas, Lavin. Forthcoming. "Events and Processes in the Philosophy of Action." http://www.tandf.co.uk/journals/authors/style/reference/tf_ChicagoAD.pdf.
Hamblin, C. L. 1971. "Instants and Intervals." *Studium Generale* 24: 127–134.
Hornsby, Jennifer. 1980. *Actions*. London: Routledge & Kegan Paul.
Hornsby, Jennifer. 2011. "Actions in their Circumstances." In *Essays on Anscombe's Intention*, edited by Anton Ford, Jennifer Hornsby, and Frederick Stoutland, 105–127. Cambridge, MA: Harvard University Press.
Hursthouse, Rosalind. 2000. "Intention." In *Logic, Cause and Action*, edited by R. Teichmann, 83–106. Cambridge: Cambridge University Press.
Hyman, John. 2001. "-ings and -ers." *Ratio* 14: 298–317.
Lavin, Douglas. 2013a. "Must There Be Basic Action?" *Noûs* 47 (2), 273–301. doi: http://dx.doi.org/10.1111/j.1468-0068.2012.00876.x.
Lavin, Douglas. 2013b. "Über das Problem des Handelns [On the Problem of Action]." *Deutsche Zeitschrift für Philosophie* 61 (3): 357–372.
McDowell, John. 1982. "Criteria, Defeasibility and Knowledge." *Proceedings of the British Academy* 68: 455–479.
Moran, Richard, and Stone Martin. 2011. "Anscombe on Expression of Intention: An Exegesis." In *Essays on Anscombe's Intention*, edited by Anton Ford, Jennifer Hornsby, and Frederick Stoutland, 33–75. Cambridge, MA: Harvard University Press.
Parsons, Terence. 1990. *Events in the Semantics of English: A Study in Subatomic Semantics*. Cambridge: MIT Press.
Rödl, Sebastian. 2012. *Categories of the Temporal: An Inquiry into the Forms of the Finite Intellect*. Cambridge, MA: Harvard University Press.
Searle, John. 1983. *Intentionality*. Cambridge: Cambridge University Press.
Sellars, Willfrid. 1991. "Empiricism and the Philosophy of Mind." In *Science, Perception and Reality*, 127–196. Atascadero, CA: Ridgeview.

Stoutland, Frederick. 2011. "Anscombe's *Intention* in Context." In *Essays on Anscombe's Intention*, edited by Anton Ford, Jennifer Hornsby, and Frederick Stoutland, 23–32. Cambridge, MA: Harvard University Press.

Thompson, Michael. 2008. *Life and Action: Elementary Structures of Practice and Practical Thought*. Cambridge, MA: Harvard University Press.

Thompson, Michael. 2011. "Anscombe's Intention and Practical Knowledge." In *Essays on Anscombe's Intention*, edited by Anton Ford, Jennifer Hornsby, and Frederick Stoutland, 198–210. Cambridge, MA: Harvard University Press.

Velleman, J. D. 2007. *Practical Reflection*. Stanford, CA: CSLI.

Vogler, Candace. 2001. "Anscombe on Practical Inference." In *Varieties of Practical Reasoning*, edited by E. Millgram, 437–464. Cambridge, MA: MIT Press.

Waterlow, Sarah. 1982. *Nature, Change and Agency in Aristotle's Physics*. Oxford: Oxford University Press.

Williamson, Timothy. 2000. *Knowledge and its Limits*. Oxford: Oxford University Press.

Wittgenstein, Ludwig. 1963. *Philosophical Investigations*. 3rd ed. Translated by G. E. M. Anscombe. New York: Macmillian.

Synchronic requirements and diachronic permissions

John Broome[a,b,c]

[a]Faculty of Philosophy, University of Oxford, Oxford, UK; [b]Department of Philosophy, Stanford University, Stanford, CA, USA; [c]Department of Philosophy, Australian National University, Canberra Australia

ABSTRACT
Reasoning is an activity of ours by which we come to satisfy synchronic requirements of rationality. However, reasoning itself is regulated by diachronic permissions of rationality. For each synchronic requirement there appears to be a corresponding diachronic permission, but the requirements and permissions are not related to each other in a systematic way. It is therefore a puzzle how reasoning according to permissions can systematically bring us to satisfy requirements.

1. Introduction

On the face of it, rationality has two aspects – a static one and a dynamic one. Rationality regulates people's mental states: some particular states, such as the state of having contradictory beliefs, are irrational and others are not. Rationality also regulates people's mental processes. In particular it regulates reasoning: there are rational and irrational ways to reason.

How are these static and dynamic aspects of rationality connected together? It is natural to assume that rational processes can help us avoid irrational states. But the two aspects of rationality have different structures. Static rationality is regulated by synchronic requirements, whereas dynamic rationality is regulated by diachronic permissions. It is hard to find a systematic connection between these two structures that satisfactorily unifies the two aspects of rationality. This paper explains the difficulty. I am sorry to say I have no solution to it.

2. Synchronic requirements

Rationality requires things of you. It requires you not to have contradictory beliefs, to intend what you believe is a means implied by an end you intend, and much else. When rationality requires something of you, and you fail to achieve it, you are not entirely rational.

The requirements I mentioned put constraints on mental attitudes that are contemporaneous with each other. In other words, they are synchronic. You may believe something at one time and believe its negation at another time, and yet be entirely rational. Only if you have those two beliefs at the same time are you necessarily not entirely rational; you violate a requirement of rationality. Similarly, if you intend an end at some time but at some other time do not intend what you believe is a means implied by that end, you may yet be entirely rational. Only if you intend an end and at the same time do not intend what you believe is a means implied by it are you necessarily not entirely rational.

There are other synchronic requirements of rationality besides the two I mentioned. Formulating them accurately is surprisingly complicated. It may seem straightforward that rationality requires you not to have contradictory beliefs. But what if you are a dialetheist? Dialetheists believe that some propositions (such as the proposition that this very proposition is false) have the special feature that both they and their negations are true. Suppose a dialetheist believes some proposition and also its negation, and also believes this is one of those special propositions. Is she necessarily irrational? It would be hard to say so. So it does not seem strictly true that rationality requires you not to have contradictory beliefs. Still, there must be some requirement of the sort. I shall not offer an accurate formulation of it in this paper (see Broome 2014, 91).

It is also hard to formulate the means–end requirement I mentioned. Here is the formulation I have arrived at after some years of development (Broome 2014, 159). It may yet be incorrect:

Instrumental Requirement. Rationality requires of N that, if

(1) N intends at t that e, and if
(2) N believes at t that, if m were not so, because of that e would not be so, and if
(3) N believes at t that, if she herself were not then to intend m, because of that m would not be so, then
(4) N intends at t that m.

This is strictly a requirement-schema rather than a requirement. A requirement is obtained by making appropriate substitutions for the schematic letters: the name of a person for 'N', a specification of a time for 't', and sentences denoting propositions for 'e' and 'm'. Informally 'e' stands for 'end' and 'm' for 'means'.

The Instrumental Requirement can be put in a slightly less forbidding form by introducing some special terms. I use 'a is a means implied by b', to mean that, were *a* not so, because of that *b* would not be so. And I use '*m* is up to *N* then' to mean that, if *N* were not then to intend *m*, because of that *m* would not be so. These are not exactly the meanings of the terms in English, but they approximate the meanings. The Instrumental Requirement can now be written:

Instrumental Requirement. Rationality requires of *N* that, if

(1) *N* intends at *t* that *e*, and if
(2) *N* believes at *t* that *m* is a means implied by *e*, and if
(3) *N* believes at *t* that *m* is up to her herself then, then
(4) *N* intends at *t* that *m*.

Many features of this formulation call for explanation (see Broome 2014, 159–69), but few of them matter to this paper. I need only draw attention to the indexical terms 'her herself' and 'then'. If *N* were to express the belief of hers described in (3), she would say '*m* is up to me now'. In indirect speech, we represent 'me' and 'now' by 'her herself' and 'then'. The first 'then' in clause (3) refers to the time when *N* has this belief. It needs to be in there; the requirement would not be correctly stated without it. Suppose you intend an end, and believe the end will not be achieved unless at some time you intend a particular means to it. But suppose you do not believe that the time has yet arrived when you need to have this intention in order to bring about the means. Then you may be entirely rational even if you do not have this intention. Only when you believe the time has arrived are you irrational in not intending what you believe to be an implied means.

> I shall use another requirement as an example in this paper: *Modus Ponens Requirement.* Rationality requires of *N* that, if *N* believes at *t* that *p*, and *N* believes at *t* that if *p* then *q*, and if *N* cares at *t* whether *q*, then *N* believes at *t* that *q*.

Why the clause about caring? Well, rationality does not require you to believe something that follows by modus ponens from things you believe if it does not matter to you. On the other hand, it does require you to have such a belief when it does matter. If things go badly for you because you do not believe something that follows by modus ponens from things you believe, that is a failure of rationality on your part. So there has to be a clause of this sort. It is debatable just what it should be, and for my purposes the precise form makes no difference. I have chosen to make it a caring clause.

Because the requirements I have mentioned are synchronic, and so are many other requirements of rationality, we human beings spend much of our lives in violation of requirements of rationality. When we form new plans or get new information, some of our beliefs and intentions change. This can put them out of line with others of our beliefs and intentions. It takes some time before those others catch up with the new situation. In the meantime we violate some requirements of rationality; we are not entirely rational. This bothers some people, and can be used as an argument against synchronic requirements. But I think human beings cannot aspire to full rationality.

3. Rationality and reasoning

Requirements of rationality do not apply to everything. For example, they do not apply to stones. Call something to which requirements of rationality apply a *rational being*. A rational being is *fully rational* if and only if it satisfies every requirement of rationality that applies to it. Otherwise it is less than fully rational. If two rational beings are subject to the same requirements, and one satisfies all the requirements that the other satisfies and at least one more, then the former is *more rational* than the latter. So requirements of rationality determine degrees of rationality, and these degrees are partially ordered. If you are to become more rational – if your degree of rationality is to increase – you must come to satisfy requirements of rationality that previously you did not satisfy.

How does it happen that you satisfy requirements of rationality? Sometimes by chance. For example, you might by chance intend to do something that you later come to believe is a means implied by something else you intend. But it can also happen through processes that systematically bring you to satisfy requirements.

Some of these processes are not acts of yours; they are not things you do. For example, suppose you believe platypuses are not mammals, but then you learn that platypuses are mammals. You acquire the belief that platypuses are mammals. If everything works as normal, at the same time, automatically, some subpersonal process causes you to drop your belief that platypuses are not mammals. This process ensures you satisfy the requirement not to have this particular pair of contradictory beliefs. It brings you to satisfy a requirement, but it is not an act of yours.

Some such processes might qualify as a sort of *reasoning*. If there are any that do, I call them *passive reasoning*. Some processes of passive reasoning might bring you to satisfy a requirement of rationality. Suppose that, as a child, you were taught to reason by modus ponens. To begin with, you had to think your way consciously through the reasoning. But with time it became automatic. Then when this process occurs in you, we might still count it as reasoning, but we might no longer count it as an act of yours because it is automatic. We might treat it as more like digesting your food than eating your food. But it can bring you to satisfy a particular instance of the Modus Ponens Requirement.

I do not insist that passive reasoning really exists. But I do insist that sometimes you can come to satisfy a synchronic requirement of rationality by a process of reasoning that is an act. Such a process is *active reasoning*. For example, you reason actively about some issue you care about, employing modus ponens, and thereby come to satisfy the Modus Ponens Requirement in this instance.

Or you come to satisfy the Instrumental Requirement in a particular instance by active instrumental reasoning.

From here on in this paper, 'reasoning' refers to active reasoning only.

What exactly is this process of active reasoning, and what makes it an act? This question is not the topic of this paper, and I shall simply take for granted my own answer to it, which appears in Broome (2014). Reasoning is a process that takes you from some attitudes (the 'premise attitudes') of yours to a new attitude (the 'conclusion attitude') that you did not previously have. For example, you reason from some existing beliefs to a new belief. (Sometimes reasoning confirms an attitude you already have, rather than leading to a new attitude, but I shall ignore these cases here.) In active reasoning, the premise attitudes and conclusion attitude are conscious. You operate on the contents of the premise attitudes to derive the content of the conclusion attitude, following a rule. The rule sets up a standard of correctness, and in following the rule you recognize this standard and are guided by it. It is because you follow a rule that reasoning is something you do. That is an outline of my account of reasoning.

4. Correctness of reasoning

Evidently, some processes of reasoning are correct and others are incorrect. What distinguishes the correct ones from the incorrect ones? This question *is* a topic for this paper and I shall spend some time on it.

Since reasoning can be a means of coming to satisfy synchronic requirements of rationality, a natural first answer to the question is that reasoning is correct if and only if it brings you to satisfy a synchronic requirement. But that is not so: correct reasoning may not bring you to satisfy a synchronic requirement of rationality, and incorrect reasoning may bring you to satisfy one.

Here are two examples where correct reasoning does not bring you to satisfy a synchronic requirement. Suppose you believe that p and you believe that if p then q, and you reason from these beliefs to a belief that q. This is obviously correct reasoning. But if you do not care about whether q, it does not bring you to satisfy a requirement of rationality. You are not required to believe everything that follows by modus ponens from everything you believe. Or alternatively, suppose that by the time you believe q you no longer believe p. This must be possible: reasoning is not instantaneous, so you may have lost a premise attitude by the time you acquire the conclusion attitude. In that case, your reasoning does not bring you to satisfy any synchronic requirement of rationality.

Here is an example where incorrect reasoning brings you to satisfy a requirement of rationality. Suppose you care about whether q, you believe that p, you believe that if p then q, you believe that if q then r, and you believe that r. Then you reason from the last two of these beliefs to acquire the new belief that q. This is reasoning by affirming the consequent, which is obviously incorrect. Yet it brings you to satisfy the Modus Ponens Requirement in relation to the first two beliefs.

These examples reveal a general difficulty with the natural first answer to the question of correctness. A criterion for correct reasoning needs to be a feature of the reasoning process itself, rather than a feature of the result of reasoning. The result can depend on contingencies that are irrelevant to the process's correctness.

For the same reason we can reject the idea that reasoning is correct if and only if the conclusion is validly derivable from the premises. In any case, this idea cannot be applied to all sorts of reasoning. It is aimed at only at the particular sort of theoretical reasoning that takes you to a belief from other beliefs. In any case, it is mistaken. You could reason to a conclusion incorrectly, but the conclusion might nevertheless be validly derivable from the premises. For example, suppose your premises are p, if p then q, if q then r, and r. You might reason from these premises to the conclusion q by affirming the consequent. This is incorrect reasoning, even though the conclusion is validly derivable from the premises.

Evidently the right account of correctness must pay attention to the reasoning process itself. My account of reasoning provides an easy first step towards what I believe is the right account. Since reasoning involves following a rule, we may take it that reasoning is correct if and only if it correctly follows a correct rule. A rule sets up a standard of correctness: you follow the rule correctly if and only if you conform to the rule. But if you are to reason correctly, the rule itself also needs to be correct. If you correctly follow the rule of affirming the consequent, your reasoning is incorrect. So a full account of correctness also needs to specify when a rule is correct.

5. Rules of reasoning

As a preliminary, I need to formulate rules of reasoning. Start with an instance of reasoning by modus ponens. Suppose you believe it is raining and that if it is raining the snow will melt, and you reason your way to believing the snow will melt. You do this by operating on the contents of your beliefs, which are propositions. The content of your first belief – that it is raining – is the antecedent of the conditional proposition – that if it is raining the snow will melt – that is the content of your second belief. You operate on these two contents following the Modus Ponens Rule. This rule tells you to construct the proposition that is the consequent of the conditional proposition. You end up believing this proposition.

The Modus Ponens Rule is:

From p

and If p then q

to derive q

Notice some things about this formulation. First, the rule is about the contents of the attitudes you reason with rather than the attitudes themselves. Your reasoning process consists in a progression from some attitudes to another attitude. But you reason *about* the contents of these attitudes, and you apply a rule to those contents.

Second, I have not formulated the rule as an imperative. A rule merely specifies what it is to conform to the rule; it does not tell you to conform to itself. Something else may tell you to conform to a particular rule by giving the rule *force*, as I put it. Rules are given force in various ways: some by the law, some by the command of an authority, some perhaps by rationality, and in many other ways. There are also rules that have no force: you have no reason to follow them. For instance, you have no reason to follow the rule of not ending a sentence with a preposition. You may even follow a particular rule that you have no reason to follow and that you do not even believe you have a reason to follow. For instance, out of habit you may avoid ending a sentence with a preposition. When walking along the street, you may follow the child's rule of not stepping on the lines, while at the same time thinking this is a stupid thing for an adult to do.

I have assumed so far that, when you do the snow reasoning, you follow the Modus Ponens Rule. But you might instead follow the more restricted rule:

From p

and If p then q

to derive q, if q is a proposition about snow

Or the stranger rule:

From p

and If p then q

to derive q if you are on Earth

and to derive Not q if you are elsewhere

According to Saul Kripke (1982), it may be indeterminate which rule you follow. The second of these rules is incorrect, whereas the first is correct and so is the Modus Ponens Rule. So if Kripke is right, it may be indeterminate whether you are reasoning correctly or incorrectly. This is odd, but I do not think it is a fatal problem for an account of the correctness of reasoning. We can have a criterion for the correctness of reasoning even if it can be indeterminate whether your reasoning meets the criterion.

So far, I have formulated rules in a way that suits reasoning from beliefs to a belief. But an account of correctness must cover other sorts of reasoning too. For example, it must cover reasoning that concludes in an intention, including instrumental reasoning. Instrumental reasoning takes you from intending an end to intending a means to the end. An example is reasoning that has as its premise states an intention to visit Venice and a belief that you will not visit Venice if you do not buy a ticket, and has as its conclusion state an intention to buy a ticket.

I take it that the content of an intention, like the content of a belief, is a proposition. For example, an intention to visit Venice has the same content as a belief that you will visit Venice: namely, the proposition that you will visit Venice. But an intention and a belief, even if they have the same content, do not play the same role in reasoning. From an intention to visit Venice, with some other premise, you could derive an intention to take a means of visiting Venice. But from a mere belief that you will visit Venice you could not derive an intention to take a means of doing so. So rules that guide reasoning must keep track of not only the propositional contents of the attitudes involved, but also the nature of the attitudes they are the contents of.

They can do so by being rules about *marked contents*. I treat a marked content as a pair consisting of a proposition that is the content of an attitude together with a 'mark', which is the type of attitude it is the content of. The marked content of a belief that you will visit Venice is the pair < I shall visit Venice; belief >. (I express the proposition in the way you would, using the pronoun 'I'.) The marked content of an intention to visit Venice is the pair < I shall visit Venice; intention >.

The instrumental reasoning I described might follow this rule:

From < I shall visit Venice, intention>

and < I shall not visit Venice if I do not buy a ticket; belief>

to derive < I shall buy a ticket; intention>

The Modus Ponens Rule should be formulated in the same way:

From < p; belief>

and < If p then q; belief>

to derive < q; belief>

This is the same rule as I presented before, but specified more fully.

At the end of section 4, I briefly outlined my account of the reasoning process. That account now needs to be modified slightly. In reasoning, you operate, not on the contents of your attitudes alone, but on their marked contents. You do so following a rule of the sort I have described.

6. Basing prohibitions

Now we know what a rule is like, we can ask what determines whether a rule is correct. It is important to recognize that this is a question about permissibility rather than requirement. For something to be correct – a rule or anything else – is for it to be permissible rather than required. It is required only if there is no permissible alternative. Also, when we are dealing with rules of reasoning, we can assume that the source of correctness is rationality. For a rule to be correct is for it to be rational – which is to say, rationally permissible – to follow it.

It is useful to start with the opposite: what rationality prohibits. A prohibition of rationality is simply a requirement of rationality with a negative content: a requirement not to do something or not to be in some state. Prohibitions have a crucial place in an account of rationality. Without them, we could not account for what Schroeder (2004) calls the 'asymmetry' of some features of rationality.

Most requirements of rationality have a conditional content. This means there is more than one way of satisfying them. You will satisfy a requirement if the consequent of its content is true or if one of its antecedents is false. Take this instance of the Instrumental Requirement from section 2:

Rationality requires of you that, if

(1) You intend to go to London, and if
(2) You believe that taking a train is a means implied by your going to London, and if
(3) You believe that taking a train is up to you now, then
(4) You intend to take a train.

You will satisfy this requirement if you intend to take a train, or if you do not intend to go to London, or if you do not believe that taking a train is a means implied by your going to London, or if you do not believe that taking a train is up to you yourself now. The requirement can be equally well satisfied in any of these ways. It is symmetrical in this respect.

A way to put this is to say that conditional requirements allow contraposition. For example, without any change in its meaning, the Instrumental Requirement may be written:

Contraposed Instrumental Requirement. Rationality requires of N that, if

1) N intends at t that e, and if
2) (4') N does not intend at t that m, and if
3) N believes at t that m is up to her herself then, then
4) (2') N does not believe at t that m is a means implied by e.

In the example:

Rationality requires of you that, if

(1) You intend to go to London, and if
(2) (4') You do not intend to take a train, and if
(3) You believe that taking a train is up to you now, then
(4) (2') You do not believe that taking a train is a means implied by going to London.

Contraposing a requirement makes it plain how it can be satisfied in various ways. But not all ways of *coming to* satisfy a requirement are necessarily rational. There is nothing irrational about satisfying clause (4) of the uncontraposed version because you satisfy clauses (1), (2) and (3). However, it would generally be irrational to satisfy clause (2') of the contraposed version because you satisfy clauses (1), (4') and (3). It seems to be irrational for your non-belief to be explained in this way by the state of your intentions. So there is an asymmetry, not in the requirement itself, but among ways of coming to satisfy the requirement.

The asymmetry needs to be stated more accurately. Suppose the story is this. You initially believe that taking a train is a means implied by going to London. You intend to go to London. But you have a standing intention not to take any train. The conflict among these attitudes causes you to think again, and the result is that you realize you can get to London by bus. So you drop your belief that taking a train is a means implied by going to London. There may be nothing irrational about this process, even though your non-belief is explained by the state of your intentions. We learn from this story that there need be nothing irrational about your non-belief's being explained causally by your intention and non-intention. We therefore need to refine the 'because' in the previous paragraph. There is irrationality only if your satisfying clause (2') is *based on* your satisfying clauses (1), (4') and (3), rather than being merely causally explained by them. The asymmetry lies in basing.

What is it for one attitude or non-attitude to be based on others? I cannot give an analysis of basing but I can make a couple of remarks about it. Basing is not mere causation, but it does imply a causal connection: the basing attitudes or non-attitudes causally explain the based one. Because causation takes time, it follows that the basing attitudes or non-attitudes exist before the based one. Basing can therefore be a diachronic relation.

You might be doubtful about diachronic basing. Even if the basing attitudes cause the based attitude, you might think that the based attitude can be based on the basing attitudes only for as long as the basing attitudes persist. But that is not so. Suppose at some time you see a light in a house, and so believe that a light is switched on in the house. Suppose on this basis you believe someone is in the house. Your belief that someone is in the house is based on your belief that a light is switched on in the house. Suppose you later see the light going off, and so at a later time no longer believe there is a light switched on in the house. But you continue to believe someone is in the house, though you acquire no further evidence of this. Then your belief at this later time that someone is in the house is based on your earlier belief whose content was that a light is switched on in the house.

When you acquire an attitude by reasoning from other attitudes, the attitude you acquire is based on the others. But basing does not always arise from reasoning. An attitude or non-attitude may be based on others as a result of processes that are not acts of yours. When you learn that platypuses are mammals and consequently drop your belief that platypuses are not mammals because of some subpersonal process, your non-belief in the proposition that platypuses are not mammals is based on your belief in the proposition that platypuses are mammals. This basing does not arise from reasoning.

Now I can state more accurately what we can learn from the example of the train to London. The conclusion is that rationality prohibits you – (rationality requires of you that it is not the case that):

> At some time you intend to go to London, and
> at some time you do not intend to take a train, and
> at some time you believe that your taking a train is up to you, and
> at some time you do not believe that your taking a train is a mean implied by your going to London, and
> your non-belief that taking a train is a means implied by your going to London is based on your intention to go to London, your non-intention to take a train, and your belief that taking a train is up to you.

This rules out not just contemporaneous attitudes and non-attitudes with a particular basing connection, but also ones that are not contemporaneous. It is a diachronic basing prohibition.

7. Basing permissions

There clearly are basing prohibitions, and they satisfactorily explain the asymmetry. The opposite of a basing prohibition is a basing permission. In Broome (2014) I said that a permission is simply the negation of a prohibition. I meant that for something to be permitted by rationality is for it not to be prohibited. I now realize that was a mistake. My own account of requirement, which is presented in Broome (2014), means I have to allow for some things that are neither prohibited nor permitted. 'Permitted' is a narrower category than 'not prohibited'. However, the distinction is technical and need not trouble us here.

> Instead, I shall take the idea of permission for granted, and go ahead to formulate a couple of basing permissions of rationality. One is: *Modus Ponens Permission*. Rationality permits N that, if N believes at some time that p, and N believes at some time that if p then q, then N believes at some time that q and N's belief that q is based on N's belief that p and N's belief that if p then q.

This formulation contains some slightly deviant grammar, but there is no harm in that. It does not specify that the time of N's belief that q is no earlier than the time of her other beliefs, which may seem odd. But doing so is not necessary because it is a feature of basing that a based belief cannot be earlier than its basing beliefs.

Another basing permission is:

Instrumental Permission. Rationality permits N that, if

(1) N intends at some time that e, and if
(2) N believes at some time that m is a means implied by e, and if
(3) N believes at some time that m is up to her herself, then
(4) N intends at some time that m and
(5) N's intention that m is based on N's intention that e, and N's belief that m is a means implied by e, and N's belief that m is up to her herself.

These two examples of permissions resemble the corresponding requirements, but differ from them in various ways (apart from being permissions rather than requirements).

First, they are *basing* permissions; they are permissions not just to have particular combinations of attitudes, but to have one attitude on the basis of others. The corresponding requirements are not concerned with basing.

Second, they are diachronic, whereas the requirements are synchronic. At least, they are potentially diachronic. They permit you to have an attitude based on attitudes you no longer have. This is necessary. In section 6, I gave the example of your belief that someone is in the house, which you have on the basis of a belief you had at an earlier time that a light is on in the house. This sort of diachronic basing is clearly permitted by rationality. Since reasoning takes time, an attitude acquired through reasoning will always be based on attitudes you had a short time previously.

Third, whereas the requirements are symmetric, the permissions are not. They cannot be contraposed. This is not to say that there are not other permissions corresponding to contraposed versions of the corresponding requirements. Consider this putative permission:

Contraposed Modus Ponens Permission. Rationality permits *N* that, if at some time *N* does not believe that *q*, and *N* believes at some time that if *p* then *q*, then at some time *N* does not believe that *p* and *N*'s non-belief that *p* is based on *N*'s non-belief that *q* and *N*'s belief that if *p* then *q*.

This formula is tricky in some ways, and I do not certify the Contraposed Modus Ponens Permission as true. But I know no conclusive argument against it. On the other hand, no permission corresponds to the Contraposed Instrumental Requirement I stated in section 7.

Fourth, the conditional clauses in the permissions are weaker than the corresponding clauses in the requirements. So the permissions apply in some circumstances where the requirements do not. It is to be expected that more is permitted than is required.

The difference in the case of the Modus Ponens Permission is that the permission does not contain the caring clause that appears in the Modus Ponens Requirement. This is as it should be. Whereas you are not required to believe everything that follows by modus ponens from anything you believe, you are permitted to believe anything that follows.

The difference in the case of the Instrumental Permission is more subtle. Clause (3) of the permission does not contain the indexical adverb 'then', whereas the same clause in the requirement does. Again, this is as it should be. It is permissible to intend means that you believe are implied by an end you intend, if you believe that achieving the means is up to you – if, that is to say, you believe the means would not come about were you not to intend it. Moreover, it is permissible to intend the means on that basis. This is permissible even if you do not believe you have to intend the means at that very moment in order for it to come about. When you see a need for intending means coming up in the future, you may permissibly plan ahead at your leisure.[1] But you are not actually required to intend the means until you have reached a time when you believe you need to intend it if it is to come about. Indeed, you must plan ahead if you are to form your intention by reasoning. Since reasoning takes time, an attitude you acquire by reasoning is based on attitudes you have at a time before you acquire it. If you wait to start your reasoning until you believe the intention is already necessary, you are therefore too late by your own lights. You will not have your intention at a time when you believe you must have it in order for the means to come about.[2] This reinforces the point that reasoning is regulated by permissions of rationality rather than requirements. And it shows that the Instrumental Permission has to have the weaker version of clause (3), without 'then'.

8. Correctness of rules and correctness of reasoning

Our question was when a rule of reasoning is correct, and we now have an answer available.

Any permission of rationality has the form:

Rationality permits N that, if

> N has attitude A at some time, and if
>
> N has attitude B at some time, and if
>
> N has attitude C at some time, and if
>
> ..., then
>
> N has attitude K at some time and
>
> N's attitude K is based on N's attitudes $A, B, C \ldots$

The 'attitudes' in this formula may include non-attitudes such as not believing. For any permission we can define a corresponding rule:

From

> $<a; A\text{–type}>$ and
>
> $<b; B\text{–type}>$ and
>
> $<c, C\text{–type}>$ and
>
> ...

to derive

> $<k, K\text{–type}>$.

A rule of reasoning is correct if and only if it corresponds to a genuine permission of rationality. That is the answer.

Reasoning is correct if and only if it correctly follows a correct rule, and a rule is correct if and only if it corresponds to a permission of rationality. This does not mean that reasoning is correct if and only if it is in accord with a permission of rationality. You may reason incorrectly (not correctly following a correct rule) but nevertheless arrive at a conclusion-attitude that is in accordance with a permission of rationality.

(Note in passing. The rule of instrumental reasoning I described in section 5 is not correct by this criterion; the rule it follows does not correspond to the Instrumental Permission. It is indeed not a correct rule. It needs some more premises. The instrumental reasoning I described in section is not correct unless it is enthymematic, with some further suppressed premises. (Broome 2014, 259–60))

9. Diachronic permissions and synchronic requirements

We have made a little progress with correctness, but more is needed. This account of correctness for reasoning simply throws the question onto permissions of rationality. How is it determined what rationality permits?

For the special case of a belief based on beliefs, there may seem to be an easy answer. It may seem that it is permissible to base a belief on other beliefs if and only if the proposition that is the content of the based belief follows validly from the propositions that are the content of the basing beliefs. But this is doubtful. Suppose you believe each of Peano's Axioms. Suppose you reason from those beliefs to believing the Goldbach Conjecture, so you end up believing the Goldbach Conjecture on the basis of your believing Peano's Axioms. And suppose that the Goldbach Conjecture follows validly from Peano's Axioms. (Nobody knows whether this is so.) It is doubtful that you reason correctly and that your belief is permissibly based, since you have no idea whether the conclusion follows from the premises.

Be that as it may, this criterion for permissibility has at best a limited scope. There are basing permissions involving other attitudes besides belief, such as the Instrumental Permission. The criterion does not extend to them. It is not true in general that it is permissible to base an attitude on others if and only if the content of the based attitude follows validly from the contents of the basing attitudes. For example, suppose you believe you will catch flu (because there is so much around) and you believe that you will not catch flu unless you are in contact with a fluey person. It would not be permissible for you to base an intention to be in contact with a fluey person on the basis of those beliefs.

Sadly, I do not have a general answer to the question of how it is determined what rationality permits. Nor do I have a general answer to the question of what rationality requires. These are serious lacks, and I wish I could overcome them. I know some constraints on requirements of rationality. For one thing they are requirements on the state of your mind, so rationality cannot require a physical act for example. But in specifying requirements and permissions I have little to go on besides intuition.

Here I shall draw attention to just one part of the question of how it is determined what rationality permits. What is the relation between requirements and permissions? This is the question I introduced in section 1. How are the static and dynamic aspects of rationality unified? I take it that reasoning is a means we have of improving our rationality. But you improve your rationality – increase your degree of rationality – only if you come to satisfy a requirement of rationality that you did not previously satisfy. Merely conforming to permissions of rationality, and avoiding prohibitions of rationality, does not directly make you more rational. If you reason correctly, you act as rationality permits you to, but that on its own does not improve your rationality. Only satisfying a new requirement does that. So how does correct reasoning achieve the end of satisfying a new requirement? Understanding the relation between requirements and permissions should answer that question.

We can take it for granted that whatever is required is permitted. So to every synchronic requirement of rationality there is a synchronic permission in which 'requires' is replaced with 'permits'. But this gives us no help. It tells us nothing about the process of coming to satisfy requirements.

It also seems plausible that, for every synchronic requirement there is a corresponding diachronic basing permission. I gave the two examples of the Modus Ponens Permission corresponding to the Modus Ponens Requirement, and the Instrumental Permission corresponding to the Instrumental Requirement. Basing permissions do tell us about processes. They determine whether or not a process of reasoning is correct. And a reasoning process that is made correct by a particular basing permission can bring you to satisfy the corresponding requirement.

But how come? First of all, why does a synchronic requirement always have a corresponding basing permission? And why is the corresponding permission such that, by reasoning in the way it permits, you can come to satisfy the requirement in particular cases. For example, reasoning in accordance with the Modus Pones Permission can be directed towards satisfying the Modus Ponens Requirement in cases where you care about the result. It is easy to see how this works in this particular case: you simply reason according to the Modus Ponens Permission to arrive at a belief in some proposition that you care about. But how come the same thing works in general?

This is puzzling because permissions differ from requirements in the various different ways I listed in Section 7, and they seem not to be related together in a systematic way. Their relation is systematic in one respect: the relevant permissions are basing permissions and they are diachronic, whereas the relevant requirements do not mention basing and they are synchronic. But the examples reveal no system in other respects.

Take the Contraposed Instrumental Requirement, for example. This is a perfectly good synchronic requirement, and we could ask what diachronic basing permission corresponds to it. But the corresponding diachronic basing permission is the Instrumental Permission set out in section 7. This is the same as the one that corresponds to the ordinary Instrumental Requirement. So in order to get from the Contraposed Instrumental Requirement to its corresponding diachronic basing permission, we first have to contrapose it to get the ordinary Instrumental Requirement, and then we have to drop the indexical 'then' from its condition (3). None of this is like what we have to do to get from the Modus Ponens Requirement to the Modus Ponens Permission.

Furthermore, instrumental reasoning has the odd feature that, if you do the reasoning at the time when the conditions of the Instrumental Requirement are satisfied, your reasoning will fail by your own lights. Instead, you have to do instrumental reasoning in accordance with the Instrumental Permission before the Instrumental Requirement itself kicks in. Again, there is nothing like this with the Modus Ponens Requirement.

So there is a puzzle.

10. Are there synchronic requirements?

One way to overcome it would be to deny that rationality has a static aspect. Perhaps there are no such things as synchronic requirements; rationality might be entirely concerned with processes. We have seen that certain processes are permitted by rationality and others are prohibited. That might be all there is to rationality. This view has what may be seen as a further merit. I explained at the end of section 2 that we are very often in violation of synchronic requirements. When you acquire a new attitude, it takes time for your other attitudes to adjust to it, and in the meantime you are not entirely rational. It is therefore impossible for a human being to be entirely rational. Some philosophers find that an undesirable conclusion.

But actually there truly are synchronic requirements. Suppose there were none. And suppose that, without going through any irrational process, you find yourself believing p, believing that if p then q, caring about whether q, but not believing q. If there were no synchronic requirements, you might be entirely rational and you might continue to be entirely rational even if you remain in this state indefinitely. That is absurd.

This argument could be resisted by a response that calls on the idea of a reason. The response is that your belief that p and your belief that if p then q together constitute a reason to believe q. Given that you have a reason to believe q, the response continues, it follows that you are not rational unless you believe q. But this goes too far. When you have a reason to believe q, it cannot follow that you are not rational just because you do not believe it. You might have a stronger reason not to believe it. (This argument is set out in more detail in Broome 2014, 79–82.)

So we cannot avoid the conclusion that there are synchronic requirements of rationality. That leaves us with the difficulty of finding a systematic explanation of how they are connected with the diachronic permissions of rationality that regulate reasoning. We still need an explanation of how the static and dynamic aspects of rationality are connected together.

Notes

1. As Geoff Brennan pointed out to me.
2. As Kieran Setiya pointed out to me.

Acknowledgements

Many thanks to Michael Bratman for his extensive comments on this paper.

Funding

This research was supported by the Australian Research Council (ARC) Discovery [grant number DP140102468].

References

Broome, John. 2014. *Rationality through Reasoning*. Oxford: Wiley-Blackwell.
Kripke, Saul. 1982. *Wittgenstein on Rules and Private Language*. Oxford: Blackwell.
Schroeder, Mark. 2004. "The Scope of Instrumental Reason." *Philosophical Perspectives* 18: 337–364.

The courage of conviction

Sarah K. Paul

Department of Philosophy, University of Wisconsin-Madison, Madison, WI, USA

ABSTRACT
Is there a sense in which we exercise direct volitional control over our beliefs? Most agree that there is not, but discussions tend to focus on control in forming a belief. The focus here is on sustaining a belief over time in the face of 'epistemic temptation' to abandon it. It is argued that we do have a capacity for 'doxastic self-control' over time that is partly volitional in nature, and that its exercise is rationally permissible.

As agents, we sometimes determine for ourselves what we will do. Some of our intentions and actions are attributable to *us*, rather than to some external influence or some automatic, subpersonal mechanism within us. And we have the capacity to be more or less self-governing over certain aspects of our practical lives, in that the extent to which our actions are the product of external forces is sometimes under our control. Can anything similar be said about our relationship to our beliefs?

According to a widespread and appealing view of agency, an action is most attributable to an agent when it expresses that agent's values, higher-order desires, or practical commitments. The idea is that the structure of a person's will is constituted by a network of such attitudes, such that when this network guides thought and behavior, the agent governs herself. It is when a person non-accidentally does what she takes to be most worth doing, or what she wholeheartedly wants to do, or what is most consistent with her plans and self-governing policies, that her agency is fully manifested. When her behavior deviates from what is called for by these lights, in contrast, her agency is diminished. This is sometimes a matter of failing to be an agent altogether, as when she is passively acted upon by psychological or environmental forces that are completely external to her will. In other cases, she is akratic; she actively does something other than what is called for by her values and other commitments.

On this view, there is a substantial role for something worth calling 'volition' in constituting oneself as an agent. For one thing, it denies that autonomous agency consists solely in responding cognitively to one's reasons for action by forming normative beliefs and acting accordingly. This is because there is – at least apparently – widespread normative underdetermination in our practical lives. There are countless incompatible things that are all worth doing, and countless ways of doing them that are equally good. Even the most angelic agent who is determined to do what is best must commit to pursuing only some of the valuable things, and to doing them in only some particular ways. There is therefore ample latitude for discretion in one's intentional actions that is consistent with one's normative reasons for action. Where this latitude exists, we face a genuine choice: there are multiple actions or intentions available, each of which would be an expression of the agent's will if that course of action were adopted.

Moreover, the wide middle ground between 'full-blooded' agency and total passivity that is afforded by the phenomenon of akrasia allows for the exercise of self-control. In cases where an agent is assailed by temptation to do something other than what she by her own lights ought to do, it is in part up to her whether she succumbs or succeeds in resisting. When she gives in and takes the second dessert, she is not simply overcome by appetite; there is a real sense in which she chooses to give in. Likewise, when she refrains, this is not merely a hydraulic process of good judgment overcoming the rogue force of desire. Though it is notoriously difficult to flesh out exactly what this capacity is, it is not merely a conative matter of one's strongest desire winning out, nor a cognitive matter of having the correct beliefs. Like determining for ourselves what to do in the face of normative underdetermination, it is a volitional matter.

In contrast, it is almost universally denied that volition plays any direct role in forming or sustaining our beliefs and other doxastic commitments. Some have argued that this is a conceptual constraint on belief, while others see it as a merely contingent psychological claim, but most agree on its truth. As William Alston puts it in his seminal discussion, 'volitions, decisions, or choosings don't hook up with anything in the way of propositional attitude [belief and withholding] inauguration, just as they don't hook up with the secretion of gastric juices or cell metabolism' (1988, 263). The explanation of why this is so is controversial, but a natural thought is that it derives from the absence of the kind of normative latitude in our epistemic lives that is present in our practical lives. There is only one kind of consideration that properly bears on the question of what to believe: considerations that bear on what is true. And because there is a univocal measure of success with respect to any particular belief – namely, truth – there is no sense in which we can actively elect to believe on the basis of epistemic reasons we know to be outweighed, in the way we can elect to pursue one genuine good while knowing that we ought to pursue a different good. As Joseph Raz writes, 'the weaker reasons are just less reliable guides to one and the same end ... because there is no possibility that the lesser reason for belief serves a concern that is not served better by the better reason there is no possibility of preferring to follow what one takes to be the lesser reason rather than the better one' (2011, 42). It has thus seemed to many that we must be 'passive' in response to (Feldman 2001, 83) or 'at the mercy' (Hedden 2015, 25) of the evidence.

To be sure, it is widely acknowledged that we can voluntarily shape what we believe in many *indirect* ways, and that non-evidential influences frequently affect what we believe. We can curate the evidence we expose ourselves to, or even change our evidence; we can choose how thoroughly to deliberate; we can develop good or bad habits with respect to the possibilities we consider. And if we are at the mercy of our evidence when we are explicitly considering what to believe, we are equally at the mercy of implicit bias, wishful thinking, fatigue, intoxication, and all sorts of other forces that influence how we see the evidence. The denial that volition plays any role in forming or sustaining a belief is specifically the claim that volition plays no *direct* role, unmediated by some distinct action.

My constructive purpose in this paper is to argue that there is more latitude for volition in constructing our doxastic lives than this traditional picture admits. I think there are important cases in which what we believe is directly up to us. This in turn grounds a dimension in which we can be more or less self-governing in our doxastic lives, just as we can in our practical lives. My destructive purpose is to argue against an increasingly influential conception of epistemic rationality, one that emphasizes 'transparency,' on which this kind of doxastic self-governance is condemned as problematically alienated.[1]

1. Transparency

The first task is to lay out more precisely the philosophical theses that I wish to challenge. My chief target will be a way of thinking about the nature of belief and epistemic rationality that I will refer to under the umbrella label 'the Transparency View,' although I do not mean to suggest that any particular philosopher has advocated for the view quite as I will present it here. I focus on this view because I find much in it that I agree with, and yet it purports to rule out what I think is the genuine possibility of believing at will. I also find the explanation it offers for why we cannot believe at will to be the most compelling of those I am aware of.[2] What I ultimately hope to show is that we can preserve much of the insight of the Transparency View without accepting its implications for the relationship between belief and volition.

The starting point is the insight that belief is an attitude that embodies a thinker's take on what is true. According to the Transparency View, this fact about belief is centrally manifested by a conceptual constraint on doxastic deliberation. The claim is that as a matter of conceptual truth, the deliberative question of whether to believe that P is transparent to the question whether P, in that the former question can only be settled by considerations bearing on the factual question of whether P is true. As Nishi Shah characterizes the thesis, it is manifest in the phenomenology of doxastic deliberation: '… as long as one is considering the deliberative question of what to believe, these two questions must be considered to be answered by, and answerable to, the same set of considerations. The seamless shift from belief to truth is not a quirky feature of human psychology, but something that is demanded by the nature of first-personal doxastic deliberation' (2003, 447). According to Shah, transparency is explained by the fact that belief is a normative concept, such that possessing the concept of belief requires that one accept the norm that it is correct to believe that P if and only if P is true. Because engaging in doxastic deliberation requires that the concept of belief be at least implicitly deployed, the disposition constitutive of accepting this norm of correctness will be activated, compelling the thinker to exclude any considerations that she does not take to bear on whether P is true.

This conceptual constraint on doxastic deliberation purports to rule out the possibility of believing at will. To believe at will, it is not enough that one voluntarily do something in order to bring it about that one has a particular belief. Rather, the belief itself would need to be the conclusion of a process explicitly aimed at issuing in a belief, but that did not appeal only to evidence. For if the thinker does appeal only to questions bearing on the truth of P, then she is simply oriented toward her belief in the ordinary epistemic way; this would not count as believing at will. On the other hand, if she appeals to non-evidential considerations in her effort to form the belief, such as that it would be worthwhile to believe that P, then she has violated a conceptual requirement for being engaged in a process aimed at issuing in a belief. By her own lights, the considerations she has mustered do not settle the question that must be positively answered if she is to believe that P – namely, whether P. Whatever issues from this process would explicitly fail to meet the correctness norm on belief, and thus would not count as that state.[3]

A second context in which transparency is often said to be manifested is in a thinker's capacity to know what she believes. The idea here is that a rational thinker need not rack her brain or theorize about herself in order to know whether she believes that P. Rather, because a rational thinker's beliefs are settled by what she takes to be true, she can come to know that she believes that P simply by reflecting on her reasons for thinking P is true and avowing her conclusion as her belief (Moran 2001; Boyle 2009). That is, the question 'do I believe that P?' is held to be transparent to the question 'is P true?' On the version of the view I am interested in, there is no inferential step between concluding that P is true and avowing it as one's belief. Rather, the claim is that when all goes well, the conclusions are not distinct; to judge that P is both to make up one's mind that P and to know that one believes that P.[4]

Perhaps surprisingly, it is meant to be consistent with both of these appeals to transparency (if not exactly highlighted) that most of us are in fact woefully irrational thinkers. We all believe many false things, and our beliefs frequently do not comport with our evidence. We are subject to all sorts of illicit influences like implicit biases, wishful thinking, neuroticism, priming effects, confirmation effects, stereotype threat, and so forth. Knowing this, how can I be justified in taking my beliefs to be settled by my evidence, let alone true? The answer, I take it, is that transparency only holds from the first-person perspective. If I adopt a 'theoretical,' third-personal point of view on myself, conceiving of myself as any other person who is subject to cognitive error and frequently mistaken, the possibility comes into view that my beliefs are false or unsupported by my evidence. But when I adopt the first-personal perspective, my potentially fallible mind is rendered invisible to me; it does not allow me to entertain the possibility that my beliefs might deviate from what fact and evidence require. As Bernard Williams famously argued, reflection about what to believe makes no essential use of the concept of the first person: 'When I think about the world, and try to decide the truth about it, I think *about the world*, and I make statements, or ask questions, which are about it and not about me' (Williams 2006, 67).

This is not to deny that it is possible, and sometimes necessary, to adopt a third-personal perspective on oneself. If my belief that P is recalcitrantly resistant to my take on whether P, I will not be in a position to know of my belief by reflecting on my evidence; I will have to theorize about myself, or pay an analyst to do it for me. And I can certainly reflect in general on my cognitive failings and devise strategies for improving my epistemic success. But the key claim here is that with respect to any particular belief, to adopt a theoretical perspective on that belief is to become alienated and estranged from it – the belief no longer seems to embody *my* take on how things are. We are sometimes so alienated, but the advocates of transparency argue that this is necessarily the exception and not the rule. It is a symptom of a rational breakdown, in that one's judgment has failed to determine one's belief in the way it ought to. Transparency is thus understood as a normative ideal for belief as well as a conceptual constraint on doxastic deliberation.

The transparency of doxastic deliberation and the transparency condition on self-knowledge might seem to be only loosely related. After all, one need not deliberate anew every time one wishes to know what one believes. Indeed, critics of the transparency condition on self-knowledge have objected that deliberating about whether P is no method at all for knowing what one already believes (e.g. Shah and Velleman 2005, 506–508). It can lead one to make up one's mind anew, but it cannot reliably tell one whether one believed that P before deliberation commenced. While true, I think this objection fails to appreciate the scope of the rational ideal that is advocated by proponents of transparency. In roughly the same way that believing against one's take on the evidence results in estrangement, some have held that alienation also arises for a thinker who takes her past beliefs to have settled for her what she now believes.

The argument for this claim appeals to the kind of answerability involved in believing. Belief is such that a thinker can always be asked for her reasons for believing that P, and even if she has no reason to offer on a particular occasion, she must acknowledge the appropriateness of the question. Matthew Boyle and Pamela Hieronymi have independently pointed out that within this practice of holding a thinker answerable for her belief, it is inappropriate to give an answer in the past tense – 'because I believed that P' or even 'because I consulted the evidence and judged that P' (Boyle 2011, 2013; Hieronymi manuscript.).[5] As Boyle puts it, 'The relevant why-question does not inquire into the explanation of [one's] coming, at some past time, to hold the belief in question, except insofar as the subject's knowledge of how he came to hold the belief speaks to the reasonableness of his continuing to hold it now. Our interest is not in his psychological history, but in the present basis of his conviction' (2011, 11). The objection is that if I take my beliefs to be passive states that I occupy now as a result of some past intervention on myself – even a past event of forming a judgment – this is more akin to programming myself than to the exercise of reason that the why-question aims to elicit.

These claims about the structure of answerability have led both Boyle and Hieronymi to conclude that beliefs must be in the metaphysical category of ongoing activities rather than passive states. The idea is that believing that P is a continuous exercise of the capacity to settle for oneself what one believes, generally (though not necessarily) by deeming one's reasons for so believing to be sufficient. At each point in time, the thinker is unalienated from her belief that P only if she *now* actively holds P to be true. And if this is right, then the two faces of transparency are connected after all. On pain of alienation, higher-order questions about what one believes should if possible be treated as deliberative questions that elicit one's current assessment of P. Questions about past beliefs might be of psychiatric or biographical interest, but something has gone wrong if they play any distinct rationalizing role in determining what one now believes.

Admittedly, the notion of 'alienation' invoked in these arguments is somewhat impressionistic, and it is at first difficult to see how the same threat of alienation should arise both from the inability to know of one's beliefs transparently and in the reliance on past judgments. The former signifies a divergence between what the thinker believes and what she takes to be true, but the latter need not. As I understand it, however, the problem with conceiving of belief as the causal product of some event of making a judgment, and thus as standing states rather than activities, also traces back to the infelicity of taking a third-personal perspective on oneself. If beliefs are states that are formed at a particular time by an event of making a judgment, the worry is that judgment becomes a matter of intervening on oneself to bring about a state of believing. And intervening on oneself is in turn understood as requiring that one adopt a third-personal perspective on oneself, treating one's own mind as a transitive object. It is indeed plausible that any belief I instill or discover from this perspective is one I am alienated from, in that it could only be self-ascribed by way of a referential stipulation that it belongs to the person who happens to be me. If this is correct, then the connection between the two manifestations of alienation is that they each involve a problematic abandonment of the first-personal perspective.

In sum, I have tried in this section to explicate several related philosophical theses (omitting many nuances, I am afraid). These are: (1) believing is necessarily involuntary; (2) reflection about what to believe makes no essential use of the concept of the first person; and (3) beliefs that are opaque to one's current take on the evidence, or that are held on the basis of a past judgment, are a rational failure and exhibit a problematic form of alienation. These claims are each meant to follow from the premise that transparency is both a conceptual constraint on doxastic deliberation and a normative ideal for belief in general. I do not claim that any particular philosopher endorses all of these theses, or the reasoning I have suggested is behind them, but I do think the spirit of this view has wide appeal. I aim in the rest of the paper to deny all three of them.

2. Epistemic temptation

In this section, I will highlight what I take to be a major drawback of belief transparency. Briefly, if the line of thought developed in Section 1 is correct, it turns out that there is no way for a thinker to weather fluctuations in her judgment in a rational manner. If the loss of transparency between belief and evidence is necessarily a rational breakdown, and especially if transparency is a conceptual constraint on treating the question of whether one believes that P deliberatively, then a rational thinker must be bound to her present perspective on her evidence even if that perspective is corrupted. The only way to avoid having one's beliefs fluctuate along with such corruptions of judgment will be to engage in estranged self-manipulation.

The kind of fluctuation I have in mind might be called 'epistemic temptation,' in that it is structurally similar to the kind of temptation that afflicts our desires and evaluative judgment. As the ancient Greeks perceptively emphasized, practical temptation often works on us in a way that is akin to suffering an illusion (though I do not mean to be endorsing the view that it is always like this). It distorts an agent's capacity to assess what she genuinely has most reason to do by distorting the perceived value or desirability of some actions or states of affairs. Whereas she would ordinarily take herself to have much better reason to get a good night's sleep than to stay up late watching 'Broad City,' the temptation of watching just one more episode corrupts her judgment and makes the value of watching the episode appear temporarily outsize. We can identify this as a distortion rather than a genuine change of mind by reference to its temporal profile, which is bookended by the reverse preferences, as well as by the fact that it tends to be caused by ease of opportunity and followed by regret.

Although it is far less frequently discussed,[6] I think the corresponding phenomenon of epistemic temptation is equally commonplace. As noted earlier, most of us are regrettably vulnerable to non-evidential influences like emotion, peer pressure, priming effects, stereotype threat, and myriad other factors. The very same evidence can strike one as supporting different conclusions depending on how it is presented, the company one is in, or the kinds of emotions one is currently experiencing. When these factors vary over time, a thinker's ability accurately to assess what her evidence supports varies with them, and can lead to a rise or fall in her confidence in a proposition without a change in the evidence she possesses. Of course, not every change in confidence without a change in evidence is a mistake; sometimes, a thinker rightly recognizes that she has incorrectly deliberated and redeliberates to a better conclusion. But some such changes can be properly classified as temptation because they are by nature temporary, caused by emotions that will pass or environmental stimuli that will eventually be escaped.[7]

Although I will ultimately argue against the claim that transparency to evidence is in any way a conceptual constraint on belief, a significant kernel of truth in that view is that it is psychologically very difficult to be clear-eyed about the effects of epistemic temptation. Even more than in the practical case, tempting influences tend to work by directly pervading and distorting the thinker's perception of the truth. They cause some subset of the evidence to become much more vivid while the rest pales, or lead the thinker groundlessly to suspect that she has deliberated unsoundly. They can also affect us at the level of the evidential standards we hold ourselves to, inclining us to alter the threshold we employ in favor of assenting more readily or withholding more strictly. Either way, rather than driving a wedge between an accurate judgment as to what one's reasons support and the akratic belief one actually forms, epistemic temptation directly pervades the thinker's perspective on the reasons themselves. It is almost irresistible to resort to visual metaphors here, as Michael Smith and Philip Pettit do: beliefs that run counter to what fact and evidence require '... will not allow those requirements to remain visible because the offending beliefs themselves give you your sense of what is and your sense of what appears to be' (1996, 448).

Because I am interested in the framework of all-out belief rather than in credences here, I will specifically focus on cases in which a thinker has formed the belief that P at some previous point in time, and later loses confidence in her previous judgment without acquiring new evidence or having specific reason to think her deliberation was flawed. Let us suppose that she is aware of a conflict between how things seemed to her before and how they seem to her now, but that she has no strong evidence one way or the other as to which perspective might be a result of some malfunction. In at least some such cases, the fact of the matter is that her previous deliberation was sound and her current loss of confidence is a result of epistemic temptation.

Consider an example: suppose that at some point in the past, I deliberated about a philosophical question, considering all the major arguments for and against the possible views. Eventually, I formed the belief that View X is the correct one, thereby coming to believe in the truth of X. But when I arrive at the conference to present on X, my confidence in my previous deliberation plummets (though I gain no specific information concerning a flaw in that deliberation). The arguments in favor of X now strike me as much less forceful than they previously did. Although my time and psychic energy could be better used by concentrating on the next session, I instead spend it by re-opening the question and deliberating anew with the same evidence I previously had, with my insecurity-infused judgment now leading me to abandon my belief in X. Finally, although I previously held that the prestige of a philosopher's home institution is no evidence at all that his or her views are correct, I now perceive the arguments of those with prestigious positions as much more compelling and form the new belief that Y is the correct view.[8]

The outcome of this episode is clearly suboptimal; I have lost a belief that I was entitled to on the basis of my evidence, ended up with a belief my evidence does not support, and wasted time and energy in the process. The interesting question is whether I could have been more autonomous or self-governed than I was: could I have maintained my previous belief throughout the conference, even though it no longer seemed during that time to be true or adequately supported by the evidence? Now, it is uncontroversial that we can exercise what I will call 'self-manipulation' to weather bouts of temptation and continue in the belief we previously had. I could have gone to sleep, drugged myself, or otherwise undermined my capacity to redeliberate. But this is not especially philosophically interesting (nor good conference etiquette); the more pressing issue is whether it is possible to exercise 'doxastic self-control' in a way that is epistemically rational, without strategic self-manipulation.

We are now in a position to see the dark side of transparency. If we are rationally or conceptually bound to treat our beliefs as transparent to our current take on what is true, then there is no way (or no unalienated way) to insulate our beliefs from temporary corruptions of judgment. For this would be a matter of actively maintaining a belief through points in time at which it does not seem true or sufficiently supported by the evidence. It might be that one has most *practical* reason to maintain one's belief, even at the cost of feeling alienated, but this is not something that the standards of epistemic rationality could directly condone.

I think this is a mistake. Before I proceed to argue against this conclusion, though, let me set aside two tempting but inadequate responses to this kind of case. First, one might attempt to assimilate instances of epistemic temptation to the examples typically discussed in the literature on higher-order evidence, concerning what a thinker should do when she has evidence that she is likely experiencing a cognitive malfunction – she is severely sleep-deprived, or has taken a drug that interferes with normal belief-forming mechanisms. The idea would be that in cases of epistemic temptation, the thinker will frequently have higher-order evidence about her own cognitive functioning that will dictate a rational response – to withhold belief, perhaps, or bracket the deliverances of any potentially compromised thought (e.g. Christensen 2010).

In my view, this response will not do on its own, since cases of epistemic temptation are often relevantly different from cases in which one is drugged or severely sleep-deprived. There will generally have been no obviously compromising event in the former kind of case, or even anything much out of the ordinary, and therefore no clear higher-order evidence about the cause of the conflict between past and present. Whereas drugs and all-nighters are not inescapable facts of everyday life (for those of us who are not rock stars or college students), having emotions and being in social situations are. I am not denying that it is possible in some cases of epistemic temptation to have conclusive higher-order evidence that one's current perspective on the truth is clouded and one's past judgment is therefore more likely to be sound. In such cases, there may be a rational response that is dictated by the combination of one's first-order and higher-order evidence. But I think there are many cases in which the thinker lacks conclusive evidence one way or the other as to which of her perspectives is corrupted. She may have some ambiguous or complex evidence, such as that she is feeling intimidated or buoyant, but this will not always suffice to tell her what to do; we cannot be required to suspend trust in ourselves whenever we are experiencing emotion.[9]

Second, it might seem that there is a simple way to incorporate one's past perspective in such cases while still maintaining transparency: treat one's past judgment that P as testimonial evidence as if from any other person. But while this may in general be admissible, it is not in fact an option in the relevant cases, in which the thinker has called the soundness of her previous deliberation into question. If she were nevertheless simply to accept the deliverances of past deliberation wholesale, treated as the testimony of another person with the same expertise in possession of precisely the same evidence, this would be a matter of continuing to believe that P against her own best judgment. This is clearly epistemically irrational. On the other hand, if she were to treat her past judgment merely as some evidence that P and factor it in to new deliberation as to whether P, then the game is all but lost – her corrupted perspective on the evidence will incline her to draw the incorrect conclusion, especially since the fact that she believed that P will not generally carry much evidential weight. Treating past judgments merely as more evidence will not solve the problem.[10] The trouble is that in cases of epistemic temptation, the thinker should not be making a current evidence-based judgment at all, even one in which higher-order evidence and the testimony of past perspectives is factored in.

3. The diachronic first-person perspective

My view is that it is possible to weather epistemic temptation in a way that is not self-manipulative, rationally impermissible, or alienated. I think that the arguments we have considered to the contrary rest on a mistaken conception of what the first-personal perspective must be.

The mistake is to presuppose that the first-personal perspective is necessarily synchronic, encompassing only the present moment. Although it is never made explicit, the ideal of transparency in fact demands this presupposition. If it were allowed that multiple, conflicting answers to the question 'Is P true?' are first-personally available, the relation between truth and belief could not be conceptually or metaphysically unmediated. And yet, memory does give us access to appearances of the truth that can differ from what now appears to be true. It may even be possible to have psychological access to a future take on what is the case. If these past and future stances were not implicitly ruled out as part of a thinker's first-personal perspective, transparency would fail; the capacity to avow the belief that P on the basis of reflection on evidence would require the mediation of a further answer to the question 'When?'

It may sound odd for me to claim even of the view that believing is an ongoing activity that it is committed to a synchronic first-personal perspective – surely activities are diachronic. But I think it is so committed: as I understand it, it is a time-slice view of believing in which the slices are maximally thin, like stop-animation. At each point in time, the activity view entails that whether the thinker believes that P in an unalienated way is entirely dependent on the synchronic fact as to whether she *now* takes some set of considerations Q to answer the question of whether P (even if in some cases, the consideration is simply 'P'). It does not matter whether she took Q to be a sufficient reason to believe P a moment ago, or whether she will do so in the next moment. Only the present moment matters, or could rationally matter, on pain of becoming estranged from that belief. As Boyle writes, 'I do not recall what I believe about whether P unless I recall what now looks to me to be the truth as to whether P. What I call to mind must be not merely my past assessment of it, but my present assessment of it – the assessment that currently strikes me as correct' (Boyle 2011, 10).

I think we should reject the idea that we are rationally limited to occupying a synchronic, present-directed perspective – that the first person is essentially indexed to 'now'. It is open to me to conceive of myself as occupying a genuinely diachronic first-personal perspective that encompasses past, present, and even future assessments of the truth as potentially my own.[11] I do not think that this diachronic self-conception is required in order to be a believer, or to possess the concept of belief, but I do not think it is ruled out either. We saw in Section 1 that according to the Transparency View, possessing the concept of belief involves accepting a norm of correctness to the effect that a belief is correct only if it is true. Let us grant that this is so. The mistake is to interpret this norm as compelling us to believe whatever the evidence *now* seems to us to require. As a reflective creature, I am in a position to recognize that my capacity to evaluate what is true vacillates over time. I can therefore see that the best way of satisfying the norm of believing P only if it is true may not be always to let my present perspective determine what I believe. A legitimately epistemic concern for the truth does not compel me to conceive of past and future judgments as akin to the testimony of another person, something that could never settle for me what to believe unless I now take the further step of deeming it to be sufficient first-order evidence. Rather, I can consider all of them mine, and therefore candidates for constituting my considered stance on what is true.

If this is right, then we should reject the thesis examined in Section 1: that as a matter of conceptual truth, the deliberative question of whether to believe that P must be settled by reasoning solely about the truth of P. Or rather, we should make a further distinction between the deliberative question of whether to *form* the belief that P and the deliberative question of whether to *continue* to believe that P. The transparency claim may well be true with respect to the first question, but I think it is false with respect to the second. For the diachronic believer, the present moment is not uniquely authoritative in determining what to believe; there is always an implicit question concerning *which* moment in time settles what the diachronic thinker believes. Normally, that question is settled simply by when the thinker takes herself to be in possession of the best evidence (whether or not she is right). But in the cases I am interested in, when P sometimes seems to me to be true and sometimes not without a change in evidence, the question is not settled in this way. It is up to me whether I continue to take my past perspective from which I judged that P as constituting my best judgment, or whether to abandon my belief and deliberate anew, thereby taking my current perspective to have primary authority.[12]

Of course, the truth contained in the doctrine of presentism about the first-personal perspective is that the question of whether to continue believing can only ever arise for the thinker *now*, and must be answered on the basis of considerations that are accessible to her now. Richard Foley dismisses the view I am advocating on this basis:

> ... insofar as one is deliberating about what to do and think, it is one's current self that is doing the deliberating. This means that conflicts between past opinions and current opinions cannot be treated by me as conflicts between a past self and a current self, where the latter is merely one more part of my temporally extended self. To view the matter in this way is to overlook the banal truth that at the current moment, if I am to have opinions at all, they will be current opinions. Correspondingly, if I am to arbitrate between my current opinion and past opinions, it will be my current self that does the arbitration. (2001, 149)

Foley concludes that 'the solution ... is not to pretend that I can somehow escape from my current perspective. It is to burrow deeper in my current perspective ...'

(151–152). But this simply does not follow. The banal truth cited is merely a formal condition of thought; the fact that the arbitration must *happen* now does not force us to suppose that the *conclusion* of that arbitration must therefore prioritize the present in cases of conflict.

What this shows is that contra Williams, the concept of the first person does make an essential contribution to rational reflection about what to believe. When I think about the world, and try to decide the truth about it, I am at the same time taking a stance on my own ability to evaluate what is true. I am at least implicitly, and occasionally explicitly, answering the question 'Which of the temporal perspectives that are accessible to me constitutes my take on what is true?'. In cases of epistemic temptation, I can elect to continue to treat my past perspective rather than my current one to speak for me and thereby refrain from changing my mind. It is the fact that I conceive of both the past and the present moment as belonging to my own diachronic first-personal perspective that allows me to avoid believing against my own best judgment.[13] Instead, I take my best judgment to consist in my earlier assessment rather than in the way things seem to me now. This is the phenomenon I have previously called 'doxastic self-control.'[14]

The possibility of retaining my grasp on my prior assessment of the truth in the face of epistemic temptation may seem ruled out by my earlier observation that epistemic temptation tends to work by directly pervading and distorting the appearance of the truth. I do not mean now to be retreating from this claim; I think epistemic temptation is exceedingly difficult to identify and overcome. To see how it is even possible, it is helpful to think of the phenomenon as a kind of cognitive illusion. Illusions generally do not dissipate merely because one starts to suspect that one is undergoing an illusion. Still, it is something one can in principle recognize and thereby refuse to believe accordingly.[15] In order to do this, the thinker need not actually retain a memory of precisely how the evidence struck her in the past. She merely needs to remember *that* she previously took herself to have sufficient reason to think P is true, and this is precisely the fact that is represented by her belief that P.[16]

Still, it is difficult to give a philosophical argument for the psychological possibility of something. At this point, I will resort to aping Alston's tactic for demonstrating that voluntary control over belief is psychologically impossible: 'simply ... asking you to consider whether you have any such powers' (1988, 122). Unlike Alston, I am hoping that you respond with a positive answer. For my part, it seems to me that I do have the power to hold fast to a previously-formed belief even when it currently does not strike me as true, by determining that my present perspective does not speak for me on this matter.

In my view, then, transparency to the present is neither a conceptual nor a psychological constraint. Exercising doxastic self-control is consistent with belief being a state that is regulated for truth, and with accepting the norm that a belief is correct only if true. The capacity for non-manipulative self-control over one's beliefs is enabled by conceiving of oneself as a thinker who takes a diachronic stance on what is true, rather than occupying only the 'ongoing present.' This self-conception allows one to entertain the possibility that the truth is independent of what seems at any given point to be true, without shifting to a spectatorial third-personal perspective on oneself. It is possible to weather epistemic temptation by taking my past perspective on the evidence, rather than my current one, to be *my* take on what is true.[17]

4. Rationality and alienation

Even if I am right that we can choose to believe against our current take on the evidence, the question remains of whether this can be epistemically rational, and whether it need involve a problematic form of alienation.

There are various substantively different notions of rationality we might be interested in here. One such notion concerns an impersonal standard by which we evaluate epistemic states, where this standard is not meant to provide guidance to the thinker herself or obey any kind of 'ought implies can' principle. However important this notion might be, I wish to set it aside here. My concern is not with ideal thinkers, but with the limited epistemic agents that we actually are. To what norms should thinkers like us be disposed to conform, and are they norms that we could reflectively endorse and be guided by? On this personal understanding of rationality, the question is whether we should accept a norm that permits the exercise of doxastic self-control.

An initially tempting thought is that once we reject a time-slice conception of the first-person perspective, with the incumbent commitment to the priority of the present, then the answer is obviously 'yes' – of course it is rational to continue in one's beliefs. To suppose that there is a philosophical puzzle about how one can rationally or autonomously take a past judgment or perspective to be authoritative for oneself might seem to just assume that different temporal stages of a person are rationally equivalent to the viewpoints of different thinkers. On the time-slice view, it is indeed puzzling how a past judgment could influence one's current beliefs without it being a matter of the past self 'programming' the future self. This is what leads us to think that past judgments must be treated as mere testimony. But once we reject this conception of what it is to be a believer, it might seem to follow that there is no philosophical puzzle here – of course a thinker can rationally and autonomously continue to believe what she judged in the past to be true, for no other reason than that the past judgment was *hers*.[18]

There is a sense in which I quite agree with this response, but I do not think it suffices in this context merely to point out that we are not time-slice believers. True, we are thinkers that occupy a point of view that is more or less unified over time, but this is not a given or a happy accident – it is an achievement that requires explanation. This is particularly the case in the circumstances under discussion, in which diachronic unity is threatened by a fluctuating perspective on the evidence. It is easy to slide into time-slice language to describe the problem, couching it as a matter of disagreement between a past and future self, but I think this is a dispensable crutch rather than an illicit assumption necessary to generate the problem in the first place. The philosophical puzzle concerns how a thinker ought to conceptualize and respond to the fact that her reasons seem to her to support different conclusions at different times. Must she always conceive of her past view as a mistake when this happens, or not? Simply pointing out that the past perspective is hers does not solve the problem, since the present perspective is also hers, and yet they conflict. More needs to be said in support of the claim that in cases like these, the present need not always trump.

And this is the relatively modest claim I wish to defend – that as long as the thinker does not take herself to have acquired significant new evidence since forming her belief, she is rationally permitted to respond to a dive in confidence by electing to accept her previous view of the evidence in place of her current view. I do not think it is rationally required, or that it is rationally forbidden to respond by withholding belief or even redeliberating and changing one's mind. There might of course be features of any given case that make one response required; the claim is merely that there is no general requirement prohibiting the exercise of doxastic self-control.

The first thing to note is that the successful exercise of doxastic self-control does not require that one believe against one's epistemic reasons, as I argue in more detail in Paul (2015). A major difficulty for explaining how self-control in the practical case could be rational is that it often does require that an agent follow through on a prior resolution even when she lacks sufficient reason in the moment to do so. This is because the effect of temptation on our desires and evaluative judgments can alter our reasons for action. In contrast, it rarely if ever alters our normative reasons for belief; it affects a thinker's perception of her reasons, but not the reasons themselves. Of course, one could exercise doxastic self-control to maintain a belief that is inadequately supported by one's reasons, but nothing in the phenomenon of epistemic temptation inherently requires this.

Second, assuming that genuine cases of epistemic temptation occur regularly (although how frequent they are will vary from person to person), a disposition to exercise doxastic self-control on at least some occasions will be more conducive to having significant true beliefs than a disposition always to withhold belief or to redeliberate and perhaps change one's mind. In such cases, the thinker's past assessment of the evidence is more likely to have been correct than her current assessment. And the beliefs in question will tend to be significant ones that the thinker has a strong interest in having if true; epistemic temptation is more likely to strike when the stakes are high. I therefore suggest that a rational prohibition on doxastic self-control would be too costly, requiring the thinker to lose significant true beliefs and transition into what will often be a less accurate doxastic state.

Further, the exercise of doxastic self-control is consistent with at least minimal internalist standards, in that the thinker will still be in possession of her original grounds for believing that P, at least obliquely. It is only possible if she recalls her past belief from memory, and is thus aware that she previously took herself to have sufficient reason to form the belief. She may not be in a position in the moment to grasp her reasons for accepting P as true, but she has access to the fact that by her own lights, there are such reasons.[19] She can thus understand her continence as an expression of her own best judgment, rather than an inexplicable impulse or moment of akrasia, in a way that should go some distance toward appeasing the internalist about rationality.

Most importantly, as claimed in Section 3, it is consistent with accepting the norm that a belief is correct only if it is true. But it will be objected that the thinker is by hypothesis not in a position to *know* whether or not her past perspective is more likely to be correct. These cases are interesting precisely because the thinker herself cannot rely purely on evidence to resolve what to do. I must therefore deny that deferring to one's past perspective requires having sufficient reason to believe that one will be correct in doing so in order to be rational, or even sufficient reason to believe that it is likely. This is not as troubling as it might seem. We are generally entitled to form beliefs on the basis of our own first-order assessment of the evidence, without needing some additional reason to believe that we are likely to be correct in doing so. The only option one can be certain will not result in a false belief is withholding judgment. And while withholding judgment is rationally permitted in these cases, I do not think it is rationally required for any but the most Cliffordian risk-averse among as. It is a way of avoiding error, but at the cost of losing many a true and important belief.

Finally, between the options of maintaining a prior belief or abandoning it, a compelling rationale can be given at the level of having a general disposition to maintain. In my view, we form beliefs in order to settle questions for ourselves precisely because we do not have the cognitive resources or the leisure constantly to be reassessing and updating credences. We need to close our deliberations even when we are not certain so that we can move forward in our investigations and act on our conclusions.[20] And beliefs do not play this cognitive role simply in the way that a heavy object is subject to inertia; they settle questions for us in part because we treat them as doing so. Creatures who go in for belief must therefore already have the cognitive disposition to maintain beliefs that have been formed. If this is right, then I think the burden is on the opponent to explain why it is rationally impermissible for this disposition to extend to cases in which the thinker herself is unsure which option would be more accurate.

That we are rationally permitted to stick with our beliefs if there has been no change in evidence is a claim that many will already be convinced of. For instance, it is entailed by the Bayesian principle of Conditionalization, which holds that a thinker's credences at t_1 should match her credences at t_0 conditional on any new evidence she has learned. If she has learned no new evidence, her credences should not change. Conditionalization has its discontents, however, since it conflicts with even mild forms of internalism about epistemic rationality (e.g. Hedden 2015). For instance, it makes no (explicit) provision for forgetting evidence one once possessed; it requires that the evidence on which one's credences are based be cumulative, even if some of that evidence is no longer mentally accessible (Williamson 2000; Titelbaum 2013). More fundamentally, one might think that to accept Conditionalization is just to assume without argument that there must be some rational requirement on how one's present credences should relate to one's past credences, where Conditionalization states what that relation is.[21] The view I have articulated here addresses only a specific subset of cases to which Conditionalization applies, does not assume that one's credences should in general match up in any way over time, and is one I think even a proponent of internalism can accept.

It might be objected that doxastic self-control as I have characterized it is merely an exercise of practical rather than epistemic rationality, and that all I have succeeded in doing is to point to a particular way in which we can employ our agency to shape our beliefs indirectly. It is uncontroversial that we can control the gathering of evidence, the duration of deliberation, and other mental activities that have bearing on what we end up believing. It may seem that doxastic self-control as I have characterized it is simply one more activity of this type. But I think this would be a misconstrual of what is going on. The question facing a thinker in the grips of epistemic temptation is 'whether to continue to believe that P'. This is just as much a question of doxastic deliberation as the question of whether to form the belief that P; the former, like the latter, is governed by the norm of truth. If the thinker elects not to abandon her belief, this is precisely a matter of continuing to take P to be true. It is not in light of considerations that show belief maintenance to be worthwhile in any other respect. This is the purview of epistemic rationality.[22]

Finally, must a thinker who has successfully exercised doxastic self-control in the way I have described stand in an alienated relation to her belief that P? The difficulty with addressing this question is that it is rarely made precise exactly what is problematic about alienation. One thing that is commonly said is that when we are alienated from a belief, we stand in a relation to it that could not be the paradigm case (e.g. Boyle 2011, 9). If this is all that is meant, then I am happy to grant that bracketing one's current perspective on the truth could not be a rational thinker's default stance. One can only exercise doxastic self-control once a belief has been formed, and one can only deliberately form the belief that P if one now takes P to be true. Deliberation about what to believe *ipso facto* accords one's present perspective epistemic authority. It follows that the capacity for doxastic self-control is parasitic on the default authority of the present.

However, as I observed a moment ago, it is equally impossible for thinkers like ourselves to function as though our beliefs are justified only by what strikes us as true in the current moment. We simply have nothing like the cognitive resources to make good on this ideal. And I have argued that even if we did, it would leave many of us epistemically worse off. Further, in exercising self-control to maintain her belief that P, the thinker still represents P as true. She elects not to change her mind, thereby recommitting herself to P and putting herself in a position to avow it as her belief. She is not forced to discover that she still believes, nor does it follow that she stands in a merely spectatorial relationship to her belief. True, she cannot avow her belief on the basis of the evidence as it currently strikes her. But if anything, this is because she is alienated from her present judgment, not from her belief.

It is also important to remember that the notion of alienation has at least one foot in the domain of the political. If I am correct that exercising doxastic self-control is an important route to achieving autonomy and self-governance in our lives, then the burden is on those who deploy the charge of alienation as a critique of the stance I have advocated here to explain further why it is something we should avoid. Let me emphasize that this is not merely an academic issue; I think the phenomenon in question is extremely common, and frequently implicated in events that are misdescribed as exemplifying a lack of willpower. There are numerous examples of differential behaviors between genders, ethnic groups, and socioeconomic classes with respect to 'stick-to-itiveness' in certain contexts. Girls are far more likely to quit sports teams they have joined than are boys; women more likely to leave STEM field jobs they have started; those in poverty more likely to abandon long-term savings plans and end up in borrowing traps. This is not best understood on the model of supposing that some groups have stronger will-muscles than others, or that those in question suddenly decide that these activities are not in themselves worthwhile. Rather, many such cases might be explained by fluctuation in the agents' beliefs concerning their abilities, the likelihood that the world will cooperate, and so forth. The capacity for doxastic self-control in such situations might be precisely what is needed to maintain confidence that continuing to pursue the activity is a sensible choice. And if this requires a kind of alienation, the alternative is much worse.

5. Belief and volition

I have argued that staying within the first-personal perspective does not conceptually, psychologically, or rationally require that one's belief as to whether P be settled by one's present take on P. Insofar as I remember having had a different take in the past, either take is a rationally permissible candidate for being *my* settled view on P, as long as I have not acquired significant new evidence in the interim. I will conclude by reflecting on the extent to which this claim makes space for an element to belief that is genuinely volitional.

First, although I have been critical of the extent to which transparency is a rational ideal, a central insight I wish to accept is that a thinker cannot voluntarily believe P if she does not take P to be true. If she is convinced that not-P, she cannot form or sustain the belief that P except by manipulating herself. This is the extent to which it is true that belief is not under voluntary control.

This does not mean that we must be passively compelled by the mere appearance of truth, however. A diachronic thinker often has more than one candidate standpoint available to constitute where *she* stands. When she has multiple standpoints available, it is up to her to determine which one constitutes her stance on what is true. In making this determination, she must take herself to be pursuing truth by believing what her best reasons now support; it cannot be done for any other practical reason. But nor can it be done for any particular epistemic reason. It is in part a volitional matter, in whatever sense the choice between multiple normatively underdetermined practical options is volitional.

This claim does not apply to all instances of belief, but it does apply widely. In cases where the thinker has taken no previous stance on the truth of P, or in which she has forgotten any stance she took, she cannot but be compelled by the evidence as she now sees it. On the other hand, it may not only be in the exercise of doxastic self-control that volition plays a role in determining what one believes. Whenever we are in a position to recognize that our evidence does not pin down a uniquely rational response, then whatever doxastic state we form will be a matter of going beyond what the evidence seems to us to require.[23] Focusing on the diachronic case is helpful because it is easier to see how the thinker might be able to have multiple takes on the evidence in view, but insofar as this is possible synchronically, then there is room for volition to play a role in such cases as well.[24]

Still, the volitional latitude I am arguing for here has strict limits. For instance, a tempting but mistaken thought is that it is possible for a thinker to have a policy or set of policies concerning which way to go in various situations. The problem is that policies are by nature general, whereas the truth norm on belief is particular. Even if such a policy were adopted solely on grounds of truth-conduciveness, this would license policies that 'traded off' a few false beliefs for many true beliefs. But trading off in this way violates the conceptual constraint that one must take *each* of one's own beliefs to be true. It is therefore impossible to adopt general policies that directly govern one's beliefs, even with respect to negotiating conflicts in perspective that are not settled (from a subjective point of view) by the evidence. To be sure, one can have policies that govern one's evidential standards, or one's deliberative and assertoric behavior, but such policies concern our beliefs only indirectly. The volitional latitude that arises from being a diachronic believer can have only a particular belief as its object.

That said, it is enough to ground the possibility of a legitimate form of doxastic autonomy or self-governance. Insofar as my beliefs are shaped by my own activity in responding to my evidence, they can be attributed to *me* rather than to some passive, subpersonal mechanism. And while in the moment of epistemic temptation, I will not be in a position to evaluate whether or not I have gotten it right in exercising doxastic self-control, I will often be able to see it retrospectively as an event of correctly resisting the influence of corrupting forces on my beliefs (although I will sometimes come to recognize it as a mistaken exhibition of dogmatism). If I manage to maintain my well-supported belief that completing a PhD in philosophy is a reasonable goal to pursue because I have the ability to write a successful dissertation, even though I am periodically assailed with self-doubt as a result of fear combined with stereotype threat, this will be in part due to me and not just to a fortunate amount of stability in my evidence. It will have been an instance of being not only self-governing with respect to my actions over time, but with respect to my beliefs.

Notes

1. This paper builds on Paul (2015) and is in part intended to be a further development of the view I sketched there, though it departs from the earlier view in some ways.
2. In particular, although discussions of doxastic voluntarism often take Williams (1973) as their starting point, the conception of 'believing at will' at work in that paper is not the one that I think should be defended, for reasons given in Shah (2002).
3. The argument here largely owes to Hieronymi (2013), though I have put some of these claims in ways that I am not sure she would accept.
4. This is importantly different from the notion Williamson (2000) terms 'luminosity'. To claim that a mental state is luminous is to claim that if you are in that state, you are in a position to know that you are in that state. Transparency is more limited; it is meant to hold only in cases where the thinker's belief is appropriately responsive to evidence. Further, it often holds not because the thinker is in a position to detect the mental state she is in, but rather because she is in a position to be in whatever state she thinks she is in.
5. To be clear, Hieronymi is not addressing questions about self-knowledge or even specifically investigating transparency; her interest is in understanding what beliefs would have to be in order to explain the kind of answerability we in fact exhibit.
6. An important exception is Lawlor (2013). Lawlor draws on a case originally offered by Foley (2001).
7. Although the word 'temptation' might suggest that it always involves finding some other belief more desirable than one's current beliefs, this is not an essential feature of the phenomenon. The parallel with practical temptation concerns the distortion of judgment, not the conative aspects.
8. I offer some other examples in Paul (2015). One might object to this example on the grounds that we should rarely if ever believe that a philosophical thesis is true. Perhaps what we ought to do is merely 'accept' the view in the context of

arguing for it at a conference, for instance, or act as if it is true. Though I cannot argue for this here, I think we should not settle for these simulacra of belief. For instance, it is plausible that there is a belief norm of assertion, such that I ought not go to the conference and assert that P unless I genuinely believe that P. The example is admittedly messy, but the real-world examples that I think should interest us generally are.

9. It might also be that after substantial experience with certain types of situations, we have a kind of evidence about how these situations can influence our judgment. This kind of insight can certainly help us deal with epistemic temptation, but I think it is a substantial achievement, and my aim here is simply to deny that it is necessary for weathering epistemic temptation in a rationally permissible way.

10. I make this argument in slightly more detail in Paul (2015).

11. Nagel (1969) argues for a similar view with respect to our desires and values over time.

12. The proponent of transparency might object here that I am interpreting the constraint too narrowly, and that the lesson to be learned from cases of epistemic temptation is simply that we should sometimes take the fact that we believed that P in the past to be a consideration that *now bears* on the truth of P. But if this suggestion is understood as claiming that the fact that I believed that P is evidence for P, in that it makes P more likely, then I think the evidence will generally be far too weak to make a difference – I have had any number of false beliefs in the past. On the other hand, if the suggestion is that it is one of the things that it is relevant to consider in thinking about what to believe, I could not agree more; my objection is to characterizing the relevance in terms of 'bearing on the truth' of P. If the bearing-on relation is understood this broadly, then the Transparency View becomes trivial.

13. Talk of 'taking' here might suggest a problematic multiplication of psychic entities. But I do not intend to be reifying a little 'taker' in the head; all we need here is the ordinary phenomenon of concluding deliberation by answering a question for oneself, however that normally happens. Thanks to Michael Bratman for raising this concern.

14. Weatherson (2008) has also discussed a notion of doxastic self-control that he thinks grounds a kind of voluntarism with respect to some beliefs. But Weatherson's sense amounts to what I would call *indirect* control of belief, and is in that sense distinct from (though compatible with) mine; it concerns the thinker's control over which possibilities she considers as live before proceeding to form a belief.

15. There is clearly more to be said here about what is involved in negotiating such situations. I am tempted to say that it involves a kind of cognitive skill or virtue, but I have no specific account to offer. I only wish to deny that it is a matter that is settled by one's evidence.

16. The memory condition is important here. I do not think it follows from what I have argued here that learning about a past perspective in some other way – by reading about it in what happens to be one's own diary, say – would suffice. The perspective has to be accessible first-personally.

17. Richard Pettigrew rightly objects that this would be the wrong response if confronted with two other people who disagree with one another about whether P on the basis of the same evidence, and where there is no univocal higher-order evidence about which person is more likely to be right. In this case, it is not permissible to simply pick one of the two people and adopt that belief. But

a central theme of my project is that we are not required to treat our own past and future 'selves' as if they were other people.
18. Nefsky and Tenenbaum (manuscript) advance a similar argument concerning the question of whether one can autonomously act on past intentions.
19. Tenenbaum's notion of 'oblique cognition' is helpful here: 'An oblique cognition is a representation of a claim or an object ... through which one understands (or seems to understand) that there are reasons to accept that the object is as one represents it, or that the claim is true' (1999, 894).
20. Holton (2014) accentuates these points.
21. Thanks to Mike Titelbaum for emphasizing this to me in conversation.
22. One might have the worry here that what I am describing is higher-order reasoning, and that this could not rationally result in a first-order attitude. But I am in agreement with the Transparency View in thinking that the deliberative higher-order question cannot be answered by appeal to reasons bearing on whether to have the attitude, and thus that it is in some sense transparent. I am simply arguing that the first-order question need not be settled by one's current assessment of the evidence. Thanks to John Broome for raising this question to me.
23. If the Uniqueness Thesis is true, then the thinker will never be *correct* in supposing that there are multiple permissible attitudes she can rationally take toward a body of evidence. Nevertheless, it might still be possible for her to do so.
24. Thanks to Richard Pettigrew for helping me to frame this point.

Acknowledgements

I'm grateful to the Massachusetts Institute of Technology, where I was employed as a visiting professor while writing this paper. Audiences at the 2015 Pacific APA, the BRAT conference at UW-Madison, UT Austin, the University of Vermont, the MIT work-in-progress seminar, the Midwest Epistemology Workshop at the University of Missouri, and Flickers of Freedom were all of great assistance. I'm especially indebted to Mike Titelbaum for written comments, countless conversations, and general inspiration. Thanks also to Richard Pettigrew, Matthew Silverstein, Nishi Shah, Berislav Marušić, Richard Moran, Matt Boyle, and Alex Byrne for very helpful comments and conversations.

References

Alston, William. 1988. "The Deontological Conception of Epistemic Justification." *Philosophical Perspectives* 2: 257–299.
Boyle, Matthew. 2009. "Two Kinds of Self-Knowledge." *Philosophy and Phenomenological Research* 78 (1): 133–164.
Boyle, Matthew. 2011. ""Making up Your Mind" and the Activity of Reason." *Philosophers' Imprint* 11 (17): 1–24.
Boyle, Matthew. 2013. "Active Belief." *Canadian Journal of Philosophy* 39 (supplemental issue): 119–147.
Christensen, David. 2010. "Higher-Order Evidence1." *Philosophy and Phenomenological Research* 81 (1): 185–215.
Feldman, Richard. 2001. "Voluntary Belief and Epistemic Evaluation." In *Knowledge, Truth, and Duty*, edited by Matthias Steup, 77–90. Oxford: Oxford University Press.

Foley, Richard. 2001. *Intellectual Trust in Oneself and Others*. Cambridge: Cambridge University Press.

Hedden, Brian. 2015. "Time-Slice Rationality." *Mind* 124 (494): 449–491.

Hieronymi, Pamela. 2013. "Believing at Will." *Canadian Journal of Philosophy* 39 (supplemental issue): 149–187.

Hieronymi, Pamela. *Minds That Matter*. Manuscript.

Holton, Richard. 2014. "Intention as a Model for Belief." In *Rational and Social Agency*, edited by Manuel Vargas and Gideon Yaffe, 12–37. Oxford: Oxford University Press.

Lawlor, Krista. 2013. "Exploring the Stability of Belief: Resiliency and Temptation." *Inquiry* 57 (1): 1–27.

Moran, Richard. 2001. *Authority and Estrangement: An Essay on Self-Knowledge*. Princeton: Princeton University Press.

Nagel, Thomas. 1969. *The Possibility of Altruism*. Oxford: Oxford University Press.

Nefsky, Julia and Sergio Tenenbaum. "Extended Agency and the Problem of Diachronic Autonomy." Manuscript.

Paul, Sarah. 2015. "Doxastic Self-Control." *American Philosophical Quarterly* 52 (2): 145–158.

Pettit, Philip and Michael Smith. 1996. "Freedom in Belief and Desire." *The Journal of Philosophy* 93(9): 429–449, p. 488.

Raz, Joseph. 2011. *From Normativity to Responsibility*. Oxford: Oxford University Press.

Shah, Nishi. 2002. "Clearing Space for Doxastic Voluntarism." *The Monist* 85 (3): 436–445.

Shah, Nishi. 2003. "How Truth Governs Belief." *Philosophical Review* 112 (4): 447–482.

Shah, Nishi, and J. David Velleman. 2005. "Doxastic Deliberation." *Philosophical Review* 114 (4): 497–534.

Tenenbaum, Sergio. 1999. "The Judgment of a Weak Will." *Philosophy and Phenomenological Research* 59 (4): 875–911.

Titelbaum, Michael. 2013. *Quitting Certainties: A Bayesian Framework Modeling Degrees of Belief*. Oxford: Oxford University Press.

Weatherson, Brian. 2008. "Deontology and Descartes's Demon." *Journal of Philosophy* 105: 540–569.

Williams, Bernard. 1973. "Deciding to Believe." In *Problems of the Self*, 136–151. Cambridge: Cambridge University Press.

Williams, Bernard. 2006. *Ethics and the Limits of Philosophy*. 2nd ed. Oxford: Clarendon Press.

Williamson, Timothy. 2000. *Knowledge and Its Limits*. Oxford: Oxford University Press.

Continuing on

Michael G. Titelbaum

Department of Philosophy, University of Wisconsin-Madison, Madison, WI, USA.

ABSTRACT
What goes wrong, from a rational point of view, when an agent's beliefs change while her evidence remains constant? I canvass a number of answers to this question suggested by recent literature, then identify some desiderata I would like any potential answer to meet. Finally, I suggest that the rational problem results from the undermining of reasoning processes (and possibly other epistemic processes) that are necessarily extended in time.

Consider this case from Titelbaum (2013, 154):

Baseball: The A's are playing the Giants tonight, and in the course of a broader conversation A's announcers Ray and Ken turn to the question of who will win the game. They agree that it's a tough matchup to call: the Giants have better pitching, but the A's have a more potent offense; the A's have won most of the matchups in the past, but the A's are weaker this year than usual. All in all, it seems like a reasonable person could go either way. Nevertheless, Ken asks Ray what he thinks, and Ray says 'I'm not certain either way, but I think it'll be the A's.' Ray then goes on to discuss how an A's win might affect the American League penant race, etc.

Five minutes later, Bill comes in and asks Ray who he thinks will win tonight's game. Ray says, 'I'm not certain either way, but I think it'll be the Giants.'

This series of responses seems puzzling, and in need of explanation. Perhaps Ray gained some new relevant information between answering the two questions – he glanced through his A's media guide and saw a crucial statistic he wasn't aware of before. Perhaps Ray remembered a relevant fact about the matchup that he hadn't thought about for a long time and wasn't taking into account when he provided his initial answer. Perhaps Ray's responses don't really reveal his beliefs, and there's some pragmatic reason why he would give a different response to Bill than to Ken. Or perhaps, Ray simply changed his mind about the game between responding to the two prompts.

Presumably there are questions we could ask Ray to test these explanations. Suppose we ask him those questions and it turns out that none of them is an accurate description of his experience between giving his two answers. We concoct some more explanations and ask him about those, but they aren't correct either. In the end, Ray admits that he just believed one thing at one time and another thing at another; in fact, he wasn't even aware that his beliefs on the matter had changed until Bill asked the later question.[1]

In that case it seems to me that there is something wrong, from a point of view of epistemic rationality, with Ray's sequence of beliefs. I hope the reader shares that intuition with me. If not, here's a piece of initial evidence for it: Observing Ray's behavior, why are we inclined to ask him the kinds of questions I mentioned above? Why do we look for an explanation of his change in position? I submit that, in Davidsonian fashion, we are attempting to *rationalize* Ray's pattern of responses. If Ray just shifted from one view to another – without any new or remembered information, or even a conscious mind-change in between – then we would level a charge of irrationality. Imputations of irrationality are a last resort in the game of interpretation, so our questions seek other viable options.

Going forward, I will take it as a datum that Ray's pattern of opinions is rationally problematic. This essay explores accounts of *why* it's problematic. I will begin by describing some of the approaches currently available, and explaining my disappointment with each. I will then lay out a list of desiderata I would like a theory of rational doxastic diachronic consistency to meet. Finally, I will tentatively propose a theory that might fit the bill.

1. Available approaches

Let's focus a bit more specifically on the questions I'll be asking. Any argument for a particular rational diachronic constraint on doxastic attitudes can be broken down into two steps: first, one establishes the existence of rational pressure for an agent's attitudes at different times to line up in *some* way; second, one argues for a specific way in which those attitudes ought to line up. The second of these steps is often the easier one. For instance, in Bayesian epistemology there are a number of good arguments that *if* rationality requires an agent's credences to line up over time, *then* updating by conditionalization is the rational way for them to align (at least for cases in which the agent's later evidence is a superset of her earlier). These arguments include Teller (1973) (the "Diachronic Dutch Book"), Greaves and Wallace (2006), Brown (1976), and my own Titelbaum (2013). Yet none of these establishes a rational demand for an agent's attitudes to line up over time in the first place.[2]

I'm interested in that first step, so I will simplify the proceedings by mostly working with cases (like Baseball) in which an agent's evidence remains constant over time. I take it that in many such cases the constancy of the agent's evidence makes it rational for her to keep her beliefs constant as well. If we can explain this rational pressure to keep one's attitudes fixed in cases of constant evidence, I think that will go a long way toward completing the first step, after which we can carry out the project of determining exactly how an agent's attitudes should change or remain constant in the face of changing evidence. So I will focus on cases in which diachronic *consistency* requires attitudinal *constancy*.

I will be asking two questions about such cases:

Architecture Question: Why is it good (from a point of view of rationality) that our cognitive mechanisms tend to keep our beliefs constant when we neither gain nor lose evidence?

Belief Question: Why is it bad (from a point of view of rationality) when our beliefs don't remain constant in the face of constant evidence?

I will say more about the interaction between these questions. But roughly speaking, my answer to the Architecture Question will be that it's rationally good that we have a particular cognitive architecture because that architecture prevents us from suffering the rational badness that would occur if our beliefs were inconstant in individual cases. So my answer to the Belief Question will provide most of the philosophical substance needed to answer the Architecture Question.

Here are some available accounts that address one or both of the two questions. I note at the outset that these accounts are not all mutually exclusive, nor are they all mutually exclusive with the proposal I will ultimately offer. Thus it's not strictly necessary to think of them all as *rivals*.

> (1) *Primitivism*. There exist primitive rational requirements. Requirements of diachronic belief consistency are among those. Such requirements can be discovered by considering cases, but they admit of no further explanation.[3]

On the primitivist account, our judgment about Ray in the Baseball case is a datum, which may help us discover theoretical rationality's diachronic demands. But past that point, nothing more can be said about why it's rationally desirable for Ray to have the same belief at both times. Primitivism answers the Belief Question by saying, 'It just is.'

I find primitivism unsatisfying; it leaves something interesting and important about rationality unexplained. Perhaps we'll have to settle for this approach in the end, but it's worth trying to see if a more rewarding answer to the Belief Question can be found.

One way to explain what primitivism leaves unexplained would be to provide a theory of reasons – specifically, a theory on which each agent has reasons to assign the same beliefs across times. Such reasons are tidily provided by our second account.

(2) *Time-slicing from uniqueness.* An agent's evidence at a given time rationally mandates a specific attitude toward any proposition; constant evidence over time therefore requires constant attitudes. Apparently diachronic rational requirements are ultimately grounded in purely synchronic requirements.

According to the Uniqueness Thesis (Feldman 2007; White 2005), for any body of evidence and any proposition there is a particular attitude that any agent with that body of total evidence is rationally required to take toward that proposition. If the Uniqueness Thesis is true, then any agent who has the same total evidence at two distinct times yet takes different attitudes toward some proposition violates the requirements of rationality at least once. We get the result that a fully rational agent keeps her doxastic attitudes constant across times when her evidence remains fixed.

This account yields the result that something is rationally wrong with Ray's attitudes in Baseball. Assuming Ray initially judged his evidence correctly, it also provides him with a reason to adopt the same attitude toward an A's win at the later time as he did at the earlier. Yet that reason isn't a reason to adopt the same attitude *as such*. Instead, his evidence provides him reason to adopt a particular attitude concerning the outcome of the ballgame at the later time. If he judged that same evidence (and therefore the same reasons) correctly at the earlier time, he will now have reason at the later time to adopt the same attitude as he did earlier. But the fact that he adopted that particular attitude earlier makes no difference to his reasons later on. While there is apparently a rational diachronic constancy norm here, it ultimately boils down to synchronic rational pressures supplied by Ray's evidential reasons.[4]

Thus, the account of diachronic constancy developed from the Uniqueness Thesis is a *time-slice view*. Kelly (forthcoming) defines 'current time-slice' theories of rational requirements so that on any such theory, facts about what an agent is rationally permitted to believe at a given time supervene on the non-historical facts obtaining at that time.[5] Relevant non-historical facts might include an agent's current attitudes, whether her faculties are currently functioning properly, what entities she can currently perceive, etc. Historical facts include attitudes the agent assigned in the past, how she came to have particular beliefs, her faculties' historical track record of reliability, etc.[6]

One need not endorse the Uniqueness Thesis to maintain a time-slice view.[7] But if a time-slicer wants to explain the rational pressure on agents like Ray to keep his attitudes fixed when his evidence remains constant, a Uniqueness-based account nicely fits the bill.

We might criticize this account by suggesting that it doesn't explain all the diachronic rational pressures it needs to. So far I've discussed cases in which an agent correctly forms the attitude rationally mandated by her evidence at the earlier time – but what about agents who assign an earlier attitude at odds with their evidence? One might suggest that even if an earlier attitude was a mistaken response to the evidence, there is still some rational pressure for the agent to maintain it going forward. If our only explanation of the rational pressure for diachronic constancy is that an agent who initially assigns the evidentially correct attitude should also line up her attitudes correctly with the evidence later on, then the Uniqueness time-slicer seems unable to explain the rational diachronic pressure on agents who make initial errors.

Of course, the time-slicer may respond that on her view no such pressure exists.[8] So I will pursue a different line of complaint: I think the Uniqueness Thesis is false. In fact, I think it's rather dramatically false: Uniqueness conjoins two claims, each of which strikes me as incorrect. First, Uniqueness asserts an evidentialism about rationality, on which the rational requirements on an agent supervene on her current total evidence. I think this evidentialism is false, for reasons supplied in Titelbaum (2010) and then further defended in Titelbaum and Kopec (forthcoming).[9] For present purposes, it suffices to say that assessing large bodies of evidence is a complex task that often involves balancing multiple considerations. For example, scientists may trade off competing epistemic features of hypotheses such as simplicity, predictive strength, and explanatory power. The conclusions a scientist draws from data depend not only on the content of her evidence but also on her weighting of these various features, and different weightings are rationally permissible.

Second, the Uniqueness Thesis asserts than in any given situation exactly one doxastic attitude is rationally permissible to adopt toward each proposition.[10] Yet I'm interested in the possibility that no matter what kinds of facts rational permissions supervene upon – present or past, evidential or otherwise – there are situations in which multiple attitudes toward a given proposition are rationally available to a particular agent. And if there are such situations, agents have the ability to perform a very special epistemic maneuver. Faced with an epistemic situation that could permissibly be resolved in multiple ways, confronted by competing considerations that must somehow be weighed, we have the power to *make up our minds*, taking some of those considerations to be compelling and forming the beliefs they support as a result.[11]

I have tried to present Baseball as one such case – a case in which Ray initially has to make up his mind between two potential conclusions, each of which is genuinely rationally open to him.[12] If the Uniqueness Thesis is false in the ways I have described, there must be at least some such cases, and I will suppose in what follows that Baseball is one of them. I'll admit that I find making up one's mind a fairly mysterious type of doxastic activity. But my concern here is: If an agent makes up her mind among genuinely rationally available options at an initial time, is there any rational pressure for her to maintain the attitude initially selected?[13]

The following accounts suggest that there is:

> (3) *Identity/self-governance.* Self-governance and/or maintaining one's identity requires constancy of belief given constancy of evidence. This provides at least a *prima facie* reason to maintain rationally permissible beliefs.

This is really an umbrella category for multiple specific accounts that could be offered. I'm imagining those accounts running parallel to accounts that have been offered in the action theory literature of rational constancy of permitted intention. One could develop an account parallel to that of Korsgaard (2009) on which belief constancy would be a constitutive norm of rational agency, the violation of which would threaten the integrity of our epistemic identity.[14] Or one could develop an account like that of Bratman (2012), on which self-governance would require belief constancy and thus provide agents who aim to be self-governing with a reason to maintain their beliefs.

While these accounts in action theory still need many details filled in (even before we get to their correlates for belief!), I find them attractive and don't think the proposal I'll make necessarily rules them out. Nevertheless, I have a couple of concerns about any account in this category. First, these accounts are *global* rather than *local*; they indict individual episodes of inconstancy on the grounds that those episodes contribute to a broader problem. Too much inconstancy, and the agent either will no longer be self-governing or will simply cease to be. I think, however, that when doxastic inconsistency is rationally deleterious, this is because of features of that instance of inconsistency taken alone, and not because of its contribution to any broader effects. Here's an analogy: Suppose you criticize me for dropping the plastic holder from a six-pack of soda on the ground at a park. I ask you what's wrong with what I did. You might offer the global response that too much plastic left in the park will make that park unusable and will generally harm the environment. Or you might say that *this particular* six-ring of plastic could get picked up by a seagull and choke it to death. The latter response identifies a local problem with my action irrespective of how it might contribute to a larger pattern.

I prefer local answers to the Belief Question, local explanations of the rational problem with diachronic inconsistency. It seems to me that there is something wrong with Ray's set of responses *considered in its own right*, regardless of whether a pattern of such responses would have troubling long-term effects.[15] This kind of explanation also avoids a problem with global approaches: When a behavior pattern is desirable because it allows an agent to maintain a particular property over the long term (or maintain her status as *that particular agent*), one-off deviations from the pattern may not threaten maintenance of the property. This might happen because the particular deviation is somehow causally isolated from the larger effect. (I happen to know that if I litter right now, you will indignantly pick up whatever I have dropped.) Yet, I imagine it's open for identity/self-governance theorists to say that in such cases diachronic inconstancy is not rationally problematic. While I happen to find that response unpersuasive, there's a trickier case in the offing: It might be that while no particular deviation is causally isolated from maintenance of the property, the property can withstand a few deviations here and there. (A park is still usable with only one or two pieces of litter.) In that case, the global theorist needs a way to say that each and every deviation is rationally problematic, even when the feared consequences for identity or self-governance are not going to appear. On the other hand, an explanation that accounts for the rational badness of inconstant episodes one at a time – on their own terms, as it were – ensures that each and every such episode will exhibit a problem.[16]

Second, if identity or self-governance accounts of rational belief are patterned after their practical brethren, they will suggest the existence of a kind of reason that I don't think exists. It's difficult to discriminate intuitively cases in which *no* reason for a course of action exists from cases in which such a reason exists but is very *small* (Schroeder 2007, Ch. 5). Nevertheless, consider Bratman's case in which he has to choose between two routes (Highway 280 and Highway 101) to reach San Francisco and each route is equally good. Suppose that far before reaching the relevant junction, Bratman makes up his mind to take 280. Now he is approaching the junction at which the decisive turn must be made. As many authors have emphasized, there are often reasons not to reconsider a settled intention.[17] But suppose Bratman re-opens the question anyway, and is considering once more which way to go. It would be awfully strange for Bratman to treat his past intention as generating any kind of consideration in favor of taking 280. Similarly, when Bill prompts Ray to think again about who will win the game, it would be odd for Ray to cite the belief he formed while talking to Ken as part of a *reason* to think the A's will win.[18] Yet the identity and self-governance accounts seem to make these earlier attitudes into reasons for later actions, or at least allow those earlier attitudes to generate reasons influencing later actions. These accounts thus posit a kind of later-time reason (even during reconsideration) of which I'm suspicious.

2. Desiderata

As has already begun to emerge, I am curious whether there is an account of the rational desirability of diachronic consistency that displays particular features. I will now lay out those features, and (where this hasn't already been addressed above) try to explain why I am interested in an account that displays them.

- *Extensional adequacy.* I am interested in an account that matches certain settled opinions about particular cases. For example, I want to maintain the result that there is a rational problem with Ray's changing beliefs in the Baseball case. Must the account detail a rational problem in *every* case in which an agent's evidence remains constant but her doxastic attitudes don't? As I will discuss below, it's not clear to me that there actually is a rational problem in every such case. So to the extent there is a distinction between belief-inconstancy cases that are rationally problematic and those that aren't, we want the account to track the contours of this extensional difference. It's also possible that in some rationally problematic belief inconstancy cases there is more than one rational problem present. Or it may be that different types of rational problem are present in different belief-inconstancy cases – there may be no single, unified account covering them all. I would like if possible to find a unified account that indicates the same kind of problem in all cases in which belief inconstancy is rationally problematic, but I am not committed to that being the only kind of rational problem present.

- *Explanatoriness.* I am also interested in an *explanation* of why there's a rational problem in diachronic inconsistency cases when such cases are problematic. Further, if there's a distinction between rationally problematic and rationally unproblematic cases of diachronic inconsistency, it would be nice for the account to explain that distinction.

- *Concerns only theoretical rationality.* I am interested to find an account that works purely in terms of theoretical rationality, without invoking concerns of practical rationality. If you like, I want to show that diachronically inconsistent beliefs are rationally flawed *as beliefs* – as a particular kind of representational mental state. In addition to their purely representational role, beliefs may also play a role in rationalizing actions and a causal role in bringing about certain consequences for agents. But I am interested to see if a diachronic consistency account can be developed without adverting to these additional roles.

  This does *not* rule out the account's attending to what I'll call the 'pragmatics' of belief management. For instance, we'll look later at an account of belief consistency centered on the limited computational and storage capacities of finite human minds. This account concerns the demands of *theoretical* rationality on a believer with limited representational abilities. It concerns the pragmatics of belief management for such an agent, but not the practical rationality of possessing certain kinds of beliefs.[19]

- *Local not global.* As discussed above, I'm curious to see whether we can find an explanation for rational flaws in instances of diachronic inconsistency that appeals only to the features of each instance as opposed to the properties of a general pattern into which the instance fits (or fails to fit).[20]

- *Compatible with a Strong Permissivism.* Earlier I indicated that I'm a 'permissivist' (to use Roger White's coinage) – I deny the Uniqueness Thesis. Moreover, I'm what I'll call a strong permissivist, in the sense that I deny *both* conjuncts of the Uniqueness Thesis. So I want an account of diachronic consistency that applies even when the agent's initial doxastic attitude was one of a number that were rationally available to her at the earlier time.

- *Genuinely diachronic.* Given this strong permissivism, I will not be interested in time-slice accounts of diachronic rationality. I think there are cases in which all the purely synchronic features of a situation underdetermine what an agent is rationally required to believe, yet there are rationally significant relations between what the agent believes now and what she made up her mind to believe in the past. Put another way, I think there are rational evaluations of agents' series of beliefs that genuinely require looking at conditions across multiple times. So I will not be opting for a time-slice account.

- *Consistent with mind-changing.* As I just noted, the strong permissivism I'm exploring here sometimes allows an agent to make up her mind among multiple options that are genuinely rationally open to her. Intuitively, if my theory of rationality is going to allow an agent to make her own doxastic bed in this fashion, it ought to allow her to re-make it later. That is, once we allow an agent to *make up* her mind at a given time, it seems we ought to allow her to *change* her mind later on.[21] I find changing one's mind no less mysterious than making it up to begin with, but the general idea here is that if making up one's mind involves, say, determining how to weigh up various considerations in a manner not entirely driven by one's evidence, then it ought to be equally rationally permissible to *re*consider one's weighting later on in a manner not entirely driven by evidence (or a change therein). So I want an account that lends some rational permissibility to mind-changing.

I'm interested in a plausible account of diachronic rational consistency that has all of the features listed above. On the other hand, I will not demand that an account display certain features that many authors simply assume are required.

- *Need not be prescriptive.* While this use of terminology may be a bit idiosyncratic, I use 'normative' as an umbrella term for an entire category of notions contrasted with the descriptive. Thus for me the normative includes both evaluations (e.g. assessments of goodness) and prescriptions (e.g. 'ought' statements). I would be perfectly happy with an *evaluative* account that explained why there is a rational flaw in sequences of doxastic attitudes that are not consistent over time even if it did not entail that an agent *ought* at the later time keep her attitudes consistent with what she had assigned earlier. I also will not demand that the account yield rational *requirements* of any kind.

- *Later reasons not provided.* In a similar vein, I do not think an account of diachronic rational consistency needs to provide the agent at a later time any *reason* to keep her attitudes in line with what she assigned earlier, especially not a reason that bears weight should she come to explicitly reconsider that earlier assignment. This was part of my point in discussing the Bratman highways example.

As I said, these last two desiderata contravene what many authors assume is the job of a story about theoretical rational diachronic consistency. For instance, Sarah Moss writes,

> The norms articulated in an epistemology classroom govern deliberating agents.... It may be true that people often chug along without deliberating, responding to any indeterminate claim as they did before, without reconsidering [the attitude] they are acting on. It may even be true that people cannot survive without acting in this way. But this does not challenge norms that tell agents what they should do when they deliberate. To compare: it may be true that people often fall asleep and hence fail to consider or assess any reasons at all, and it may even be true that people cannot survive without sleeping. But this fact about human nature does not challenge ordinary norms governing lucid agents. (2015, 184)

I don't know whether consideration of non-deliberators should influence the norms we apply to deliberating agents. I want to challenge the passage's first sentence, and suggest that there are norms worth articulating in the epistemology classroom that do something other than govern deliberating agents.[22] For instance, a theory of rationality might criticize an agent who fails to deliberate at all on important occasions (perhaps she takes a nap instead). This is a genuinely normative negative evaluation of the agent or of her cognitive processes, yet its content bars it from governing agents who are (already) deliberating.

A similar point could be made about the rational assessment of memory loss. I don't know whether it's ever rationally problematic for an agent to forget something. But if norms of rationality must provide the agent with reasons in deliberation, we can generate an impressively quick argument against the possibility of genuinely diachronic rational memory norms. Suppose an agent forms the belief that p at t_1 and then forgets that she did so by t_2. She cannot at t_2 have any reason to believe that p related to her t_1 belief, because she does not remember having assigned that earlier belief.[23] So there's the argument: Norms of rationality must provide reasons in deliberation, the forgetful agent can't have any reasons while deliberating at the later time to retain her earlier belief, so there are no norms of rationality related to memory loss.

This brief bit of reasoning does not seem to me to settle the subtle matter of whether there is ever anything rationally bad about forgetting. But that's in part because I reject the premise tying all rational norms to reasons in deliberation. On the other hand, Luca Ferrero accepts an argument fairly similar to this one.

Assessing the possibility that there might be an irreducibly diachronic constraint of structural rationality against forgetfulness, he writes

> A systematic failure to retain judgment-sensitive attitudes – like beliefs and intentions – is a failure in securing the necessary background for the proper functioning of the rational psychology of temporally extended agents like us. But it does not seem to me that, for each particular judgment-sensitive attitiude that one might have at any particular time t_1, one is under a rational constraint to preserve it at a later time t_2. (2012, 153)

The 'But' here reflects a crucial step in the argument. Ferrero grounds his denial that there exists *any* diachronic structural constraint related to memory loss in a denial that the agent is under a rational constraint to preserve the attitude in question at t_2. This move succeeds only given the assumption that if there is an extant diachronic constraint in place, it must issue a rational prescription applying directly to the agent at t_2.

One might grant that the assumptions I'm questioning here are indeed assumptions, yet still maintain that they flow naturally out of an intuitive understanding of the metanormative landscape. After all, how can we have a diachronic norm of rationality relating two times without its generating prescriptions for the agent at the later time, or at least *reasons* for the agent at that time? I'll try to demonstrate the possibility of a normative account that sheds these assumptions by providing one later on. But for the time being, let me try another analogy about what goes on at the park:

> Suppose that after picking up my litter, I lay out cones to mark the goals for a soccer game. As the game is being played, it's important that those cones stay where they are. (You'd be annoyed, for instance, if a young child picked one up and started moving it around.) But if we stop the game to have a discussion about moving the cones (perhaps I chose a hilly spot, or the sun is in one team's eyes), the fact that they're already in a particular location provides no reason to keep them there. If we decide in the end to move the cones, the child may be confused about why we were angry at him for doing so earlier. But that's because he doesn't understand the normative structure of the situation: Playing soccer is a downstream activity that depends on the cones' maintaining a constant location. In the course of that activity, the fixity is important for reasons that aren't dependent on the cones' particular coordinates. But if we halt that activity and turn to assess the coordinates themselves, the fixity no longer has any normative significance.

It seems to me that in this case it is genuinely bad if the cones move while we are playing soccer. Yet if, say, at half-time we deliberately reconsider their location, the fact that they have been in one place so far provides no reason not to move them. (Setting aside the slight effort it would take to pick them up and set them down.) So we have a genuinely normative evaluation dependent on a cross-temporal relation that nevertheless provides no reason to maintain that relation under deliberate reconsideration. I will exploit precisely this kind of pattern in my account of diachronic attitudinal consistency.[24]

3. A positive account

I will now try to develop an account that explains a rational flaw that occurs in many cases of diachronic inconsistency. I offer this account tentatively, and honestly don't know if I believe all the particulars myself. But even if it fails, I hope it will indicate that there is logical space for a kind of normative account that satisfies the desiderata laid out in the previous section.

The first thing to note about Ray's succession of beliefs in Baseball is that it's weird. Typical human cognitive architecture is such that once we adopt a particular attitude toward a proposition, we generally keep it – especially over a short period of time. In fact, I think it's an interesting question about the metaphysics of mind whether a mental state must have some nontrivial duration in order to even *count* as a belief. That will depend on whether beliefs are functional states, computational states, etc. and on whether such states could be realized only momentarily. But setting that question aside, humans are certainly built to have beliefs that persist. And it's possible that our negative intuitive reaction to Baseball is simply a reaction to Ray's behaving in a manner people typically don't.[25]

Yet I think there's more to it than that. As the Architecture Question indicates, I think that it's good – good from a point of view of theoretical rationality – that we are built such that our beliefs typically remain constant once we adopt them. Or at least, it would be bad if we didn't have that feature.

At this point, someone will inevitably bring up computational limitations. Because of our limited cognitive capacity, we can't recalculate all our beliefs from our evidence (or whatever else) every time we need one of them. So it's useful to be able to settle a matter and then retain that settlement for use at later times.

While I think that's true, one might object that this is only an argument for *having* beliefs about propositions one has considered before, not for keeping those beliefs *constant*. Imagine a creature who, once she adopts a doxastic attitude toward a proposition, always has an attitude toward that proposition at future times. But imagine that this creature's attitudes toward propositions slide around over time: if she has degrees of belief, their numerical values drift; if she has binary beliefs, some of them might flip from belief to suspension to disbelief or *vice versa* at random. Since this creature always has attitudes toward propositions at the ready, she need not calculate a new stance on a proposition should it rearise. But this creature certainly doesn't display the belief constancy we're interested in.

Let's be clear what exactly this objection comes to. I am trying to point out rational benefits of our tendency to keep beliefs constant. The objection proposes that the same benefits could be achieved by a mental architecture lacking such constancy. But that's fine – showing that some other architecture also achieves those benefits doesn't deny that our architecture does too, nor does it undermine the claim that it's a good thing for us that we have the architecture we do. An analogy: For the sake of navigating our environment, it's good for us that we can see. The ability to see isn't any less beneficial in navigating our environment just because it would also be possible to navigate using echolocation.

Nevertheless, I do think there's another aspect of belief constancy that's crucial for theoretical rationality, and this aspect really depends on the *constancy*. Consider first the synchronic requirements of theoretical rationality. Rationality requires an agent's beliefs to be consistent, and requires her to believe (at least some of) the consequences of what she believes. A rational agent attempts to make her beliefs consistent, and attempts to believe (at least some of) the consequences of what she believes. The rational agent need not think of her efforts to meet these constraints as such. For instance, after Ray forms his belief that the A's will win tonight's game, he goes on to consider the consequences of an A's win for the playoff race. This is an exercise in forming beliefs that follow from what he believes, but Ray probably doesn't think of it that way. Instead, he simply thinks about what follows from the proposition that the A's will win (or really, what follows from *the A's winning*). Similarly, Ray might at some point consider how the A's manager will arrange his lineup to face the Giants' pitching. Once he sorts that matter out, Ray may wonder how his new conclusions mesh with his prediction of an A's win. This is an exercise in maintaining belief consistency.

While the norms here are synchronic, an agent puts herself in a position to satisfy them by engaging in various processes – in particular, *reasoning processes*. Since reasoning is a causal process, it extends over time.[26] And this creates a need for belief stability. Consider an agent who believes p and wants to determine some consequences of that belief. She begins reasoning from p to various conclusions that follow. As her train of reasoning continues, she considers the consequences of those conclusions, and the consequences of those consequences. She may no longer be mentally attending to p at all. But now suppose that as her reasoning worked through these further consequences, the agent's attitude toward p swung around so that she believed $\sim p$. (I realize this doesn't happen to normal human agents – the point is to see why it would be bad if it did.) An abrupt change in belief like that would vitiate the agent's reasoning from p; the reasoning process would no longer be one of drawing out consequences of her beliefs. A similar thing goes for checking belief consistency: imagine how difficult it would be to draw a large cluster of beliefs into harmony if they kept changing as you went along. (An analogy to herding cats feels appropriate here.)

There are other temporally-extended epistemic processes for which it's important that our beliefs remain constant. Sometimes a belief prompts us to launch an investigation out in the world. Sir Arthur Eddington was one of the earlier purveyors and defenders of general relativity. He famously organized a 1919 expedition to confirm the theory by measuring the sun's bending of starlight during a solar eclipse. Now imagine that once the expedition had been organized and launched, Eddington's allegiance had suddenly switched to a theory compatible with any amount of bend. Again we have a situation in which inconstancy of belief would rob an ongoing process (in this case quite a costly one) of its significance for an agent. While I don't want to put too much emphasis on such external investigations – and will continue to make my argument largely in terms of internal reasoning – it's worth considering the significance of belief constancy in making them possible.

So there's the core of the account: reasoning is a crucial rational activity; being causal, it extends over time; instability of belief would vitiate reasoning's efficacy.[27] I will now expand upon this account in the course of explaining how it satisfies the desiderata I listed above (though not in the order in which I presented them).

Hopefully it's clear that this account, if correct, is Explanatory of at least one problem that occurs when beliefs do not remain constant over time. It also Concerns Only Theoretical Rationality – the explanation has to do with the pragmatics of coming to meet theoretical rationality's synchronic requirements. Further, the explanation is Local not Global: If an agent were to start reasoning from her belief that *p*, then cease to have that belief while the reasoning was still ongoing, this would generate a problem *in that specific case* – not because of any contribution it made to a larger phenomenon.

Assessing the account's Extensional Adequacy is a bit more complicated. It gets the Baseball case right: Being a baseball broadcaster, Ray engages in all sorts of reasoning downstream from his opinion about who will win the game, which is then undermined when that opinion changes out from under the reasoning. This explanation of the rational problem with a change in belief is Compatible with Strong Permissivism; the explanation still goes through if Ray's initial opinion about the game was not rationally required of him. (In fact, it goes through even if Ray's initial opinion was rationally *forbidden* given his evidence at the initial time.)

But what about other examples of diachronic inconsistency? One might object that all I've done is argue for the rational constancy of *some* of our beliefs *while* we're engaged in reasoning that depends on them. Thus, I haven't provided a full explanation of why diachronic inconsistency is rationally bad in general.

I have two responses to this objection. First, one of my goals is to answer the Architecture Question, to exhibit what's rationally good about a cognitive architecture that keeps beliefs intact over time. One way of reading the objection is that I haven't explained why that sort of cognitive architecture is better than an architecture that only keeps beliefs constant while we're engaged in reasoning dependent on them. Now it's a bit difficult to imagine a cognitive architecture that would achieve this trick without going *any* farther – in determining which beliefs to keep constant, such an architecture would have to track exactly what's involved in ongoing chains of reasoning, which investigations have been put into the field, and which beliefs are and are not in consistency relations with other ongoing beliefs. But more to the point, this is the echolocation objection again. The fact that another kind of cognitive architecture could achieve the feature being considered here doesn't change the fact that that feature is a good feature of the architecture *we* have.

Second response: As an answer to the Belief Question, my account may be getting the extension of the phenomenon correct. Typical human mental faculties certainly don't keep all beliefs intact for all time. Intuitively, some of those losses seem problematic, some less so, and some perhaps not at all. I find quick, repeated belief flip-flops to be much more objectionable than changes over an extended period.[28] It also seems worse to flip on central issues than on trivial matters or matters on the cognitive periphery. The latter asymmetry might be explained by notions like centrality to epistemic identity. But both of these differences could also be explained by the potential of a switch to undermine ongoing reasoning and investigative processes. If I have some trivial belief – say, about the name of the guy who took my order at the coffee place this morning – and over the course of a week it switches from 'Stan' to 'Steve,' that's not a horrible problem. This tracks the fact that during that interval I probably don't have many ongoing reasoning processes or investigations involving this belief, nor is it heavily tied into relations of consistency with my other beliefs. On the other hand, when I imagine a case in which an agent's beliefs rapidly flip all over the place while she is engaged in actively deliberating about their consequences, that seems cognitively crippling. A spectrum of cases lies in-between.

The account may also explain another asymmetry in our intuitive assessments of diachronic inconstancy. In Baseball, we negatively evaluate Ray's belief switch in part because it seems to have taken place without his noticing. On the other hand, if he were to explicitly reconsider his opinion about the game's outcome, and come to change his mind about which way the evidence points, that wouldn't seem as rationally problematic. My account of diachronic inconsistency is Consistent with these intuitions about Mind-Changing: reconsidering whether to believe *p* is a process of explicitly reasoning *about p*, not a process during which *p* is taken as a premise while another proposition is considered. So changing one's opinion about *p* via explicit reconsideration does not have the same negative rational fallout as if one's opinion about *p* had drifted without one's attending to it.

The account therefore explains what I call the Eyes-On Asymmetry concerning belief consistency. *Very* roughly, it's rationally odd for an agent's beliefs to switch when she doesn't have her eye on them, but when a belief is the explicit focus of a reasoning process, change in that belief is much less rationally problematic. The latter category includes not only cases in which an agent consciously changes her mind, but also cases in which she gains new evidence and changes her belief as a result, and cases in which she discovers that her belief conflicts with other beliefs she possesses and modifies her opinions for that reason.[29] Though I'm not sure whether this gets my intuitions about the rational status of different types of belief change exactly right, something does seem right to me about this Eyes-On Asymmetry.

The asymmetry also makes a great deal of sense in light of an analogy between this account of diachronic consistency and the soccer cones example from earlier. It's bad if a kid moves the cones while you're busy playing soccer, but it's perfectly fine for you to explicitly reconsider their location and move them during half-time. Reasoning from a premise is a downstream activity that relies on the fixity of that premise in your set of beliefs. But if we come to explicitly reconsider the premise itself, its fixity is no longer necessarily desirable.

This analogy can also help us understand the normative structure of the rational verdicts yielded by my account. The account doesn't generate anything like a general rational requirement that an agent who adopts a particular doxastic attitude *ought* to retain that attitude as long as her evidence remains constant. At best, we get that it's rationally harmful when an agent's attitudes shift around in certain kinds of cases. The rational verdict is evaluative, Not Prescriptive. Moreover, Later Reasons are Not Provided. When we reconsider the cones' location at half-time, their current position provides us with no reasons influencing our decision. Similarly, the fixity of an agent's doxastic attitudes is rationally significant when she is engaged in downstream reasoning. But when she explicitly reconsiders her attitude toward a particular proposition, my account of diachronic constancy does not provide her with any reason to keep her old opinions intact.[30]

One might have a different type of Extensional Adequacy concern: One might worry that my account hasn't captured the intuition that there is something problematic *with changing one's beliefs over time* when one's evidence remains constant. At best, I've shown that if an agent's beliefs shift around, and she nevertheless continues processes of reasoning based upon those beliefs, then this *combination* is rationally problematic. But perhaps there's nothing wrong with the belief-shifting; perhaps the agent's mistake lies entirely in carrying on with her reasoning after the shift occurred.[31]

The complaint here can't be that my account reduces to the nearly trivial 'You shouldn't continue a piece of reasoning once you've stopped believing its premises.' Because of the Eyes-On Asymmetry, the cases with which I'm concerned are precisely those in which the agent is unaware that the premises have been dropped. So the rational problem in the rationally problematic cases can't be that the agent has failed to properly enact this prescription. Yet one might still maintain that a negative *evaluation* of the reasoning is appropriate: while there's nothing wrong with the agent's having dropped the premises, we may negatively evaluate her continuing to reason based upon them.

This sounds to me a bit like the kid at the soccer game saying, 'There wasn't anything wrong with my moving the cones! *You guys* shouldn't have kept playing once I moved them!' Be that as it may, in answering the Belief Question I am primarily concerned to explain why something rationally bad happens in cases of belief inconstancy. I don't feel a need to demonstrate that *the bad thing* was the belief inconstancy itself as opposed to the resultant vitiated reasoning or a combination of the two. Certainly such a demonstration isn't necessary to answer the Architecture Question: As long as something bad happens somewhere in cases of belief inconstancy, it can be a good thing that our architecture helps us avoid such cases. Moreover, I'm not sure my intuitions about cases like Ray's are fine-grained enough to demand that I locate the rational problem in one particular place rather than another.[32]

Final desideratum: Is my account Genuinely Diachronic? This is a bit subtle, for on one level my account is driven by synchronic concerns. An agent engages in reasoning to meet particular synchronic demands: to make her beliefs consistent, to believe what follows from her other beliefs, to square her beliefs with her evidence. The account explains the rational value of diachronic consistency in terms of what's required for such reasoning to be effective. Yet I don't think this kind of grounding in synchronic norms makes the account a time-slice view. The diachonic norms I've discussed certainly don't *reduce* to synchronic norms as they do on a Uniqueness account. And the rational evaluations in question supervene on genuinely diachronic relational facts. While the driving demands behind the account may be synchronic constraints on belief, much of the view's substance derives from the pragmatic problems of an agent who must develop and maintain such representational attitudes through temporally-extended causal processes. So I would characterize the account as genuinely diachronic, but amenable to those primarily concerned with synchronic norms.[33]

Perhaps an agent's ability to keep her beliefs intact is something like an 'executive virtue' – given the rest of her cognitive equipment, this ability helps the agent achieve synchronic features that are significant for theoretical rationality. And thinking along the lines of virtues may illuminate the relevant normative landscape as well. We are willing to recognize a character trait as virtuous or vicious even when we understand that an agent who possesses that trait may be incapable of changing it (or at least incapable any time soon). When an agent's beliefs go missing, or change without her noticing, there may be nothing she can do about that fact. (Or nothing she can do about it *after the fact*.) But that shouldn't bar us from evaluating the episode as rationally unfortunate.[34]

Notes

1. The previous two paragraphs are adapted from my discussion of the Baseball case in Titelbaum (2013).
2. For what it's worth, a similar point could be made about rational constraints on how an agent's various attitudes should relate at a *given* time. Arguments that rational credences satisfy Kolmogorov's probability axioms typically begin by *assuming* that there's some rational pressure for an agent's synchronic credences in different propositions to line up with each other. The assumption is rarely commented upon only because it seems so obviously true.

3. Thanks to Greg Novack for helping me better articulate this position.
4. There is a small logical step here from the synchronic to the diachronic: Just because one is required to have attitude A at time 1 and one is required to have attitude B at time 2, that doesn't necessarily mean that there's a requirement to have *A at 1 and B at 2*. The details will depend on one's deontic logic of rational requirements.
5. This is not Kelly's *definition* of time-slice views, for two reasons: First, Kelly works with facts about justification rather than facts about rational permission. Second, Kelly ultimately defines a current time-slice theory as one on which the normative facts are *grounded* in non-historical facts. Moving from supervenience to grounding helps Kelly deal with cases in which certain non-historical facts are themselves grounded in historical facts. Yet clearly the grounding definition implies the supervenience condition in the text above. Moss (2015), meanwhile, defines time-slice epistemology in terms of two claims: (1) 'what is rationally permissible or obligatory for you at some time is entirely determined by what mental states you are in at that time'; and (2) 'the fundamental facts about rationality are exhausted by these temporally local facts.' I slightly prefer Kelly's definition because it leaves open the possibility that non-historical facts other than facts about an agent's attitudes might affect what is rationally permissible for the agent. (See also Hedden (2015) for another approach to defining time-slice views.)
6. Kelly notes that on some epistemologies the constitution of an agent's current total evidence will count as a historical fact (or as grounded in historical facts). For instance, an epistemology might combine Williamson's (2000) position that evidence is knowledge with a theory of knowledge invoking the etiology of beliefs. Yet most time-slicers assume that evidential facts are non-historical, so I will go along with that assumption here.
7. Hedden (2015) does, while Moss (2015) doesn't.
8. Instead, she might respond that an agent who forms a rationally-incorrect initial belief will *take* it to be correct, and so will think there is some rational pressure to maintain that belief later on because she will continue to take it to be what's (synchronically) required. In other words, the agent who initially errs is actually under no rational requirement to remain diachronically consistent, but our intuitions about her can be explained by the fact that in some sense it's reasonable for her to *think* she's under such a requirement. This line of response strikes me as unpromising, because we can always ask about cases in which the agent does not maintain her initial belief, nor does she remember its content. If there is a rational problem with the agent's adopting a different belief in response to the same evidence in at least some such cases – as it will emerge I think there is, even when the initial belief was an incorrect response to the evidence – the time-slicer's response will fail to account for that problem.
9. For additional arguments against the Uniqueness Thesis, see Kopec (forthcoming), Kopec (2015), Meacham (2014), Schoenfield (2014), and Kelly (2014).
10. Some formulations of Uniqueness replace 'exactly' with 'at most' to allow for doxastic rational dilemmas.
11. Sometimes the expression 'make up my mind' is used as follows: 'I wanted to go to graduate school for a long time, but in the fall of 2002 I finally made up my mind to do so.' I'm not sure whether this use of the expression (to indicate resolution, as it were) is different from the use just indicated in the main text, but if so let me stipulate that this isn't the sort of mind-making I'll be discussing in this essay.

12. Moreover, I've tried to make Baseball *acknowledgedly permissive*: not only are there multiple conflicting beliefs rationally available to Ray when he makes his initial judgment; Ray is also aware of this permissiveness in his own situation. For the significance of acknowledgedly permissive cases, see Ballantyne and Coffman (2012) and Titelbaum and Kopec (forthcoming).
13. The 'selection' talk may be a bit misleading here; I don't want to take a stand on whether making up one's mind need be or can be a volitional activity. Moreover, my anti-Uniqueness stance doesn't require the outcome of making up one's mind to be underdetermined by *causal* factors – there may be a perfectly deterministic story by which I could look at your brain right now and figure out how you're going to make up your mind about any given issue. I merely want to maintain that the *epistemically* relevant factors bearing on a particular instance of belief-formation may rationally underdetermine which direcion a given agent goes.
14. The type of epistemic identity maintained in part by belief constancy need not be one of the types of identity considered in the personal identity literature, nor in the metaphysics of identity more generally. To my mind, Hedden's (2015) attacks on the identity approach assimilate it too quickly to these potentially independent discussions.
15. Earlier, I suggested that my answer to the Belief Question has a certain sort of priority over my answer to the Architecture Question. How does this interact with my preference for local vs. global answers to the Belief Question? Answer: Not at all, as far as I can see. The local/global issue is: Given a rationally problematic instance of belief inconstancy, is it rationally problematic only because (and when) it fits into a larger, undesirable pattern? This is different from the Architecture Question about the rational properties of cognitive architectures that causally *generate* constant or inconstant beliefs. One could give either a local or a global answer to the Belief Question and still consider that answer prior to one's answer to the Architecture Question.
16. Compare the traditional problem with rule-utilitarian theories that agents may on occasion be able to break a rule without causing the general harm that's supposed to motivate that rule. We may think that even in such cases breaking the rule is wrong, but the rule-utilitarian struggles to explain why that's the case.
17. See especially Holton (2008) on the reconsideration of intention, and Paul (2015) for investigation of related questions in the belief case.
18. If Ray is uncertain at the later time what would be a rational response to his initial evidence, yet is fairly confident he was thinking rationally at the earlier time, he might take the fact that he settled on the A's at the earlier time as evidence that that belief was supported by his evidence at that time. But then Ray's later body of total relevant evidence isn't the same as his initial body of evidence, because it includes an evidentially significant fact about his earlier attitudes.
19. Here's one way to think about the distinction: Imagine a purely receptive entity (agent?) whom I'll call the 'passive believer.' The passive believer takes in information about the world, is concerned to develop the most accurate representations of that world that it can, yet has no ability to act in the world as a result. If finite, the passive believer will still have pragmatic theoretical rationality concerns about how to best manage its representational resources, but presumably there are no demands of practical rationality on a passive believer.
20. Compare Ferrero's use of 'local' terminology in his (2012) and the fourth desideratum he lists in Section 1.3 (which he in turn attributes to Bratman (2012, Section 1.5) and Bratman (2010, 10–11 and 20–21)). Elsewhere in the action theory literature, a 'local'/'global' distinction is sometimes used to frame

the question of whether a rational requirement that an agent displays certain general properties over time can generate requirements on particular attitudes considered singly. Notice that even if this question is answered in the affirmative, the resulting account of rational requirements on individual attitudes would not be 'local' in my sense.
21. To quote Jeff van Gundy on a May 2nd, 2014 broadcast of the NBA playoffs: 'Man's greatest right is to change his mind.'
22. Compare Nomy Arpaly's distinction between theorizing about rationality that creates a 'rational agent's manual' and theorizing that creates an 'account of rationality.' As she puts it, 'Not everything which is good advice translates into a good descriptive account of the rationality of an action, or vice versa' (2000, 489).
23. Here, I'm availing myself of the distinction between reasons that apply to an agent (so to speak) and reasons that the agent *has*. One might be willing to grant that the agent's t_1 belief makes it the case that there *is* some reason for the agent to believe p at t_2, but because the agent is unaware of any such reason it's not a reason that she *has*.
24. While I don't, some people *define* the normative in terms of the presence of reasons. If we want to satisfy such a definition, we will have to find a reason *somewhere* in the vicinity of the soccer example, or else the statement that it would be bad for the cones to move during the game cannot be genuinely normative. Here's a suggestion: We have a reason to tell the young child not to move the cones while we're playing soccer. While this reason couldn't appropriately figure in our half-time deliberations, it nevertheless is a reason somewhere in the normative mix of the situation, and seems to pair nicely with the claim that it'd be bad if the cones were moved. Later on I'll point out where we could make a similar move (if we felt the need to do so) in my account of diachronic consistency.
25. Sarah Moss suggested this to me in conversation.
26. John Broome writes, 'When you acquire a new attitude – for instance you learn something or you make a decision – many of your other attitudes may need to adjust correspondingly, to bring you into conformity with various synchronic requirements of rationality.... That some of our attitudes take time to catch up is a limitation of our human psychology.... Ideally rational beings would instantly update their attitudes when things change.' (2013, 153) Broome therefore sets aside the time lag in reasoning because the rational requirements he is considering are based on ideal agency.

    Given that human minds are realized in physical brains, human reasoning must be a causal process. (One might argue that as the *generation* of one attitude from another, reasoning would have to be a causal process even if minds weren't physically realized. But I don't know how to argue about causality among the non-physical.) And I believe it's a metaphysical truth that causal processes take time. My conception of rational ideality does not involve idealizing away from the physical realization of minds. So even if we grant that considerations of rationality should attend to the conditions of ideal agency, I do not agree with Broome that ideally rational beings could update instantly.
27. While I came up with the basics of this account independently, it bears strong affinities to some of what John Broome says in his (2013, especially Ch. 10). Kelly (forthcoming) also discusses the relevance of reasoning processes to time-slicing. Meanwhile, Abelard Podgorski has in a number of works developed the idea of reasoning as a temporally-extended process into a much broader account of diachronic rationality.

28. Though this is a general tendency, not an ironclad rule. And that may be tied to the fact that some reasoning processes are extremely extended over time. Philosophers are certainly familiar with mulling over a particular argument or piece of reasoning over the course of *years*.
29. One might worry that even these cases are rationally dangerous: Given the requirement to keep one's beliefs consistent, there's always the risk that a given belief change will generate unnoticed inconsistencies with some of the agent's other beliefs. Yet that seems to me just a cognitive fact of life. The key point here is that my account lumps the threat level of mind-changing in with that of the other two reasoning processes listed, and does *not* put it in the same boat as background flips-flops of opinion.
30. So (going back to the potential concerns of note 24), are there reasons involved at *any* level in my account of rational diachronic consistency? If one wanted, one could say that my answer to the Architecture Question provides reasons at the level of Bratmanian 'creature construction': I have explained some reasons why a designer of cognitive creatures like us might want to provide them with a cognitive architecture that keeps beliefs intact.
31. I'm grateful to Sarah Moss, Michael Bratman, and Sergio Tenenbaum for discussion of this concern.
32. Forget about the *target* of the rational problem; one might complain that I still haven't explained what the *nature* of that problem is. What exactly *is* this 'vitiation' that occurs when a reasoning process loses its premises? I haven't answered that question because I think a number of possible answers are available, and I haven't settled on one that I like best. But just because it's interesting, here's one option: We might see reasoning as an attempt not just to generate new beliefs that follow from one's other beliefs, but instead to generate new beliefs *grounded* or *based* in the appropriate way on one's other beliefs. Viewed this way, reasoning is a process of constructing a cognitive state with a particular justificatory structure. If that's right, then the disappearance of the beliefs from which a process of reasoning began makes it impossible for that reasoning to be successful.
33. Going back to the last point of the Extensional Adequacy discussion, one might worry that if the rational flaw in cases of belief inconstancy lies entirely with the continuation of reasoning, this will open the door once more for a time-slicing account. The thought would be that it's a purely synchronic matter whether one is engaged at a given time in processes of reasoning whose premises one believes. Yet shifting the locus of negative evaluation in cases of diachronic inconstancy to reasoning processes seems to me like a bad move for the time-slicer. A reasoning *process* is a temporally extended affair; evaluations of such processes seem intrinsically diachronic to me. Podgorski's work is once more illuminating on this point.
34. I am grateful to Sarah Paul for copious discussion of this essay and for suggestions concerning many of the references. I am also grateful to audiences at the spring 2014 Informal Formal Epistemology Meeting and the fall 2015 conference on Belief, Rationality, and Action over Time, both held at UW-Madison.

References

Arpaly, N. 2000. "On Acting Rationally Against One's Best Judgment." *Ethics* 110: 488–513.
Ballantyne, N., and E. Coffman. 2012. "Conciliationism and Uniqueness." *Australasian Journal of Philosophy* 90: 657–670.

Bratman, M. E. 2010. "Agency, Time, and Sociality." *Proceedings of the American Philosophical Association* 84: 7–26.

Bratman, M. E. 2012. "Time, Rationality, and Self-governance." *Philosophical Issues* 22: 73–88.

Broome, J. 2013. *Rationality through Reasoning*. Oxford: Wiley Blackwell.

Brown, P. M. 1976. "Conditionalization and Expected Utility." *Philosophy of Science* 43: 415–419.

Feldman, R. 2007. "Reasonable Religious Disagreements." In *Philosophers without Gods: Meditations on Atheism and the Secular Life*, edited by L. M. Antony, 194–214. Oxford: Oxford University Press.

Ferrero, L. 2012. "Diachronic Constraints of Practical Rationality." *Philosophical Issues* 22: 144-164.

Greaves, H., and D. Wallace. 2006. "Justifying Conditionalization: Conditionalization Maximizes Expected Epistemic Utility." *Mind* 115: 607–632.

Hedden, B. 2015. "Time-slice Rationality." *Mind* 124: 449–491.

Holton, R. 2008. *Willing, Wanting, Waiting*. Oxford: Oxford University Press.

Kelly, T. 2014. "Evidence may be Permissive". In *Contemporary Debates in Epistemology*, edited by M. Steup, J. Turri, and E. Sosa, 298–311. West Sussex: Wiley-Blackwell.

Kelly, T. (Forthcoming). "Historical versus Current Time Slice Theories of Epistemic Justification". In *Goldman and His Critics*, edited by H. Kornblith and B. McLaughlin. Blackwell.

Kopec, M. 2015. "A Counterexample to the Uniqueness Thesis." *Philosophia* 43: 403–409.

Kopec, M. (Forthcoming). "A Pluralistic account of Epistemic Rationality." Unpublished manuscript.

Korsgaard, C. M. 2009. *Self-constitution: Agency, Identity, and Integrity*. Oxford: Oxford University Press.

Meacham, C. J. G. 2014. "Impermissive Bayesianism." *Erkenntnis* 79: 1185–1217.

Moss, S. 2015. "Time-slice Epistemology and Action Under Indeterminacy". In *Oxford Studies in Epistemology*, edited by T. S. Gendler and J. Hawthorne, Vol. 5, 172–194. Oxford: Oxford University Press.

Paul, S. K. 2015. "Doxastic Self-control." *American Philosophical Quarterly* 52: 145–158.

Schoenfield, M. 2014. "Permission to Believe: Why Permissivism is True and What it Tells us About Irrelevant Influences on Belief." *Noûs* 48: 193–218.

Schroeder, M. 2007. *Slaves of the Passions*. Oxford: Oxford University Press.

Teller, P. 1973. "Conditionalization and Observation." *Synthese* 26: 218–258.

Titelbaum, M. G. 2010. "Not Enough There There: Evidence, Reasons, and Language Independence." *Philosophical Perspectives* 24: 477–528.

Titelbaum, M. G. 2013. *Quitting Certainties: A Bayesian Framework Modeling Degrees of Belief*. Oxford: Oxford University Press.

Titelbaum, M. G., and M. Kopec. (Forthcoming). "Plausible Permissivism." Unpublished manuscript.

White, R. 2005. "Epistemic Permissiveness." *Philosophical Perspectives* 19: 445–459.

Williamson, T. 2000. *Knowledge and its Limits*. Oxford: Oxford University Press.

Memory, belief and time

Brian Weatherson

Department of Philosophy, University of Michigan, Ann Arbor, MI, USA

ABSTRACT
I argue that what evidence an agent has does not supervene on how she currently is. Agents do not always have to infer what the past was like from how things currently seem; sometimes the facts about the past are retained pieces of evidence that can be the start of reasoning. The main argument is a variant on Frank Arntzenius's Shangri La example, an example that is often used to motivate the thought that evidence does supervene on current features.

I know a lot about the past. I know, for instance, that the Chicago White Sox won the 2005 baseball World Series. I remember that's true. I don't remember the event. I was in Australia, and it wasn't on television. I don't even remember the event of learning that the White Sox won. But I remember that they won. And to remember something is to, *inter alia*, know it is true. And to know something is to, *inter alia*, have a rational belief that it is true.

So I have a rational belief that the White Sox won the 2005 baseball World Series. In virtue of what is this belief of mine rational? That's too big a question to answer here, so let's start narrowing it down. Is this belief rational in virtue of facts about how I now am, or historical facts about me? Call the former view a temporally local theory of rationality, and the latter a temporally extended view. Which of those is correct?

I'm going to defend the temporally extended view. In this respect, I'm following recent work by Barnett (2015), though being a philosopher I'll quibble about his argument, put forward alternate reasons, and so on. But I'm agreeing with his big conclusion.

At least, I'm going to agree with a version of that conclusion. I'm an evidentialist about rationality, in a sense that I'll try to make clearer as we progress through the paper. So it's natural to convert the core question into a question about evidence, and about evidence acquisition. What is my evidence that the White Sox won the 2005 World Series, and in virtue of what do I have that evidence? Is it the correct fact that it mnemonically seems to me that the White Sox won, perhaps supplemented with some knowledge I have about the reliabiity of my mnemonic seemings? Or is it something more temporally extended? I'm going to argue that it is the latter.

My positive view, inspired to some extent by the *evidence is knowledge* view defended by Williamson (2000), is that the fact the White Sox won became part of my evidence some time in 2005, and has stayed in my evidence ever since. At the time, this belief, and this knowledge, was grounded in further evidence, presumably perceptual evidence of what some computer screen looked like. But I came to know the White Sox won, and this became part of my evidence. An alternative view is that the visual seemings from 2005 are part of my evidence still. That's what the view of Lewis (1996) implies. And yet another view is that the content of those perceptions, perhaps that ESPN is telling me the White Sox won, is still in my evidence. I don't like either of these latter views, but I'm not going to argue about them here. Rather, the focus is on whether evidence is contemporary or historical, and I want to argue for the class of historical theories over the class of contemporary theories.

Evidentialism

I'm interested in memory because it raises challenges for the evidentialist theory I'd like to defend. Evidentialism, as we'll start construing it, says that the doxastic attitudes it is rational to have depend entirely on the evidence one has. This is a version of evidentialism. I'm taking this to be a thesis both about partial beliefs, what are commonly called credences in the philosophical literature, and full beliefs. I have a lot to say elsewhere about the relationship between full and partial belief (Weatherson 2012), but I won't be relying on those views here.

I am construing the 'dependence' in the statement of evidentialism rather weakly. It is just a claim that the evidence one has, and the attitudes it may be rational to hold, co-vary. Put another way, the rationality of doxastic attitudes supervenes on one's evidence, at least throughout worlds similar enough to this one. I am not defending the stronger claim that facts about what evidence one has are always explanatorily prior to facts about what doxastic attitudes it is rational to hold.

It is easy enough to imagine epistemologies that aim for this more ambitious, priority, thesis. Lewis (1996), for instance, suggests we should understand evidence in terms of phenomenal states; two agents with the same phenomenology over time have the same evidence. It's arguable that facts about phenomenology are metaphysically prior to facts about rationality. So, if one was an evidentialist with Lewis's theory of evidence, it would be natural to think that facts about evidence didn't just subvene facts about rationality; the former provided full and perhaps reductive explanations for the latter.

I hold out no such hope for reductive explanations. Indeed, I'm closer in spirit to the kind of view you might read into Williamson (2000). As noted above, Williamson holds that one's evidence is all and only what one knows. This thesis has become known as $E = K$. The notation here is instructive. It is commonplace to introduce new terms by definition by putting the new term on the left-hand side of an equality sign. $A =_{df} B$ means that A is defined to be identical to B, not the other way around. The $E = K$ thesis suggests a form of evidentialism where evidence is in fact explanatorily posterior to rationality. Something is part of one's evidence in virtue of the fact that one knows it, and arguably one only knows what one rationally believes.

I've been a bit coy in the previous paragraph about what I'm attributing to Williamson, and what I'm just saying can be read into him. That's because the view Williamson defends is not that rationality has explanatory priority, but that knowledge does. As he says in the first line of his book, his view is 'knowledge first' (Williamson 2000, v). And it's consistent with 'knowledge first' to say that the explanatory relationship between evidence and rationality is complicated and multidirectional. Although I don't endorse the knowledge first programme, I agree with that last conclusion. The explanatory relationship between evidence and rationality is complicated and multidirectional. Evidentialism should not be construed as denying this claim.

The other way in which my version of evidentialism is weaker than it may be is that it really is restricted to being a claim about rationality. It isn't a claim about justification. For all I say here, maybe something other than evidence determines whether a doxastic attitude is justified. For example, it may be that only true beliefs are justified. I don't think that's true, but if it is, it would be consistent with evidentialism as I'm construing it.

More importantly for what follows, evidentialism also isn't a claim about wisdom. It is very important to keep evaluations of agents apart from evaluations of acts or states. It is attitudes or states that are in the first instance rational or irrational. We can talk about rational or irrational agents, but such notions are derivative. Rational agents are those generally disposed to have rational attitudes, or be in rational states. Wisdom, on the other hand, is in the first instance a property of agents. Again, we can generalise the term to attitudes or states. A wise decision, for instance, is one that a wise person would make. But the wisdom of agents is explanatorily and analytically prior to the wisdom of their acts, judgements, decisions and attitudes. (I think that everything I've said in this paragraph is true of ordinary English. But I'm not committed to that, and it doesn't matter if I'm wrong. You can read this paragraph as stipulating that 'rational' is to be used as a term that in the first instance applies to states, and 'wise' is to be used as a term that in the first instance applies to agents, and little will be lost.)

Evidentialism is not a claim about the nature of wise agents. Perhaps a wise agent is one who always has rational attitudes. If so, then evidentialism will have quite strong implications for what wise agents are like. But that connection between wisdom and rationality is far from an obvious conceptual truth. For all I've said, it may well be wise to have doxastic attitudes that do not track one's evidence. That is consistent with evidentialism, provided we understand the relevant situations as being ones where it is unwise to have rational attitudes.

The most important recent work on the connection between rationality and wisdom is by Lasonen-Aarnio (2010, 2014b). And I agree with almost everything she says about the connection. The biggest difference between us is terminological. She uses 'reasonable' and 'reasonableness' where I use 'wise' and 'wisdom'. In my idiolect, I find it too easy to confuse 'rational' and 'reasonable'. So I'm using a different term, and one that, to me at least, more strongly suggests a focus on agents, not states. But this is a small point, and everything I say about the distinction draws heavily on Lasonen-Aarnio's work.

Finally, I'm not taking evidentialism to be committed to any kind of uniqueness thesis. It may be that different agents with the same evidence can have different views about p, and both be rational. That's fine, as long as any agent with just that evidence could have either view about p and be rational. The view is that there's a function from evidence and attitude to rational evaluation, not that there's a function from evidence to rational attitude.

Memory and testimony

It's natural to think about theories of memory by analogy to theories of testimony. Indeed, we see this strategy used in otherwise very different work by Moss (2012) and Barnett (2015). Moss and Barnett have very different views on memory, and very different views on the relationship between memory and testimony, but they both find it worthwhile to situate views about memory in relation to views about testimony. And I will follow this lead.

For an evidentialist, there are three interesting classes of theories of testimony. These almost, but not quite, track onto familiar categories of theories in the literature on testimony. I'll use slightly idiosyncratic names for them, just to indicate that the categories aren't exactly the same. In all cases, speaker S says that p on the basis of evidence E, and hearer H hears (and understands) the speaker. (And I'll assume S is a she, and H a he.) I'm going to start with the case where S knows that p, and H has no reason to doubt S's testimony; we'll look at the complications that ensue when those assumptions are dropped presently.

The classes I'm interested in are divided by their answers to two questions:

(1) Is the evidence that H gets, in the first instance, that p, or that S said that p?
(2) If the evidence is only that S said that p, is the fact that S said that p a 'self sufficient' reason to believe that p, or does it need to be supplemented?

The term 'self sufficient' is borrowed from Malmgren (2006), who uses it in describing work by Wright (2002, 2004), Pryor (2004) and White (2005). Wright, Pryor and White are primarily concerned with whether perceptual appearances are self-sufficient reasons to believe their contents, or they need to be supplemented. That isn't the focus here; like Malmgren, I'm focusing on testimony and memory.

Here are the three classes of views that you get from the natural answers to those questions.

- *Indirect Theories of Testimony*. The evidence is that S said that p, and this is not a self-sufficient reason to believe that p. This class closely corresponds to the class of so-called reductionist theories of testimony. Lackey (2008) provides an important recent indirect theory.
- *Direct Theories of Testimony*. The evidence is that S said that p, and this is a self-sufficient (though defeasible) reason to believe that p. Many theorists who reject reductionism about testimony endorse what I'm calling a direct theory. Coady (1995) provides an important recent direct theory.
- *Transmission Theories of Testimony*. The evidence is that p, so it doesn't matter how we answer the second question. Schmitt (2006) provides an important recent transmission theory.

Transmission theories need not deny that H also gets the evidence that S said that p. And they need not take a stand on how good that evidence is as evidence that p. And direct theories need not deny that H may have independent evidence that if S says that p, then p is true. But in the other direction, I'm taking it as characteristic of the theories that they deny the core claims of the ones that come after them. So indirect theories deny that H immediately gets evidence that p, or that S says that p is a self-sufficient reason to believe p. And direct theories deny that H immediately gets evidence that p.

The direct and transmission theories just say that a certain thing is possible. I haven't said yet what they have to say about when it is possible. To make matters a little less abstract, I'll focus for now on theories that abide by the following constraints.

- S saying that p is only reason to believe that p in the absence of evidence against p, and in the absence of evidence against S's reliability.
- H only gets to add p to their stock of evidence if it was in S's stock of evidence to start with; testimony doesn't generate evidence, except for evidence about what is said.

A direct theory that didn't comply with the first constraint really would be a charter for gullibility. Even with this constraint, direct theories possibly are too gullible, as Fricker (1994) has argued, but without this constraint, they certainly are. And a transmission theory that didn't comply with the second constraint would not deserve the name transmission; it would be a generative theory.

We can use these categories to draw three similar categories of memory. Here the case is that M forms a belief that p at t_1, and has an apparent memory of p at t_2. As we might put it, her memory reports that p at this time. As above, start with the simple case where M knows p at t_1, and there is no counterevidence, or reason to doubt her own reliability, at later times. We'll come back, in great detail, to cases where those assumptions are relaxed. What evidence does M get, in these simple cases, when her memory reports that p, and how good is this evidence?

- *Indirect Theories of Memory.* The evidence is that M's memory reports that p, and this is not a self-sufficient reason to believe that p
- *Direct Theories of Memory.* The evidence is that M's memory reports that p, and this is a self-sufficient reason to believe that p.
- *Transmission Theories of Memory.* The evidence is that p.

The first two theories are temporally local, in the sense I started with, and the last is temporally extended. Again, we'll put some restrictions in place.

- Memory's reporting that p is only a self-sufficient reason to believe that p in the absence of either evidence against p, or evidence that memory is unreliable.
- Memory only transmits evidence that p if p was genuinely among M's pieces of evidence at an earlier time. And that requires, I'm assuming, that M knew that p at the earlier time.[1]

Since I want to defend a temporally extended theory, that means I'm defending the transmission theory. And like Barnett, I do so while rejecting the corresponding theory of testimony.[2] But once we set things out this way, we see that there are two distinct temporally local theories, and they fail for slightly different reasons. Before we get to why they fail, we'll look at a reason for thinking one or other of them must work.

Shangri La

The Shangri La case introduced by Arntzenius (2003) can be used to generate an argument that evidentialists are committed to the temporally local approach to evidence. This isn't exactly how Arntzenius introduced it; he introduced it as a puzzle for conditionalisation. But the argument I'm interested in is related to the puzzle Arntzenius introduced. Here is how Michael Titelbaum describes the example.

> You have reached a fork in the road to Shangri La. The guardians of the tower will flip a fair coin to determine your path. If it comes up heads, you will travel the Path by the Mountains; if it comes up tails, you will travel the Path by the Sea. Once you reach Shangri La, if you have traveled the Path by the Sea the guardians will alter your memory so you remember having traveled the Path by the Mountains. If you

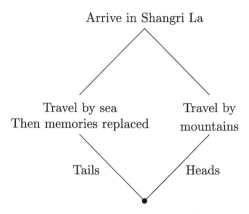

Figure 1. Original Shangri La game; Hugh takes the right-hand path.

> travel the Path by the Mountains they will leave your memory intact. Either way, once in Shangri La you will remember having traveled the Path by the Mountains. The guardians explain this entire arrangement to you, you believe their words with certainty, they flip the coin, and you follow your path. What does ideal rationality require of your degree of belief in heads once you reach Shangri La. (Titelbaum 2014, 120)

The name of the person Titelbaum's narrator is addressing isn't given, so we'll call him Hugh. And we'll focus on the case where Hugh actually travels by the Mountains (Figure 1).

There is something very puzzling about Hugh's case. On the one hand, many philosophers (including Arntzenius and Titelbaum) report a strong intuition that once in Shangri La, Hugh should have equal confidence that he came by the mountains as that he came by the sea. On the other hand, it's hard to tell a dynamic story that makes sense of that. When he is on the Path by the Mountains, Hugh clearly knows that he is on that path. It isn't part of the story that the paths are so confusingly marked that it is hard to tell which one one is on. Then Hugh gets to Shangri La and, well, nothing happens. The most straightforward dynamic story about Hugh's credences would suggest that, unless something happens, he should simply retain his certainty that he was on the Path by the Mountains.

And you might think evidentialism is committed to the same thing as that dynamic story. To see why, imagine that Hugh is being terrifically sneaky, and wearing a small camera in his glasses. The camera is tracking what he sees, and Laurie is watching it on a distant TV monitor. The guardians can't do anything to Laurie's memory, so they don't, just like they don't do anything to Hugh. That night, it might seem Hugh and Laurie have the same evidence. Yet, according to some intuitions, it is rational for Laurie to believe that Hugh took the Path by the Mountains, and not rational for Hugh to believe this.

Here's a natural way out of that bind. Say that the evidence Hugh and Laurie have does not consist of what they saw as Hugh was ascending, but their current mnemonic seemings. Now their evidence is different. Hugh has the evidence that it seems to Hugh that Hugh ascended via the mountains, and Laurie has the evidence that it seems to Laurie that Hugh ascended via the mountains. And it is common knowledge that in either this world or a nearby one, Hugh's mnemonic seemings are unreliable, while Laurie's are reliable in all nearby worlds. So the temporally local theories can handle the problem, while one might think temporally extended theories cannot.

The most straightforward way to explain the common intuition about Shangri La is via the indirect theory of memory. On that theory, Hugh won't know that he came to Shangri La via the mountains. That's because the report of his memory, 'We got here via the mountains, Hugh!', would be the same however he came up, and Hugh knows it. There is no basic entitlement, on this theory, to move from *My memory says that p* to *p*, and since Hugh does not even believe that a correlation obtains in practice between what he believes about his method of ascent and how he actually ascended, there is no earned entitlement.

It is a little tempting to read some of the published arguments that Hugh can't know he came via the mountains as reasoning in just this way. Here is Arntzenius's central argument. (Assume Arntzenius is talking to Hugh here, so 'you' picks out Hugh.)

> For you will know that he would have had the memories that you have either way, and hence you know that the only relevant information that you have is that the coin was fair. (Arntzenius 2003, 356)

Moss (2012) makes a similar claim about the case. (Again, her narration is addressed to Hugh.)

> Intuitively, even if you travel on the mountain path, you should have .5 credence when you gets to Shangri La that the coin landed heads. This is a case of abnormal updating: once you arrive in Shangri La, you can no longer be sure that you traveled on the mountain path, because you can no longer trust your apparent memory. (Moss 2012, 241–242)

Now it isn't immediately clear why the fact that Hugh would have the same apparent memories in the two cases should matter. As far as I can see, the only way it could matter is if the following two things were true. First, we are using a temporally local theory, so the evidence is what Hugh's memory reports when he is in Shangri La, not the evidence he acquired on the trip up the mountain. And second, what those appearances support is solely a function of things internal to the agent, and not, say, their connection to the truth. As an evidentialist, I'm committed to a version of that second assumption – at least, I'm committed to saying that things that override evidence must themselves be evidence.

Let's focus for now on the assumption of temporal localism behind the arguments here. I'm going to offer a series of arguments against it, starting with a variant on the Shangri La case.

Iterated Shangri La

Here's a slightly more complicated variant of the Shangri La example.

> Sati walks up to the base of the paths to Shangri La. 'Have some toast and yeast extract,' says one of the attendants, somewhat stiltedly.
>
> 'Yeast extract?' says Sati.
>
> 'Yes, yeast extract. Vegemite or Marmite, your choice.'
>
> 'Must I?' says Sati.
>
> 'You must.'
>
> 'Well, Vegemite then,' says Sati, recalling fond memories of having Vegemite in Australia, and dire memories of that trip to the English countryside.
>
> 'Good choice,' says the attendant. Sati has her Vegemite on toast, and heads up the mountain path to Shangri La, as directed. On the way, she notices a worried looking person standing in front of a priest about to flip a coin. When she gets to Shangri La, she asks the attendant about that.
>
> 'Oh,' says the attendant, 'he chose Marmite.' Sati looks confused as to why this is relevant, so the attendant continues. 'The priests don't like people who choose Marmite, but they still must let them through. So they flip a coin to decide whether they will go by the sea or the mountains. Then, if they went by the sea, they will wipe the memory of that trip, and replace it with a memory of going through the mountains.'
>
> 'I'm glad that didn't happen to me. Lucky I chose Vegemite.'
>
> 'Recently,' continued the attendant, 'the priests decided to make things more complicated. They decided they would also wipe the memory of having eaten the Marmite, and hence facing the coin flip. Instead they would implant a false memory of having chosen Vegemite, indeed false memories of having preferred Vegemite to Marmite in the past, plus a false memory of seeing some other poor sap facing the coin flip. They really really don't like Marmite eaters.'
>
> 'So all the Marmite eaters get memories wiped?' asked Sati.
>
> 'No, only if the coin lands the wrong way. So some people get to the top thinking they liked Marmite. But we only tell that memories of going by the sea will be wiped. In fact, knowing they chose Marmite is evidence they went by the Mountains, but they don't know that.'
>
> 'It all sounds horrible,' says Sati. 'I'm so glad I remembered I liked Vegemite more than Marmite.'
>
> 'Have a good day!' said the attendant, grinning.

I think that Sati's last statement is correct; she does remember that she likes Vegemite more than Marmite. Indeed, she knows this in virtue of her memory. But it's not clear how a temporally local theory, either direct or indirect, can get that answer.

Imagine someone, call him Joe, who starts off in the same situation as Sati at the base of the mountain. Sadly, due to an unfortunate unbringing, he prefers Marmite to Vegemite, so he takes that. And then the coin lands the wrong way,

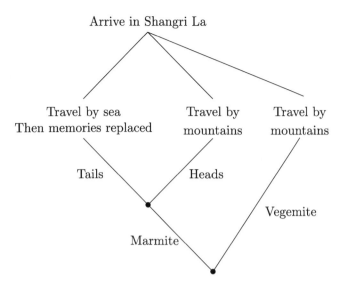

Figure 2. Revised Shangri La game; Sati takes the right-hand path, Joe the left-hand path.

and he is sent by the sea. Then his memories are wiped and replaced with fake memories when he gets to Shangri La (Figure 2).

If a temporally local theory is correct, then presumably Sati and Joe have the same evidence. And that means if evidentialism is true, then it is rational for them to believe the same things. Yet that is implausible; Joe should not be very confident that he had the Vegemite, came by the mountains, and so on.

On the other hand, it is overdetermined that Sati can know she came by the Mountains. The crucial difference between Sati and Hugh comes from the defeasibility conditions on the transmission theory. Past memories that p transform into current evidence that p unless they are forgotten, or the agent gets some good reason to suspect that her memory is unreliable. Hugh has such a reason; he is a coin flip away from having faulty memories. Sati does not have such a reason. She knows that had she had a very different kind of upbringing, and had she been on the bad end of a coin flip, she would have had faulty memories. But a reason to think that had things been different she would have reason to distrust her memories is not, itself, a reason to distrust her memories.

Sati's case is not meant to be a close call. There are lots of relevant ways in which her case is different than cases in which the defeasibility clause is triggered. The fact that two different kinds of things need to have gone wrong here is relevant. And the fact that the first requires things going wrong for a long long time into the past is relevant. And the fact that the first is only a problem in very different possible worlds to actuality is relevant. In short, any plausible kind of defeasibility condition whatsoever on the transmission theory will mean that Joe's memories of going by the sea are not transmitted, but only an implausibly strong defeasibility condition will prevent Sati's memories from being transmitted.

Note that I have not said that Sati can trust her memories because the probability of them being unreliable is so low. That is not the way to formulate defeasibility conditions. The sense of probability that is relevant here is evidential probability. And evidential probability is, as the name suggests, explanatorily posterior to evidence possession. We should not use evidential probability in our theory of what evidence the agent has. Sati knows she grew up liking Vegemite, despite the Shangri La shenanigans. But that's not because it is so improbable that she had her memories wiped. Rather, it is improbable she had her memories wiped because she knows she does not meet the conditions under which memories are wiped.

So temporally extended theories can distinguish Sati's case from Joe's, as intuition requires that they be distinguished. But temporally local theories seem to have a problem here. Perhaps the problem here is not with the theory of mnemonic evidence that the temporally local theories hold, but with evidentialism. Perhaps, that is, this is a case where we should say that Sati and Joe have the same evidence, but that this evidence supports different beliefs, given the different reliability of their memories.

But there is little to be said to motivate such a theory. If we aren't going to be evidentialists, it isn't clear what the relevance of a theory of evidence is. And if we are going to say that historical events, like the fact that Joe's memories were wiped and Sati's weren't, are relevant to contemporary rationality, it isn't clear what we gain by having a temporally local theory of evidence. Either way, we have said that the existence of past events is relevant to the rationality of current beliefs. At this point, we aren't engaged in much more than a terminological dispute with the temporally extended theories.

Against indirect theory

As Steup (2013) argues, the indirect theory of memory is implausible. It says that when one remembers that, say, the Chicago White Sox won the 2005 World Series, there are two things that are needed in order to ground the rational belief. The first is the apparent memory, and the second is some kind of reason to think that the memories are reliable. But the only reasons we could have for believing the second comes from what we have learned about the track record of memory, or perhaps of the role of memory in human functioning. And we couldn't be rational in believing those things unless we could rationally rely on memory in forming beliefs. So we can never rationally form any belief on the basis of memory unless we antecedently have reason to trust memory. And that, plus the indirect theory of memory, leads to a vicious regress, and hence to an implausible scepticism.

The argument here is similar in form to an argument that has often been levelled against the indirect theory of testimony. This argument traces back at least to Coady (1995). The argument is that children can rely on testimony to get knowledge, and hence rational belief, but they don't have the information or the cognitive capacity to rationally judge who is and isn't reliable. So it can't be, contra the indirect theorist, that such judgements of reliability are required in order to get rational belief and knowledge from testimony.

One problem with such an argument in the case of testimony is that it has relied, historically, on a very impoverished view of the cognitive capacities of young children. It is true that the capacity shown for explicit reasoning by children is often very weak. But they have rather amazing capacities for implicit reasoning, and there isn't any reason to think they could not judge and track reliability of informants.[3]

The issue here is not capacity, it is information. No matter how much capacity you have, you can't make rational judgements about the reliability of memory without information about memory. And you can't have that information without being able to use memory. That's the key problem.

We can use this idea to strengthen the arguments in the previous section about Sati. If the indirect theory of memory is wrong, we have to be a bit careful about why Hugh can't know he came by the mountain path. It can't just be that he lacks a reason to think his memories are reliable. Rather, it must be that what he was told at the bottom of the mountain is a reason to think his memories are not reliable. It must be the presence of reasons to doubt memory, not the absence of reasons to trust, that is doing the work.

And, as noted, this is a big difference between Hugh's case and Sati's. Sati does not have any positive reason to doubt her memory. She is several steps removed from the situation where her memories would be in doubt. It's true that her mnemonic beliefs are insensitive to the truth in a certain way. Arguably, the nearest world in which she came to Shangri La by the sea is one where she still believes she came by the mountains. But any kind of defeasible, direct theory of memory will allow for some rational but insensitive belief.

Assume that our theory says that S can rationally use her memory to believe that p unless defeaters D are triggered. And S uses her memory to (accurately) remember D. That is, she remembers that she is not in a situation where those defeaters are triggered. Presumably if D were true, her memory would be unreliable; that's what makes D a defeater. So there isn't any reason to think that this mnemonic belief in D is sensitive; she may well still have had it were D true. But the direct theory implies this doesn't matter, and the direct theory is the only theory on the table, given that the indirect theory leads to implausible scepticism.

Could it be that Sati should not trust her memory because she is, and she knows she is, in a class of people whose memories are unreliable? Well, the mere fact that she is in such a class is not interesting. She knows, after all she is a member of the class consisting of her and all people with unreliable memories, and the memories of that class are as a group unreliable. But that's not a reason to distrust her memory. Or, at least, it can't be on pain of scepticism. What must matter is that she is in such a class, and it is epistemologically significant. But the significant class around here seems to be the class of people whose memories have been erased, or who have reason to suspect their memories have been erased. And that doesn't include Sati. She knows she likes Vegemite, and has for a long time, and she knows that only Marmite-likers in Shangri La had their memories erased.

Here's what is true of Sati. She is, right now, phenomenally indistinguishable from a possible person whose memories are unreliable. But why should that matter? We all know brain in vat cases are possible, and each of us is phenomenally indistinguishable from such an unreliable 'person'. But that isn't on its own grounds for doubt about memory. All that she learns from the attendant is that another kind of brain in vat case is possible. But she knew they were possible all along. The case isn't actual and, unless we come up with a trigger for the defeater in the theory of memory, she has no reason to think it is actual.

Argument from a priority

There is another argument against the temporally local theories, and against both the direct and indirect theories, that we can derive from the work of Burge (1993, 1997). (I should note that there is considerable dispute about how best to interpret Burge. I'm not claiming that what follows is the best interpretation, or the only interpretation, just that it is an interesting argument inspired by, and quite arguably contained in, his work.)

Tamati is doing a proof. At one stage in the proof he appeals to Fermat's Little Theorem, which says for any natural number n, and any prime p, $n^p \equiv p$ (mod n). Using this theorem, Tamati completes his proof, and derives a nice result M. Intuitively, Tamati has not just come to know M, but he has come to know M a priori.

But assume, now, that either kind of temporally local theory is true. At one stage of the proof, Tamati had to, at least implicitly, reason as follows. It seems to me that I remember that $n^p \equiv p$ (mod n), so (perhaps with an extra premise), $n^p \equiv p$ (mod n). And that can't be a priori reasoning, since the premise about how things seem to Tamati is contingent and a posteriori. If the indirect theory of memory is right, the extra premise needed about the reliability of Tamati's memory will also be contingent and a posteriori.

It would be a very strange and revisionary theory of the a priori to say that any proof is not a priori if it relies on remembered theorems without, perhaps, memory of the proof of that theorem. The proof of Fermat's Little Theorem isn't difficult, but it does go through several steps. It is hard to keep the whole proof in mind at once. Even proving it, that is, requires a little memory. On the temporally local theory, it isn't clear that it could ever be a priori knowable for any normal person. And any theorem that required using it would similarly be a posteriori.

Perhaps it could be said that Tamati's reasoning is a priori because it doesn't rely on sense perception, only on perception of how things seem to Tamati. But some such perception of how things seem yields a posteriori knowledge. If Tamati has a headache, and notices this at the same time he remembers Fermat's Little Theorem, he gets a posteriori knowledge of the contingent truth that he has a headache, and a priori knowledge of the necessary truth of the theorem.

In short, a transmissive theory of memory is required to get the result that Tamati gets a priori knowledge of the mathematical theorem. As Burge argues, a transmissive theory of testimony gets the exciting result that when Tamati goes on to tell his friend about *M*, the friend gets a priori knowledge of *M* as well. If one thinks it is intuitive that the friend's knowledge is a priori, that's a good reason to favour a transmissive view of testimony. But that the friend's knowledge is a priori is not as intuitively obvious as that Tamati's knowledge is a priori, so it isn't obvious we must treat memory and testimony the same way here.

I'll end this section with a note about the dialectic. What would the argument of the paper lose if the arguments of this section didn't work? This is an important question because of arguments, such as those by Sgaravatti (2012, Ch. 3), that the a priori/a posteriori distinction can't do the epistemological work that it is traditionally taken to do. The answer is that we'd lose one of the best arguments against the direct version of the temporally local theory, while the argument against the indirect version would not be significantly affected.

Assume for now that one is happy with Tamati's knowledge, and indeed all non-trivial mathematical knowledge, being a posteriori in this way, because it relies on mnemonic knowledge about one's earlier self. There is still the question of how one gets from this knowledge about one's earlier self to knowledge of mathematics. On this indirect theory, this goes via reasoning about the reliability of one's earlier self. But that reasoning will have to use some non-trivial mathematics, and we'll be back in the kind of circle we warned about in the previous section. On the direct theory, this won't be a problem, since there isn't any challenge in getting from *I have an apparent memory that p* to *p*. That inference is perfectly sound, as long as one lacks reasons to distrust it. It is still, I think, puzzling that we have to analyse mathematicians as reasoning this way, and generating a posteriori knowledge. But they key dialectical point is that sense of puzzlement is only relevant to thinking about the direct version of the temporally local theory; the indirect version is beset by a host of further and more serious problems.

Argument from laundering

The arguments involving Sati and Tamati were designed to show that not all rational mnemonic belief relies on inference from the existence of a current mnemonic seeming. But neither argument suggested that there was anything wrong with such inferences. It is fully compatible with what I said about both Sati and Tamati that they could also try to infer from how things seem to them to facts about how they got to Shangri La, or about modular arithmetic.

Barnett's argument for a temporally extended view takes the opposite tack. He thinks there is something problematic about these inferences, or at least a special class of them. And because of this, he infers that the inference from present seeming can't be explanatorily important. And that gets him to a version of a temporally extended theory.

So what's the problem? Here's the schematic case that he focusses on.

Two Beliefs

On Monday you came to believe that p for good reasons that justified your belief, and on Tuesday you came to believe that q for bad reasons that failed to justify it (where p and q are independent). It is now Wednesday, and you have forgotten nothing, reconsidered nothing, and learned no new relevant evidence. You recall each conclusion without occurrently recalling your original reasons for those conclusions. (Barnett 2015, 15)

Again, it's a bit of an annoyance to use 'you', especially since you, dear reader, would not do anything so foolhardy as come to believe q. So let's assume Barnett's narration is directed at Kim. And the question is, is Kim's belief that q, on Wednesday, rational? Assume, to make the case most interesting, that this mistaken inference to q is completely out of character. Kim is, and knows he is, a very reliable processor of information, who rarely makes this kind of mistake.

The worry is that any temporally local theory will say that Kim's belief on Wednesday is rational. After all, Kim has an apparent belief that q, and not only lacks evidence of his unreliability, but knows he is reliable. Great! But, intuitively, his belief doesn't go from being irrational to being rational just by the passage of time. It can't get its irrationality laundered out in this way.

But it isn't clear how big a problem this really should be. Note that Kim is supposed to have forgotten nothing. So the evidence on which q was based is still there. Now allow the temporally local theory a principle that they should want on independent grounds. That principle is that evidence screens judgment; the evidential force of the fact that an agent made a judgment is completely screened, for that agent, by the evidence the judgment was based on.[4] I just stated that principle synchronically, so it doesn't immediately have implications for Kim's case. But it is plausible to say that as long as the judgment remains, its evidential force is screened off by the evidence it was based on.

Now whether one has a direct or indirect theory, Kim is not obviously compelled to hold on to her belief that q. And whether or not one believes the screening principle, the fact that Kim has forgotten nothing means that there is no symmetry between the cases of p and q. The relevant evidence is different in the two cases. The only theorist who has a challenge here is one who thinks that only occurrent states are evidence, and that is a particularly implausible addition to the indirect theory.

Barnett's case is different in a couple of respects than an example Harman (1986, Ch. 4) uses to draw rather different conclusions. Working through the differences between them allows us to see something interesting about rational dilemmas, even if it isn't immediately relevant to the debates about memory.

In Harman's example, Karen first draws a conclusion q. This is actually rational for her to draw given her evidence, but her evidence was extremely misleading. She then forgets why she came to believe q, and gets new evidence that would show her the old evidence was misleading. But since she doesn't remember why she believed q, she doesn't know that this new evidence affects her grounds for belief in q, and retains the belief.

Harman says that this is rational. Karen isn't required to keep track of her evidence for each thing she believes. That seems right. It is hardly a rational failing of mine to not remember precisely why I think that the White Sox won the 2005 World Series; I don't need to keep that level of detail in mind. And if Karen does not do that, she can't be expected to adjust her beliefs when the evidence that, unbeknownst to her, they are based on is undermined.

Harman thinks that our original intuition about Karen's case is that her belief in q is irrational once it has been undermined. But he also thinks reflection on real life cases like Karen's shows this intuition to be mistaken. The lesson he draws from this is that something like the direct theory is right; Karen can trust her memories unless she has a special reason to doubt them, even if in fact she couldn't put together a positive argument for their reliability.

Barnett's case of Kim is different than Harman's case of Karen in two respects. Kim retains his evidence; Karen loses hers. And Kim makes an irrational mistake; Karen is rationally misled by misleading evidence. Are those differences enough to think we should treat the cases differently? Or should we be worried that Karen's case, like perhaps Kim's, is one where intuition is not a reliable guide?

I don't actually have a firm view on this. The differences are significant. Harman himself thinks that the intuition in Karen's case is driven by the mistaken assumption that Karen will track and retain her evidence. That's not true in normal cases like Karen's. But it is true, by stipulation, in Kim's. So that is one big reason for treating the cases differently. Still, I do worry a little that we're drifting into areas where intuition is unreliable.

To make that worry a little more concrete, consider this argument for the conclusion that Kim's belief in q is actually rational.

(1) It would be irrational for Kim to re-open inquiry into whether q, given that it was settled, and no new evidence has come in.
(2) It would be irrational or impossible for Kim to intentionally forget q.
(3) Kim cannot change his attitude to q without either re-opening inquiry into whether q, or by forgetting q.
(4) There is some rational attitude towards q that Kim can take.
(5) So, Kim is rational to retain belief in q, since any other possible path would involve irrationality of some kind.

Premises 2 and 3 aren't, I think, particularly controversial, especially if 'inquiry' is read so broadly that any re-evaluation of q counts as re-opening inquiry. The issues are premises 1 and 4. Premise 4 is a no dilemmas principle. We'll return to it later, though in this context it is notable that Barnett himself endorses it, as do many other epistemologists (Barnett 2015, 10).

The big issue is premise 1. I think it is true. It is a mistake to go around constantly reconsidering things that one has settled. Once a decision has been reached, it should be held, unless a reason comes along to reconsider it. That reason may be evidence that the decision was faulty, or reason to think the decision was badly made. But the mere passage of time is not a reason to reconsider, and nor is the fact that if inquiry were (properly) conducted, it would yield a different conclusion.

The picture I'm putting forward here owes a lot to Holton (1999, 2009, 2014), as well as to a related idea due to Wright (2004). Holton argues that if one has an intention, rationality requires one to maintain that unless a good reason comes along to reconsider it. The fact that one would not form the intention again were one to reconsider it is not, he thinks, itself a good reason. Strikingly, he says that even in Kavka's toxin puzzle (Kavka 1983), the agent who intends to drink the toxin should not reconsider, because they have no reason to do so (Holton 2009, 162–165). And he suggests that we should think of belief along similar lines (Holton 2014). To believe something is to commit to its truth, and we need a positive reason to give up our commitments. Wright argues that the sceptic tries to lure us into opening inquiries we can tell will not be completed. We should resist the lure. We have no reason to open the broad ranging inquiry into our own competencies that the sceptic wants us to hold, and good reason to avoid it.[5]

We can perhaps motivate the application of these ideas to cases like Kim's by thinking of a similar case involving action.

> Ned has been thinking about buying a new bed. He is deciding between a wood bed and a metal bed. And he just decided to get the wood bed. This is a bad mistake. He will like the metal bed much better, and this is in fact clear from the evidence available to Ned. But he's made up his mind. The wood bed store is five miles east, the metal bed store is five miles west. And there's Ned in his car, driving eastward. What does rationality require of Ned now?

I think Ned's in a rational dilemma. It is irrational to drive to the wood bed store and buy a wood bed. He won't like it, and it is predictable that he won't. What a mistake. But it is irrational to reopen inquiry. He's made up his mind, and now he should focus on the road. He hasn't received any new evidence about the qualities of the bed, or any reason to think he mis-evaluated the old evidence. And we can't go around second guessing our past decisions all the time. That includes those of us (presumably all of us) who make mistakes. It is irrational to be fickle.

So what can Ned rationally do? The arguments of the previous paragraph suggest he's in a rational dilemma. If you want to act rationally, you shouldn't start where Ned is. If he keeps driving to the wood bed store, he'll irrationally buy a sub-optimal bed. If he thinks again about the issue, he'll be irrationally fickle. Rationality requires something that is practically impossible; changing his mind about what to buy without reopening the issue of what to buy.

This is a dilemma for Ned, but it is one he could have avoided. He could have not made the mistaken decision in the first place. It may or may not be unfair if rationality makes incompatible demands on an agent without any chance to avoid them. But it isn't unfair to think that agents who make mistakes at t_1 are, in virtue of those mistakes, left without any good options at t_2. Mistakes have consequences.

Is this inconsistent with evidentialism? I said above that evidentialism says the rational status of a belief supervenes on the evidence that the agent has. Yet now I'm saying Ned is irrational to change his mind. But if he had, with the very same evidence, believed that he should get the metal bed, that would have been rational. This looks like a counterexample to evidentialism.

Here's why it isn't a counterexample. What is irrational for Ned is reopening inquiry into what bed to get. It is the activity of engaging in further consideration of the question that it is irrational. Moreover, this is irrational because the evidence that is available to make this decision does not support it. Should Ned irrationally engage in this activity, there is a uniquely rational way to finish it, which is to change his mind. But that's not the same as saying that he should, rationally, change his mind.

I am making a big assumption here, but one I think is true. Careful consideration involves thinking through a large amount of evidence. Decisions to engage in careful consideration must be made on the basis of flimsier amounts of evidence. After all, to bring all the evidence one has to bear on a question is to engage in careful consideration. So a decision to engage in such consideration must not use all that evidence. So evidentialism must say that the rationality of a belief, credence, decision, etc. must depend on, i.e. supervene on, the evidence available to the agent when they make that decision. And when deciding whether to carefully consider or reflect on the evidence, very little is available.

That's why I think Ned isn't a counterexample to evidentialism. And nor is Kim a counterexample to evidentialism, even if there is no way she can rationally lose her belief in q. For Kim too faces a dilemma, of just the same kind. So the argument I gave for the rationality of Kim's continuing to believe q goes wrong at step 4. Kim has gotten herself into a mess, and there are no rational ways out.

But note that last conclusion cuts across the theories of memory we've considered here. The temporally extended theory has, as its distinctive claim, that some agents have a kind of evidence that the temporally local theory says no agent has. But Kim is not one of those agents. The evidence in question is evidence one gets when one acquires a piece of knowledge, and keeps that token mental state across time. And the relevant fact about Kim is that he has a belief in q that is well and truly not a piece of knowledge. So it doesn't look like the case should tell the local and extended theories apart.

What it does is show that there is a new kind of argument for the possibility of rational dilemmas. People make mistakes. When they do, there might be no good way to undo the effect of the mistake. And then they're in a dilemma. We don't avoid that conclusion by giving people who don't make mistakes more evidence.

Conclusion and future research

I've argued for a transmissive, temporally extended, view of memory and the evidence it provides. When I remember that the White Sox won in 2005, it is the fact that they won which is my evidence, not my apparent memory. The role of memory is to preserve this fact in evidence, not to give me new evidence for it. Saying this invites any number of questions. I'll end with a list of several ones that I find fascinating, but which I'm a long way from having answers to, divided up loosely into questions about metaphysics, and questions about epistemology.

Preservation

What is it for memory to preserve a belief? Bernecker (2008) has written on this at length, and the issue turns out to be much more complicated than we might first suspect. I'm particularly unsure about cases like this one,

Ankati: I haven't had to change planes at O'Hare for over five years. That makes me happy.

Bojan: Are you sure? What about the trip to Vancouver? Or the one to Hong Kong?

Ankati: Vancouver was a direct flight. And I went to Hong Kong via New York. But, oh, you're right, I came back via O'Hare. Sad face.

At the end, Ankati remembers that she flew home from Hong Kong via O'Hare. Is this a belief that was stored in memory ever since it happened? If so, we have to say that Ankati had inconsistent beliefs at the start of the conversation. If not, then I think it is hard to say that the relevant evidence for the belief that saddens her is the fact that she transferred at O'Hare. In such a case, it seems to me that the temporally local theory is more plausible than in more usual cases.

Initial evidence and over-riding

The following two questions are related:

- What past states can constitute present evidence?
- What present states can over-ride, or defeat, past evidence?

My instinct is to defend an extremely restricted answer to this pair of questions. In particular, S's attitude towards p at t_1 can only be evidence for her at t_2 if the following conditions obtain.

(1) S knows that p at t_1.
(2) S does not receive a significant amount of evidence against p between t_1 and t_1.
(3) S does not receive (undefeated) reasons to distrust her ability to preserve information between t_1 and t_2.

But every one of these points is problematic.

The first point might imply some counterintuitive things about people who trust misleading evidence, such as 'Karen' in the earlier cited example by Gilbert Harman (1986, Ch. 4). Let's focus on an even simpler case than Harman's. Unlike me, my doppleganger Nairb believes that the Astros beat the White Sox in the 2005 World Series. That's because his web browser had been hacked on that crucial October morning, and it reported the wrong results. He hasn't seen any relevant evidence since. He has forgotten why he thinks the Astros won in 2005, but has held on to the belief. Is this belief rational, and what's his evidence for it?

The evidence can't be that the Astros won in 2005; they didn't. And it can't be that his computer reported that; he's forgotten that fact. Let's say that it is his apparent memory that they won, which seems to be the only remaining option. That would mean that the rationality of his forming the belief in the first place is independent of whether his current belief that the Astros won is rational. That's better than the alternative options, but it isn't particularly happy either.

The second point leads us into the version of the dogmatism puzzle that Lasonen-Aarnio (2014a) has developed. Assume that significant evidence can factor into insignificant parts. Pazu knows that p, then gets three pieces of evidence e_1, e_2 and e_3 that tell against p. The conjunction is significant evidence, the individual parts are not. But the parts come in sequentially. When e_1 comes in, Pazu still knows p; after all, it is insignificant evidence. So Pazu can conclude, i.e. know, that it is misleading evidence. And, intuitively, we can ignore evidence we know to be misleading. So he ignores e_1. And for similar reasons he ignores e_2. Then e_3 comes in. Should he still ignore it? Presumably; it is on its own insignificant, and the only other evidence was known to be misleading, and so ignored. But it is odd that Pazu can hold onto his knowledge in p in the face of these three pieces of evidence, while he would have lost knowledge had they come in at once.

Finally, we need to explain why evidence of unreliability of mnemonic processes can block mnemonic knowledge. If memory was a source of evidence, rather than a preserver of evidence, that would be an easy problem. In general, a source does not provide evidence to an agent if the agent has reason to believe that it is unreliable. The problem is how to motivate an extension of that principle to memory, which is in general not a source of evidence, but a preserver of it.

We could simply insist that the Shangri La case shows that the preservative role of memory can be defeated, given sufficient grounds to doubt its accuracy. I think that's right, we can insist that. But there is a puzzle still about why this should be so. And that puzzle remains work for another day, as do the other puzzles in this section.

Externalism

Finally, there are some tantalising possibilities for new angles into familiar epistemological debates between internalists and externalists. It is hardly news that this is possible; Goldman's 'problem of forgotten evidence' is a familiar challenge to (certain) internalists (Goldman 1999). But there might be other ways to make memory relevant to familiar debates.

If the temporally extended theory is true, then what is rational depends on something that is, well, extended. And if what is rational depends on something that is extended in time, we might think it is less surprising that is also depends on something that is extended in space. And that suggests the way to a kind of externalism.

We can do a bit better than that hand-waving metaphor though. There are versions of the New Evil Demon problem for transmissivism. If transmissivism is true anyway, that means those problems have solutions. Then we just have to find what those solutions are, and see if they generalise to solutions to the spatial version of the New Evil Demon problem. And if they do, we might have new ways to defend externalist theories of rationality, or at least new motivations for familiar ways to defend those theories.

Notes

1. As with the transmissive view on testimony, I don't take it to be essential to the transmissive view that all mnemonic knowledge is transmitted. Perhaps, as Lackey (2005) argues, memory can sometimes generate new knowledge. Even so, as long as it sometimes plays a purely preservative role, the transmissive theory is true.
2. Dummett (1994) also defends a transmissive account of memory, though the analogy between testimony and memory is important in his argument. Dokic (2001) endorses Dummett's position on memory.
3. On children's capacities to learn, see Saffran, Aslin, and Newport (1996a, 1996b) and Gopnik et al. (2001). For applications of this directly to the judgements of credibility, see among many others, Koenig, Clement, and Harris (2004) and Harris and Corriveau (2011). Jaswal, McKercher, and VanderBorght (2008) show that children don't just track credibility of informants, they trade off credibility of informant against credibility of what is currently being said. In general, the lesson from the last 10–20 years of research is that children have more than enough capacity to perform the cognitive tasks that indirect theorists require of them.
4. I haven't actually defended this in print yet, but it is correctly attributed to me by Horowitz (2013, 25).

5. Hamilton (2001, 78) says that this idea, that it is wrong to open an inquiry you know you can't complete, plays a central role in the epistemology of the important Nyāya philosopher Gotama. The discussion of forecasting in Tetlock and Gardner (2015) might cast doubt on whether the kind of conservatism I'm endorsing here is empirically sound. There is a suggestion there that people who tinker with their credal states more frequently end up with more accurate credences. This is a topic that deserves revisiting as more data comes in.

Acknowledgements

Thanks to Maria Lasonen-Aarnio, Ishani Maitra, and the participants at the excellent Belief, Action, and Rationality over Time conference for helpful comments on this paper. Special thanks to Jonathan Weisberg, whose comments on the version of the paper presented at Madison saved me from a number of mistakes.

References

Arntzenius, Frank. 2003. "Some Problems for Conditionalization and Reflection." *Journal of Philosophy* 100 (7): 356–370.
Barnett, David James. 2015. "Is Memory Merely Testimony from One's Former Self?" *Philosophical Review* 124 (3): 353–392. doi:10.1215/00318108-2895337.
Bernecker, Sven. 2008. *The Metaphysics of Memory*. New York: Springer.
Burge, Tyler. 1993. "Content Preservation." *The Philosophical Review* 102: 457–488.
Burge, Tyler. 1997. "Interlocution, Perception, and Memory." *Philosophical Studies* 86 (1): 21–47.
Coady, C. A. J. 1995. *Testimony: A Philosophical Study*. Oxford: Clarendon Press.
Dokic, Jérôme. 2001. "Is Memory Purely Preservative?" In *Time and Memory. Issues in Philosophy and Psychology*, edited by Christoph Hoerl and Teresa McCormack, 213–232. Oxford: Oxford University Press.
Dummett, Michael. 1994. "Testimony and Memory." In *Knowing from Words*, edited by A. Chakrabarti and B. K. Matilal, 1–23. Dordrecht: Kluwer.
Fricker, Elizabeth. 1994. "Against Gullibility." In *Knowing from Words*, edited by Bimal Krishna Matilal and Arindam Chakrabarti, 125–161. Dordrecht: Kluwer.
Goldman, Alvin. 1999. "Internalism Exposed." *The Journal of Philosophy* 96 (6): 271–293.
Gopnik, Alison, David M. Sobel, Laura E. Schulz, and Clark Glymour. 2001. "Causal Learning Mechanisms in Very Young Children: Two-, Three-, and Four-year-olds Infer Causal Relations from Patterns of Variation and Covariation." *Developmental Psychology* 37 (5): 620–629. doi:10.1037//0012-1649.37.5.620.
Hamilton, Sue. 2001. *Indian Philosophy: A Very Short Introduction*. Oxford: Oxford University Press.
Harman, Gilbert. 1986. *Change in View*. Cambridge, MA: Bradford.

Harris, Paul L., and Kathleen H. Corriveau. 2011. "Young Children's Selective Trust in Informants." *Philosophical Transactions of the Royal Society B: Biological Sciences* 366: 1179–1187. doi:10.1098/rstb.2010.0321.

Holton, Richard. 1999. "Intention and Weakness of Will." *The Journal of Philosophy* 96 (5): 241–262.

Holton, Richard. 2009. *Willing, Wanting, Waiting*. Oxford: Oxford University Press.

Holton, Richard. 2014. "Intention as a Model for Belief." In *Rational and Social Agency: Essays on the Philosophy of Michael Bratman*, edited by Manuel Vargas and Gideon Yaffe, 12–37. Oxford: Oxford University Press.

Horowitz, Sophie. 2013. "Epistemic Akrasia." *Noûs Early View*: 1–30. doi:10.1111/nous.12026.

Jaswal, Vikram K., David A. McKercher, and Mieke VanderBorght. 2008. "Limitations on Reliability: Regularity Rules in the English Plural and Past Tense." *Child Development* 79 (3): 750–760.

Kavka, Gregory S. 1983. "The Toxin Puzzle." *Analysis* 43 (1): 33–36 (Oxford University Press).

Koenig, Mellisa A., Fabrice Clement, and Paul L. Harris. 2004. "Trust in Testimony: Children's Use of True and False Statements." *Psychological Science* 15 (10): 694–698. doi:10.1111/j.0956-7976.2004.00742.x.

Lackey, Jennifer. 2005. "Memory as a Generative Epistemic Source." *Philosophy and Phenomenological Research* 70 (3): 636–658.

Lackey, Jennifer. 2008. *Learning from Words: Testimony as a Source of Knowledge*. Oxford: Oxford University Press.

Lasonen-Aarnio, Maria. 2010. "Is There a Viable Account of Well-founded Belief?" *Erkenntnis* 72 (2): 205–231. doi:10.1007/s10670-009-9200-z.

Lasonen-Aarnio, Maria. 2014a. "The Dogmatism Puzzle." *Australasian Journal of Philosophy* 92 (3): 417–432. doi:10.1080/00048402.2013.834949.

Lasonen-Aarnio, Maria. 2014b. "Higher-order Evidence and the Limits of Defeat." *Philosophy and Phenomenological Research* 88 (2): 314–345.

Lewis, David. 1996. "Elusive Knowledge." *Australasian Journal of Philosophy* 74 (4): 549–567. doi:10.1080/00048409612347521.

Malmgren, Anna-Sara. 2006. "Is There a Priori Knowledge by Testimony?" *Philosophical Review* 115 (2): 199–241.

Moss, Sarah. 2012. "Updating as Communication." *Philosophy and Phenomenological Research* 85 (2): 225–248. doi:10.1111/j.1933-1592.2011.00572.x.

Pryor, James. 2004. "What's Wrong with Moore's Argument?" *Philosophical Issues* 14: 349–378.

Saffran, Jenny R., Richard N. Aslin, and Elissa L. Newport. 1996a. "Statistical Learning by 8-month-old Infants." *Science* 274 (5294): 1926–1928.

Saffran, Jenny R., Richard N. Aslin, and Elissa L. Newport. 1996b. "Word Segmentation: The Role of Distributional Cues." *Journal of Memory and Language* 35: 606–621.

Schmitt, Frederick F. 2006. "Testimonial Justification and Transindividual Reasons." In *The Epistemology of Testimony*, edited by Jennifer Lackey and Ernest Sosa, 193–224. Oxford: Oxford University Press.

Sgaravatti, Daniele. 2012. "Down to Earth Philosophy: An Anti-exceptionalist Essay on Thought Experiments and Philosophical Methodology." PhD thesis, University of St Andrews.

Steup, Matthias. 2013. "Is Epistemic Circularity Bad?" *Res Philosophica* 90 (2): 215–235. doi:10.11612/resphil.2013.90.2.8.

Tetlock, Philip E., and Dan Gardner. 2015. *Superforecasting: The Art and Science of Prediction*. New York: Crown.

Titelbaum, Michael. 2014. *Quitting Certainties: A Bayesian Framework for Modeling Degrees of Belief*. Oxford: Oxford.
Weatherson, Brian. 2012. "Knowledge, Bets and Interests." In *Knowledge Ascriptions*, edited by Jessica Brown and Mikkel Gerken, 75–103. Oxford: Oxford University Press.
White, Roger. 2005. "Explanation as a Guide to Induction." *Philosophers' Imprint* 5 (2): 1–29.
Williamson, Timothy. 2000. *Knowledge and Its Limits*. Oxford: Oxford University Press.
Wright, Timothy. 2004. "Warrant for Nothing (and Foundations for Free)?" *Proceedings of the Aristotelian Society, Supplementary* 78 (1): 167–212.
Wright, Crispin. 2002. "(Anti-)Sceptics Simple and Subtle: G.E. Moore and John McDowell." *Philosophy and Phenomenological Research* 65 (2): 330–348. doi:10.1111/j.1933-1592.2002.tb00205.x.

A defense of objectivism about evidential support

Brian Hedden

Department of Philosophy, University of Sydney, Sydney, Australia.

ABSTRACT
Objectivism about evidential support is the thesis that facts about the degree to which a body of evidence supports a hypothesis are objective rather than depending on subjective factors like one's own language or epistemic values. Objectivism about evidential support is key to defending a synchronic, time-slice-centric conception of epistemic rationality, on which what you ought to believe at a time depends only on what evidence you have at that time, and not on how you were at previous times. Here, I defend a version of objectivism about evidential support on which facts about evidential support are grounded in facts about explanatoriness.

1. Introduction

My aim in this paper is to defend the claim that evidential support is an objective matter against a challenge from subjectivists. Subjectivists about evidential support hold that a body of evidence only supports a given hypothesis relative to some subjective factor, like a set of evidential standards, or standards for evaluating evidence, and that there is no privileged set of evidential standards. For subjectivists, the only case where there is a non-relative fact of the matter about the degree to which evidence supports a hypothesis is the trival one where the evidence entails the hypothesis or its negation, for this is a case where all permissible evidential standards agree on the degree to which the evidence supports the hypothesis. By contrast, objectivists hold that whether and to what extent a body of evidence supports a hypothesis is an objective matter, so that a body of evidence supports a hypothesis to a given degree *simpliciter*, not just relative to a choice of evidential standards. (Objectivists can endorse talk of evidential standards; they'll just hold that there is a single privileged choice of evidential standards, whereas subjectivists think there are no such privileged standards.) Objectivists think of evidential support as a two-place function, taking as arguments a body of evidence and a hypothesis (and outputting a degree of evidential support), while subjectivists think that evidential support must be a three place function, taking as arguments a body of evidence, a hypothesis, and a set of evidential standards.

The debate between objectivism and subjectivism about evidential support is closely related to, but not identical with, another debate in epistemology – the debate over Uniqueness and Permissivism. Uniqueness theorists hold that there is a unique doxastic state that it is rational for one to be in, given a body of total evidence. Permissivists hold that for at least one body of total evidence, there is more than one doxastic state that it is rational for one to be in.

These two debates – between objectivism and subjectivism about evidential support, and between Uniqueness and Permissivism – are in turn central to the debate over diachronic norms on belief. Here's why. First, objectivism about evidential support is plausibly a necessary condition for Uniqueness to be true. If subjectivism were true, and so there were different equally permissible evidential standards, then it would be difficult to resist the thought that different agents could use different such evidential standards in arriving at their beliefs and still qualify as perfectly rational. Now, objectivism isn't quite a sufficient condition for Uniqueness. One might deny (one version of) the evidentialist thesis, which says that the only reasons for belief are evidential reasons. For instance, if there were pragmatic reasons for belief, then which doxastic states are perfectly rational would not be solely determined by facts about one's evidence (Kopec ms takes something like this approach, treating epistemic rationality as a species of instrumental rationality and hence sensitive to practical considerations). One might also accept evidentialism but adopt a comparatively undemanding view of rationality. Perhaps the facts about evidential support are extremely precise, while agents cannot be reasonably expected to have such precise degrees of belief, either because they cannot know such precise facts about evidential support, or because they cannot achieve such fine-grained doxastic attitudes.[1] Still, objectivism about evidential support seems necessary for Uniqueness. If objectivism were false, it is difficult to see how Uniqueness could nonetheless be true.

Second, Uniqueness is plausibly a necessary condition for denying the existence of diachronic norms governing belief (and doxastic states more generally). Suppose we take it as a datum that it is irrational for an agent to have wild fluctuations in her beliefs (at least, unless her evidence likewise fluctuates wildly). To take one example, if she had the same evidence throughout the day but vastly different (*de dicto*) beliefs at different times in the day, this would be irrational.[2] The Uniqueness theorist can account for this datum without appealing to diachronic norms. Let the Uniqueness theorist espouse just the synchronic norm stating that at each time, your degree of belief in a proposition ought to be the degree to which that proposition is supported by your evidence at that time. If the agent has the same body of total evidence throughout the day but different doxastic states at different points, then at least most of the time, her doxastic state was not the uniquely rational one, given her evidence. But this explanation is unavailable to the Permissivist, for she denies that there is always a uniquely rational doxastic state to be in, given a body of evidence. Instead, she must appeal to diachronic norms to proscribe wild fluctuations in belief. Suppose that each of the doxastic states the agent has during the day is individually permissible, given her total evidence. For instance, each is based on a different, but permissible, set of evidential standards. The Permissivist might then appeal to a diachronic norm stating that it is a rational requirement that one always base one's doxastic state on the same set of evidential standards (and that at any given time, one ought to have the doxastic state which is proportioned to her evidence, given that set of evidential standards). Different agents could rationally have different doxastic states in response to the same body of total evidence, but a single agent at different times could not.[3]

This point can be made precise in a Bayesian framework. We can think of a set of evidential standards as being represented by a prior probability function (or a *prior*, for short). Objectivists about evidential support think that there is a privileged prior which represents the privileged evidential standards. Subjectivists think that there are multiple permissible priors, since there are multiple permissible sets of evidential standards. Extreme subjectivists will hold that all probabilistically coherent priors are permissible, while more moderate subjectivists will hold that the set of permissible priors excludes some probabilistically coherent priors (the crazy ones), but is nonetheless not a singleton.

Our Uniqueness theorist, who is also an objectivist about evidential support, can give the following theory about rational belief, which includes only synchronic norms: Let P be the privileged prior. If at some time an agent has total evidence E, then she ought to be in the doxastic state represented by the probability function $P(-\mid E)$. This theory will proscribe wild fluctuations in belief that aren't due to wild fluctuations in evidence. If an agent's probability function changes dramatically, and this isn't due to a dramatic change in her evidence, it must be due to her sometimes not using the privileged prior P.

Our Permissivist, however, will give a theory which includes some diachronic norm. Conditionalization is the most popular one. It says, in effect, that once one adopts a prior as one's own, one must stick with it. More precisely, it says that if at time t_0 one has probability function P_0, and at t_1 one gains evidence E (and nothing stronger), then at t_1 one's probability function should be $P_1(-) = P_0(-\mid E)$.[4]

A small caveat: Uniqueness and Permissivism, as well as objectivism and subjectivism about evidential support, can be located on a spectrum. Permissivists can vary in just how wide they take the range of permissible doxastic state to be in any given evidential situation. For instance, very moderate Permissivists might think that it is permissible to assign some proposition a probability anywhere between 0.6 and 0.62, while more extreme Permissivists might hold that the permissible range is significantly wider, with the most extreme ones holding that any probability assignment between 0 and 1 is permissible. An analogous point can be made about subjectivism about evidential support. Moderate subjectivists will hold that there are some objective facts about evidential support that make it determinately the case that the evidence supports a given hypothesis to a degree that is somewhere in a fairly narrow range, but that only subjective factors, like the exact weights that one gives to various epistemic values (e.g. simplicity) could narrow things down further. More extreme subjectivists, by contrast, will hold that objective factors rule out far less. Whether the opponent of diachronic norms could settle for a very moderate form of Permissivism, and hence perhaps also a very moderate form of subjectivism, depends on why changes in one's doxastic state without changes in one's evidence are supposed to be irrational. If it is just that certain wild changes in one's doxastic state are intuitively irrational, the opponent of diachronic norms could perhaps be happy with a very moderate Permissivism. After all, such a moderate Permissivism would, even absent diachronic norms, allow only very minor fluctuations in one's doxastic state, and these aren't obviously intuitively irrational. If, by contrast, the theorist wants to prohibit non-evidence-driven changes in doxastic state on the grounds that such changes leave one vulnerable to exploitation along the lines of the diachronic Dutch Book for Conditionalization (Teller 1973, Lewis 1999), then the theorist must reject even very moderate Permissivism, since even very small fluctuations in one's doxastic state, without changes in evidence, will leave one in principle vulnerable to exploitation. Either way, the further along the spectrum toward full objectivism, the better for the opponent of diachronic norms. Going forward, then, I will be focusing on full objectivism, but it is important to keep in mind that the opponent of diachronic norms might be able to settle for something short of these extreme position.[5]

My aim in this paper is to defend objective evidential support against a certain sort of objection, pressed most forcefully by Titelbaum (2010). According to this objection, the fundamental facts about evidential support – what the privileged evidential standards are – must be *a priori* in order for evidential support to play the role in epistemology that objectivists want it to play, but the only plausible candidate factors that might determine the privileged evidential standards are *a posteriori* ones. (Throughout this paper, I use 'determines' in a metaphysical, rather than an epistemic sense, to mean something like 'grounds' rather than something like 'discovers.') Therefore, objective evidential support is either non-existent or cannot play the role that many of its advocates want (myself included), namely helping to determine what agents ought to believe. I will concede that it must be an *a priori* matter what the evidential support relation is, but I will argue that the most plausible factors that might determine this evidential support relation are not *a posteriori* ones after all.

2. Evidential support, a priori, and language dependence

The fundamental facts about evidential support must be *a priori*. The qualifier 'fundamental' is important here. Of course, it is often an empirical, *a posteriori* whether and to what extent some particular piece of evidence supports a given hypothesis. It is an empirical matter whether the evidence that there are dark clouds on the horizon supports the hypothesis that it will rain soon. For this depends on what other background evidence one possesses. This is compatible with the claim that it is an *a priori* matter whether and to what extent a given body of *total* evidence supports some hypothesis. Equivalently, it is compatible with the claim that it is an *a priori* matter what the objective evidential support relation is, or what the privileged evidential standards are. In my view, these fundamental facts about evidential support must be *a priori*.

Before saying why that is, let me say how I am understanding the *a priori*. Following Field's (2000) characterization, some proposition is *a priori* if one has justification for believing it without empirical evidence, and this justification is not defeasible on empirical grounds. Similarly, a belief-forming method, like a set of evidential standards, counts as *a priori* just in case one has justification for using it that doesn't depend on empirical evidence supporting the method (call this 'default' justification), and moreover this justification for using it is not defeasible on empirical grounds. (If you dislike this characterization of the *a priori*, just replace '*a priori*' with 'Field-*a priori*' in what follows. For it is his notion of *a priority* that I think the evidential support relation must, and does, satisfy.)

Why, then, must the objective evidential support relation (if such exists) be *a priori*? I think there are two reasons, corresponding to each of Field's two conditions. First, the *a priority* of the objective evidential support relation may be necessary in order to avoid a pernicious epistemic circularity. If what the evidential support relation is depends on some fact F, and if it's an empirical matter whether F is true, then in order to proportion one's beliefs to one's evidence, one has to know whether F is true, but one would already have to know whether F is true in order to proportion one's beliefs to one's evidence (Titelbaum 2010). So, the idea is that in order for facts about evidential support to be able to play the role of determining what one ought to believe, they must be knowable *a priori*. Now, I am somewhat skeptical that one actually has to know what the evidential support relation is in order to (justifiably) proportion one's beliefs to one's evidence. Justified belief at the first order is compatible with lack of knowledge or justified belief at higher levels; one may justifiably believe H without knowing or even justifiably believing that H is supported by one's evidence, and certainly without knowing all the other facts about evidential support. Similarly, one might justifiably make various deductive inferences without knowing what rules one is following and without knowing that they are valid inference rules.

Still, it is plausible that what one ought to believe supervenes on one's mental states.[6] (This is a characterization of what Conee and Feldman (2001) call 'mentalist internalism,' which to my mind is more plausible that 'access internalism,' according to which what one ought to believe depends on factors to which one has some sort of special access.) If evidential support determines what one ought to believe, this means that what evidential standards one ought to employ in proportioning one's beliefs to one's evidence should supervene on one's mental states. The most obvious (though not the only) way for this to happen is for it to be necessary what the privileged evidential standards are. Of course, this isn't quite to say that they must be *a priori*; in principle they could be necessary *a posteriori*. But it would be worrying for defenders of objective evidential support if we didn't at least have default justification for employing these necessarily privileged evidential standards in forming one's beliefs. This corresponds to the first clause in Field's characterization of the *a priori*.

Second, it is a desideratum on any set of belief-forming rules, or any 'inductive method,' that it treat its most basic principles as empirically indefeasible. This corresponds to Field's second clause. The argument comes from Lewis (1971) (see also Elga 2010). Say that an inductive method is *immodest* if it always recommends itself over any competitors. It never recommends that, in response to a given piece of evidence, you adopt some other inductive method instead. Lewis cashes this out in terms of estimated accuracy: an inductive method is immodest just in case, given any body of total evidence, the inductive method's estimate of the accuracy of believing in accordance with that inductive method is at least as great as its estimate of the accuracy of believing in accordance with any competitor inductive method. Lewis (1971, 56) argues that any inductive method that is not immodest would thereby fail to deserve your trust:

> Suppose you did trust some non-immodest method. By definition, it estimates some competing method to be more accurate than itself. So if you really did trust your original method, you should take its advice and transfer your trust to one of the competing methods it recommends. It is as if *Consumer Bulletin* were to advise you that *Consumer Reports* was a best buy whereas *Consumer Bulletin* itself was not acceptable; you could not possibly trust *Consumer Bulletin* completely thereafter.

An immodest inductive method treats itself as empirically indefeasible. So if there's an inductive method such that we have default justification for employing it, then while it can treat its non-basic methodological principles as empirically defeasible, it must treat its most basic such principles as not subject to revision on empirical grounds. If evidential support is to play the role of determining what one ought to believe (so that the relevant inductive method is to believe a hypothesis to the extent that it is supported by one's evidence), then what the privileged evidential standards are must not be subject to revision on empirical grounds.

So, objectivism about evidential support is committed to the claim that the privileged evidential standards are *a priori* in the sense that we have default justification for employing them in proportioning our beliefs to our evidence, and that the privileged evidential standards are not revisable on empirical grounds.

Can an evidential support relation meet this requirement? What factors could determine the evidential support relation (or, equivalently, the privileged evidential standards), subject to this constraint?

It is useful to divide candidate facts into two broad types: formal (or syntactic) factors, on the one hand, and substantive factors on the other. Substantive factors are just non-syntactic ones. We'll get into some specific proposals later, but possible substantive factors might include simplicity (if this isn't cashed out formally), explanatoriness, naturalness, beauty, and the like.

Carnap (1950) famously sought a theory on which substantive factors played no role, and instead formal, purely syntactic, factors would be sufficient to determine the degree to which a hypothesis is supported by some body of evidence. By espousing only formal factors, Carnap's theory would qualify as an inductive *logic* to stand alongside deductive logic. After all, deductive logic is often taken to be the theory of logical consequence. That is, it is the study of which sentences are consequences of which others purely in virtue of their form or syntactic structure. A sentence that follows from another partly in virtue of the meanings of its non-logical terms would not count as a *logical* consequence of it. 'All bachelors are messy' is a consequence of 'All unmarried men are messy,' but this is so partly in virtue of the meanings of 'bachelors' and 'unmarried men.' If we swapped out one of these predicates for another with a different meaning, the consequence relation might no longer hold. So what Carnap was seeking was a characterization of the confirmation or evidential support relation which was sensitive only to the syntactic structures, and not the meanings, of the sentences involved. If one sentence supports another to a given degree, then so should the result of swapping out all occurrences of some predicate 'F' in the two sentences with a new predicate 'F*' which doesn't occur in the original sentences.

It would be great for objectivists if formal factors were sufficient to determine an objective evidential support relation. For then, it would be very plausible that the evidential support relation would meet the requirement of *a priority*, for the same reason that deductive logic is *a priori*.

But unfortunately, formal factors aren't enough. Goodman (1955) gave an example which convinced many that the prospects for such an inductive logic were dim. Start with the datum that observing 1000 green emeralds and no non-green ones is strong evidence that all emeralds are green. So an inductive logic should assign 'All emeralds are green' a high degree of evidential support, relative to the evidence 'Emeralds 1–1000 are all green, and they are all the emeralds we have observed.'

Now introduce a new predicate 'grue' which applies to an object if and only if that object is green and has been observed or else is blue and has not been observed.[7] Crucially, any observed emerald that is green is also grue. If we then replace all occurances of 'green' with 'grue' in the evidence and hypothesis sentences mentioned above, our inductive logic must assign a high degree of evidential support to 'All emeralds are grue' relative to the evidence 'Emeralds

1–1000 are all grue, and they are all the emeralds we have observed.' But this is plainly the wrong result. Observations of grue emeralds (and lack of observation of any non-grue emeralds) don't support the claim that all emeralds are grue to anything like the degree to which observations of green emeralds (and lack of observation of any non-green ones) support the claim that all emeralds are green.[8] In Goodman's terms, 'green' is a projectible predicate whereas 'grue' is not.

As Titelbaum (2010, 479) observes, Goodman's example is suggestive but isn't an airtight proof that no inductive logic is possible. For instance, it might be that once we take into account the other sentences that will be among the agent's evidence in any natural spelling-out of Goodman's case, facts about the syntactic features of these other evidence sentences will suffice to secure the result that 'green' is projectible while 'grue' is not.

However, in an important result, Titelbaum (2010; see also his 2011) proves that Goodman's language-dependence problem will infect any purely formal theory of evidential support. With some plausible auxiliary assumptions, he proves that no evidential support relation can be both substantive (in the sense of sometimes favoring one hypothesis over another despite being logically independent of both) and formal (in the sense of being invariant under permutations of predicates). In order to be substantive, the evidential support relation must be sensitive to more than just the syntactic form of the sentences in question. It must play favorites among predicates.

Some philosophers might immediately jump to the stronger conclusion that there can be no substantive evidential support relation at all. They make the background assumption that such a relation must be purely formal if it's to be worth any salt. Such philosophers might be motivated by two different concerns. The first is epistemic. If the evidential support relation can't be characterized formally, how can we know about it? I won't go into detail about the concern here (after all, much of the remainder of the paper deals with this epistemic issue) except to note that in ethics, most theorists take it that there can't be a formal characterization of moral reasons, but they don't become nihilists or error theorists on that account. Rather, they espouse a wide variety of metaethical positions – naturalism, non-naturalism, expressivism, and the like – that each give subtle answers to the question of how we can know about moral reasons absent any formal characterization of them. The second is a worry about normative force. Facts about evidential support are supposed to constrain what it's rational to believe. But some philosophers are skeptical about the normative force of any rational requirement that can't be motivated by something akin to a Dutch Book argument showing that if you violate the requirement, then there are cases where your attitudes license you to act in a way that is to your own acknowledged, predictable disadvantage. And as it happens, only purely formal rational requirements appear to be amenable to motivation via a Dutch Book argument. Hence, if the evidential support relation isn't purely formal, it's doubtful whether it can have any normative force. I think such philosophers are mistaken, and indeed I am skeptical of whether Dutch Book arguments themselves are probitive (see Hedden 2013, 2015a), though again I won't argue for this point here. Rather, I'll just take my target audience to be people who aren't already skeptical of the possibility of a substantive (i.e. non-formal) rational requirement having normative force.

The challenge for objectivists about evidential support is therefore to say what substantive factor or factors determine the evidential support relation, subject to the constraint that they be *a priori*.

A quick caveat, though, before plunging ahead. While I will be exploring approaches on which there is just a single substantive factor that does all the work of determining the evidential support relation, it is also open to the objectivist to be a primitivist or a pluralist about evidential support. On a primitivist view, facts about evidential support are brute facts that aren't determined by other, explanatorily prior facts. Of course, we would still be able to give rules of thumb or *ceteris paribus* principles (e.g. simpler hypotheses tend to be better supported by the evidence) for getting a grip on the evidential support relation, but there aren't further facts that ground the evidential support relation. On a pluralist view, there are multiple substantive factors that together ground the evidential support relation. For instance, facts about simplicity, explanatoriness, beauty, naturalness, and perhaps others besides are given weights and then aggregated to determine the degree to which a given body of total evidence supports some hypothesis. Both primitivism and pluralism strike me as eminently reasonable positions. But before retreating to either of these positions, I want to examine the prospects for a more monolithic[9] conception of objective evidential support. Still, it is important to remember that these are very live options. Even if a monolithic view of evidential support is implausible in the end, objectivism is not yet defeated.

3. Naturalness

Start with perhaps the most popular proposed solution to the Goodman's grue paradox. This view posits a distinction between natural properties and unnatural ones, and, more generally, posits degrees of naturalness for properties. Natural properties are ones that carve nature at its joints, so that sharing a natural property makes for objective similarity, whereas sharing an unnatural property needn't do so. In Goodman's case, greenness is a fairly natural property, while grueness is a horribly unnatural one. So here is a proposal about evidential support more broadly: the substantive factors that determine the evidential support relation are the degrees of naturalness of the properties involved in the hypotheses in question. In general, hypotheses with natural properties received higher degrees of evidential support than hypotheses with unnatural properties.[10]

Lewis (1983) posits a distinction between natural and unnatural properties to do a host of jobs, from helping to fix the laws of nature to contributing to determining the referents of our terms. But for present purposes, the most important role of naturalness that Lewis discusses involves its connection to rationality, and in particular its potential to solve Goodman's grue paradox. Lewis holds that part of the reason we in fact have beliefs about greenness rather than grueness (at least until we've read our Goodman) is that beliefs that involve projecting greenness are more rational than beliefs that involve projecting grueness, and this in turn is because greenness is more natural than grueness. Here are a couple representative passages:

> The principles of charity will impute a bias toward believing that things are green rather than grue, toward having a basic desire for long life rather than for long-life-unless-one-was-born-on-Monday-and-in-that-case-life-for-an-even-number-of-weeks. (Lewis 1983, 375)

> We think that some sorts of belief and desire ...would be unreasonable in a strong sense ...utterly unintelligible and nonsensical. Think of the man who, for no special reason, expects unexamined emeralds to be grue. ...What makes the perversely twisted assignment of content incorrect, however well it fits the subject's behavior, is exactly that it assigns ineligible, unreasonable content when a more eligible assignment would have fit behavior equally well. (Lewis 1986, 38–39)

Lewis' solution to Goodman's paradox, and the broader theory of rationality it yields, has generated widespread interest, much of it sympathetic, in the literature. Here is Jenkins (2013, 100) discussing the use of naturalness in responding to Goodman's paradox, though I hasten to add that she does not ultimately endorse the proposal:

> Empirical evidence alone could be construed as underdetermining whether all emeralds are green or all emeralds are grue, but [a theory of rationality on which beliefs involving projecting natural properties are more rational] holds out hope of a solution, provided that it can be argued that the proposition s: *All emeralds are green* is more natural than r: *All emeralds are grue*.

Similarly, Weatherson argues that we should view naturalness as playing a role in determining reference (so that our words tend to refer to natural rather than unnatural properties) in virtue of the role it plays in the theory of rationality and hence in the determination of mental content. His is an exegetical essay on Lewis' own theory, but Weatherson also endorses the interpretation of Lewis that he favors:

> But why is it more charitable to attribute beliefs about greenness to beliefs about grueness? I think it is because we need more evidence to rationally form a belief that some class of things are all grue than we need to form a belief that everything in that class is green. And that's because, ceteris paribus, we need more evidence to rationally form a belief that all *F*s are *G*s than that all *F*s are *H*s when *G* is less natural than *H*. (Weatherson 2012, 3)

Goodman and Titelbaum have argued that an evidential support relation has to play favorites among properties, but if we believe in a distinction between natural and unnatural properties, this should come as no great surprise. The evidential support relation should play favorites: it should favor natural properties over unnatural ones.

3.1. Is naturalness a priori?

While the naturalness theorist seems to have a nice solution to the problem of language dependence, Titelbaum (2010) argues that it ultimately fails. This is because he thinks that it's an empirical matter what the natural properties are (and, more generally, which properties are more natural than which). If that's right, then his epistemic circularity worry looms: Beliefs about what the natural properties are must be determined on the basis of our evidence, but they aren't themselves entailed by our evidence. If facts about what one's evidence supports are determined in part by facts about what the natural properties are, this means that in order to figure out what one's evidence supports, one must first figure out what the natural properties are, and to do that, one must figure out what one's evidence supports, but to do that one must figure out what the natural properties are. And round and round we go.[11]

Now, we might resist this circularity worry by holding that facts about naturalness can determine what you ought to believe even if you're not in a position to know these facts.[12] But even so, facts about naturalness will fail to supervene on one's mental states, at least assuming that the empirical status of facts about naturalness means they're also contingent. The particular supervenience worry dissolves if they are necessary *a posteriori*, though I think it would still threaten the plausibility of the claim that one has default justification for employing naturalness-based evidential support relation in arriving at one's beliefs.

How about the second reason for thinking that facts about evidential support must be *a priori*, namely that inductive methods (or, in our terminology, evidential support relations) must be immodest? Well, if the proposal is that (to use Goodman's phrase) one ought to project the properties that are in fact natural, regardless of whether your evidence supports the hypothesis that those are the natural properties, then the naturalness theorist's evidential support relation needn't be immodest. But if the proposal allows for defeaters, so that while you ought to start out by projecting the properties that are in fact natural, you should no longer project them if you later get misleading evidence that they aren't natural, then it won't be immodest.

In any event, it is possible to resist the thought that facts about naturalness are empirical. To preview, my suggestion will be that it is *a priori* which properties, if instantiated, would be natural (or which possible properties are more natural than which), even though it's clearly empirical which properties are actually instantiated. To use Hawthorne and Dorr (2013) helpful way of putting it, the view is that it is *a priori* which properties are possibly natural, and being possibly natural and actually instantiated is necessary and sufficient for being natural.

(More generally, it is *a priori* whether some property is possibly natural-to-such-and-such-degree, and being possibly natural-to-such-and-such-degree and actually instantiated is necessary and sufficient for being natural-to-such-and-such-degree.) However, I will ultimately argue (Section 3.2) that the question of the empirical status of naturalness is a red herring, for naturalness is not the most promising substantive factor for determining the evidential support relation. Therefore, the impatient reader can skip ahead without losing the thread.

Start with why one might think it's empirical what the natural properties are (ignoring for the moment whether the empiricality lies in whether a property would be natural if instantiated, or just in whether a property is in fact instantiated). Certainly, prominent proponents of the natural/unnatural distinction emphasize the empirical nature of naturalness. Lewis and Armstrong both take the sciences, and physics in particular, to be guides to what the natural properties are. For instance, Armstrong (1979, 8), who takes natural properties to be the *only* properties there are, writes, 'What properties and relations there are in the world is to be decided by total science, that is, by the sum total of all enquiries into the nature of things.' And he emphasizes the special role of physics: '...I look for the genuine universals, the genuine properties and relations, in the fundamental notions of physics' (1988, 105–106).[13] In the same vein, Lewis (1984, 228) holds that 'physics discovers which things and classes are the most elite [i.e. natural] of all' and takes the most plausible version of the naturalness thesis to be 'one that give[s] a special elite status to the 'fundamental physical properties': mass, charge, quark color and flavor.'[14] And van Fraassen (1989), a prominent critic of the natural/unnatural distinction, likewise assumes that empirical evidence can be our only guide to what the supposedly natural properties are: 'if laws are to be what science hopes to provide in the end, then science had better hope to formulate its theories in a correct language [i.e. one whose predicates refer to natural properties]. And the guardians of this correctness can only be the scientists themselves.'

This empirical conception of naturalness has stuck. In a recent critical survey, Hawthorne and Dorr (2013, 18) identify empiricism as one of the central roles played by the notion of naturalness: 'The right method for identifying actually instantiated perfectly natural properties is empirical.' Even authors who question the privileged role assigned to fundamental physics hold that it is an empirical matter what the natural properties are. For instance, Schaffer (2004) holds that all sciences are in the business of discovering the natural properties.

So much for appeals to authority. What is the actual motivation for thinking that it is an empirical matter what the natural properties are? Apart from a background Quinean holism, the main motivation seems to me to be that a central theoretical role of natural properties is to constitute a minimal supervenience base, and it is plausible that it is an empirical matter which properties constitute such a minimal supervenience base.

But it is not clear that having natural properties constitute a minimal supervenience base requires it to be an empirical matter whether some property is possibly natural, as opposed to just an empirical matter whether some given possibly natural property is in fact instantiated. Natural properties could constitute a minimal supervenience base in each world even if it was a different set of natural properties in each world, provided just that all the possibly natural properties in each world where they are instantiated are part of a minimal supervenience base for that world.[15]

Other roles to be played by natural properties seem to outright conflict with thinking of science, and especially physics, as discovering what the natural properties are. I will mention just two. First is independence: perfectly natural properties are supposed to be mutually independent, in the sense that it is metaphysically possible for any combination of them to be instantiated by some object. Lewis (2009, 209) espouses a combinatorial principle on which every recombination of parts of reality is possible. The relevant parts of reality 'include not only spatiotemporal parts, but also abstract parts – specifically, the fundamental [i.e. natural] properties.' The problem is that the properties figuring in fundamental physics don't seem to be mutually independent. For instance, in the above quote, Lewis mentions mass as a plausible perfectly natural property in virtue of its role in physics. Presumably, the property in question is not (or not only) *having mass*, but rather (or rather also) the infinitely many determinates of that determinable: *having mass 0.298743 grams*, and the like. For part of the naturalness role is supposed to be that perfect duplicates share all there perfectly natural properties, and perfect duplicates cannot have different masses (Hawthorne and Dorr 2013, 44). But these determinate mass properties are not mutually independent. Similarly, if there turn out to be multiple fundamental particles, as seems like, and if each fundamental particle corresponds to a perfectly natural property (*being a quark, being a lepton, being an anti-quark, being an anti-lepton*, and the like), then the perfectly natural properties won't be mutually independent.

Second, consider the role supposed to be played by naturalness in determining laws of nature. One might think that this clearly requires that naturalness be empirical, but not so fast. Here is Lewis's take on naturalness and laws. He endorses a Mill/Ramsey-style best system account of laws of nature. A system is a set of propositions (or alternatively, sentences) purporting to describe the world. A suitable system is:

> one that has the virtues we aspire to in our own theory-building, and that has them to the greatest extent possible given the way the world is. It must be entirely true; it must be closed under strict implication; it must be as simple in axiomatization as it can be without sacrificing too much information content; and it must have as much information content as it can have without sacrificing too much simplicity. A law is any regularity that earns inclusion in the ideal system. (Lewis 1983, 367)

However, Lewis notes that an immediate problem arises:

> Different ways to express the same content, using different vocabulary, will differ in simplicity. The problem can be put in two ways, depending on whether we take our systems as consisting of propositions (classes of worlds) or as consisting of interpreted sentences. In the first case, the problem is that a single system has different degrees of simplicity relative to different linguistic formulations. In the second case, the problem is that equivalent systems, strictly implying the very same regularities, may differ in their simplicity. (ibid)

Lewis's solution is to bring in naturalness:

> We should ask how candidate systems compare in simplicity when each is formulated in the simplest eligible way; or, if we count different formulations as different systems, we should dismiss the ineligible ones from candidacy. An appropriate standard of eligibility [is] not far to seek: let the primitive vocabulary that appears in the axioms refer only to perfectly natural properties ... [Then] laws will tend to be regularities involving natural properties. Fundamental laws, those that the ideal system takes as axiomatic, must concern perfectly natural properties.(ibid)

I take it that science, and especially physics, is supposed to discover the (perfectly) natural properties by discovering the laws of nature, and then we take the natural properties to be those that figure in those laws. But then a potential circularity looms. What the natural properties are depends on what the laws of nature are (if they are whatever properties figure in those laws), but what the laws of nature are depends on what the natural properties are (since laws are regularities in the ideal system, and ideality depends in part on simplicity when the system is formulated in a language whose predicates refer to natural properties). If naturalness is supposed to help settle which system is ideal, and hence what the laws are, then the naturalness facts must be prior to facts about what the laws are and hence cannot hold in virtue of facts about what the laws are. Of course, naturalness could play this role in helping determine what the laws are if it's *a priori* which properties are possibly natural but *a posteriori* which possibly natural properties are actually instantiated.

So the theoretical roles meant to be played by naturalness do not seem to require, and in some cases conflict with, the view that it's an empirical matter which properties are possibly natural, and not just empirical which possibly natural properties are instantiated. Thinking that it's an empirical, or at least a contingent, matter which properties are possibly natural also raises some uncomfortable questions:

> Among the properties which are not in fact perfectly natural, which ones could be perfectly natural? One possible view is that every property whatsoever could have been perfectly natural. While it seems like an attraction of this view that it enables us to dodge the need for making a distinction between the possibly perfectly natural properties and the rest, plenty of other awkward questions remain. For example, assuming that it is still necessary that no perfectly natural property supervenes on all the rest, there must be limits on which sets of properties can be perfectly natural *together*; and it is hard to think of a good way to answer questions like 'Which properties are such that they could be perfectly natural in a world where *being a spoon* was perfectly natural?' (Hawthorne and Dorr 2013, 32–33)

As I noted above, there is room in logical space for the view that it is necessary but *a posteriori* which properties are possibly natural (to-such-and-such-degree). But I think the most attractive view on which such facts are necessary is one on which they come out *a priori* as well.[16] First, note that for non-perfectly-natural properties, it is already plausible that it is *a priori* which are more natural than which. For instance, it is plausible that it is *a priori* that greenness is more natural than grueness. So the tough cases concern scientific theoretical properties. But here, it is tempting to adopt a view on which, were the laws of nature much different – or perhaps even *any* different – from how they are now, the actually instantiated properties figuring in our best scientific theories wouldn't be instantiated at all. If massive bodies didn't attract (ignoring other forces), then they wouldn't count as massive (and more generally, no mass properties would be instantiated). If protons weren't composed of quarks, they wouldn't be protons (and the property of being a proton wouldn't be instantiated). And if quarks were composed of smaller particles, then they wouldn't be quarks (and the property of being a quark wouldn't be instantiated).

On this view, it is plausibly *a priori* that if the property *being a proton* is instantiated at all, then it's natural (more generally, natural-to-such-and-such-degree), since in order for that property to be instantiated, the scientific theory in which it figures must be true, and this is all that's required in order for it to count as natural.

If this is right, then we could have our objective evidential support relation involve the constraint that one only project possibly natural properties (which may or may not be actually instantiated).[17] No circularity worry arises, since if it is *a priori* whether a property is possibly natural, then one needn't do induction in order to find out what properties are possibly natural, and hence in order to find out how to do induction.

3.2. The shortcomings of naturalness

However, in the final analysis I think that the question of whether naturalness is an empirical matter is a bit of a red herring. This is because naturalness is narrowly targeted at enumerative induction, but cannot be the whole story in determining the privileged evidential standards more broadly. While it is reasonably clear to see how an appeal to natural properties would help solve Goodman's grue paradox, and perhaps even the more general problem of justifying *enumerative* induction, it is doubtful whether it would be of much use in justifying induction more broadly.

Why can't naturalness be the whole story? Jenkins (2013, 102) points out that naturalness seems impotent to solve the problem of skepticism about the external world. In order for it to do so, it would have to be the case that the property of being such that one's perceptions are veridical counts as a more natural property than the property of being a brain in a vat being fed non-veridical perceptual experiences (or something along those lines). But insofar as I have a grip on the distinction between natural and unnatural properties in the first place, I don't find myself with any strong judgment either way about which property is more natural than the other. So insofar as one thinks of the problem of skepticism about the external world as a kind of skepticism about induction, namely about inductive reasoning from evidence concerning perceptual experiences to hypotheses about the external world, naturalness can't be the whole story about induction.

Now, this might not be so bad, for there are attractive solutions to the problem of skepticism about the external world whose diagnosis is that beliefs about the external world aren't inductive after all. To give just one example, consider Williamson's (2000) thesis that your evidence consists of all and only the propositions that you know (E=K). Assuming that you know that you have hands (or some other external world proposition), then by believing that you have hands you are not going beyond what's entailed by your evidence. On this diagnosis, Cartesian skepticism about the external world is a different problem, and admits of a different solution, than Humean skepticism about induction.

But even setting aside Cartesian skepticism, appeals to naturalness fall short of what is required to ground an objective evidential support relation. Consider cases of non-enumerative induction (sometimes called 'abduction'). Seeing that the sky is filled with dark clouds, I conclude that it will rain shortly. How is naturalness supposed to be relevant here? The property of being such that it will rain isn't obviously any more natural that the property of being such that it won't rain. (Similarly for the other properties you might think are involved in this case – the property of being such that there are dark clouds and it will rain isn't clearly more natural than the property of being such that there are dark clouds and it won't rain.) Then there are the sorts of inductive inferences common in the sciences. From the evidence that the organism have such-and-such phenotypic property, the scientist concludes that it probably is it heterozygous at a given locus rather than homozygous for the dominant allele. But the property of being heterozygous is not more natural than being homozygous for the dominant allele.

If we're worried about induction and evidential support in general, rather than just with enumerative induction and Goodman's grue paradox, then an appeal to naturalness can't be the full story, even if it can avoid Titelbaum's circularity objection.[18] Of course, this leaves open the possibility that an appeal to naturalness might be part of the story of what grounds facts about evidential support. But in the next section I will argue that there is a more promising approach to the problem of underdetermination that, if successful, would render appeals to naturalness superfluous.

4. Explanationism

My proposed alternative solution is a familiar one: explanationism. Facts about what evidence supports what hypotheses to what degree ultimately turn on explanatory considerations. Explanationism tends to go under the name 'inference to the best explanation,' but this name might misleadingly suggest that evidence can only support a hypothesis when the hypothesis is the best possible explanation of the evidence. But a given body of evidence can also support a hypothesis in cases where the hypothesis, if true, would be well explained by the evidence. This would be a sort of 'inference from the best explanation,' to use Lipton's (1991) term. More generally, two propositions can each be evidence for the other, even though explanation is asymmetric. Nevertheless, these observations are compatible with the claim that there is an objective evidential support relation, and that this relation is determined by explanatory considerations.

4.1. *Explanation as a general response*

Explanationism can succeed where appeals to naturalness failed. It has the potential to account not only for how not only intuitively good instances of enumerative induction can be rational, but also for how good instances of induction more generally can be rational. My discussion here will be programmatic. I won't be saying nearly enough to demonstrate that explanationist treatments of all cases of induction are correct. Instead, I just want to show that explanationism is promising as a general solution to the problem of induction, rather than being narrowly aimed at enumerative induction.

First, explanationism may be able to serve as a solution to the problem of skepticism about the external world. Bonjour has argued that the best explanation of the coherence and stability of our perceptual beliefs is that the experiences they are based on are by and large veridical:

> The coherence-cum-stability of a system of beliefs is complicated and fragile, easily disrupted or destroyed, and thus it is inherently unlikely that a system of beliefs which is constantly receiving [observational inputs] would remain coherent from moment to moment without constant revisions which would destroy its stability. Some explanation is therefore needed for why it continues to do so, and the obvious one is that the beliefs of the system match the independent reality which they purport to describe closely enough to minimize the potential for disruptive input. (Bonjour 1985, 171)

I don't want to hang my hat on Bonjour's proposal (see Vogel 2010 for criticism of Bonjour's argument). Note also that even if the general explanationist thrust of his proposal is right, we might dispute the details. For instance, Bonjour takes the relevant explanandum to be the long-run coherence and stability of our perceptual beliefs. An alternative explanationist solution to the skeptical challenge might take the explananda to be propositions like *that I am having an experience as of a hand in front of me* and then to argue that the best explanation for why I'm having this particular experience is that there is in fact a hang in front of me.

Even if an explanationist solution to skepticism about the external world fails, this needn't be terribly worrying, for as I have noted, there are other solutions on offer, such as Williamson's E=K thesis, that treat beliefs about the external world as not inductive at all (at least in the good case).

More importantly, explanatory considerations are clearly relevant to garden variety cases of non-enumerative induction where appeals to naturalness are impotent. In the case of the cloudy sky, the best explanation for why there are dark clouds covering the sky would also be a good explanation of why it will rain (if in fact it does rain). Here we are inferring to the best explanation of the dark clouds, and then inferring from that best explanation to the conclusion that it will rain. Similarly, insofar as our scientist's inference is a good one, this is plausibly because being heterozygous at the relevant locus is a better explanation for having the given phenotype than is being homozygous for the dominant allele.

Explanatory considerations also have the potential to provide an attractive solution to Goodman's grue paradox, which would render appeals to naturalness superfluous. White (2005) proposes that one explanatory virtue is stability: an explanation of some fact F is stable to the extent that, according to this explanation, F couldn't easily have failed to obtain, and stability is a good-making feature of an explanation to the extent that its explanandum calls out for explanation.

You've observed a bunch of emeralds, and all of them have been green. By definition, this means that all observed emeralds have also been grue. Nonetheless, White argues that the hypothesis that all emeralds are green is a better explanation of the fact that all observed emeralds have been green/grue than is the hypothesis that all emeralds are grue. The reason is that the all-green hypothesis is more stable than the all-grue hypothesis. Properties like grueness are 'counterfactually dependent on observation,' whereas ordinary colour properties are not:

> Whereas an unobserved green thing would still have been green had we observed it, an unobserved *grue* think would have been *bleen* [i.e. blue if observed and green otherwise] had we observed it. For if something is grue and unobserved then it is blue, and would have been observed and blue and hence bleen. Similarly, an unobserved bleen thing would have been grue had we observed it. For if something is bleen and unobserved then it is green and would have been green had we observed it, in which case it would have been green and observed and hence grue. (White 2005, 18)[19]

Importantly, it was arbitrary which emeralds we happen to have observed.[20] Had we happened to have observed different emeralds, then some actually unobserved emeralds would have been observed. The hypothesis that all emeralds are green has the consequence that even had we observed some of the actually unobserved emeralds, our explanandum – that all observed emeralds are green/grue – would still have obtained. By contrast, the hypothesis that all emeralds are grue doesn't have this consequence. If all emeralds are grue, then had we observed some actually unobserved emeralds, then it wouldn't be true that all observed emeralds are green/grue, for these emeralds would be blue/bleen.

There is of course much more to be said here, and I refer the reader to White's paper for further discussion. But I do think that White's explanationist response to the grue paradox is on the right track, and if that's right, then appeals to naturalness are superfluous, and explanatory considerations have the potential to be the whole story in grounding facts about evidential support. This would be a monolithic picture of evidential support which deals which yields a treatment of enumerative induction as just a special case of induction more generally (though see footnote 20 for a caveat on which naturalness may still have a role to play). In this I am simply echoing the line taken in Harman (1965, 88) seminal paper on inference to the best explanation: 'all warranted inferences which may be described as instances of enumerative induction must also be described as instances of the inference to the best explanation.'

4.2. Explanationism and the a priori

So far we have seen that explanationism has the potential to be a response to worries about underdetermination in general, whereas appeals to naturalness seem to help only with enumerative induction. Now I want to argue that an explanationist approach to evidential support avoids the circularity objection that Titelbaum levels against the naturalness approach. For it is plausible that the most basic explanatory standards are *a priori*. (I don't say 'our most basic explanatory standards,' for it is doubtful whether the standards that we fallible humans have adopted are the correct ones.)

Importantly, this is not to say that whether something is in fact a good explanation of a given body of evidence is an *a priori* matter. For starters, something can't count as a good explanation of anything unless it is true (or at least approximately true), and this will almost always be an empirical matter (mathematical explanations being perhaps the lone example, which we can set aside since we're concerned with induction). Moreover, on many familiar accounts of explanation, it will be an empirical matter whether a given set of propositions, even if true, would constitute an explanation of the evidence in question (Ludlow 1991, 60). For instance, on the deductive-nomological model (Hempel and Oppenheim 1948), an explanation must include a lawlike statement, but even holding fixed that the statement is true, it will be a contingent, empirical matter whether it is a law or instead an accident. Similarly, on causal accounts of explanation, even granting that some event occurred (so that the corresponding proposition about its occurrence is true), it will be a contingent, empirical matter whether it caused the evidence. Better to say, following Ludlow, that a potential explanation of some evidence is one that does explain that evidence in some possible world or other.

One might also think that it is an empirical matter what the best potential explanation of some body of evidence will be, since which potential explanation looks best will depend on our background knowledge, much of which is empirical. For instance, it is an empirical matter whether the best potential explanation of the sidewalk's being wet is that it recently rained or that someone washed it down with a hose. But this is compatible with thinking that it is an *a priori* matter which hypothesis is the best potential explanation of a body of *total* evidence.

My suggestion, then, is that it is an *a priori* matter what the privileged explanatory standards are, and hence what the best potential explanation of a given body of total evidence is. We have default justification for employing those explanatory standards, and those explanatory standards are not defeasible on empirical grounds.

I won't attempt to give an analysis of explanatory goodness. Indeed, I doubt whether such an analysis is possible. But as a first pass, the most basic explanatory virtues, the features that make a potential explanation a good one, include the extent to which the potential explanation is simple,[21] unified (if this is different from simplicity), and stable (in White's sense, above).

In suggesting that the most basic explanatory standards are *a priori*, I want to make two points. First, unlike facts about what the natural properties are, there is little pull toward thinking of physics (or the sciences in general) as being in the business of discovering facts about the importance of simplicity, unification, stability, and the like in judging the goodness of a potential explanation. Science discovers how simple the world in fact is, but not how important simplicity is to a good explanation. Indeed, if we adopt an expressivist approach to epistemology,[22] there won't be any such facts at all. (A caveat: expressivists are typically keen to earn the right to talk just like realists and hence to be able to talk of facts about the relevant normative domain, but these 'facts' won't be the sort of facts that are discoverable by scientific means.)

Second, it is difficult to come up with a case in which the most basic explanatory standards should be revised on empirical grounds. Where there is a case of methodological change on empirical grounds, it seems unlikely that the jettisoned principle was a *basic* explanatory principle in the first place. This is to be expected, of course, if explanationism is the whole story about evidential support, since any adequate evidential support relation must be immodest and hence treat itself as unrevisable on empirical grounds.

Take an example from the history of science. Prior to Newton, scientific standards had it that appeals to action at a distance were a cost of a scientific theory, even a major cost. But afterwards, the methodological principle of avoiding appeals to action at a distance was dropped. Now, a first thing to note is that it's not clear that this methodological principle was dropped on *empirical* grounds, as opposed to conceptual ones. Perhaps it was Newton's conceptual progress in formulating an elegant, mathematically precise theory involving action that predicted the extant evidence at least as well as its competitors that led to the dropping of this methodological principle, rather than any new empirical evidence. But regardless of whether the methodological principle was dropped on empirical or conceptual grounds, the preference against theories involving action at a distance is not plausibly regarded as having enjoyed the status of a basic principle of inductive methodology. Better to view the case of Newton and action at a distance as one where more basic explanatory standards led to the dropping of a non-basic explanatory principle. The fact that Newton's theory was simple and provided a unified treatment of terrestrial and heavenly motion (favoring simplicity and unification being plausible components of our basic explanatory standards), and that this theory involved action at a distance, meant that the non-basic explanatory principle proscribing appeals to action at a distance had to be dropped.

Here is a purely hypothetical, example from Field that makes the same point:

> Presumably our empirical methodology includes a bias for simplicity. We recognize that insofar as we can account for all past and present observations by our present body of theory T, we could account for it equally well by an alternative T* according to which T holds until Jan 1 [2016], after which Aristotelian physics, Lamarckian biology, etc., take over. Why do we rule out T*, and base our predictions instead on the approximate truth of T? ...presumably it's that T is a vastly simpler way of accommodating our evidence than is T*. But now it might seem that our methodology of choosing the simpler is empirically revisable (either by revising the principle 'choose the simpler' or by revising the simplicity judgments that give this slogan its content). Suppose we had evidence that in each past year on New Year's day, the laws of nature drastically changed; that would seem like good inductive evidence that they'd change on New Years in [2016] too. Doesn't this show that our empirical methodology...is itself empirically revisable?
>
> No, it doesn't show this at all. What it shows is only that we regard theories T** according to which the laws of nature change every year as more plausible than corresponding theories T*** according to which the laws change every year until 2004, but don't change then. It seems that we have two pre-existing biased: one for T over T*, which licenses a belief that the laws won't change in [2016] given evidence that they haven't changed in the past; the other for T** over T***, which would license a belief that the laws will change in [2016] were we to be given evidence that they have changed in the past. So the fact that the laws of nature haven't changed drastically in the past is indeed inductive evidence that they won't change drastically in [2016]; but this fact is based on a fixed bias (for T over T* and for T** over T***) which there is no obvious way to undermine by empirical evidence. (Field 2005, 75)

And even if we could find a case where we really do revise the weight we assign to simplicity (or unification, or stability) on empirical grounds, this might just be take to show that simplicity wasn't a basic explanatory or inductive virtue. Some more basic explanatory principles stand in the background and govern how the weights assigned to simplicity, unification, and stability should change given changes in evidence.[23]

So here's why a broadly explanationist treatment of evidential support doesn't fall prey to a version of Titelbaum's circularity objection. First, the most basic explanatory standards – favoring simplicity, unification, stability, and the like – aren't the sorts of things that science is in the business of discovering.

Science employs such explanatory standards, but doesn't discover facts about which are the right ones. Second, it's not clear how to come up with a case in which the most basic explanatory standards should be revised on empirical grounds. This is for good reason – a good inductive method must be immodest and hence treat its most basic methodological principles as empirically indefeasible. If the most basic methodological principles are explanatory ones, this would explain why the most basic explanatory standards, whatever they are, aren't subject to revision on empirical grounds.

5. Conclusion

The evidential support relation cannot be characterized in purely formal terms. This is the lesson of Goodman's grue paradox and Titelbaum's related proof. So if there is such a thing as evidential support, there must be substantive (i.e. non-formal) constraints on what counts as evidence for what. But these substantive constraints must be *a priori* ones in order for evidential support to play its role in determining what one ought to believe. Some philosophers have proposed that these substantive constraints are to be found in the distinction between natural and unnatural properties: only natural properties are projectible. But even we can defend the claim that it's *a priori* which properties are possibly natural, naturalness can't be the whole story about evidential support. Better to adopt an explanationist approach, which has the potential to handle not just enumerative induction, but evidential support more broadly. Such an explanationist approach avoids Titelbaum's circularity objection, since the most basic facts about explanatoriness are a priori.

If successful, this defense of objective explanatory support is an essential part of defending the claim that all requirements of epistemic rationality are synchronic. For objective explanatory support is necessary for defending Uniqueness, and Uniqueness is plausibly necessary for defending such a purely synchronic picture of epistemic rationality, on which the only norm is one stating that your beliefs at a time ought to be the ones that are supported by your evidence at that time.

Notes

1. Note, however, that Uniqueness theorists may also simply deny that the facts about evidential support are so fine-grained. They might hold that the degree to which a body of evidence supports a hypothesis is sometimes to be represented by an interval of real numbers rather than by a single real number, for instance. Uniqueness theorists might also hold that it is sometimes indeterminate the degree to which a body of evidence supports a hypothesis, so that it is indeterminate what degree of belief an agent with that evidence should have in that hypothesis.

2. Of course, the opponent of diachronic norms could also deny the alleged datum. Perhaps, for instance, it is permissible to change one's beliefs without a change in one's evidence if this change is driven by the adoption of a different set of epistemic standards. For instance, it might be permissible to come to give greater weight to simplicity in evaluating evidence, and this will lead one to revise one's beliefs without gaining or losing any evidence. Moss (2014) takes something analogous to this approach in discussing imprecise credences. She holds that an agent with imprecise credences (where her doxastic state is represented by a set of probability functions rather than by a single probability function) must identify with one member of that set of probability functions, and use that member as the basis for practical decision-making. She holds that it is permissible for that agent to come to identify with a different member of that set, where such a change is analogous to a rationally permissible change in her (practical) values. While Moss is discussing a change in which aspect of one's doxastic state one uses for practical decision-making, rather than a change in one's doxastic state itself (since she is assuming that one's overall imprecise credal state remains constant absent changes in evidence), one could go further and say that it is also permissible to undergo a change in one's doxastic state without a change in evidence due to a similar change of heart. Christopher Meacham (personal communication) tells me that he is sympathetic to this sort of position.
3. Note that on this sort of Permissivist picture, epistemic rationality isn't all that much less demanding than on a Uniqueness picture. After all, maintaining the exact same evidential standards over time and always having the beliefs that those standards recommend is no mean feat!
4. See Meacham's contribution to this volume for detailed discussion of subtleties involved in interpreting Conditionalization.
5. In earlier work (Hedden 2015a, b), I have defended a time-slice-centric picture of rationality on which all requirements of rationality are synchronic and impersonal. Obviously, this involves commitment to more than just Uniqueness, and hence objectivism about evidential support. For even if there are no diachronic norms governing what you ought to believe, there might be diachronic norms governing, say, the temporally extended process of reasoning, or evidence-gathering, or doxastic (as opposed to propositional) justification. Hlobil (2015) and Podgorski (forthcoming) argue that there may be diachronic requirements of rationality such as requirements governing the temporally extended process of reasoning, even if there are no diachronic norms governing what you ought to believe at a particular time. And even if there are no diachronic norms governing belief, there might be diachronic norms governing preferences, intentions, or actions, for instance. And even if there are no diachronic norms whatsoever, there might be norms that nevertheless fail to be impersonal, such as synchronic norms saying that you should defer to the attitudes that you *now believe* your early or later selves had or will have. Still, if objectivism about evidential support, or at least something close to it, is false, the whole edifice comes crashing down.
6. Indeed, this supervenience consideration is one of my main arguments for a time-slice-centric picture of rationality in Hedden (2015b, c).
7. This definition of 'grue' is slightly different from Goodman's. His 'grue' applies to an object just in case it is green and was first observed before *t* (for some unspecified time *t*) or blue and first observed after *t*. I drop reference to *t* for simplicity.
8. It would go too far to say that observations of grue emeralds don't support the claim that all emeralds are grue *at all*. After all, such observations rule out various hypotheses which are incompatible with the hypothesis that all emeralds are

grue. For instance, they rule out the hypothesis that all emeralds are red. So they must support the claim that all emeralds are grue to at least some small degree.

9. I owe this term to Jonathan Weisberg, who recently used it in a lecture on objective Bayesianism.

10. Titelbaum (2010) holds that his proof shows that the naturalness proposal, or something very close to it, is a necessary condition for objectivism to be true. The reason is that if a substantive evidential support relation cannot treat evidential support as invariant under permutations of predicates, it can seem that any such evidential support relation must treat some predicates (or the properties to which they refer) as special, whether we call this specialness 'naturalness' or something else. But in my view, the fact that the evidential support relation cannot be invariant under permutations of predicates does not entail that it must treat some predicates (or properties) as special *in and of themselves*, such that the appearance of certain predicates in the evidence and hypothesis always makes for greater evidential support. Instead, it could be that the evidential support relation cares about the *relationship* between the predicates and the object terms of which they are predicated; that is, it must care about the meaning of the proposition as a whole (and about the relationship between the evidence proposition and the hypothesis proposition). This is akin to the Moore (1903) notion of an organic unity. Consider the fact that chocolate and strawberries (together) taste better than chocolate and salmon. This doesn't mean that the presence of strawberries *in and of itself* makes for a better dish than does the presence of salmon. After all, salmon and greens tastes better than strawberries and greens. It's the relationship between the two that matters. For this reason, naturalness isn't the only game in town when it comes to objective evidential support. In fact, as I will argue shortly, it isn't even the most promising approach.

11. As Titelbaum (2010, 485) puts the point, the problem is that any substantive evidential support relation 'displays a bias toward certain properties that is prior to and independent of the influence of any evidence. But supplying such a bias was the job the natural properties were supposed to do! In order for the list of natural properties to play its envisioned role in shaping the evidence favoring relation, it cannot be determinable from an agent's evidence.' One might attempt to invoke reference magnetism to escape Titelbaum's circle. According to one interpretation of the idea of reference magnetism, it is a brute constraint on interpreting the meanings of terms in a language that they tend to refer to natural rather than unnatural properties. So, if you just project the predicates that are already in your language, you're likely to be projecting a natural property. Now, Titelbaum worries that there is still a problem, since despite a general preference for natural properties to serve as the referents of predicates, one's language is still likely to contain plenty of predicates referring to unnatural properties as well. So one will still need empirical evidence to know which of the predicates in one's language to project. Of course, the naturalness theorist might respond that in any case *most* of one's predicates will refer to natural ones due to the general constraints imposed by reference magnetism, and so by adopting a general policy of projecting any and all predicates in one's language, one makes it likely that in any particular instance one will be projecting natural properties. Even so, there is a deeper problem with this escape route. For arguably, it is in virtue of facts about rationality, and in particular about evidential support, that predicates in one's language tend to refer to natural rather than unnatural properties. Weatherson (2012) makes a compelling case that this is the order of explanation in Lewis' philosophy of language, at least. There, the idea is that facts about mental content

are explanatorily prior to facts about linguistic meaning, and facts about mental contents are themselves determined in part by facts about rationality. It's easier to have rational attitudes toward propositions involving natural properties, so there's pressure to interpret agents as having attitudes toward such propositions rather than propositions involving unnatural properties. And that's why linguistic predicates tend to refer to natural rather than unnatural properties. But this Lewisian picture is one we can't endorse if we hold that the fact that one's terms tend to refer to natural properties is itself what explains how and why it is rational to project natural properties.

12. Titelbaum considers this possibility in Section 5 of his 2010.
13. These two quotes are highlighted in Schaffer (2004).
14. Another representative quote: Lewis (1986, 60) writes that 'What physics has undertaken ... is an inventory of the *sparse* [i.e. natural] properties of this-worldly things.'
15. There may also be grounds for ditching or demoting the supervenience role of the natural/unnatural distinction. For as Schaffer (2004, 99) argues, there may be possible worlds in which there is no minimal supervenience base, and instead, 'properties might be endlessly supervenient upon lower level properties.'
16. Lewis himself certainly thought that it was a non-contingent matter which properties are possibly natural, though it is unclear whether he thought this was also *a priori*. He writes that, 'The name [natural] has proved to have a drawback: it suggests to some people that it is supposed to be *nature* that distinguishes the natural properties from the rest; and therefore that the distinction is a contingent matter, so that a property might be natural at one world but not at another. I do not mean to suggest any such thing. A property is natural or unnatural *simpliciter*, not relative to one or another world' (1986, 60, fn 44).
17. Of course, if one cannot refer to uninstantiated but possibly natural properties, this complicates matters. Take one of Titelbaum's central examples, that of phlogiston theory at a time when it was still a live possibility. On some views, phlogiston necessarily doesn't exist. It wouldn't exist even if the Ramsey sentence corresponding to phlogiston theory were true. If that is right, the same difficulties arise in modeling the doxastic states of phlogiston theories and interpreting their language that arise for fictional terms like 'Santa Claus.' I won't go into these matter here.
18. A caveat: Hawthorne and Dorr (2013) mention the possibility of evaluating entire probability functions for naturalness, with the result that facts about evidential support boil down to facts about which probability functions are most natural. I won't pursue this possibility here.
19. Note that the fact that gruesome properties are counterfactually dependent on observation is independent of whether we start with non-gruesome predicates and define gruesome ones therefrom, or if we instead start with gruesome predicates and define non-gruesome ones therefrom. Even if we define 'green' as 'grue if observed and bleen if unobserved,' if remains the case that an unobserved green thing (which is therefore bleen) would still have been green had we observed it (in which case it would have been grue).
20. What about cases where it isn't wholly arbitrary which emeralds we've observed? Consider a different property grue+, where something is grue+ just in case it is green and first observed before AD 2500 or blue and first observed (if ever) after AD 2500. Suppose also that for any given emerald we don't observed AD 2500, the reason it doesn't get observed until then it that it's on an exoplanet, and we don't get the technology to mine on exoplanets until after AD 2500. Then, the

hypothesis that all emeralds are grue+ provides a fairly stable explanation of why we've observed only grue+ emeralds. If all emeralds are grue+, then even if we'd made somewhat different observations than we in fact did, this wouldn't involve our mining on exoplanets in the twenty-first century, and so we still would have observed only grue+ emeralds. I think there are three things to say about this sort of case. First, even if the hypothesis that all emeralds are grue+ is a rather stable explanation of our evidence, it is still a bit a less stable explanation than the hypothesis all emeralds are green. If the former hypothesis is true, then it is still possible for us not to have gotten the evidence that we've observed only grue+ emeralds, even if we have to go to fairly dissimilar possible worlds to get cases where we lack this evidence. So the grue+ hypothesis may be a lot better than the standard grue hypothesis in terms of explanatory stability, but it's still not as good as the green hypothesis. Second, we know that by around the late twenty-fifth century, we (i.e. later humans) will start heavily favoring the green hypothesis over the grue+ hypothesis (and White's story explains why this would be justified), so reflection-style reasoning suggests we should favor the green hypothesis now. Third, even if there are gruesome property where While's explanationist story breaks down (consider the property grue++, which applies to things that are green unless they're in some causally inaccessible region of the universe), we can still fall back on an appeal to naturalness, provided that it's *a priori* which properties are possibly natural, as I have suggested. This would amount to a retreat from a monolithic picture of evidential support, on which explanatory considerations do all the work, to a pluralist approach on which there are a variety of substantive factors that together determine the evidential support relation.

21. One might worry that facts about simplicity will depend on facts about naturalness, for the reason given by Lewis in his discussion of laws of nature. If simplicity is a matter of, say, the number of symbols needed to state the hypothesis, then how simple a hypothesis is will depend on the language used to express it. So we need to fix on a canonical language in which to evaluate the simplicity of different hypotheses, and one option would be for the canonical language to be one in which the predicates refer to natural properties. But if facts about which properties are possibly natural-to-such-and-such-degree are *a priori*, as suggested above, then this doesn't threaten to make facts about simplicity, and hence explanatoriness, empirical. An alternative option, which I won't pursue here, would be to conceive of simplicity in non-syntactic terms.

22. See Field (2009) for a defense.

23. Perhaps no evidence could simultaneously call into question the preference for simplicity, unification, and stability (or whatever one's candidate basic explanatory standards are). In that case, at least one such explanatory standard would be treated as empirically indefeasible in that particular situation, and would be used to determine how to modify the methodological principles that are called into question. This would amount to a picture on which at least one methodological principle is treated as *a priori* relative to a given body of evidence, even though no methodological principle is treated as *a priori* relative to all possible bodies of evidence. (Compare citeauthorbib2 (citeyearbib2) on the law of contradiction in logic.) Of course, provided that there is a uniquely rational way to determine which principles to treat as indefeasible for present purposes, and how to revise those principles that are called into question, it is tempting to say that really, the most basic methodological principles are those that determine this uniquely

rational way to proceed with methodological change, even if we find it difficult or impossible to actually articulate those most basic principles.

References

Armstrong, David. 1979. *A Theory of Universals*. Cambridge, MA: Cambridge University Press.

Bueno, Otávio, and Mark Colyvan. 2004. "Logical Non-apriorism and the Law of Non-contradiction." In *The Law of Non-contradiction: New Philosophical Essays*, edited by Beall Priest and Armour-Garb, 156–175. New York, NY: Oxford University Press.

Carnap, Rudolf. 1950. *The Logical Foundations of Probability*. Chicago: University of Chicago Press.

Conee, Earl, and Richard Feldman. 2001. "Internalism Defended." In *Epistemology: Internalism and Externalism*, edited by Hilary Kornblith, 231–260. Oxford: Blackwell Press.

Elga, Adam. 2010. "How to Disagree about How to Disagree." In *Disagreement*, edited by Richard Feldman and Ted Warfield, 175–186. New York: Oxford University Press.

Field, Hartry. 2000. "Apriority as an Evaluative Notion." In *New Essays on the A Priori*, edited by Paul Bogghosian and Christopher Peacocke, 117–149. New York: Oxford University Press.

Field, Hartry. 2005. "Recent Debates about the a Priori." In *Oxford Studies in Epistemology*, edited by Tamar Szabo Gendler and John Hawthorne, Vol. 1, 69–88. Oxford: Oxford University Press.

Field, Hartry. 2009. "Epistemology without Metaphysics." *Philosophical Studies* 143 (2): 249–290.

Goodman, Nelson. 1955. *Fact, Fiction, and Forecast*. Cambridge, MA: Harvard University Press.

Harman, Gilbert. 1965. "The Inference to the Best Explanation." *The Philosophical Review* 74 (1): 88–95.

Hawthorne, John, and Cian Dorr. 2013. "Naturalness." In *Oxford Studies in Metaphysics*, edited by Karen Bennett and Dean Zimmerman, Vol. 8, 3–77. Oxford: Oxford University Press.

Hedden, Brian. 2013. "Incoherence without Exploitability." *Noûs* 47 (3): 482–95.

Hedden, Brian. 2015a. "Options and Diachronic Tragedy." *Philosophy and Phenomenological Research* 90: 423–51.

Hedden, Brian. 2015b. "Time-Slice Rationality." *Mind* 124 (494): 449–491.

Hedden, Brian. 2015c. *Reasons without Persons: Rationality, Identity, and Time*. Oxford: Oxford University Press.

Hempel, Carl, and Paul Oppenheim. 1948. "Studies in the Logic of Explanation." *Philosophy of Science* 15 (2): 135–175.

Hlobil, Ulf. 2015. "There are Diachronic Norms of Rationality." *Thought* 4 (1): 38–45.

Jenkins, Carrie. 2013. "Justification Magnets." *Philosophical Studies* 164 (1): 93–111.
Lewis, David. 1971. "Immodest Inductive Methods." *Philosophy of Science* 38 (1): 54–63.
Lewis, David. 1983. "New Work for a Theory of Universals." *Australasian Journal of Philosophy* 61 (4): 343–377.
Lewis, David. 1984. "Putnam's Paradox." *Australasian Journal of Philosophy* 62 (3): 221–236.
Lewis, David. 1986. *On the Plurality of Worlds*. Oxford: Blackwell Press.
Lewis, David. 1999. "Why Conditionalize?." In *His Papers in Metaphysics and Epistemology*, 403–407. Cambridge: Cambridge University Press.
Lewis, David. 2009. "Ramseyan Humility." In *Conceptual Analysis and Philosophical Naturalism*, edited by David Braddon-Mitchell and Robert Nola, 203–222. Cambridge, MA: MIT Press.
Lipton, Peter. 1991. *Inference to the Best Explanation*. New York: Routledge.
Moore, G. E. 1903. *Principia Ethica*. Cambridge, MA: Cambridge University Press.
Moss, Sarah. 2014. "Credal Dilemmas." *Noûs* (early view). doi:10.1111/nous.12073.
Podgorski, Abelard. Forthcoming. "A Reply to the Synchronist." *Mind*.
Schaffer, Jonathan. 2004. "Two Conceptions of Sparse Properties." *Pacific Philosophical Quarterly* 85 (1): 92–102.
Teller, Paul. 1973. "Conditionalization and Observation." *Synthese* 26 (2): 218–258.
Titelbaum, Michael. 2010. "Not Enough There There: Evidence, Reasons, and Language Independence." *Philosophical Perspectives* 24 (1): 477–528.
Titelbaum, Michael. 2011. "Symmetry and Evidential Support." *Symmetry* 3: 680–98.
van Fraassen, Bas. 1989. *Laws and Symmetry*. New York, NY: Oxford University Press.
Weatherson, Brian. 2010. "The Role of Naturalness is Lewis's Theory of Meaning." *Journal for the History of Analytic Philosophy* 1 (10): 1–19.
White, Roger. 2005. "Explanation as a Guide to Induction." *Philosophers' Imprint* 5 (2): 1–29.

Don't stop believing

Jennifer Rose Carr

Department of Philosophy, University of Illinois at Urbana–Champaign, Champaign-Urbana, IL, USA.

ABSTRACT
It's been argued that there are no diachronic norms of epistemic rationality. These arguments come partly in response to certain kinds of counterexamples to Conditionalization, but are mainly motivated by a form of internalism that appears to be in tension with any sort of diachronic coherence requirements. I argue that there are, in fact, fundamentally diachronic norms of rationality. And this is to reject at least a strong version of internalism. But I suggest a replacement for Conditionalization that salvages internalist intuitions, and carves a middle ground between (probabilist versions of) conservatism and evidentialism.

Epistemic rationality requires two kinds of coherence. Broadly speaking, an agent's beliefs must fit well together at a time, and also fit well together over time. At any particular time, we should avoid believing contradictions, believe the consequences of our beliefs, and so on. And over time, we should respect the evidence we've received and adapt our beliefs to new evidence.

The traditional Bayesian picture of epistemic rationality is simply the conjunction of a synchronic claim and a diachronic claim:

Synchronic coherence: Rational belief states form a probability function and are rationalized by one's evidence.

Diachronic coherence: Rational belief states evolve by retaining old certainties and conditioning on new evidence.Recently, a number of philosophers have pushed for the abandonment of diachronic coherence norms. Norms like conditionalization, that have traditionally been understood as constraints on beliefs at different times, have lately been reinterpreted as purely synchronic constraints. On this view, the norms of epistemic rationality apply only to time-slices of individuals.

I want to resist this movement. I'll argue for the following claim:

Diachronic Rationality: There are diachronic norms of epistemic rationality. The problem that the opponent of diachronic rationality poses is this: diachronic norms of epistemic rationality are in tension with some form of *epistemic internalism*. Epistemic internalism, generically, is the view that whether or not an agent is epistemically rational supervenes on facts that are 'internal' to the agent. The relevant sense of 'internal' can be cashed out in a variety of ways, generating a variety of internalist theories. If there are diachronic norms of epistemic rationality, then whether an agent is epistemically rational *now* is partly determined in part by the agent's past. Facts about the past are not, in some epistemically important sense, internal.

I argue that the rejection of diachronic norms incurs a number of serious problems: most importantly, that it permits discarding evidence, and that it treats intuitively irrational agents as epistemically ideal.

In Section 1, I explain the framework in which much of my discussion takes place, i.e. the Bayesian view of rationality. I then flesh out the objection to diachronic epistemic norms, some of its common motivations, and how the debate is situated within epistemology. I introduce a few important distinctions.

In Section 2, I offer a series of objections to time-slice internalism. First, Sections 2.1 and 2.2 argue that time-slice rationality entails that discarding evidence and erratically changing one's beliefs without new evidence are rational. Then in Section 2.3 I argue against the view that epistemic *ought*-implies-*can*, and address the claim that cognitive limitations somehow limit our epistemic liability. I describe a notion of relative rationality, which allows us to accommodate many of the intuitions cited in favor of time-slice internalism. Section 2.4 argues that there are normative differences between agents who conform to diachronic norms and those who don't. The opponent of diachronic norms is committed to a strong claim: that no agent can ever be rationally worse than another in virtue of purely diachronic differences between them. There are intuitive counterexamples to this generalization. I discuss the ways in which the diachronic position can be weakened while still maintaining the existence of diachronic norms of epistemic rationality. Finally, in Section 2.5, I discuss the conception of rationality as subjective epistemic good, and the elaboration of this theory in epistemic decision theory.

Section 3 discusses an objection to diachronic norms prohibiting information loss. What if one can ensure a net gain in information only at the cost of losing some information? I discuss diachronic norms that can accommodate the idea that this sort of informational tradeoff can be rational. I conclude briefly in Section 4.

1. The conflict

1.1. Bayesianism

I will assume a partial belief framework. (Nothing hinges on this.) On this view, beliefs come in degrees ('credences'). Credences fall in the interval [0, 1], where credence 1 represents certain belief and credence 0 represents certain disbelief. A person's total belief state is represented by a credence function, i.e. a function from propositions to real numbers in the unit interval.

According to the classical Bayesian picture, rational agents conform to both synchronic and diachronic rationality constraints. The primary Bayesian synchronic constraint is probabilism:

Probabilism: a rational agent's credences form a probability function.[1] The traditional diachronic Bayesian constraint is conditionalization:

Conditionalization: let E be the strongest proposition an agent learns between t and t'. Then the agent's credences should update such that[2]

$$Cr_{t'}(\cdot) = Cr_t(\cdot \mid E)$$

One of the consequences of conditionalization is that once an agent rationally learns a proposition, she can't rationally unlearn it. One can't rationally lose information. (The set of live possibilities only shrinks.)

There are analogs to conditionalization in the full belief framework. For example, Friedman (2000), defends the following norm of inquiry: when a question has been closed, don't reopen it. This is a close analog to conditionalization's controversial consequence: that possibilities with credence 0 cannot recover positive probability. Other diachronic norms are weaker: for example, some forms of epistemic conservatism say that if an agent rationally believes a proposition at an earlier time, then it remains rational for her to continue believing it at later times, as long as she doesn't receive any new, disconfirming evidence.

In this paper, I discuss a number of general diachronic norms that cross-cut whether we treat belief states with the full belief framework or the partial belief framework, and also cross-cut whether we treat the overriding diachronic norm as conditionalization, or whether we accept alternative diachronic norms on credences (e.g. Jeffrey conditionalization).[3] Here is one candidate:

Diachronic evidentialism: An rational agent will only change her epistemic state by updating on new evidence. A consequence of diachronic evidentialism is that when we speak of 'an agent's evidence,' we are speaking of all of the evidence the agent has received, not merely the evidence that is accessible to the agent, or internal to the time-slice. It would therefore be question-begging to motivate time-slice internalism by claiming that agents sometimes lose evidence and are only responsible for believing what it supported by 'their evidence at a time.' By the lights of the diachronic evidentialist, 'evidence at a time' is just all the evidence the agent has received by that time.

Note that this is, on its face, a fairly strong norm. One needn't endorse this strong a norm in order to accept that there are diachronic constraints on rationality. But we'll start with the strong claim and see what can be said in favor of it, before considering weakenings.

1.2. The rejection of diachronic rationality

Arguments against the existence of diachronic epistemic norms appear in Talbott (1991), McGrath (2007), Christensen (2000), Williamson (2000), Meacham (2010), Moss (2014), and Hedden (2015). There are a variety of motivations for a time-slice-first epistemology. Some, e.g. Williamson, simply find diachronic constraints like Diachronic Evidentialism implausible. For others, time-slice internalism follows from a more general principle – in particular, some form of epistemic internalism. Here, for example, is Meacham (2010):

> In Bayesian contexts, many people have appealed to implicitly internalist intuitions in order to support judgments about certain kinds of cases. But diachronic constraints on belief like conditionalization are in tension with internalism. Such constraints use the subject's beliefs at other times to place restrictions on what her current beliefs can be. But it seems that a subject's beliefs at other times are external to her current state. (87)[4]

There are a number of different forms of epistemic internalism. The two varieties that are perhaps most familiar are *mentalist internalism* and *access internalism*.

Mentalist Internalism: the facts in virtue of which a subject is epistemically rational or irrational supervene the subject's mental states.

Access Internalism: the facts in virtue of which a subject is epistemically rational or irrational supervene on those of the subject's mental states that she has *access* to, in some epistemically relevant sense.

Neither of these immediately conflicts with diachronic constraints on rationality, at least as stated. After all, it might be that what's rational for an agent to believe at one time supervenes on her mental states at another time, or her mental states at many different times, or currently accessible mental states from other times, or mental states that were at one time or other accessible.[5]

Opponents of diachronic norms often appeal to a form of access-internalism: facts about our past mental states are irrelevant to our current rationality because they are, at least in some circumstances, inaccessible to us.[6] However, not all opponents of diachronic norms accept access internalism, in the sense of access noted above. So the form of internalism endorsed by the opponent of diachronic norms should be characterized neutrally:

Time-slice Internalism: the facts in virtue of which a subject is epistemically rational or irrational *at a particular time t* supervene on the subject's mental states *at t*.

Here's an example statement of this sort of internalism:

> Whether it is rational to retain or abandon a belief at a time is a matter of which of these makes sense in light of your current epistemic perspective, i.e. in light of what you currently have to work with in revising your beliefs. (McGrath (2007), 5)

Time-slice internalism is typically taken to entail that the norms governing epistemic rationality are purely synchronic, and hence Diachronic Rationality is false.

In some instances (e.g. Meacham (2010), Hedden (2015)), the motivations for time-slice internalism draw on an analogy between facts about the past and facts about the external world. Our access to our past mental states is, at least in principle, limited in just the same way as our access to the external world.

In particular, this form of time-slice internalist emphasizes the analogy between an internally coherent agent who's deceived about the external world and a synchronically coherent agent whose memories are periodically systematically scrambled. Both agents are doing the best they can under strange, externally imposed circumstances. What more could rationality demand?

The proponent of diachronic norms responds that the scrambled agent should instead be understood on analogy to someone who is given a drug that makes him believe contradictions. They are both doing the best they can under strange, externally imposed circumstances – but nevertheless, they are not ideally rational. I'll argue for this claim in greater detail in Section 2.3. First, however, I'll discuss some general objections to any form of time-slice internalism, including those that are access externalist.

1.3. Diachronicity in normative theories

I will ultimately defend a comparatively weak claim: that there are diachronic norms of epistemic rationality. Advocating diachronic epistemic norms does not entail advocating conditionalization.

There are weaker diachronic requirements that could constrain rational belief: for example, that one shouldn't reduce or increase confidence in a proposition (in which her previous credence was rational) unless she receives new evidence *or* loses evidence. The time-slice internalist endorses a strong claim: that rationality is in no way sensitive to diachronic features of agents.

The framework for epistemic normativity that I use in this paper is epistemic utility theory. Following Berker (2013), I distinguish three components of this form of epistemic consequentialism: a theory of final value, a theory of overall value, and a deontic theory. In epistemic utility theory, the theory of final value is encoded in the epistemic utility function: a function from epistemic outcomes to cardinal utilities. Typically, in epistemic utility theory, epistemic outcomes are characterized in terms of the (gradational) accuracy of a doxastic state. The theory of overall value delivers a ranking of epistemic options, as a function of epistemic utility and other parameters, e.g. probabilities. For example, options may be ranked in terms of their expected epistemic utility. Finally, the deontic theory delivers verdicts about what's epistemically required, permissible, and impermissible. For example, expected utility maximization might require choosing an option with highest expected utility.

All three elements of the theory are normative, not simply the deontic theory. And so diachronic normativity could enter into the framework at any of the three points. There could, in principle, be diachronic norms that affect the theory of overall value (ranking of options) without affecting the deontic theory. (For example, diachronic consistency could be universally supererogatory.) For this reason, it's useful to frame the discussion in terms of the facts in virtue of which an agent is *more or less* epistemically rational.

The opponent of diachronic norms under discussion opposes diachronic norms entering at any point within the normative theory. It's not obvious that any actual opponents of diachronic norms endorse this strong claim, or instead the weaker claim that diachronic norms don't affect the deontic theory. Absence of an explanation for why diachronic normativity in the theory of overall value shouldn't affect the deontic theory, it seems most likely that actual opponents of diachronic rationality defend the stronger claim: diachronic facts have no effect on an agent's rationality.

2. Problems for time-slice rationality

2.1. Problem #1: permissibly discarding evidence

One of the benefits that time-slice internalists claim for their view is that, by rejecting conditionalization, they are able to vindicate the idea that forgetting doesn't render a person irrational. If conditionalization applies, without qualification, over the whole of an agent's life, then any instance of forgetting would be sufficient for irrationality.[7]

The flip side is that time-slice internalism also makes any instance of discarding evidence epistemically permissible. Discarding evidence is, at least prima facie, a canonical example of a violation of epistemic norms. The reason that time-slice internalism has this effect is that discarding evidence is a fundamentally diachronic phenomenon. At some time, you receive evidence. At a later time, your attitudes fail to reflect the fact that you've received that evidence.

Discarding evidence

Suppose an agent has strong beliefs about whether capital punishment has a deterrent effect on crime. Then he learns of a study that provides evidence against his view. So he should reduce his confidence in his belief. But instead our agent (involuntarily) discards the evidence; he loses any beliefs about the study; it has no enduring effect on his attitudes regarding capital punishment. Now he can go on confidently endorsing his beliefs without worrying about the countervailing evidence.

This is a standard example of irrationality. One might object: an agent like this is epistemically irrational only if he voluntarily discards the evidence. But cognitive biases are not voluntary; so this objection would have the consequence that cognitive biases never result in irrational belief. I take this to be uncontroversially false.

Another possible objection: it's not the discarding of evidence as such that's irrational, but rather the disposition to discard evidence. This disposition is possessed at a time-slice. So the time-slice internalist has the means to explain the irrationality of discarding evidence.

Two replies: first, it seems to me that an agent who is disposed to discard evidence but never manifests this disposition is not epistemically irrational. It's the discarding itself, not the disposition to discard, that is irrational. Second, as Hedden (2015) points out, an agent might discard evidence and afterward lose her disposition to discard evidence. The time-slice internalist has no explanation for the epistemic non-ideality of such an agent.[8]

Discarding evidence is epistemically irrational. Therefore, there are diachronic norms of epistemic rationality. There's not much more to say about this. But to my mind it is a serious challenge to time-slice internalism; perhaps the most serious.

2.2. Problem #2: erratically changing beliefs without new evidence

Some kinds of belief change are plausibly described as deviating from some sort of epistemic ideal, even when no synchronic norms are violated. It might be controversial whether, by virtue of deviating from the ideal, the agent is irrational. Nevertheless, if there are purely diachronic epistemic ideals to deviate from, it follows that there are diachronic epistemic norms.

Consider again an agent whose total belief state is entirely overhauled at regular, and perhaps frequent, intervals (every minute? every second?). At every instant her credences are probabilistically coherent. And they uphold any other synchronic constraints on rational belief: for example, they are appropriately sensitive to chance information, they reflect whatever the epistemically appropriate response is to whatever phenomenological inputs the agent has at that instant, etc. However strong you make the norms of synchronic rationality, our agent obeys all of those norms at each instant.

But her total belief state at one moment is largely different from her total belief state at the next. If you asked her a minute ago where she was from, she'd say Orlando; if you asked her now, she'd say Paris; if you ask her a minute from now, she'll say Guelph. These changes are random.

The time-slice internalist is committed to the claim that such an agent can be *ideally rational*. I think this is false. Whether or not the agent rises to the level of rationality, it is clear that she is epistemically subideal: with respect to epistemic rationality, she is doing worse than someone whose credences are more stable over time.[9]

Objection: If her evidence changes with each belief overhaul, then perhaps it is rational for her to overhaul her beliefs so frequently.

Reply: In order to assess whether her evidence changes with each belief overhaul, we would need to say more about what 'her evidence' is. For example, if you believe her evidence is what she knows[10] – i.e. $E = K$ – then we can stipulate that it too will overhaul, since her beliefs overhaul. It might just be that she irrationally stops believing various propositions that she previously knew.

Similarly for other views wherein what an agent's evidence is depends at least in part on her beliefs.

For a toy example, suppose an agent initially knows the outcomes of 50 independent tosses of a coin that is biased either 3/4 toward heads or 3/4 toward tails. Unfortunately, the coin happens to have fallen about half heads over the 50 tosses, so the information the agent has received happens not to be informative about the bias of the coin. If our agent stops having beliefs about the outcome of most of the tosses where the coin landed heads, she'll come to be confident that the coin is biased toward tails; vice versa if she stops having beliefs about most of the tosses that landed tails. If she alternates between these two states of mind, then she will change from confidence that the coin is biased toward heads to confidence that the coin is biased toward tails, back and forth, as quickly as you like. Because she loses belief, she loses knowledge; because she loses knowledge, on this conception of evidence, she loses evidence.

Imagine having a conversation with someone like this about the coin. I take it the person would seem more than merely confused. She would not seem like a paragon of rationality.

On any conception of evidence where some of an agent's beliefs count as evidence (because they count as knowledge, or for some other reason), it's unclear how the time-slice internalist can make such beliefs rationally mandatory. In losing those beliefs, the agent loses evidence; if she loses evidence, the time slicer says, then it's permissible to change beliefs. The proponent of $E = K$ owes us some story about how beliefs that are knowledge can ever be rationally mandatory even at a time-slice: in other words, a story about why one *should* have evidence.[11] Moreover, this toy case shows that endorsing *Uniqueness* – the thesis that anybody of total evidence determines a unique rationally permissible doxastic state – does not prevent wild fluctuations in belief when 'evidence' is interpreted synchronically.

On the other hand, if diachronic evidentialism is correct, then 'an agent's evidence' is *all the evidence the agent has received*. It is not just the evidence that is accessible to her in the moment, or internal to a time-slice. As for the agent whose beliefs overhaul every second, the proponent of diachronic evidentialism will say: her evidence does not dramatically change. So it's irrational for her beliefs to dramatically change.

2.3. Epistemic ought implies can

One might object: so much the worse for any of diachronic norms! 'Ought' implies 'can.' Consider one of the primary motivating cases for time-slice internalism: forgetting.

Forgetting is not irrational; it is just unfortunate. (Williamson (2000), 219).

But forgetting is not merely unfortunate. it's *epistemically* unfortunate. 'Epistemic misfortune' is simply a gentler name for epistemic subideality.

'Ought'-implies-'can' principles are questionable in epistemology. Our friend in his tinfoil hat can't make himself stop overtly believing contradictions. That doesn't mean he's doing what he epistemically ought to do. It is a commonplace in epistemology that a person can be irrational even when she is doing the best she can.[12]

Indeed, even if the epistemic *ought*-implies-*can* argument were successful against ideals like deductive closure, probabilism, or precise credences, it's not clear that it applies to forgetting. A norm against forgetting would prescribe maintaining one's current state (except in response to new evidence). Unlike deductive closure, probabilism, or precise credences, it's not physically or psychologically impossible to be in the recommended belief state. After all, the relevant agent has already been in the recommended belief state.

The relevant 'can' for 'ought'-implies-'can' principle is difficult to provide a semantics for. It's a challenge for the proponent of 'ought'-implies-'can' arguments against e.g. conditionalization to provide truth conditions for the relevant sense of 'can.'

Importantly, the relevant 'can' must not be the 'can' of practical rationality, whereby the relevant acts are under the agent's immediate voluntary control. Beliefs are not subject to immediate voluntary control.[13] So an inability to immediately control forgetting is consistent with an epistemic obligation not to forget.

Finally: suppose the 'ought'-implies-'can' argument was successful against strong diachronic norms like conditionalization or the more general diachronic evidentialism. This would be no argument against diachronic epistemic requirements. Even if 'not can' implies 'not ought,' still: sometimes 'can' and 'ought.' We are sometimes capable of retaining information over time. When we can avoid forgetting, ceteris paribus, epistemic rationality favors doing so. To say that diachronic constraints have exceptions is not to say that there are no diachronic constraints.

One fear we might have about accepting epistemic principles that ordinary agents can't perfectly realize is that we would then have to accept that the norms of rationality are, in some sense, only for ideal agents; they don't apply to any actual agents.

But that's rather like saying that if you're not ideally law abiding – you've already gotten a speeding ticket; there's nothing you can do to change that fact – then traffic laws no longer apply to you. Suppose the traffic laws say:

(1) Don't get speeding tickets;
(2) If you get speeding tickets, pay the speeding tickets;
(3) If you don't pay your speeding tickets, go to your court hearing;
(4) ...Then this set of legal norms generates different 'levels' of law-abidingness. 'Ideal law-abidingness' amounts to obeying *all* of these (where everything after 1 you satisfy trivially by virtue of satisfying 1). Still, if you *can't* obey all of the laws, you're legally required to obey 2, 3, ...; and

if you *can't* obey 2, then you're legally required to obey 3, etc.. What the traffic laws require of you in particular circumstances is relativized to what you are capable of. Still, though, if you are not capable of satisfying all of the laws, then you are not *ideally* law-abiding.

We can represent the norms of rationality as having a similar structure:

(1) Be diachronically *and* synchronically coherent.
(2) If you can't be both, be synchronically coherent.
(3) ...etc.So, like law-abidingness, we can think of rationality as *relative* – in particular, relative to our cognitive limitations. Ideal rationality is a special case of relative rationality: it is the case where there are no limitations.

2.4. Rationality and epistemic ideality

The aim of this paper was to defend the claim that there are diachronic epistemic norms. Here are two stronger claims:

Rationality = Ideal Rationality In order to be epistemically rational, one must satisfy all epistemic norms, synchronic or diachronic;or even stronger:

Rationality Requires Lifelong Information Retention Epistemic rationality requires never having lost any information through the course of one's life.[14]One could resist these extensions of diachronic rationality. For example, it might be that being immune to information loss would make an agent epistemically better, but that it isn't necessary for rationality. Or it might be that information retention is rationally required over stretches of time, but not an agent's entire life. Perhaps it's required between instances of some psychological event of forgetting, where this might be psychologically distinguished from discarding evidence. Perhaps whenever it's psychologically possible for an agent to retain information, she should. These hypotheses are not remotely as demanding as the strong claims above.

The opponent of diachronic norms defends a universal generalization: she insists that no one is *ever* rationally subideal by virtue of diachronic facts. The proponent of diachronic norms defends an existential: there need be only one instance where, e.g. discarding evidence is rationally subideal.

2.4.1. Diachronic normativity within an epistemic deontic theory

First, there's a case to be made that diachronic norms should affect our epistemic deontic theory: that is, our assessments of whether an agent is rational or irrational.

A sociological observation: formal and informal epistemologists tend to talk about rationality in quite different ways. For many informal epistemologists, the majority of people are basically rational. It is common to think, e.g. that one is not rationally required to believe all the consequences of one's beliefs (though perhaps doing so would be epistemically better). By contrast, among formal epistemologists, it is more common to use 'irrational' to mean *rationally imperfect*. To be epistemically irrational, in their sense, is to deviate from epistemic ideals.

Formal epistemologists often accept that all of us are irrational. Because of our cognitive limitations – for example, the fact that we can't believe all mathematical truths – actual agents' beliefs are never actually closed under deduction. Deductive closure remains an epistemic ideal. Similarly for probabilism, which entails that we must, e.g. have credence 1 in all necessary truths. Probabilism also entails that we must have infinitely precise credences: that there be a difference between having credence .2 and credence .20000000000001. But because of our cognitive limitations, on the most plausible theories of mind, actual human agents never have infinitely precise credences. Moreover, canonical forms of epistemic irrationality are also a consequence of cognitive limitations. Irrationality is involuntary. Confirmation bias, hypoxia, and paranoid delusions are involuntary.

So, the proponent of diachronic evidentialism might conclude, because of our cognitive limitations, no actual agents are epistemically ideal. There's no obvious reason to treat forgetting any differently. Why should we classify the misfortune of being a forgetter differently from how we classify the misfortune of confirmation bias? The time-slicer should provide an explanation for why some epistemic misfortunes do not constitute irrationality, while others do.

2.4.2. Diachronic normativity within an epistemic theory of overall value

Second, there's a case to be made that diachronic norms should affect our epistemic theory of overall value: that is, our assessments of an agent's comparative epistemic ideality.

This form of diachronic epistemic norm is less demanding than those that infect our deontic theory. It won't immediately follow from this hypothesis that anyone is irrational by virtue of diachronic facts. One might agree with Williamson that forgetting is rationally permissible – but still hold it to be epistemically subideal.

One might, for example, have a *satisficing* deontic theory of epistemic rationality, according to which rational permissibility doesn't require ideal rationality. Traditionally, this form of deontic theory isn't common among formal epistemologists. Formal epistemologists tend to accept that rationality just is ideal rationality, and so accept that none of us is rational. But satisficing views are commonly presupposed informal epistemology. For example, informal epistemologists typically accept that it's not rationally required that we believe all the consequences of our beliefs, while also accepting that we would be rationally better if we did.

Still, there is common ground between these views. The satisficing and maximizing epistemologists can agree on comparative assessments of epistemic ideality. These comparative assessments form a (possibly partial) ranking of epistemic acts, states, or agents. The satisficer and maximizer endorse different functions from rankings to sets of permissible acts. The maximizer permits all and only maximally ranked acts, while the satisficer appeals to some permissibility threshold. The ranking is normative: it represents the extent to which different acts compare in terms of value. If the satisficer and maximizer agree on the ranking, they agree on some of the normative facts.

For example: perhaps the satisficer and maximizer can agree on the following ranking of epistemic properties in terms of ideality:

(1) Omniscience
(2) Conformity to some epistemically privileged diachronic and synchronic constraints[15]
(3) Conformity to the synchronic constraints
(4) Conformity to the synchronic constraints except where one is susceptible to involuntary biases and delusions

Each property entails the subsequent properties. The omniscient agent is epistemically ideal; the non-omniscient agent who nevertheless obeys both synchronic and diachronic norms (e.g. probabilism and conditionalization) does worse, epistemically, than the omniscient agent, but better than someone who only obeys synchronic norms, who in turn does better than someone who sometimes disobeys the synchronic norms because of biases and delusions.

Where in this ranking do we draw the line between what's necessary for *rationality* and what isn't? It is uncontroversial that omniscience is epistemically ideal but not necessary for rationality. It is also uncontroversial that some involuntary biases and delusions are sufficient for irrationality. So the question is whether to draw the rationality line between 1 and 2 (with the friend of diachronic norms) or between 2 and 3 (with the foe of diachronic norms).

The time-slicer worries that requiring 2 for rationality slippery-slopes into requiring 1. She perhaps allows that it's epistemically better to conform to diachronic norms, but maintains that it's not necessary for rationality. Otherwise, what's to stop us from requiring agents simply to be more knowledgeable? Meanwhile, the proponent of diachronic norms worries that permitting 3 slippery-slopes into permitting 4. If we treat information loss (forgetting or discarding evidence) as rationally permissible, what's to stop us from permitting other involuntary biases and delusions? Why not allow that it's epistemically rational to fully believe a contradiction, so long as you can't help it? Most – perhaps all – forms of irrationality are involuntary; should we thereby conclude that no one, or virtually no one, is ever irrational?

What's important to note, however, is that friends and foes of diachronic norms can still agree on this ranking – part of a theory of overall epistemic value[16] – while disputing the *deontic* epistemic theory. It's at the deontic stage that we make judgments of rational permissibility or impermissibility. But if the diachronic facts make a difference to the theory of overall value, then there are diachronic epistemic norms that affect the comparative assessment of epistemic acts.

Suppose we all accept that the agent who loses information (by forgetting or discarding evidence) is doing worse, with respect to overall (not final) epistemic value, than the agent whose credences only change by rational update on new evidence. Then for my purposes, it doesn't matter whether we call the information loss irrational or rational. It might be that diachronic norms do not factor into the deontic theory: the determination of whether an agent is on–off rational. Still, though, diachronic facts are relevant to an agent's epistemic status. You might think that rationality is comparative or comes in degrees, or you might accept an on–off view of rationality. But at the level over overall epistemic value – where comparative or degreed rationality comes into play – the ranking above are plausible, and plausibly reflect diachronic norms.

2.5. Subjective and objective epistemic value

I have emphasized that there's a clear sense in which the subject who violates diachronic norms is doing worse, epistemically, than the subject who doesn't. But the time-slice internalist might object: the person who happens to *know* less is also doing worse, epistemically, than a person who knows more. But that doesn't mean that the person who knows less is *irrational*. So, the time-slice internalist might conclude, not all epistemic norms are norms of rationality.

There is a natural way of drawing a distinction between norms of epistemic rationality and other epistemic norms. In the practical realm we sometimes distinguish 'objective' and 'subjective' norms. In epistemology, it's often accepted that objective epistemic value is determined as a function of accuracy: the value of believing (or having high credence in) true propositions and disbelieving (or having low credence in) false proposition. The norms of rationality, by contrast, are subjective in some sense to be spelled out. At minimum, they do not require omniscience. Where do diachronic norms fall on this divide? Which of the epistemic norms are norms of epistemic rationality?

I'll suggest two hypotheses about how to address this question that are friendly to the proponent of diachronic norms.

The first is the less conservative. There is no binary subjective/objective divide. Motivations for this view have received more attention in the semantics of deontic modals (e.g. Kolodny and MacFarlane (2010)), but are generalizable beyond the linguistic and the practical. Diachronic norms are more 'subjective' than the norm of truth, but more 'objective' than some synchronic norms (like probabilism), which are in turn more 'objective' than other synchronic norms. Defending this hypothesis is outside of the scope of this paper.

Second, and more conservatively:

Schwarz (2012) defended conditionalization with this analogy: suppose we want to build a robot to gather information for us in whatever environment it ends up in. We have the option of programming it to obey diachronic evidentialism. Should we? It seems fairly obvious that we should. Then the robot will not lose information, and so will end up with more information.

One of the ways of cashing this out: the epistemic norms are the constraints that characterize the epistemic states of the ideal information gatherer. The ideal information gatherer is non-omniscient; none of her beliefs is guaranteed to be true except on the basis of evidence.

Epistemic rationality involves having beliefs that approximate the truth as much as possible, given our non-omniscience. On this view, though, there's no reason to think of diachronic norms as somehow external to rationality. Retaining information will, by and large, help you keep your belief state more accurate.

Accuracy-centered epistemology (e.g. James (1896); more recently, in epistemic utility theory, Rosenkrantz (1981), Joyce 1998, 2009, Greaves and Wallace (2006), Leitgeb and Pettigrew (2010)) supports this hypothesis. Objective epistemic norms are encoded in scoring rules, which characterize objective epistemic utility in terms of gradational accuracy. Subjective norms are decision rules, e.g. expected inaccuracy minimization or accuracy dominance avoidance. These norms can constrain not only doxastic states at a time, but the relation between doxastic states at different times. Epistemic rationality is a matter of believing in accordance with epistemic decision rules that tend to promote accuracy. Accuracy-centered epistemic utility theory provides a formal precisification of the hypothesis that the norms of rationality are the norms of the ideal information gatherer.[17]

3. Rational information loss

3.1. Losing information to gain information

There are complaints against conditionalization that have nothing to do with information loss: for example, that it only allows update when evidence justifies credence 1 in some new proposition (unlike, e.g. Jeffrey conditionalization), and that it doesn't allow believers to lower their credence in any proposition from 1 even in circumstances where no forgetting takes place (e.g. in Arntzenius (2003) Shangri-La example). But neither of these objections extends to diachronic evidentialism; so these considerations simply invite us to find a suitable diachronic replacement for conditionalization.

There's another argument against conditionalization that extends to diachronic evidentialism. Like Arntzenius, Christensen (2000) argues that we're not merely rationally permitted to violate conditionalization, but in fact in some cases conditionalization violations are rationally mandatory. Unlike Arntzenius' argument, Christensen's argument involves rationally mandatory information loss.[18]

First, note that it can't be that losing information *necessarily* makes an agent's belief state less accurate. For example: suppose that, by chance, you happen to forget only misleading evidence. Losing information thereby makes your belief state more accurate. But retaining information makes it more likely that your credences will be more accurate, roughly speaking. For example, it increases the expected accuracy of your credences.

Now, conditionalizing on new information is an example of pure information gain. And forgetting and discarding evidence are examples of pure information loss. But what should we say about mixed cases?

We can define an *informational tradeoff* as a case where an agent gains some information at the cost of losing some other information. If taking an informational tradeoff can be rationally permissible, then some strong diachronic epistemic norms are false. For example, conditionalization is false: rational informational tradeoffs would require rational information loss.

Christensen (2000) uses an example with the following structure to argue against the view that there are diachronic epistemic norms:

Doxastic downloader

Suppose you know that someone knows more than you about some topic. You know a few things she doesn't know, but on the whole she's more informed on the topic. Unfortunately, it would be gauche to ask her about the topic. Fortunately, you have the option of using a doxastic downloader to replace your credences on the topic with hers. Is it permissible for you to do so?

Christensen invites us to judge that it is indeed permissible.

It should be clear that this is at best an argument against *some* diachronic norms, not against diachronic rationality in general. But one interesting fact about this case is that if you take the tradeoff, you violate conditionalization – but you also increase the expected accuracy of your credences. So, if epistemic rationality consists in maximizing expected accuracy, then conditionalization can't be a norm of epistemic rationality.

Note that there are two possible objections one could make against conditionalization on the basis of this example.

Objection #1. Taking the tradeoff maximizes expected accuracy. So you're rationally required to violate conditionalization. This shouldn't trouble the proponent of conditionalization. The norms of epistemic rationality govern only epistemic states, not actions like using a credence downloader. If we were rationally required to perform actions that maximize the expected accuracy of our credal states, then we would, for example, be rationally required to perform constant experiments, to read all of Wikipedia, etc.

Objection #2. If you do take the tradeoff, your resulting epistemic state is rational. So it must be permissible to violate conditionalization. This objection is more troubling for the proponent of conditionalization. If this objection is correct, then conditionalization is false. At most, conditionalization holds across periods of time where no worthy informational tradeoffs are available.

There are the two options, then, for the proponent of diachronic norms:

(1) She can endorse conditionalization and reject the claim that there are epistemically rational informational tradeoffs.
(2) Alternatively, she can adopt diachronic norms that are more liberal that conditionalization.
There's little more to be said about the first option. Let's explore the second option. But first, we should say a little bit more about what expected accuracy is.

3.2. Epistemic utility theory

Epistemic utility theory formalizes the idea that rational credences are governed by epistemic decision rules that tend to promote epistemic utility. The aim of epistemic utility theory was to use the tools of decision theory, combined with an epistemic version of value, in order to give a foundational justification for various epistemic norms.

The most widely discussed epistemic utility functions are *gradational accuracy* measures. The accuracy of a credence is its nearness to the truth (by some measure). A credence function with maximal accuracy would assign credence 1 in all truths and credence 0 in all falsehoods. In other words, it would be omniscient.

Decision rules are adapted from decision theory, e.g. expected utility maximization and dominance avoidance. Paired with accuracy as the relevant measure of utility, we end up with epistemic decision rules:

Accuracy Dominance Avoidances: adopt a credence function that is not accuracy dominated. A credence function Cr dominates a credence function Cr' iff, at all worlds w in a possibility space $\mathcal{W}$, $U(Cr) > U(Cr')$.

Maximize Expected Accuracy: adopt a credence function that has maximal expected accuracy, by your own lights.[19] The expected accuracy of a credence function is standardly calculated as the sum of a credence function's accuracy in each world, weighted by the probability of that world. In symbols:

$$EU^{Cr}(Cr') = \sum_{w_i \in \mathcal{W}} Cr(w_i) U(Cr', w_i)$$

With each of these decision rules, various results can be proven. Greaves and Wallace (2006) and Leitgeb and Pettigrew (2010) proved that from an agent's own perspective, given the choice of all possible update policies, conditionalization uniquely maximizes expected accuracy. Similarly, Briggs (2013) and Robert and Williams (2006) argue that conditionalization provides an update strategy that is uniquely accuracy non-dominated. So, one might conclude hastily, in order to be an ideal information gatherer, your credences should update by conditionalization. Hereafter, we'll focus on expected accuracy maximization.

But the doxastic downloader case is intuitively a case where an agent is in a position to expect that some other credences than her own will maximize expected accuracy from her point of view. The agent rationally expects an increase in accuracy only if she updates by accepting an informational tradeoff, thereby violating conditionalization. Does that example conflict with the results of epistemic utility theory?

3.3. Assessing informational tradeoffs

No. There's no conflict between the idea that there could be rational informational tradeoffs (violating conditionalization) and the epistemic utility theoretic result that conditionalization is the only update policy that maximizes expected utility.

The reason: the epistemic utility theoretic results apply in cases where the relevant space of epistemic acts includes only credence functions, specified *de re*. But it's a feature of informational tradeoffs that you do not know, in advance, what credences you will adopt as a result of taking the tradeoff. (If you did, then you could update on that information directly, which would amount to pure information gain.) Indeed, on common assumptions,[20] it cannot be the case for any particular credence function that you can rationally assign it higher expected accuracy than your own credence function. But if you have the option of adopting some member of a set of possible credence functions – adopting a credence function specified *de dicto* as whichever satisfies some constraint – then that option can maximize expected accuracy from your perspective.

Let's consider a particular case of an informational tradeoff, specifying some of the details from the doxastic downloader case.

Coin toss

Suppose a particular coin is either fair or biased (with a $\frac{3}{4}$ heads bias), and it will land either heads or tails. You are uncertain about both matters. Now, you and your colleague start with the same priors:

$$w_{FH}: \text{fair, heads} \quad Cr_0(w_{FH}) = \frac{1}{4}$$

$$w_{FT}: \text{fair, tails} \quad Cr_0(w_{FT}) = \frac{1}{4}$$

$$w_{BH}: \text{biased, heads} \quad Cr_0(w_{BH}) = \frac{3}{8}$$

$$w_{BT}: \text{biased, tails} \quad Cr_0(w_{BT}) = \frac{1}{8}$$

Then you learn whether the coin lands heads or tails. Your colleague learns whether the coin is fair or biased. Both of you conditionalize on your respective evidence. You are not permitted to know the answers to both questions.

Suppose you learn that the coin lands heads. You have a credence downloader that will allow you to perform the informational tradeoff. Is it epistemically rational for you to give up your knowledge in order to gain your colleague's?

Applying expected utility maximization isn't straightforward. Since we don't know what your colleague has learned, we don't know which credence function to assess. So it's not obvious how we can even determine the expected accuracy of your colleague's credence function.

Here is my suggestion: we can introduce a new kind of epistemic action. Call it *learning the answer to a question*. Learning the answer to a question involves taking an epistemic option when you're not in a position to know what credence function it will result in your adopting.

This kind of epistemic tool isn't just for science fictional cases where you are offered informational tradeoffs. We can do other things with our new epistemic acts. For example, they can be useful in decisions over whether it would be more informative to perform one experiment or another, in circumstances where it is impossible, or at least costly, to perform both. However, these cases don't involve informational tradeoffs in the relevant sense: they don't involve partial information loss.

For a question Q (i.e. a partition over the set of epistemically possible worlds), let Cr_Q be Cr_0 conditionalized on whatever the true answer to Q is (that is, whichever proposition in Q is true at the world of assessment).

In our example, we can call whatever credence function your colleague has after learning whether the coin is biased or fair $Cr_{Q_{BF}}$. Note that '$Cr_{Q_{BF}}$' is a description: it picks out different credence functions in different worlds. Ex hypothesi, your colleague updates on B in B-worlds and on F in F-worlds.

Now, with a concrete example in hand, and a new tool (the epistemic act of learning the answer to a question), we can ask: should you take the tradeoff? We need to explain how to calculate the expected accuracy of $Cr_{Q_{BF}}$ from your point of view:

(1) Calculate the accuracy of Cr_B at B-worlds and Cr_F at F-worlds.
(2) Sum the values, weighted by their probability according to Cr_H. In symbols:

$$EU^{Cr_H}(Cr_{Q_{BF}}) = \sum_{w_i \in \mathcal{W}} Cr_H(w_i) U(Cr_{Q_{BF}}, w_i)$$

In this case, with plausible assumptions about the accuracy function U, taking the tradeoff maximizes expected accuracy. Retaining your current credences does not.[21]

This isn't surprising. Knowing that the coin landed heads isn't particularly informative about whether the coin is fair or biased, since it would be unsurprising either way. On the other hand, if you had instead learned that the coin had landed tails, then it would maximize expected accuracy to reject the tradeoff. After all, knowing that the coin landed tails gives you fairly strong evidence in support of the coin's being fair.

So, we have a concrete case where taking an informational tradeoff maximizes expected accuracy, and a decision rule for assessing informational tradeoffs.

3.4. Discussion

Again, the defender of diachronic norms has two options for responding to an objection like this. If she endorses conditionalization, then she must reject the claim that it's rational to accept informational tradeoffs. This might involve rejecting the idea that we should perform those epistemic acts that maximize expected accuracy, or it might involve rejecting the idea that taking an informational tradeoff is appropriately understood as an epistemic act.

On the other hand, if we allow informational tradeoffs as epistemic options, then accepting tradeoffs can lead to maximizing expected accuracy. And if we accept that this is rational, then we should reject conditionalization. The defender of diachronic rational norms should replace conditionalization with a more liberal diachronic rule.

These two options provide us with different pictures of what an ideally rational agent's credences will look like over time. On the conditionalization picture, the ideal rational agent's stock of information will strictly increase. But if we allow for violations of conditionalization in informational tradeoffs, then the ideally rational agent will in some circumstances take epistemic risks. These risks have two salient features that distinguish them from obeying conditionalization. First, they involve sure loss of information; second, they may lead to decreases in the agent's expected accuracy (from the perspective of her post-tradeoff credences).

Here is a candidate liberal diachronic norm (which is a variant on diachronic evidentialism):

Liberal norm: An ideally rational agent's credences change only in order to maximize their expected accuracy. Note that for cases of pure information gain, conditionalization will still hold. Furthermore, rational tradeoffs arguably only occur in sci-fi cases.[22] In ordinary cases, the verdicts of the liberal norm will coincide with the verdicts of the traditional, strict norm:

Strict norm (diachronic evidentialism): An ideally rational agent's credences only change in response to new evidence.

4. Conclusion

I've argued that there is a conflict between diachronic norms of epistemic rationality and a form of epistemic internalism. I've also argued that diachronically coherent agents are epistemically better. We should think of epistemic rationality as providing constraints that allow us to be more informed about our environment, whatever our environment happens to be like.

The diachronic norms I've advocated are at a middle ground between epistemic internalism and externalism: they are sensitive to facts that are external to the time-slice, but not necessarily external to the person. Contrast this sort of view with process reliabilism, which is concerned with whether some belief-forming process *actually* conduces toward the truth. Whether it does will depend on contingent facts about the agent's environment. A norm like expected accuracy maximization is concerned with whether an update method is *likely* to conduce toward the truth, by the believer's own lights.

If we take the option of maintaining conditionalization, we are also given at a middle ground between epistemic conservatism and evidentialism. Like conservatism, conditionalization permits us to continuing to believe a proposition if we already believe it (with certainty). In fact, conditionalization requires it. But unlike conservatism, conditionalization doesn't permit continuing to believe a proposition after the evidence for it has been forgotten. Conditionalization requires remembering the evidence as well. Conditionalization doesn't permit violations of diachronic evidentialism. Hence, what we're required to believe is always determined by what our evidence supports.

Notes

1. That is, an rational agent's credences conform to the following axioms: where $\mathcal{W}$ is the set of all worlds under consideration (which I suppose throughout this paper to be finite):

   (1) *Nonnegativity:* for all propositions $A \subseteq \mathcal{W}$, $Cr(A) \geq 0$
   (2) *Normalization:* $Cr(\mathcal{W}) = 1$
   (3) *Finite additivity:* if A and B are disjoint, then $Cr(A \vee B) = Cr(A) + Cr(B)$

2. $Cr(A \mid B)$ is usually defined as follows:

$$Cr(A \mid B) = \frac{Cr(A, B)}{Cr(B)}$$

3. Indeed, while I will defend conditionalization against the time-slice internalist's objections, it seems to me obvious that *de se* information of the sort discussed in Arntzenius (2003)s Shangri-La case are successful objections to conditionalization. Note, however, that these cases are not counterexamples to the norm I call 'diachronic evidentialism.'

4. Note that while Meacham argues that there is a conflict between conditionalization and internalism, and provides a synchronic alternative to

conditionalization, he is (at least in his (2010) not committed to the denial of traditional diachronic conditionalization.
5. These interpretations depend on a non-tensed reading of the principles, which I take to be charitable (since otherwise their synchronic commitments would be undefended).
6. Christensen's objection to diachronic norms, which I discuss in Section 3, doesn't require appeal to either mentalist or access internalism. Williamson and Moss both explicitly reject access internalism. Note: if evidence need not be accessible, then it's no longer clear what motivates restricting the evidence an agent's belief states should respect to evidence that is internal to a time-slice. Moss (p.c.) suggests that this restriction is not motivated by any more general principle and is normatively primitive.
7. Meacham (forthcoming) distinguishes *sequential* and *interval* updating rules. A sequential updating rule tells an agent how to adjust her doxastic attitudes whenever she receives a piece of new information. An interval updating rule tells an agent how her credences should harmonize over arbitrary intervals, given the cumulative information that she receives during an interval. Conditionalization has both sequential and updating interpretations. Both are properly diachronic. Interval conditionalization is a stronger norm than sequential conditionalization, since the latter doesn't rule out changes in belief that aren't responses to new evidence: for example, forgetting.
8. Hedden (2015) accepts that such an agent is rational.
9. Of course, it's entirely appropriate that an agent's beliefs should continuously change *a little* all the time: she should update on new information about, e.g. the passage of time, new events that she encounters, etc. But in the example I'm concerned with, a much greater proportion of her beliefs change, and not simply because she's exposed to new evidence.
10. See Williamson (2000) for the canonical defense of this identity.
11. On conceptions of evidence where one's own beliefs aren't evidence, there need be no epistemic norms on evidence possession – only on doxastic responses to evidence.
12. In a 2012 AAP talk (no manuscript currently exists), Wolfgang Schwarz argued, similarly, that the motivation for rejecting diachronic norms derives from the idea that they cannot be action-guiding, and this turns on an illicit conflation of the practical with the epistemic.
13. Agents can take actions to induce beliefs, e.g. gathering evidence, or take actions to slowly indoctrinate themselves over time. But there is an important sense in which one cannot believe a proposition merely by trying.
14. In Bayesian terms, this would amount to obeying conditionalization with respect to every past time-slice. This is a simplification: again, *de se* information and its effects on *de dicto* information make clear that lifelong conditionalization is not epistemically ideal. I will (temporarily) speak as though conforming to lifelong conditionalization is epistemically better than not doing so for ease of exposition (and because it's not obvious what the best update rule for de se information is).
15. I don't specify which diachronic constraints in the interest of generality (but at the possible expense of clarity).
16. It's consistent with this hypothesis that we treat *final* epistemic value as, e.g. true or comparative gradational accuracy.
17. As Titelbaum (2006) pointed out, the Greaves and Wallace (2006) defense of conditionalization isn't properly understood as diachronic. Rather, it provides

a justification for *planning* or *intending* to update by conditionalization in light of future evidence. But imagine we are programming our robot to be an ideal information gatherer. We have the option of programming it to plan to update by conditionalization and the option of programming it actually to update by conditionalization. We will choose the latter. Programming our robot to update by conditionalization is the best means of gathering information, from the (third personal) perspective of us, the theorists.
18. Fuller discussion of Arntzenius' counterexample to conditionalization would require framework for de se belief update, which would take the present discussion too far afield.
19. Carr (1997) argues against the conception of expected accuracy used by epistemic utility theorists. For the purposes of addressing this objection to diachronic rationality, though, I will take the appeal to accuracy at face value.
20. Namely, that epistemic utility functions must be *proper* in the sense that they yield the result that any coherent credence function maximizes expected accuracy by its own lights.
21. See Joyce (2009) and Leitgeb and Pettigrew (2010) for plausible constraints on epistemic utility functions.
22. One might make the case that clutter avoidance is a more psychologically realistic version of an informational tradeoff; see Harman (1986).

Disclosure statement

No potential conflict of interest was reported by the authors.

References

Arntzenius, Frank. 2003. "Some Problems for Conditionalization and Reflection." *The Journal of Philosophy* 100 (7): 356–370.
Berker, Selim. 2013. "The Rejection of Epistemic Consequentialism." *Philosophical Issues* 23 (1): 363–387.
Briggs, Rachael. (manuscript) "An Accuracy-dominance Argument for Conditionalization."
Carr, Jennifer. (manuscript) "How to Expect When You're Expecting."
Christensen, David. 2000. "Diachronic Coherence versus Epistemic Impartiality." *Philosophical Review* 109 (3): 349–371.
Friedman, Jane. (manuscript) "Inquiry and Belief."
Greaves, Hilary, and David Wallace. 2006. "Justifying Conditionalization: Conditionalization Maximizes Expected Epistemic Utility." *Mind* 115 (459): 607–632.
Harman, Gilbert. 1986. *Change in View: Principles of Reasoning*, Cambridge, MA: MIT Press.
Hedden, Brian. 2013. "Options and Diachronic Tragedy." *Philosophy and Phenomenological Research* 87 (1): 423–451.
Hedden, Brian. 2015. "Time-slice Rationality." *Mind* 124 (494): 449–491.
James, William. 1896. "The Sentiment of Rationality". In *The Will to Believe and Other Essays in Popular Philosophy*, 63–110. Norwood, MA: Synthèse.
Joyce, James. 1998. "A Nonpragmatic Vindication of Probabilism." *Philosophy of Science* 65 (4): 575–603.
Joyce, James, Franz, Huber and Christoph, Schmidt-Petri, eds. 2009. "Accuracy and coherence: Prospects for an alethic epistemology of partial belief". Vol. 342, In *Degrees of Belief*, New York: Synthese, Springer, 263–297.

Kolodny, Niko, and John MacFarlane, . 2010. "Ifs and Oughts." *The Journal of Philosophy* 107 (3): 115–143.

Leitgeb, Hannes, and Richard Pettigrew. 2010. "An Objective Justification of Bayesianism: The Consequences of Minimizing Inaccuracy." *Philosophy of Science* 77 (2): 236–272.

McGrath, Matthew. 2007. "Memory and Epistemic Conservatism." *Synthese* 157 (1): 1–24.

Meacham, Chris. Forthcoming. "Understanding Conditionalization." Vol. I.

Meacham, Christopher J.G., Tamar Szabo, Gendler, John, Hawthorne, eds. 2010. "Unravelling the tangled web: Continuity, internalism, non-uniqueness and self-locating beliefs". Vol. 3, In *Oxford Studies in Epistemology*, 86–125. Oxford: Oxford University Press.

Moss, Sarah. 2014. "Credal Dilemmas." *Noûs* 48 (3): 665–683.

Rosenkrantz, R. 1981. *Foundations and Applications of Inductive Probability*, Atascadero, CA: Ridgeview Press.

Schwarz, Wolfgang. 2012. *Worms first! in defence of diachronic rationality*, Wollongong: Unpublished AAP talk

Talbott, W. J. 1991. "Two Principles of Bayesian Epistemology." *Philosophical Studies* 62 (2): 135–150.

Titelbaum, Michael. 2006. "Comments on greaves & wallace". In *Pacific APA*,

Robert, J. and G. Williams, . (manuscript) "A Nonpragmatic Dominance Argument for Conditionalization."

Williamson, Timothy. 2000. *Knowledge and its Limits*, Oxford: Oxford University Press.

Understanding Conditionalization

Christopher J. G. Meacham

Department of Philosophy, University of Massachusetts, Amherst, MA, USA.

ABSTRACT
At the heart of the Bayesianism is a rule, Conditionalization, which tells us how to update our beliefs. Typical formulations of this rule are underspecified. This paper considers how, exactly, this rule should be formulated. It focuses on three issues: when a subject's evidence is received, whether the rule prescribes sequential or interval updates, and whether the rule is narrow or wide scope. After examining these issues, it argues that there are two distinct and equally viable versions of Conditionalization to choose from. And which version we choose has interesting ramifications, bearing on issues such as whether Conditionalization can handle continuous evidence, and whether Jeffrey Conditionalization is really a generalization of Conditionalization.

1. Introduction

At the heart of the Bayesian account of rationality is a rule – Conditionalization – which tells us how to update our beliefs in light of evidence. At a first pass, one might characterize this rule as follows:

Conditionalization: If a subject with credences cr gets evidence E, she should adopt new credences cr_E such that $cr_E(\cdot) = cr(\cdot|E)$, if defined. This formulation of the rule is adequate for most purposes, but it leaves open a number of questions. And, by answering these questions in different ways, we get different versions of Conditionalization.

In this paper, I'll explore these questions. My focus here will be on questions regarding the logical form of Conditionalization. There are, of course, many other interesting questions to ask about the rule, such as how to understand the notions of 'credence' or 'evidence' the rule employs. But I won't try to address those kinds of questions here. Instead, I'll restrict myself to questions regarding logical form.[1]

The rest of this paper will proceed as follows. In Section 2, I'll sketch some background. In the following sections, I'll consider three questions left open by formulations of Conditionalization like the one given above. In Section 3, I'll consider the time of evidence question. In Section 4, I'll consider the sequential vs. interval updating question. In Section 6, I'll consider the narrow vs. wide scope question. For each question, I'll present and assess some plausible answers. For two of these three questions, I'll argue that one of the answers is better than the rest. But for one of these questions – the sequential vs. interval updating Question – I'll suggest that there are two viable answers. Thus I'll suggest that, at the end of the day, there are two viable versions of Conditionalization for us to choose from.

My examination of these three questions does not, of course, guarantee that there aren't further open questions regarding the logical form of Conditionalization that haven't been answered. In order to do this, we would need to provide a logically precise formulation of Conditionalization. So to ensure that no more details of formulation are left unspecified, I'll conclude in Section 7 by presenting two formal characterizations of Conditionalization, one corresponding to each of the two viable versions of Conditionalization mentioned above. (Readers who would like to be forewarned about what formulations of Conditionalization I'll endorse can skip ahead and skim Section 7 before reading the rest of the paper.)

2. Background

Let a subject's *credences* be an assignment of real numbers to propositions representing the subject's confidence in those propositions, where an assignment of 0 indicates that the subject is virtually certain the proposition is false, and an assignment of 1 indicates that the subject is virtually certain the proposition is true.[2] Note that we are not assuming that a subject's credences assign numbers to every proposition; there may be some propositions in which a subject doesn't have a credence.

One popular normative constraint on credences is *Probabilism*, a constraint on what a subject's credences should be like at a time:

Probabilism: A subject's credences should be probabilistic.[3] A second popular normative constraint on credences is *Conditionalization*, a constraint on how a subject's credences should change over time in light of evidence. At a first pass, we can characterize Conditionalization as follows:

Conditionalization: If a subject with credences cr gets evidence E, she should adopt new credences cr_E such that $cr_E(\cdot) = cr(\cdot|E)$, if defined.

I've appended the '(v0)' to this formulation to highlight that this is only a first pass approximation; we'll consider more precise formulations of Conditionalization in the sections to come.[4] Intuitively, Conditionalization tells us that upon receiving evidence E, we should assign E a credence of 1 and renormalize; that is, shift all of our credence to E, and distribute that credence among the propositions entailing E in a way that keeps the ratios between them the same.

One common complaint about Conditionalization is that it requires us to adopt a credence of 1 in our evidence. In some situations, it's been suggested, it seems like we get 'uncertain' evidence – evidence to which we should assign a credence of less than 1. For example, if a subject sees her friend through the window, and the lighting outside is poor, then it might seem like she should assign the proposition that her friend is outside a value less than 1. Worries of this kind motivate another popular normative constraint on credences, *Jeffrey Conditionalization*.

Like Conditionalization, Jeffrey Conditionalization is a constraint on how a subject's credences should change over time in light of evidence. But on this picture, one's evidence isn't a proposition E; instead, it's a weighted partition of propositions $S = \{(E_1, x_1), (E_2, x_2), \ldots\}$ (where $E_1 - E_n$ are mutually exclusive and jointly exhaustive propositions, and the weights $x_1 - x_n$ are real numbers in the [0,1]-interval that sum to 1). Given such evidence, Jeffrey Conditionalization tells us to update as follows:

Jeffrey Conditionalization (v0): If a subject with credences cr gets evidence partition $S = \{(E_1, x_1), (E_2, x_2), \ldots\}$ she should adopt new credences cr_S such that:

$$cr_S(\cdot) = \sum_i x_i \cdot cr(\cdot | E_i), \text{ if defined.}$$

Intuitively, Jeffrey Conditionalization tells us that upon receiving evidence partition S, we should assign each E_i a credence of x_i, and then renormalize; that is, move our credence in the E_is to the indicated amount, and then distribute the credence assigned to each E_i among the propositions entailing E_i in a way that keeps the ratios between them the same.

Jeffrey Conditionalization is generally taken to be a generalization of Conditionalization that yields Conditionalization as a special case. This is because when we plug in simple evidence partitions of the form $S = \{(E, 1), (\neg E, 0)\}$, we get:

$$cr_S(\cdot) = \sum_i x_i \cdot cr(\cdot | E_i),$$
$$= 1 \cdot cr(\cdot | E) + 0 \cdot cr(\cdot | \neg E),$$
$$= cr(\cdot | E),$$

which is just what Conditionalization prescribes.

Call a view *Bayesian* if it takes both Probabilism and Conditionalization to impose normative constraints on credences. For the purposes of this paper, I'll be assessing the question of how to understand Conditionalization under the assumption that some Bayesian view is correct.

Although the discussion in this paper is couched in terms of questions about Conditionalization, the same questions can be raised regarding Jeffrey Conditionalization. Likewise, the same answers to these questions can be offered, and the same considerations for and against these answers obtain. (With one exception in Section 4.1 – but I'll flag this difference when we come to it.) So, although the following discussion will focus on Conditionalization, most of the conclusions of this paper will apply to both updating rules.

3. The time of evidence question

Conditionalization (v0) makes reference to three events: the subject having credences cr, the subject receiving evidence E, and the subject adopting new credences cr_E.[5] How are the times of these events – call them $t(cr)$, $t(E)$ and $t(cr_E)$ – related?[6] Certain constraints are clear: the time at which a subject adopts cr_E should not be before the time at which she receives E as evidence, and she should adopt cr_E at some point after she has cr. But are there other constraints on the timing of these events?

Let's focus here on the relation between $t(E)$ and $t(cr_E)$. (We'll consider the relation between these times and $t(cr)$ at the end of Section 3.1.)

Q3. The Time of Evidence Question: How is the time at which the subject receives her evidence related to the time at which she should adopt her new credences?[7]

Answers to this question fall into two camps. First, one might hold that subjects should adopt their new credences after they've received their new evidence, so that $t(E) < t(cr_E)$. Because time is *dense* – given any two distinct times there will be some time in-between – it follows that if $t(E) < t(cr_E)$, there are times in-between $t(E)$ and $t(cr_E)$. That is, there will be a temporal gap between $t(E)$ and $t(cr_E)$:

Answer 1 (Posterior). The subject should adopt her new credences some finite amount of time after she gets her evidence. We can make this understanding explicit by adding times to our formulation, following the usual convention of using time indices to reflect the differences between these times (e.g. t_1 is one unit of time after t_0, according to some linear measure):

Conditionalization (v1.1): If a subject with credences cr gets evidence E at t_0, she should adopt new credences cr_E at t_1 such that $cr_E(\cdot) = cr(\cdot|E)$, if defined.

Second, one might hold that subjects should receive E and adopt cr_E simultaneously:

Answer 2 (Concurrent). The subject should adopt her new credences at the same time as she gets her evidence. Again, we can make this understanding explicit by inserting the appropriate times into our formulation of the rule:

Conditionalization (v1.2): If a subject with credences cr gets evidence E at t_1, she should adopt new credences cr_E at t_1 such that $cr_E(\cdot) = cr(\cdot|E)$, if defined.

3.1. The time of evidence question: assessing the answers

Now, let's turn to assess each of these answers.

The posterior answer, that the subject should adopt cr_E some amount of time after receiving E, leads to implausible verdicts. Consider a subject who receives evidence E at t_0. Given the posterior answer the subject shouldn't adopt cr_E until some later time t_1. And, if she adopts cr_E at t_0 she's epistemically deficient for having 'jumped the gun'. But this seems like an odd verdict. After all, a subject who adopts cr_E at t_0 is in a strictly better position, epistemically speaking, than the subject who doesn't – she's taken all of her evidence into account. And, it's hard to see why it's epistemically irrational to take all of one's evidence into account as soon as one has it.[8]

The posterior answer is also in tension with the popular account of evidence endorsed by Howson and Urbach (1993), where a subject's evidence is the strongest proposition in which they have a credence of 1. Suppose a subject receives evidence E at t_0. What should her credences be at t_0? Since she isn't required to adopt her new credences until t_1, the most natural option is to maintain that her credences at t_0 are still cr. But, since cr generally won't assign 1 to E, this option is incompatible with Howson and Urbach's picture of evidence. Of course, there are other options one might try, but none of them are satisfactory. For example, one might maintain that at t_0 a subject should assign a credence of 1 to E (as Howson and Urbach's account requires), but should otherwise assign the same values as cr does. But since this credence function will generally violate the probability axioms, this option's incompatible with Probabilism. Alternatively, one might maintain that at t_0 a subject should adopt cr_E. But this is to abandon the posterior answer for the concurrent answer, as this entails that one should receive E and adopt cr_E simultaneously. So if we want to hold on to the posterior answer, it seems we must say that the subject's credences at t_0 should be cr. And this is incompatible with Howson and Urbach's account of evidence.

Now consider the concurrent answer, that subjects should adopt cr_E at the same time as they receive E. One worry for the concurrent answer is that it places too strong a demand on subjects like us. In particular, one might worry that this answer is incompatible with the principle that ought implies can. If subjects like us aren't capable of updating instantaneously, then how can we be obligated to do it?

Of course, this is not a fair criticism of the concurrent answer if the posterior answer also has this problem. And, as given, the posterior answer doesn't take the cognitive capacities of subjects into account either. It states that a subject's new credences should be adopted some amount of time after the subject gets her evidence, but it doesn't say anything about what this later time is, or whether it's possible for the subject to adopt those credences at that time.

But one might naturally think that one can modify the posterior answer so that it does take the cognitive capabilities of subjects into consideration. And if, by modifying the posterior answer, we can get a plausible formulation of Conditionalization that avoids these kinds of ought-implies-can worries, then we have a reason to favor the posterior answer over the concurrent answer. Let's see whether this is true: by modifying the posterior answer, can we get a plausible version of Conditionalization that avoids these kinds of ought-implies-can worries?

Here's a natural way to modify the posterior answer to take the updating time lag of cognitively limited subjects into account:

Answer 1a (Posterior-a). The subject should adopt her new credences *as soon as possible* after receiving her evidence.

Conditionalization (v1.1a): If a subject with credences cr gets evidence E at t_0, she should adopt new credences cr_E at t_1 such that $cr_E(\cdot) = cr(\cdot|E)$ (if defined), where t_1 is the earliest time following t_0 at which the subject is capable of adopting cr_E. This formulation of Conditionalization is sensitive to the temporal limitations of subjects with limited cognitive capacities. But it yields inconsistent prescriptions. Suppose a subject with prior credences cr gets evidence E at t_0, and evidence F at $t_{1/2}$. And suppose the subject is cognitively limited in such a way as to not be able to update her credences until t_1. But at t_1, she's capable of changing her credences in any way she likes. Because the subject gets E at t_0, Conditionalization (v1.1a) requires her to adopt new credences equal to $cr(\cdot|E)$ at t_1, since t_1 is the first time at which she's capable of updating on E. Likewise, because the subject gets F at $t_{1/2}$, Conditionalization (v1.1a) requires her to adopt new credences equal to $cr(\cdot|F)$ at t_1, since her credences at $t_{1/2}$ will still be cr, and t_1 is the first time at which she's capable of updating on F. But these two prescriptions will usually be inconsistent.

The problem here is that Conditionalization (v1.1a) doesn't take into account the possibility that a subject might receive further evidence besides E between t_0 and t_1. So, we might repair our formulation of Conditionalization by adding a clause which rules out this possibility:

Conditionalization (v1.1b): If a subject with credences cr gets evidence E at t_0, she should adopt new credences cr_E at t_1 such that $cr_E(\cdot) = cr(\cdot|E)$ (if defined), where t_1 is the earliest time following t_0 at which the subject is capable of adopting cr_E, and the subject doesn't get any other evidence between t_0 and t_1. This rule avoids making inconsistent prescriptions in the kinds of 'multiple evidence cases' described above by simply falling silent in such cases. But an adequate formulation of Conditionalization should give us some guidance in these cases – it shouldn't just fall silent. So this rule is too weak.

We can get around this problem by adding a further clause which tells us what credences to adopt in these cases:

Conditionalization (v1.1c): If a subject with credences cr gets evidence E at t_0, she should adopt new credences cr_E at t_1 such that $cr_E(\cdot) = cr(\cdot|E)$ (if defined), where t_1 is the earliest time following t_0 at which the subject is capable of adopting cr_E, and assuming she hasn't gotten any other evidence between t_0 and t_1. If she has gotten other evidence, she should update on the conjunction of all of the evidence $E_1 - E_n$ she's received up to t_1; i.e. she should adopt credences $cr_{E_1...E_n}(\cdot) = cr(\cdot|E_1 \wedge ... \wedge E_n)$.

This formulation avoids the inconsistent prescriptions worry, and offers prescriptions in multiple evidence cases. But it avoids these worries by sliding back toward the concurrent answer to the time of evidence question. For, like the concurrent answer, Conditionalization (v1.1c) effectively takes into account all of the evidence the subject receives up until the time at which she should adopt her new credences. And in doing so, Conditionalization (v1.1c) runs afoul of the same kinds of ought-implies-can worries that prompted these modifications of Conditionalization in the first place. Consider a multiple evidence case like the one described above, but with the following modification: at t_1, the subject isn't capable of changing her credences in any way one likes. Instead, she can only update on one of the pieces of evidence she's received, and so can only adopt new credences equal to either $cr(\cdot|E)$ or $cr(\cdot|F)$. Since Conditionalization (v1.1c) requires the subject to adopt $cr(\cdot|E \wedge F)$, such a subject isn't capable of satisfying the prescriptions the rule makes.

One might continue to finesse the formulation of Conditionalization, but there are some more general reasons why this strategy won't work. First, the intuitive idea we're trying to capture is that subjects should update on as much as they can, as soon as they can. But in order to capture this idea, a rule would need to be considerably more complex than the formulations offered above, having to provide verdicts regarding choices between updating on different batches of evidence, choices between updating sooner on less evidence versus updating later on more, and so on. And it's hard to see how any such rule could remain similar enough to the formulations given above to plausibly be identified with Conditionalization, the norm that people have been talking about in the Bayesian literature.

Second, it's not clear that subjects *should* update on their evidence as soon as they can. For example, suppose a subject who gets evidence E also violates some other epistemic norm, such as the Principal Principle – roughly, the claim that your credences should line up with what you think the chances are.[9] And suppose she is only capable of doing one thing at a time – either updating on E, or altering her credences so that they satisfy the Principal Principle. In this case, it's not clear that she should update as soon as she can – it could well be that she should alter her credences to satisfy the Principal Principle first. So even the general idea that subjects should conditionalize on their evidence 'as soon as they can' seems too simplistic to yield the desired prescriptions, given the variety of situations and cognitive limitations facing imperfect subjects.

To sum up, in order to make allowances for the restricted capacities of cognitively limited subjects, we need a very complex updating rule. And no plausible understanding of Conditionalization is this complex.

The moral is that it's a mistake to think of Conditionalization as a norm which is supposed to provide guidance to cognitively limited subjects. Instead, following Christensen (2004), we should think of Conditionalization as an ideal toward which to aim, a description of optimal performance in the epistemic realm.[10]

To borrow Christensen's analogy, we should think of Bayesian norms as like the norms describing perfect tournament chess play. Better tournament chess players can make better moves in less time, and in the limit, ideal tournament chess players would make perfect moves in no time. But even though this is a good description of perfect tournament chess play, we wouldn't expect any actual subject to be able to live up to this ideal. These 'ideal performance' norms aren't the kinds of norms to which ought implies can generally applies. And once we properly understand Conditionalization as an ideal performance norm, we can see that ought-implies-can worries regarding it are misplaced.[11]

A different worry that one might raise for the concurrent answer is that it's incompatible with plausible 'procedural' requirements on rational belief. Following Simon (1976), let us distinguish between two kinds of rational requirements: *substantive* rational requirements, which concern the rationality of the result, and *procedural* rational requirements, which concern the rationality of the process by which one obtains those results. Thus, when assessing whether a subject is epistemically rational, we might not only want her to have the right beliefs (i.e. to satisfy the relevant substantive requirements), but also to come to have those beliefs in the right way (i.e. to satisfy the relevant procedural requirements).

Conditionalization imposes a substantive requirement on rational updating: it requires subjects to come to have the right beliefs given their evidence and prior beliefs. Conditionalization doesn't care about how subjects came to have those beliefs – it doesn't care whether their beliefs were formed by reflecting on their evidence or whether their beliefs were formed by random quantum mechanical fluctuations. Now, one might think there are further requirements on rational updating beyond those imposed by Conditionalization. For example, one might also take there to be procedural requirements which require that a subject's evidence be the cause of her changing her beliefs in this way, or require that she come to have her new beliefs by reasoning about her evidence. And, one might worry that the concurrent answer to the time of evidence question is incompatible with such procedural requirements. For if a subject needs to update on her evidence instantaneously, then it doesn't seem like she *can* come to have those credences in the right way – via some causal process initiated by the receipt of her evidence, or by reasoning in light of her evidence. For any such process requires a non-zero amount of time.[12]

But this worry is misplaced. For these substantive and procedural requirements aren't actually in conflict. There isn't anything logically incoherent about a subject who instantaneously comes to have the right beliefs for the right reasons. It's true that subjects like *us* can't do this. But that's only a reason to think that these can't be rational requirements if we're assuming something like ought implies can. And, as we've seen, once Conditionalization is understood in the right way – as a description of optimal performance – this kind of reasoning is not compelling. For ideal performance norms aren't the kinds of norms to which ought implies can generally applies.[13]

Thus, all things considered, the concurrent answer is the best way to understand Conditionalization. The posterior answer yields implausible prescriptions, by effectively requiring subjects not to take all of their evidence into account, and is in tension with some popular accounts of evidence. And while the concurrent answer appears to face ought-implies-can worries and to conflict with procedural requirements, further reflection makes it clear that these worries are unreasonable (in the first case) and mistaken (in the second).[14]

Adopting the concurrent answer also settles the relationship between $t(cr)$, $t(E)$ and $t(cr_E)$. As we noted earlier, we want $t(cr) < t(cr_E)$. If we adopt the concurrent answer, so that $t(cr_E) = t(E)$, then it follows that $t(cr) < t(E)$ as well. Thus, the right relationship between these three times is: $t(cr) < t(E) = t(cr_E)$.

Building this into our formulation gets us the following rule:

Conditionalization (v1): If a subject with credences cr at t_0 gets evidence E at t_1, she should adopt new credences cr_E at t_1 such that $cr_E(\cdot) = cr(\cdot|E)$, if defined.

4. The sequential vs. interval updating question

Conditionalization (v1) says, roughly, that if a subject has credences cr at $t(cr)$, and gets evidence E at $t(E)$, then she should adopt cr_E at $t(cr_E) = t(E)$. But suppose a subject receives evidence F at some time between $t(cr)$ and $t(E)$. Then, as written, Conditionalization will still tell the subject to adopt credences $cr_E(\cdot) = cr(\cdot|E)$ at $t(E)$. But one might worry that this is the wrong prescription – after all, the subject also received F as evidence, and cr_E doesn't seem to take that into account!

There are two natural ways to reply to this worry. The first is to place a further constraint on $t(cr)$. Namely, require $t(cr)$ to be a time such that the subject *doesn't* receive any evidence between $t(cr)$ and $t(E)$. The second is to place a further constraint on the content of E. Namely, require that E incorporate (i.e. entail) any other evidence the subject gets between $t(cr)$ and $t(E)$.

These two replies lead to two different ways of thinking about Conditionalization. The first reply depicts Conditionalization as a rule which tells us how to update whenever we get a new piece of evidence. On this conception, $t(cr)$ is some time before the subject gets E but after she's received any of her other evidence, and E is the evidence the subject receives at $t(E)$. We might call this the 'sequential updating' picture, since on this picture we determine what a subject's credence should be, given some earlier credence function, by sequentially applying the rule to each of the pieces of evidence the subject receives.[15]

The second reply depicts Conditionalization as a rule which tells us, for any interval of time, how our credences at the endpoints of that interval should be related given the evidence received in the interim. On this conception, $t(cr)$ and $t(E)$ can be any times we like, and E is the cumulative evidence the subject receives during this interval.[16] We might call this the 'interval updating' picture, since on this picture the rule tells us how to update over arbitrary intervals.

So which of these two pictures of Conditionalization should we adopt?

Q3. The Sequential vs. Interval Updating Question: Does the rule tell subjects how to update whenever they get a piece of evidence? Or does it tell them how to update over arbitrary intervals, given the cumulative evidence they've received during that interval?[17] The first answer to this question takes the rule to be telling us how to update our credences whenever we get a piece of evidence:

Answer 1 (Sequential). The rule tells a subject how to update when she gets a piece of evidence. Thus $t(E)$ is the time after $t(cr)$ at which they next get evidence, and E is the evidence they get at $t(E)$. If we adopt the sequential answer, we need to add a clause to our formulation of the rule that states that the subject hasn't received any other evidence after $t(cr)$ prior to receiving E:

Conditionalization (v2.1-): If a subject with credences cr at t_0 gets evidence E at t_1 (*and no evidence between t_0 and t_1*), then she should adopt new credences cr_E at t_1 such that $cr_E(\cdot) = cr(\cdot|E)$ if defined. This formulation puts constraints on what a subject's credences should be at $t(E)$ given her credences at $t(cr)$. But it doesn't place any constraints on what her credences between $t(cr)$ and $t(E)$ should be. Since any deviations from cr during this period would amount to evidence-less belief changes – something we presumably want the rule to forbid – we'll also want to add a clause requiring the subject's credences between $t(cr)$ and $t(E)$ to remain the same:

Conditionalization (v2.1): If a subject with credences cr at t_0 gets evidence E at t_1 (*and no evidence between t_0 and t_1*), then *her credences should remain cr between t_0 and t_1* and she should adopt new credences cr_E at t_1 such that $cr_E(\cdot) = cr(\cdot|E)$, if defined. The second answer to this question takes the rule to be telling us how to update over any interval of time. We choose a time interval, plug in our credences at the start of that interval and the cumulative evidence we receive during that interval, and the rule tells us what our credence should be at the end of this interval.

Answer 2 (Interval). The rule tells a subject how to update over an arbitrary interval, given the evidence received during that interval. Thus $t(cr)$ and $t(E)$ are the endpoints of an arbitrary interval, cr is the credence function of the subject at the start of the interval, and E is the cumulative evidence she receives during that interval. We can make this understanding of the rule explicit by adding the appropriate clause to our formulation, as follows:

Conditionalization (v2.2): If a subject with credences cr at t_0 gets cumulative evidence E in the $[t_0, t_1]$ interval, then she should adopt new credences cr_E at t_1 such that $cr_E(\cdot) = cr(\cdot|E)$, if defined.

4.1. The sequential vs. interval updating question: assessing the answers

Both of these answers to the sequential vs. interval updating question have uncomfortable consequences.

If we adopt the sequential answer, and think of Conditionalization as telling subjects how to update whenever they get a piece of evidence, then the rule can't accommodate cases in which subjects get evidence continuously. This understanding of Conditionalization requires a 'no evidence between t_0 and t_1' clause. Thus, the rule requires a pair of distinct times t_0 and t_1 between which the subject doesn't get any evidence. But if the subject continuously receives evidence, then there is no such pair of times – between *any* two distinct times, there will be times in-between at which the subject gets evidence. So if we adopt a sequential understanding of Conditionalization, the rule simply goes silent in cases in which subjects receive continuous evidence.

But we also face some uncomfortable consequences if we adopt the interval answer, and think of Conditionalization as telling subjects how to update over arbitrary intervals, given the cumulative evidence they receive during that interval. In particular, the interval answer is incompatible with the conjunction of two widely held claims:

(1) Conditionalization is a special case of Jeffrey Conditionalization.
(2) The formalism of Jeffrey Conditionalization is neutral with respect to whether evidence is 'credence-dependent'.

First, there's the claim that Conditionalization is a special case of Jeffrey Conditionalization. The thought here is that Jeffrey Conditionalization is just a generalization of Conditionalization, one that returns Conditionalization in the special case in which all of one's evidence partition takes the form $\{(1, E), (0, \neg E)\}$

. This understanding of the relationship between Conditionalization and Jeffrey Conditionalization is a standard part of the Bayesian lore.[18]

Second, there's the claim that the formalism of Jeffrey Conditionalization is neutral with respect to whether evidence is 'credence-dependent'. On one way of thinking about evidence, the evidence partition a subject receives is determined by factors that are independent of her credences. For example, one might take a subject's evidence partition to be determined solely by her sensory information. On another way of thinking about evidence, the evidence partition a subject receives is determined by factors that are dependent on her credences. For example, one might take the evidence partition a subject receives to be a function of both her sensory information and her beliefs about what this kind of sensory information suggests. Thus, if the subject sees a figure through the window who looks like her friend, the proposition that her friend is outside might be assigned a large value by her evidence partition if she believes her friend is coming over to visit, but a small value if she believes her friend is out of the country. But while various considerations have convinced many people to favor the second picture of evidence over the first, the formalism of Jeffrey Conditionalization itself has generally been taken to be neutral with respect to these two ways of thinking about evidence.[19]

We can see that these two claims and the interval answer are inconsistent as follows. Suppose that the interval answer is true: we should understand Conditionalization as a rule which tells us how to update over arbitrary intervals, given the cumulative evidence we've received during that interval. Given the first claim – that Conditionalization is a special case of Jeffrey Conditionalization – Jeffrey Conditionalization should also be understood this way; as a rule which tells us how to update over arbitrary intervals, given the cumulative evidence we've received during that interval. Given the second claim – that the formalism of Jeffrey Conditionalization is neutral with respect to whether evidence is credence-dependent – it follows that this interval understanding of Jeffrey Conditionalization should be consistent with credence-independent evidence.

But it isn't. If we adopt this interval understanding of Jeffrey Conditionalization, then Jeffrey Conditionalization must yield (on pain of inconsistency) the same prescriptions regardless of what intervals we choose to update on. (For instance, updating on the evidence received during the $[t_0, t_1]$ interval and then updating on the evidence received during the $[t_1, t_2]$ interval had better yield the same result as updating all at once on the evidence received during the $[t_0, t_2]$ interval.) But as I show in Appendix A, if evidence is credence-independent, then Jeffrey Conditionalization's prescriptions *will* depend on what intervals we choose to update on. So the interval understanding of Jeffrey Conditionalization is not consistent with credence-independent evidence.

Thus the interval answer and these two claims are jointly incompatible. Given this answer, Conditionalization is an interval rule. Given the first claim, it follows that Jeffrey Conditionalization is also an interval rule. But given the second claim, it follows that Jeffrey Conditionalization can't be an interval rule – for if evidence is credence-independent, Jeffrey Conditionalization will yield inconsistent verdicts depending on what intervals we choose to update on.

To sum up, there are compelling reasons in favor of both answers. The sequential answer, which adopts a sequential-updating understanding of Conditionalization, allows us to retain the familiar picture of how Conditionalization and Jeffrey Conditionalization are related, without having to accept the surprising claim that the formalism of Jeffrey Conditionalization requires evidence to be credence-dependent. The interval answer, which adopts an interval-updating understanding of Conditionalization, allows us to apply Conditionalization to cases in which subjects get evidence continuously. And neither of these reasons clearly trumps the other.

So the sequential vs. interval updating question leaves us with two viable ways to understand Conditionalization. There's the understanding suggested by the sequential answer:

Sequential Conditionalization (v2): If a subject with credences cr at t_0 gets evidence E at t_1 (and no evidence between t_0 and t_1), then *her credences should remain cr between t_0 and t_y and she should adopt new credences cr_E at t_1 such that $cr_E(\cdot) = cr(\cdot|E)$, if defined.* And there's the understanding suggested by the interval answer:

Interval Conditionalization (v2): If a subject with credences cr at t_0 gets *cumulative evidence E in the $[t_0, t_1]$ interval*, then she should adopt new credences cr_E at t_1 such that $cr_E(\cdot) = cr(\cdot|E)$, if defined.

5. Interlude: deontic logic

In preparation for the final two sections, let's pause to say a bit more about the deontic operators that Conditionalization employs. This will provide us with the tools to discuss some natural answers to the third question we'll consider in Section 6, and it will provide us with some of the vocabulary we'll need to spell out the rule precisely in Section 7.

In standard deontic logic, the permission and obligation operators mirror the possibility and necessity operators in modal logic.[20] We begin with a set of worlds and an accessibility relation over these worlds, where the accessible worlds are intuitively the 'best' worlds that one can get to from that world. A proposition A is then permissible at w iff it's true at some world accessible to w, and obligatory at w iff it's true at all worlds accessible to w.

On the standard approach, deontic claims are true or false at a world. Thus the same deontic claims apply to every subject at a world, and at every time at that world. But it's natural to want to allow for different subjects at a world to have different obligations, and to allow a subject at different times to have different obligations.[21] And we can allow for such variations by taking deontic operators and accessibility relations to be subject and time-indexed.[22]

The move to subject and time-indexed deontic operators makes it natural to modify our formulations of Conditionalization in order to make these indices explicit. One natural way to do this is to understand the rule as making prescriptions that are indexed to the subject whose credences we're considering, and to the time at which cr_E should be adopted, as follows:[23]

Sequential Conditionalization (v2): If a subject s with credences cr at t_0 gets evidence E at t_1 (and no evidence between t_0 and t_1), then her credences should$_{s,t_1}$ remain cr between t_0 and t_1, and she should$_{s,t_1}$ adopt new credences cr_E at t_1 such that $cr_E(\cdot) = cr(\cdot|E)$, if defined.

Interval Conditionalization (v2): If a subject s with credences cr at t_0 gets cumulative evidence E in the $[t_0, t_1]$ interval, then she should$_{s,t_1}$ adopt new credences cr_E at t_1 such that $cr_E(\cdot) = cr(\cdot|E)$, if defined. I will understand Conditionalization along these lines from now on.[24]

In order to avoid cluttering the text with subscripts, I'll leave these subject and time-indices implicit when tracking them isn't important, or context makes it clear what they are.

6. The narrow vs. wide scope question

Both versions of Conditionalization (v2*) are conditional norms. That is, they have the form: 'If a subject ..., then she should ...'. Let A be the antecedent clause, C the consequent clause, and O the obligation operator. Then this phrase can be understood to have one of two logical forms: $A \to O(C)$ or $O(A \to C)$.[25] In which of these two ways should Conditionalization be understood?

Q5. The narrow vs. wide scope question: Does the obligation operator apply to the consequent, or to the entire conditional?[26] One way of answering this question takes the obligation operator to take narrow scope, applying to just the consequent:

Answer 1 (Narrow). The rule has the form $A \to O(C)$. On this understanding, the rule tells us that if a subject actually satisfies A, then she satisfies C at all of the best worlds.

The other way of answering this question takes the obligation operator to have wide scope, applying to the entire conditional:

Answer 2 (Wide). The rule has the form $O(A \to C)$. On this understanding, the rule tells us that at all of the best worlds, the subject satisfies the conditional $A \to C$.[27]

There's a literature on whether we should understand fundamental rational requirements as narrow or wide scope norms in general.[28] And one might think that the question of whether Conditionalization should be understood as narrow or wide scope should be deferred to this literature, and to the general question of whether rational requirements should be understood as narrow or wide scope. I'm inclined to think that this is a mistake. Different considerations come into play for different norms, and we shouldn't expect there to be one general answer to how all norms should be understood.[29] In any case, in what follows I'll only consider whether one particular rational requirement – Conditionalization – should be understood as a narrow or wide scope norm.

6.1. The narrow vs. wide scope question: assessing the answers

At least at first glance, both answers seem reasonable. The narrow answer is natural when we're thinking of Conditionalization primarily as an updating rule, a constraint on what one's posterior credences should be given one's prior credences. The wide answer is natural when we're thinking of Conditionalization primarily as a diachronic credence constraint, a constraint on how one's prior and posterior credences should line up.

Some people have argued that we should understand all fundamental rational requirements as narrow scope norms.[30] Perhaps the most popular argument against wide scope rational requirements is that such rational requirements make symmetrical prescriptions, and it's argued that this symmetry is implausible. Thus, in the case of Conditionalization, the wide scope version of the rule $O(A \rightarrow C) \equiv O(\neg A \vee C)$ requires that subjects either satisfy $\neg A$ or satisfy C, and the rule treats these two options symmetrically: the rule gives us no reason to prefer satisfying C over satisfying $\neg A$. But, it's argued, satisfying C should be preferred to satisfying $\neg A$. If, somehow, we were given a choice between adopting the appropriate new credences given our prior credences and evidence, or adopting whatever new credences we like and having whatever prior credences and evidence would yield these new credences, we should prefer the former option to the latter. And it's argued that the wide scope formulations of rational requirements cannot accommodate this fact. Insofar as these kinds of arguments are compelling, and insofar as we want Conditionalization to be a fundamental norm, this gives us a reason to favor the narrow answer.[31]

That said, there also seem to be considerations that tell against the narrow answer.[32] The narrow understanding of the rule takes the form $A \rightarrow O(C)$. Thus, it tells us that if a subject actually satisfies A, then they will satisfy C at all of the best worlds. But this claim seems strange, since it requires the subject to satisfy C at all of the best worlds, regardless of whether the subject satisfies A at those worlds. And it's hard to see why the subject should have to satisfy C at best worlds in which they don't satisfy A.

In light of this worry, one might modify this answer by adding A to the consequent as well:

Answer 1a (Narrow-a). The rule has the form $A \rightarrow O(A \wedge C)$. This formulation of the rule gets around the above worry, since it tells us that a subject who actually satisfies A should satisfy both A and C at all of the best worlds.

But this isn't what we want the rule to say. If $A \wedge C$ is true at all of the best worlds, then A is true at all of the best worlds. So the above norm entails that $A \rightarrow O(A)$. But we don't want A's actually obtaining to entail that A ought to obtain. In the case of Conditionalization, this would mean that the subject's actually having credences cr and getting evidence E entails that she should have credences cr and get evidence E. And this is implausible.

In light of this, one might consider a second way of salvaging the narrow answer, inspired by the ethics literature, that leaves the form of the rule the same: $A \rightarrow O(C)$.[33] The idea is to avoid the difficulties sketched above by adding certain background assumptions. We will go through this in more detail in a moment, but here's a preliminary sketch of how the story will go.

One can avoid the first worry – that the rule implausibly requires C to be true at all best worlds, even those where A is false – by adding assumptions which entail that if A is currently true, then A is also true at all of the best worlds. Now, this way of avoiding the first worry leads to the second worry: if the current truth of A entails that A is true at all of the best worlds, then the current truth of A entails that A is obligatory. One can blunt this second worry by distinguishing between 'trivial' and 'non-trivial' oughts, and showing that A only entails that A is obligatory in a trivial sense.

Let's go through this in more detail. Standard deontic logic employs a notion of accessibility, call it *O-accessibility*, that determines what things are permissible and obligatory. Let's add to this another notion of accessibility, call it *C-accessibility*, that determines what things we have the capacity to influence.[34] So while O-accessibility intuitively picks out the normatively 'best' worlds, C-accessibility intuitively picks out the worlds that one is capable of getting to.

With these two notions of accessibility in hand, we can impose a constraint that implements the idea that 'ought implies can':

Ought Implies Can: For any world w, the worlds that are O-accessible$_{s,t}$ from w are a subset of the worlds that are C-accessible$_{s,t}$ from w. It follows from this that a proposition can only be obligatory for a subject if she's capable of bringing about a state of affairs in which that proposition is true.

Given Ought Implies Can, there will be many propositions that are strictly speaking obligatory, but only in an uninteresting sense. For example, take the proposition that 1+1=2. This proposition will be true at every world, and *a fortiriori* at all of the best worlds. Thus the proposition that 1+1=2 will be obligatory. But it is only obligatory in a trivial sense. Since it's inevitable, nothing a subject can do has any bearing on whether 1+1=2 turns out to be true or not. I'll call oughts of this kind *trivial oughts*. A proposition A is *trivially obligatory iff* it's true at both every O-accessible world (making it obligatory) and every C-accessible world (making it inevitable).

Contrast this with the interesting obligations that subjects have, obligations towards propositions which are not inevitable. These are the obligations we normally talk about, such as the obligation to save a drowning baby, or to adopt the appropriate credences. I'll call these *non-trivial oughts*. A proposition A is *non-trivially obligatory iff* it's true at every O-accessible world (making it obligatory) but not true at every C-accessible world (making the subject capable of falsifying it).

Introducing the notion of C-accessibility also allows us to impose a constraint that implements the idea that the past is immutable:[35]

The past is immutable: For any world w, the only worlds that are C-accessible$_{s,t}$ to w are worlds that agree with w about the state of the world before t. It follows from this that we can't change what's in the past. (Note that if we didn't take the accessibility relation to be relativized to times, we couldn't formulate a constraint like this.) Finally, let's suppose that the posterior answer to the time of evidence question is true. I argued in Section 3.1 that we should adopt the concurrent answer, and maintain that subjects should get E and adopt cr_E simultaneously. But now let's suppose that we adopt the posterior answer instead, and hold that subjects get E some amount of time before they adopt cr_E.[36]

With all this in hand, let's turn back to the Narrow vs. Wide Scope question. Suppose we adopt the narrow answer to this question, and maintain that the rule has the form $A \rightarrow O(C)$. We now have the resources to get around the first worry raised for the narrow answer: that the rule requires C to be true at all of the best worlds, regardless of whether A is true at those worlds.

Given the posterior answer to the time of evidence question, A concerns solely facts that occur at t_0 – the subject's having credences cr at t_0 and the subject getting evidence E at t_0. So the truth value of A will be fixed by the state of the world before t_1. Given the past is immutable, it follows that A will be true at all of the C-accessible$_{s,t_1}$ worlds, and thus (given Ought Implies Can) at all of the C-accessible$_{s,t_1}$ worlds. Thus, given this set-up, the first worry no longer arises: if A is actually true, then A will be true at all of the best$_{s,t_1}$ worlds too, and the rule won't have the awkward consequence of potentially requiring C to be true at best$_{s,t_1}$ worlds where A is not.

Now, this way of avoiding the first worry leads to the second worry raised above for answer 1a: that if A is true at all of the best worlds, then A is obligatory, which seems implausible. But we now have the resources to explain away this worry too. For while it's true that on this account A is obligatory, it's only *trivially* obligatory, since it's true at all of the C-accessible worlds. So it won't be the case that A is obligatory in any sense that should bother us.

Thus if we adopt this set-up, we can lay out a way of understanding the narrow answer that avoids the worries raised above. Furthermore, this set-up fits nicely with the motivations for the posterior answer to the time of evidence question. Since the posterior answer is largely motivated by ought-implies-can worries, it's a natural fit with this way of fleshing out the narrow answer, which also appeals to ought-implies-can-like considerations.

This is, I think, the closest one can get to a viable narrow scope understanding of Conditionalization. But ultimately, even this account does not give us a compelling reason to adopt the narrow answer. First, given this account, we have no reason to favor a narrow scope over a wide scope understanding of Conditionalization. As I show in Appendix C, given the assumptions we've been making, the narrow and wide scope formulations of Conditionalization are equivalent.[37] And this equivalence undercuts the arguments that have been offered in favor of narrow over wide scope understandings of rational requirements. For example, the argument that wide scope understandings yield implausibly symmetric prescriptions while narrow scope understandings do not won't work since both understandings will yield the same prescriptions.[38]

Second, this account inherits the demerits of the posterior answer to the time of evidence question. So even this version of the narrow answer carries some unpleasant baggage.

Third, all of the versions of the narrow answer we've considered, including this one, yield implausible verdicts in cases in which the subject's t_0 credences are irrational.[39] Consider a variant of an example we discussed in section 3.1. Suppose a subject both violates the Principal Principle and receives evidence E. The subject can conditionalize on E, or adopt credences that satisfy the Principal Principle, but it's impossible for her to do both (since conditionalizing on E yields credences that violate the Principal Principle). The narrow answer yields the undesirable result that this subject must always update on E. ($A \rightarrow O(C)$ will be true iff either A is false or at all best worlds C is true; and since A is true, it follows that at all best worlds C must be true.) By contrast, the wide answer yields the desired result that the subject needn't update on E. ($O(A \rightarrow C)$ will be true iff at all best worlds either A is false or C is true; and since A commits the subject to irrational credences, A will be false at all best worlds. So it doesn't follow that C must be true at all (or even any) best worlds.)[40]

So, when all is said and done, we're left with little motivation to adopt the narrow answer. In the best case scenario for the narrow answer, the narrow and wide answers are equivalent. And even in this best case scenario, the narrow answer has unpleasant consequences, as it inherits the demerits of the posterior answer and yields implausible verdicts in cases in which a subject's starting credences are irrational.

So the wide scope understanding of Conditionalization is the better of the two options. Making the wide scope understanding explicit gives us the following formulations:

Sequential Conditionalization (v3): It should$_{s,t_1}$ be the case that if a subject s with credences cr at t_0 gets evidence E at t_1 (and no evidence between t_0 and t_1), then her credences will remain cr between t_0 and t_1 are cr, and she will adopt credences cr_E at t_1 such that $cr_E(\cdot) = cr(\cdot|E)$, if defined.

Interval Conditionalization (v3): It should$_{s,t_1}$ be the case that if a subject s with credences cr at t_0 gets cumulative evidence E in the $[t_0, t_1]$ interval, then she will adopt credences cr_E at t_1 such that $cr_E(\cdot) = cr(\cdot|E)$, if defined.

7. Precise formulations

In the previous sections, we considered three questions about how Conditionalization should be understood. And if we adopt the answers I suggested, we end up with two viable formulations of Conditionalization: the Sequential and Interval (v3) formulations. But one might reasonably worry about whether we've addressed all of the open questions regarding how to formulate Conditionalization. After all, the formulations of Conditionalization I've provided are in English. And until we've spelled out these rules in logical form, it's reasonable to worry that there may be further ambiguities, and thus further questions, that we've missed. So let's conclude by providing formal characterizations of these two rules.

To start, let's introduce the non-logical vocabulary that we need to formulate these rules.

First, we need a predicate that characterizes what a subject's credences are. Let the *credence* predicate C(s,t,f) represent a 3-place relation holding between a subject s, a time t, and a function f which assigns real numbers to (at least some) propositions. Intuitively, C(s,t,f) holds *iff* s's credence function at t is f.

Second, we need a predicate that ensures that the conditional credence function to be prescribed is well-defined. Let the *well-defined* predicate W(f,E) represent a 2-place relation between a function f that assigns real numbers to propositions, and a proposition E. Intuitively, W(f,E) holds *iff* f(.|E) is well-defined; i.e. iff f is a probability function which assigns a non-zero value to E.

Third, we need a predicate that characterizes what evidence a subject gets, where this will depend on what version of Conditionalization we're considering. For use in the sequential formulation of Conditionalization, let the *sequential evidence* predicate SE(s,t-,t,E) represent a 4-place relation between a subject s, a time t-, a time t after t-, and a proposition E. Intuitively, SE (s,t-,t,E) holds *iff* either (i) s doesn't receive any evidence in the [t-,t) interval, and receives E as evidence at t, or (ii) s doesn't receive any evidence in the [t-,t] interval, and E is the trivial proposition Ω. (The second clause is needed to ensure that the rule not only requires subjects to change their credences in the right way when they get evidence, but to also not change their credences when they don't get evidence.)

For use in the interval formulation of Conditionalization, let the *interval evidence* predicate IE(s,t-,t,E) represent a 4-place relation between a subject s, a time t-, a time t after t-, and a proposition E. Intuitively, IE(s,t-,t,E) holds *iff* E is the cumulative evidence s receives during the interval [t-,t].

Finally, with all of this in hand, we can formulate our two versions of Conditionalization in logical form as follows:

Sequential Conditionalization (final):

$$\forall E, \forall f, \forall s, \forall t, \forall t\text{-} < t, \, O_{s,t}\Big(C(s,t\text{-},f) \wedge SE(s,t\text{-},t,E) \wedge W(f,E) \rightarrow C(s,t,f(\cdot|E))\Big)$$

Interval Conditionalization (final):

$$\forall E, \forall f, \forall s, \forall t, \forall t\text{-} < t, \, O_{s,t}\Big(C(s,t\text{-},f) \wedge IE(s,t\text{-},t,E) \wedge W(f,E) \rightarrow C(s,t,f(\cdot|E))\Big)$$

These, I maintain, are the two best ways to understand Conditionalization.[41]

Notes

1. Of course, questions of how to understand the concepts the rule employs and questions of how to formulate the rule aren't entirely distinct. For example, different choices regarding how to think of credences can have a bearing on the logical form of the predicate one uses to represent (say) having a certain credence in a proposition. Likewise, different choices regarding how to formulate the rule can make certain views regarding how to think about credences more or less attractive. But, the discussion that follows will be focused primarily on questions of logical form.

2. The 'virtually' caveat is required because of the potential gap between having a credence of 1 in something and being certain of it. (E.g. one should have a credence of 1 that a countably infinite number of fair coin tosses will land tails at least once, but one shouldn't be certain of this.)

3. That is, a subject's credences should assign values to propositions that form a Boolean algebra – a set of propositions closed under conjunction and negation – and the values it assigns should satisfy the (finite) probability axioms: (i) $cr(\cdot) \geq 0$, (ii) $cr(\Omega) = 1$ (where Ω is the trivially true proposition), (iii) if A and B are mutually exclusive, then $cr(A) + p(B) = cr(A \vee B)$.

4. Of course, there are a number of different formulations of Conditionalization in the literature to choose from. I've chosen this one because it leaves all three of the questions I'll be exploring open. In order to figure out how to best formulate Conditionalization, we need to assess the different possible answers to these questions. And, a formulation of Conditionalization which leaves all three of these questions open, like the one given above, provides us with an ideal place to start.

5. In the next section, we'll be considering whether we should be thinking of E as something you get at a particular time, or as the cumulative evidence one receives over some interval of time. In the latter case, I'll undertstand '$t(E)$' as the final time over which one gets E; i.e. the future endpoint of this interval.

6. I'm assuming in the text that there's a time $t(E)$ at which one gets E as evidence and a time $t(cr_E)$ at which one should first adopt cr_E. But, this needn't be the case. It could be that the temporal interval during which one has E as evidence is an open interval, so that there is no initial time at which E is received. Likewise, it could be that the temporal interval during which one should have credences cr_E in an open interval, so that there is no first time at which cr_E should be adopted. Although these possibilities complicate things, they don't end up changing the dialectic in any interesting way (see footnote 14). So, I'll put these possibilities aside.

7. The formulations of Conditionalization given in the literature vary widely with respect to this question: some assume the posterior answer (e.g. Earman 1992,

Howson and Urbach 2006), some assume the concurrent answer (e.g. (e.g. Lewis 2010 and Strevens 2015), and some are silent on the matter (e.g. Easwaran 2011 and Weisberg 2011).

8   I'm assuming here that the time at which a subject 'gets' evidence is the time at which the evidence becomes relevant to our epistemic evaluation of the subject. But I do not take this to be controversial, since this assumption is shared by virtually everyone. (Consider: if this were not the case, then the oft repeated truism that a subject's beliefs should take all of her evidence into account (the so-called 'Principle of Total Evidence') would be untenable. If, for example, one characterized 'receiving evidence' such that the time at which a subject received visual evidence was one minute (or one year, or one century) before the light struck her eyes, it would be implausible to say that she should take all of her evidence into account.)

9   See Lewis (1980).

10 Other proponents of this kind of stance regarding epistemic norms include Feldman (2001) and Wolterstorff (2010).

11 One might reasonably want to hear more about what, exactly, it means to say that Conditionalization is 'an ideal at which to aim' or an ideal performance norm', and about how this understanding of Conditionalization interacts with things like a subject's cognitive capabilities and ought-implies-can. I describe one natural way of spelling out these notions and their interaction, using the framework of Kratzer (1991), in Appendix B.

12 Of course, this kind of worry won't arise given certain natural pictures of what receiving and updating on evidence is like. For example, suppose one adopts an account of evidence (such as Howson and Urbach's 1993 or Williamson's 2000) according to which receiving evidence E is, at least in part, a matter of coming to believe E. And, suppose one takes such belief changes to be global and concurrent. That is, just as stepping on to a trampoline changes the elevation of both the place one's standing and the surrounding area, getting E as evidence changes both one's credence in E and one's credence in the 'surrounding' propositions. And just as the full change in elevation of the place one steps doesn't happen *before* any of the other changes in elevation take place – the changes in elevation of different parts of the trampoline are (roughly) concurrent – getting E as evidence doesn't take place before these other belief changes take place, these belief changes are concurrent. On this picture, Conditionalization is naturally thought of as describing what the shape of these global concurrent belief changes should be like. And, the worries regarding potential conflicts between instantaneous updating and procedural norms described in the text won't arise on such a picture.

13 In making this reply, I assume that in order for a set of norms to provide a coherent standard of ideal performance, or a coherent ideal for us to aim at, it only has to be logically possible to satisfy them. But one might wonder why these ideals shouldn't also have to be *metaphysically* possible to live up to. And if they do, and if instantaneous causation is metaphysically impossible, then it seems that these natural procedural norms and the concurrent understanding of Conditionalization *are* in conflict after all. (Having the right beliefs (those prescribed by Conditionalization) in the right way (via some causal process initiated by the receipt of evidence) seems to require instantaneous causation, since one's beliefs must instantly change in light of one's evidence. Thus, if instantaneous causation is metaphysically impossible, then so is jointly satisfying Conditionalization and these procedural norms. And if jointly satisfying Conditionalization and these procedural norms has to be metaphysically possible in order for these norms

to be jointly true, then they can't be jointly true.)6 So why do I require these ideals to be logically possible, but not metaphysically possible? Here is why. For something to usefully serve as an ideal at which to aim, it needs to be something which we can approach by degrees; something for which we can discern paths of states that lead to it such that each state along the path gets closer to satisfying the ideal. Thus, metaphysically impossible norms can serve as useful ideals at which to aim: one can make sense of moving toward or away from the ideal of updating instantly by updating more or less quickly. But it's hard to see how logically impossible ideals could serve as useful ideals at which to aim: it's not clear how one could move closer or father away from the ideal of being a round square, or a married bachelor.

14 As noted in footnote 6, I've simplified this discussion by assuming that there are particular times $t(E)$ and $t(cr_E)$ at which a subject receives her evidence and should adopt her new credences. But this needn't be the case (e.g. if the period during which a subject should have cr_E is an open interval). Introducing these possibilities complicates the dialectic in two ways, but these complications end up effectively canceling each other out. The first complication is that these possibilities leave us with *three* natural ways to group answers to the question of how the receipt of E and the adoption of cr_E are related:

(1) E is received before cr_E is adopted, and there is a gap between the receipt of E and cr_E.
(2) E is received at the same time as cr_E is adopted, and thus there's no gap between them.
(3) E is received before cr_E is adopted, but there is no gap between the receipt of E and cr_E (e.g. E's received at some time t, and cr_E is adopted at the open endpoint of an interval starting at t).

(1) and (2) correspond to the posterior and concurrent answers considered in the text, while (3) is a possibility which only comes into view once we drop the simplifying assumption. The second complication is that these possibilities allow us to see that the worries raised for the different answers track slightly different issues. The worries regarding total evidence and fit with Howson-and-Urbach-like pictures of evidence arise for any view on which E is received before cr_E is adopted (thus applying to (1) and (3)). The worries regarding ought implies can and substantive and procedural requirements arise for any view on which there's no gap between the receipt of E and the adoption of cr_E (thus applying to (2) and (3)). But together these complications allow us to see that no interesting positions are left out by simplifying and ignoring (3). For (3) is strictly less appealing than (1) and (2), as it is subject to the worries raised for both.

15 Of course, it's a well known feature of Conditionalization that conditionalizing on E and then on F yields the same result as conditionalizing on the conjunct $E \wedge F$. So one could obtain the result either way. But, on this understanding of the rule, what's really going on 'under the hood' is a sequence of updates; updating on the conjunction is merely a convenient calculational short cut.

16 The notion of 'cumulative evidence' is best thought of as one of the basic notions that this interval updating understanding of conditionalization employs. (I.e. whereas the 'sequential updating' picture takes as basic a notion of getting a piece of evidence at a particular time, the 'interval updating' pictures takes as basic a notion of getting cumulative evidence over an interval.) Of course, when discussing Conditionalization, we have the option of understanding the *cumulative evidence* a subject receives during an interval as the logically weakest proposition that entails all of the evidence she receives during that interval (or, equivalently, the conjunction of all of the evidence she receives during that interval). This would allow both sequential and interval updating understandings of Conditionalization to take as basic the notion of getting a piece of evidence at a particular time. But when we turn discuss Jeffrey Conditionalization, in Section 4.1, we lose the option of providing a reductive understanding of the notion of 'cumulative evidence', since Jeffrey Conditionalization deals with weighted evidence partitions to which the notions of entailment and conjunction don't apply.

17 The formulations of Conditionalization given in the literature vary widely with respect to this question: some assume the sequential answer (e.g. Earman 1992; Howson and Urbach 2006), others assume the interval answer (e.g. Lewis 2010), and yet others are silent on the matter (e.g. Earman 1992; Weisberg 2011; Strevens 2015).

18 Though see Christensen (1992) for a notable dissent: '[Jeffrey Conditionalization] is thus not simply an elegant generalization of [Conditionalization], a pure improvement which merely removes some gratuitous idealization. It removes idealization, but at a price. The additional cases covered by the liberal model are not covered in the same way; and consequently, the account as a whole must be given a different philosophical interpretation' (547).

19 A number of people, including Levi (1967), Carnap (in Jeffrey 1975), Field (1978), Christensen (1992) and Lange (2000), have maintained that what evidence partition a subject receives should depend on what the subject's credences are. But they've argued for this under the assumption that it's a substantive question left open by the formalism. And thus they've appealed to various intuitive and epistemic considerations to make their case. If the formalism of Jeffrey Conditionalization itself required evidence to be credence-dependent, then the kinds of considerations that Christensen and others have offered in support of this claim would be superfluous. No interesting discussion needs to take place to establish that evidence is credence-dependent if the formalism itself entails it.

20 For discussions of standard deontic logic, see Aqvist (2002) and McNamara (2010).

21 See Feldman (1986) for some reasons for wanting to have this kind of subject and time sensitivity in the context of ethics.

22 A different (and more powerful) way to allow for such variations is to take deontic operators to range over centered worlds instead of worlds. But since this approach raises complications orthogonal to the issues at hand, I employ the more traditional approach of subject and time indexing the deontic operators in the text.

23 Recognizing the time-indexed nature of the obligation operator could be seen as raising a fourth question, in addition to the three questions discussed in the text: a 'Time of Obligation' question, regarding what times the obligation operators should be indexed to. One answer is that they're indexed to the initial time we're considering (t_0), another is that they're indexed to the final time we're considering (t_1), and a third is that they're indexed to all times – the norm requires a subject to satisfy this constraint at every time, regardless of the times the prescription

involves. I tentatively favor the second and third answers over the first, since according to the first answer, it will never be the case that a subject's obligated to adopt cr_E at the time at which she's supposed to adopt it – by the time t_1 rolls around, she'll only have obligations to adopt some further credences in the future. And I adopt the second answer (instead of the third) in the text because the most plausible version of the narrow scope answer, which I'll be arguing against in section 6, requires this time to be t_1. (Looking ahead: we need the time to be t_1 in order to ensure that the antecedent is true at all C-accessible worlds and yet the consequent is not.) So adopting the second answer allows me to stack the deck in favor of my opponents.

24 In linguistics, the standard framework for formalizing claims involving modals is the framework developed by Kratzer (1991). Although the discussion in the text assumes we're using standard deontic logic, everything I say can be translated into Kratzer's more sophisticated framework. Indeed, moving to Kratzer's framework offers some benefits, for it provides us with the tools to spell out several things that it's difficult to flesh out using standard deontic logic. Since working out these details takes a bit of time, I've relegated my discussion of how to set things up using Kratzer's framework to Appendix B.

25 See Broome (1999).

26 In the literature, Conditionalization is generally presented in a way that is neutral with respect to this question (such as in Earman 1992; Howson and Urbach 2006; Lewis 2010; Easwaran 2011; Weisberg 2011; Strevens 2015).

27 Broome (2007) shows that changing a norm from narrow to wide scope or vice versa won't change whether the actual world is one of the best worlds. Given this, one might worry about whether there's anything substantive at stake here. But these two answers are logically distinct. (E.g. if A is false and at all of the best worlds A is true and C is false, then the narrow scope conditional will be true but the wide scope one false; while if A is false and at all of the best worlds A and C are false, then the narrow scope conditional will be false but the wide scope conditional true.) And, as we'll see, these two answers will have importantly different implications.

28 For some of the recent literature bearing on this issue, see Broome (1999), Schroeder (2004), Broome (2007), Kolodny (2007), Bedke (2009), Brunero (2010), Way (2011), Brunero (2012), Lord (2013), Shpall (2013), and Titelbaum (forthcoming). (The reason it's *fundamental* rational requirements that are of interest is because one might be able to derive some wide scope norms from narrow scope norms or vice versa. So the interesting claims aren't whether there are any wide/narrow scope rational requirements, but rather whether the are any fundamental (i.e. non-derivative) wide/narrow scope rational requirements.)

29 For example, in the next section, certain questions regarding how we understand Conditionalization (such as how we answer the Time of Evidence question) will bear on the plausibility of wide vs. narrow scope understandings of the rule. We wouldn't expect the same dialectic to play out for other norms – the shape of this dialectic is particular to Conditionalization.

30 For examples of arguments in favor of narrow scope understandings of fundamental rational requirements, see Schroeder (2004), Kolodny , (2009). It's worth noting that the terms 'narrow scope' and 'wide scope' are used somewhat equivocally in this literature; see Titelbaum (forthcoming). But everyone calls norms of the form $A \rightarrow O(C)$ narrow scope, and norms of the form $O(A \rightarrow C)$ wide scope, so we can skirt these complications here.

31 For discussions of these kinds of symmetry arguments, see Way (2011), Brunero (2012), Lord (2013) and Shpall (2013).
32 In the text, I focus on worries regarding whether the narrow answer has the right normative profile. For further kinds of arguments against narrow scope understandings of rational requirements, see Brunero (2010) and Shpall (2013).
33 In particular, this proposal follows many of the ideas regarding how to set up deontic structure laid out in Feldman (1986), chapter 2.
34 The notion of 'C-accessibility' is the same as the notion of accessibility described in Feldman (1986), chapter 2.
35 Though see Feldman (1986), Section 2.1.1 for some reasons against adopting such a constraint.
36 The reason we need to assume the posterior answer is that it ensures there's a temporal gap between the events described in the antecedent A (having credences cr and receiving evidence E) and the events described in the consequent C (adopting credences cr_E). And this temporal gap is crucial to getting the maneuver described in the text to work. (Briefly: we need A to be in the past to ensure that A is true at all best worlds but only trivially obligatory, and we need C to not be in the past to ensure that C isn't trivially obligatory.)
37 It's important to not confuse this result with the result shown by Broome (2007) and discussed in footnote 27. Broome's result is both broader and weaker. Broome shows that, in general, switching narrow and wide scope formulations of a rule won't change whether the actual world is one of the best worlds. This result yields the stronger conclusion that the narrow and wide scope formulations will logically entail each other, but only in a narrower class of cases (those in which the norm is Conditionalization, and the assumptions we've been making hold).
38 In a similar fashion, this equivalence undercuts Kolodny's (2007) 'Problem of Conflict' for wide scope understandings of Conditionalization, the worry that '[s]ome requirements of formal coherence not only are not explained by a concern for the true and the good, but moreover would forbid what that concern requires'. (Kolodny 2007, 231) This kind of argument cannot support the narrow over wide scope understandings of Conditionalization, since the two understandings make the same prescriptions, and thus 'forbid' the same things. Likewise, it undercuts Kolodny's (2007) 'Problem of Normativity' for wide scope understandings of Conditionalization, the worry that there's no plausible explanation for how wide scope rational requirements could have normative force. Since the narrow and wide scope understandings of Conditionalization are equivalent, any considerations that one could use to justify one of these sets of prescriptions could also be used to justify the other.
39 See Brunero (2010) for a more general version of this worry for narrow scope norms.
40 This assumes that we don't adopt the additional assumptions sketched above. If we do adopt those assumptions, then the wide answer will yield the same undesirable results as the narrow answer (as one would expect, since given these assumptions the narrow and wide answers are equivalent).
41 I'd like thank the May 2014 UMass Brown Bag Presentation group and the audience of the 2015 Belief, Rationality and Action over Time conference for helpful comments and discussion. In addition, I'd like to thank Jennifer Carr for flagging the third worry for the narrow answer discussed in Section 6.1, Brian Hedden for discussion about the ways of thinking about evidence mentioned in footnote 12, Sarah Moss and Ralph Wedgewood for discussion about Kratzer semantics and the issues discussed in Appendix B, Miriam Schoenfield for suggesting the names

for the answers to the Time of Evidence Question, and for pushing me to address the issues discussed in footnote 13, and Michael Titelbaum for pushing me to get clearer on what one might mean by things like 'an ideal at which to aim' (which I now try to do in Appendix B). Finally, I owe special thanks to Lisa Cassell, Maya Eddon, and Alejandro Perez-Carballo, for detailed comments on the entire paper, which led to more substantive improvements than I could reasonably list.

42 I think these are plausible assumptions for the ordering base corresponding to the notions of epistemic obligation and permission. But not everyone would agree. For example, Christensen (2007) argues that there are inconsistent epistemic ideals.

43 For simplicity, I talk here as if we were taking the modal base and ordering source to be functions from worlds to set of propositions, and to not be indexed to anything. But I think our final account will want these functions to be indexed to subjects and times (or to be functions from centered worlds); see Section 5.

44 To see that these two thoughts are equivalent: given the assumption about the modal base, the formulations of Conditionalization given in the text will entail that at every ideal world subjects conditionalize (in the manner specified by that formulation), and thus that the ordering source must entail that subjects conditionalize. Going the other way, if the ordering source entails that subjects conditionalize (in the manner corresponding to some formulation), then it follows that subjects conditionalize at every ideal world, and thus (given the assumption about the modal base) that subjects *should* conditionalize, which is just what the corresponding formulation of Conditionalization asserts.

45 Of course, none of the formulations of Conditionalization we'll consider specify what this range of weaker propositions is. But this isn't something we should expect from Conditionalization – spelling out how to best decompose the proposition that subjects conditionalize into these weaker claims is a task which requires a lot more information than a simple rule like Conditionalization could provide.

46 The wide scope rule requires that $\neg A \vee C$ be true at all O-accessible worlds. If $O(A)$ is true, then the first part of that disjunct ($\neg A$) will be false at all O-accessible worlds, and thus the second part of the disjunct (C) must be true at all O-accessible worlds. Thus $O(C)$ is true.

References

Aqvist, L. 2002. "Deontic Logic". In *Handbook of Philosophical Logic*, edited by D. M. Gabbay and F. Geunther. Dordrecht, Netherlands: Kluwer Academic Publishers.

Bedke, M. S. 2009. "The Iffiest Oughts: A Guise of Reasons account of Endgiven Conditionals." *Ethics* 119 (4):672–698.

Broome, J. 1999. "Normative Requirements." *Ratio* 12 (4):398–419.

Broome, J. 2007. "Wide or Narrow Scope?" *Mind* 116 (462):359–370.

Brunero, J. 2010. "The Scope of Rational Requirements." *Philosophical Quarterly* 60 (238):28–49.
Brunero, J. 2012. "Instrumental Rationality, Symmetry and Scope." *Philosophical Studies* 157 (1):125–140.
Christensen, D. 1992. "Confirmational Holism and Bayesian Epistemology." *Philosophy of Science* 59 (4):540–557.
Christensen, D. 2004. *Putting Logic in its Place: Formal Constraints on Rational Belief*. New York, NY: Oxford University Press.
Christensen, D. 2007. "Does Murphy's Law Apply in Epistemology? Self-Doubt and Rational Ideals." *Oxford Studies in Epistemology* 2:3–31.
Earman, J. 1992. *Bayes or Bust?* Cambridge, MA: MIT Press
Easwaran, K. 2011. "Bayesianism I: Introduction and Arguments in Favor." *Philosophy Compass* 6 (5):312–320.
Feldman, F. 1986. *Doing the Best We Can: An Essay in Informal Deontic Logic*. Dordrecht, Netherlands: D. Reidel Publishing Company.
Feldman, R. 2001. "Voluntary Belief and Epistemic Evaluation". In *Knowledge, Truth, and Duty: Essays on Epistemic Justification, Responsibility, and Virtue*, edited by M. Steup. 77–92. Oxford: Oxford University Press.
Field, H. 1978. "A Note on Jeffrey Conditionalization." *Philosophy of Science* 45 (3):361–367.
Hacquard, V. 2011. "Modality". In *Semantics: An International Handbook of Natural Language Meaning*, edited by C. Maienborn, K. von Heusinger, and P. Portner. 1484–1515. Berlin: Mouton de Gruyter.
Howson, C., and P. Urbach. 1993. *Scientific Reasoning: The Bayesian Approach*. Chicago: Open Court.
Howson, C., and P. Urbach. 2006. *Scientific Reasoning: The Bayesian Approach*, Chicago: 3rd ed. Chicago: Open Court.
Jeffrey, R. C. 1975. "Carnap's Empiricism." *Minnesota Studies in the Philosophy of Science* 6:37–49.
Kolodny, N. 2007. "How does Coherence Matter?" *Proceedings of the Aristotelian Society* 107 (1pt3):229–263.
Kratzer, A. 1991. "Modality". In *Semantics: An International Handbook of Contemporary Research*, edited by D. W. Arnim von Stechow. 639–650. Berlin: W. de Gruyter.
Lange, M. 2000. "Is Jeffrey Conditionalization Defective by Virtue of being Non-commutative? Remarks on the Sameness of Sensory Experiences." *Synthese* 123 (3):393–403.
Levi, I. 1967. "Probability Kinematics." *British Journal for the Philosophy of Science* 18 (3):197–209.
Lewis, D. 1980. "A Subjectivist's Guide to Objective Chance". In *Studies in Inductive Logic and Probability*, edited by R. C. Jeffrey. Vol. 2, 83–132. Berkeley: University of California Press.
Lewis, D. 2010. "Why Conditionalize". In *Philosophy of Probability: Contemporary Readings*, edited by Antony Eagle, 403–407. London: Routledge.
Lord, E. 2013. "The Real Symmetry Problem(s) for Wide-Scope accounts of Rationality." *Philosophical Studies* 3:1–22.
McNamara, P. 2010. "Deontic logic". In *Stanford Encyclopedia of Philosophy*, edited by E. Zalta. Published April 21, 2010. Accessed September 1, 2015. http://plato.stanford.edu/entries/logic-deontic/
Schroeder, M. 2004. "The Scope of Instrumental Reason." *Philosophical Perspectives* 18 (1):337–364.
Shpall, S. 2013. "Wide and Narrow Scope." *Philosophical Studies* 163 (3):717–736.

Simon, H. A. 1976. "From Substantive to Procedural Rationality". In *Method and Appraisal in Economics*, edited by S. Latsis 129–148. Cambridge, MA: Cambridge University Press.
Strevens, M. 2015. *Notes on Bayesian Confirmation Theory*. Unpublished.
Swanson, E. 2008. "Modality in Language." *Philosophy Compass* 3 (6):1193–1207.
Titelbaum, M. G. 2015. "How to Derive a Narrow-Scope Requirement from Wide-Scope Requirements." *Philosophical Studies* 172 (2): 535–542.
Way, J. 2011. "The Symmetry of Rational Requirements." *Philosophical Studies* 155 (2):227–239.
Weisberg, J. 2011. "Varieties of Bayesianism". In *Handbook of the History of Logic*, edited by D. Gabbay, S. Hartmann, and J. Woods. Vol. 10, 477. Elsevier.
Williamson, T. 2000. *Knowledge and its Limits*. Oxford: Oxford University Press.
Wolterstorff, N. 2010. *Practices of Belief*. Cambridge: Cambridge University Press.

Appendix A

In Section 4.1, I stated that if evidence is credence-independent and we adopt an interval understanding of Jeffrey Conditionalization, then Jeffrey Conditionalization's prescriptions will depend on what intervals we choose to update on. Let's see why this is the case. If evidence is credence-independent, Jeffrey Conditionalization can only yield the same prescriptions regardless of what intervals we update on if the following claim is true:

Cumulative Evidence: For any sequence of evidence partitions $S_1 - S_n$, there is a 'cumulative' evidence partition S such that, for any credence function, consecutively Jeffrey Conditionalizing on $S_1 - S_n$ will yield the same results as Jeffrey Conditionalizing on S. We see that Cumulative Evidence is false by constructing a counterexample.

For simplicity, let's focus on a simple case where the subject's credences are only defined over four possibilities, each corresponding to one of the possible truth values for a pair of propositions A and B. Let S_1 be the evidence partition $\{(A, 1/2), (\neg A, 1/2)\}$, and S_2 the

cr_0	B	$\neg B$
A	1/10	2/10
$\neg A$	3/10	4/10

evidence partition $\{(B, 1/2), (\neg B, 1/2)\}$.
To start, consider a subject whose initial credences cr_0 over these possibilities are:

cr_1	B	$\neg B$
A	1/6	2/6
$\neg A$	3/14	4/14

Jeffrey Conditionalizing cr_0 on S_1 gives us cr_1:

cr_2	B	$\neg B$
A	7/32	7/26
$\neg A$	9/32	6/26

And Jeffrey Conditionalizing cr_1 on S_2 gives us cr_2:

What evidence partition S would gets us from cr_0 to cr_2 in one step? Well, recall that Jeffrey Conditionalization keeps the ratios of credences within each element of an evidence partition the same. So unless S is maximally fine-grained – unless S is an evidence partition which puts each of these four propositions in a different element – some of the ratios between the credences of cr_0 and the credences of cr_2 will be the same. Since none of the ratios between the credences of cr_0 and the credences of cr_2 are the same, S must be an evidence partition which puts each of these four propositions in a different element of the partition.

If one updates on such a partition, one will adopt the credences it assigns to each of these elements. So the only partition that will get us directly from cr_0 to cr_2 is the one that assigns each of these values directly. Thus, if we want an evidence partition S to yield the cr_0-to-cr_2 transition in one step, then S must be

cr_0^*	B	$\neg B$
A	1/4	1/4
$\neg A$	1/4	1/4

$\{(A \wedge B, 7/32), (A \wedge \neg B, 7/26), (\neg A \wedge B, 9/32), (\neg A \wedge \neg B, 6/26)\}$.

Now consider a subject who starts out with a different initial credence function, cr_0^*: Jeffrey Conditionalizing cr_0^* on S_1 gives us cr_0^* again. And Jeffrey Conditionalizing cr_0^* on S_2 gives us cr_0^* again. So updating cr_0^* on S_1 and then S_2 will leave the subject's credences unchanged. But Jeffrey Conditionalizing cr_0^* on S will give us cr_2, which changes the subject's credences quite a bit.

So there is no evidence partition which, for any credence function, will yield the same results as consecutively updating on S_1 and S_2. For the only evidence partition that will yield the same results as updating on S_1 and S_2 if we start with cr_0 is S, and S will not yield the same results as updating on S_1 and S_2 if we start with cr_0^*. Thus Cumulative Evidence is false.

Appendix B

Although the proposed understanding of Conditionalization presented and defended in the text is characterized using standard deontic logic, one can also characterize this proposal using Kratzer (1991) account of the semantics of modals. And doing so provides us with a natural way to flesh out some more details regarding this proposal, details that it's hard to provide using standard deontic logic.

On Kratzer's framework, the truth values of deontic modals are determined by two functions from worlds to sets of propositions. First, a *modal base*, which yields sets of propositions representing constraints on the range of possibilities – we use the modal base to pick out the relevant worlds by selecting all and only those worlds at which these propositions are true. Second, an *ordering source*, which yields sets of propositions representing the 'ideal' – we use the ordering source to provide a a partial ordering over worlds, one that ranks worlds according to how close they are to this ideal (i.e. according to how many of these propositions are true). For simplicity, let's adopt the Limit Assumption (that in any set of worlds there's always a highest ranked subset, instead of a infinite ascending sequence of more highly ranked worlds). Then the thought is that one should A iff A is true at all of the highest ranked accessible worlds. (For a more detailed presentation of Kratzer's framework, see Kratzer (1991), Swanson (2008) and Hacquard (2011)).

In what follows, I'll assume that the ordering source yields the same set of propositions at every world (i.e. that there's a single uniform ideal), and that all of the propositions in the ordering source can be jointly satisfied (i.e. that the ideal is consistent).[42]

Given this framework, we can accept the formulations of Conditionalization provided in the text, as long as we understand them as implicitly requiring the modal base to be broad enough to admit at least one ideal world – a world at which all of the propositions in the ordering source are true. The formulations given in the text then assert that, given such a modal base, the highest ranked worlds (and thus the worlds a subject should aim for) will be worlds at which subjects satisfy that formulation of Conditionalization.[43] This is equivalent to thinking of these formulations of Conditionalization as providing partial descriptions of the ordering source. In particular, we can think of these formulations as requiring the propositions in the ordering source to entail that subjects conditionalize (in the manner specified by that formulation).[44]

I didn't say that the ordering source *consists* of the proposition that subjects conditionalize for two reasons. First, if one thinks that there are other epistemic norms that bind subjects (e.g. the Principal Principle) then propositions concerning these norms will appear in the ordering source as well; so the ordering source won't *just* consist of propositions regarding Conditionalization. Second, if one wants a detailed ranking which takes into account things like partially satisfying the requirement to conditionalize, or approximately conditonalizing to a greater or lesser degree, then one won't want the claim that subjects conditionalize to appear as a single proposition in the ordering source. Instead, one will want to use a batch of weaker propositions that together entail that subjects conditionalize – this allows one to assess the magnitude of deviations from this ideal, by seeing how many of these weaker propositions are violated.[45]

This framework allows us to give the claim that Conditionalization is 'an ideal at which to aim' a precise meaning. At the ideal worlds, in which all of the propositions in the ordering source are satisfied, subjects will conditionalize. And given an appropriate decomposition of the claim that subjects conditionalize into weaker propositions, the ordering source will tell us how to move closer or farther from this ideal – i.e. it will tell us in what direction to aim.

Likewise, this framework provides a way to spell out the relationship between a subject's cognitive limitations and the rule's ability to provide guidance and satisfy ought-implies-can. A norm can only provide a subject with guidance and satisfy ought-implies-can if that subject is cognitively capable of 'getting to' the highest ranked worlds picked out by the modal base. And since Conditionalization, as I'm understanding it, implicitly requires us to work with a modal base that admits at least one ideal world, this norm will only provide guidance and satisfy ought-implies-can for subjects whose cognitive capabilities are powerful enough to allow them to get to ideal worlds. So the norm won't provide guidance or satisfy ought-implies-can for more cognitively limited subjects like ourselves. (If we can complete the difficult task of working out what exactly to put in the ordering base, we can construct a norm that provides guidance to *any* subject: we simply require the modal base to admit all and only worlds that the subject is cognitively capable of getting to, and then direct her towards the subset of those worlds that are highest ranked. This norm would have the same 'normative heart' as Conditionalization, since it makes prescriptions based on the same ordering source. But, unlike Conditionalization, it would not always tell subjects to conditionalize, since many subjects aren't capable of doing so. (If we distinguish between 'evaluative' and 'guidance' norms, then we can think of Conditionalization as the evaluative norm suggested by this ordering source, and this other norm as Conditionalization's 'guidance counterpart' – the guidance norm suggested by the same ordering source.))

Appendix 3

Appendix C

Suppose that Ought Implies Can, that the Past is Immutable, and that the posterior answer to the Time of Evidence Question is correct. Then the narrow and wide scope formulations of Conditionalization will be equivalent.

Let's see why this is so. To begin, recall that since the time of evaluation is t_1 and The Past is Immutable, it follows that anything true before t_1 will be true at all C-accessible$_{s,t_1}$ worlds, and *a fortiriori* (given that Ought Implies Can) at all O-accessible$_{s,t_1}$ worlds. Given the posterior answer to the Time of Evidence question, A only describes events at t_0, so it follows that if A is true then $O_{s,t_1}(A)$ is true, and likewise if ¬A is true then $O_{s,t_1}(¬A)$ is true. For legibility, let's suppress the s and t_1 indices on the O operators. We can now see that the narrow scope answer (A → O(C)) entails the wide scope answer (O(A → C)). At the actual world, either A or ¬A is true. If A is true, then it follows from the narrow scope rule that O(C) is true. Thus O(¬A ∨ C) ≡ O(A → C) is true. On the other hand, if ¬A is true, then O(¬A) is true. Thus O(¬A ∨ C) ≡ O(A → C) is true. Either way, if the narrow scope rule is true, then the wide scope rule is true as well.

Likewise, given the above, the wide scope answer (O(A → C)) entails the narrow scope answer (A → O(C)). At the actual world, either A or ¬A is true. If A is true, then O(A) is true. If O(A) is true, it follows from the wide scope rule that O(C) is true as well.[46] Thus ¬A ∨ O(C) ≡ A → O(C) is true. On the other hand, if ¬A is true, then it follows immediately that ¬A ∨ O(C) ≡ A → O(C) is true. Either way, if the wide scope rule is true, then the narrow scope rule is true as well. So, given these assumptions, the narrow scope and wide scope understandings are equivalent.

Risk, rationality and expected utility theory

Richard Pettigrew

Department of Philosophy, University of Bristol, Bristol, UK

ABSTRACT
There are decision problems where the preferences that seem rational to many people cannot be accommodated within orthodox decision theory in the natural way. In response, a number of alternatives to the orthodoxy have been proposed. In this paper, I offer an argument against those alternatives and in favour of the orthodoxy. I focus on preferences that seem to encode sensitivity to risk. And I focus on the alternative to the orthodoxy proposed by Lara Buchak's risk-weighted expected utility theory. I will show that the orthodoxy can be made to accommodate all of the preferences that Buchak's theory can accommodate.

1. Introduction

Philosophers, psychologists and economists have known for a long time that there are a number of decision problems for which the preferences over the available options that seem rational to many people cannot be accommodated within orthodox decision theory in the natural way. In response to this observation, a number of alternatives to the orthodoxy have been proposed (Allais 1953; Quiggin 1982; Schmeidler 1989; Buchak 2013). In this paper, I offer an argument against those alternatives and in favour of the orthodoxy. This argument is very general: it is effective against any deviation from the orthodoxy. As a result, we need some account of the preferences that seem rational and yet which this

---

This paper began life as my contribution to the Author Meets Critics session on Lara Buchak's *Risk and Rationality* at the Pacific APA in San Diego in April 2014. I received extremely helpful feedback from Lara at that point and then later, when I came to write up the paper for publication. I would also like to thank Jason Konek, Rachael Briggs, Ralph Wedgwood, Greg Wheeler, and Ben Levinstein for further comments on this paper. The work on this paper was supported by the European Research Council Seventh Framework Program (FP7/2007-2013) Starting Researcher Grant (308961-EUT), Epistemic Utility Theory: Foundations and Applications.

orthodoxy cannot accommodate naturally: we need an error theory for our intuition that they are rational, or a way of making the orthodoxy accommodate them. I will focus here on those preferences that seem to encode sensitivity to risk. And I will focus on the alternative to the orthodoxy proposed by Lara Buchak's *risk-weighted expected utility theory*, which is intended to accommodate these preferences (Buchak 2013). I will show that, in fact, the orthodoxy can be made to accommodate the preferences in question; and I will argue that this is in fact the correct way to accommodate them. Thus, the paper has two parts: the first is a general objection to any non-expected utility theory; the second is a specific account of how to accommodate within the orthodoxy the preferences that Buchak's theory permits.

2. The argument for orthodox expected utility theory

2.1. Decision problems and the framework of decision theory

Here's a decision problem. An agent is choosing between two options: on the first, which we will call *Safe*, she is guaranteed to receive £50; on the second, which we will call *Risky*, a fair coin will be flipped and she will receive £100 if the coin lands heads and £0 if the coin lands tails. There are three components of this decision problem. First: the states of the world, namely, the state in which the coin lands heads and the state in which the coin lands tails. Second: the outcomes, namely, £0, £50, £100. Third: the acts between which our agent is choosing, namely, *Safe* and *Risky*. In general, a decision problem consists of these three components:

- S is the set of *states* (or *possible worlds*). Thus, in our example, $S = \{Heads, Tails\}$.

Degrees of belief or *credences* will be assigned to a finite algebra $\mathcal{F}$ of subsets of the set of states S. These are propositions represented as sets of states or possible worlds.[1]

- $\mathcal{X}$ is the set of *outcomes*.

Thus, in our example, $S = \{£0, £50, £100\}$. We will take outcomes to be entire descriptions of the world, rather than merely changes in the agent's wealth. Thus, £0 is really *Status quo* + £0; £50 is really *Status quo* + £50; and so on. But we will continue to denote them just by the change in the status quo that they represent. *Utilities* will be assigned to the elements of $\mathcal{X}$.

- $\mathcal{A}$ is the set of *acts*.

Thus, in our example, $\mathcal{A} = \{Safe, Risky\}$. We represent acts as finite-valued functions from S to $\mathcal{X}$. That is, they take ways the world might be and return the outcome of the act if the world were that way. Thus, for our purposes, we can represent an act f in the set of acts $\mathcal{A}$ using the following notation:

$f = \{E_1, x_1; \ldots; E_n, x_n\}$, where $x_1, \ldots, x_n$ are the values that the function f might take – that is, the possible outcomes of the acts – and, for each $i = 1, \ldots, n$, the proposition E_i says that f will have outcome x_i. Thus, if we represent propositions as sets of possible worlds, as we did above, $E_i = \{s \in S : f(s) = x_i\}$. So E_i is the set of states of the world in which f has outcome x_i. Thus, in our example above, $Safe = \{Heads \vee Tails, £50\}$ and $Risky = \{Heads, £100; Tails, £0\}$. We assume that all such propositions E_i are in the algebra $\mathcal{F}$. For each outcome x in $\mathcal{X}$, there is an act in $\mathcal{A}$ – which we write $\bar{x}$ – that has outcome x regardless of the state of the world. That is, representing the act $\bar{x}$ as a function from states to outcomes, $\bar{x}(s) = x$ for all states s in $\mathcal{S}$. We call $\bar{x}$ the *constant act on x*. Let $\bar{\mathcal{X}} = \{\bar{x} : x \in \mathcal{X}\} \subseteq \mathcal{A}$ be the set of constant acts. They will prove particularly important in Section 5.2 below.

2.2. The business of decision theory

With this framework in place, we can state the business of decision theory. It is concerned with the relationship between two sorts of attitudes, which I will call *external attitudes* and *internal attitudes*.[2] The external attitudes are typically taken to be represented by the agent's preference ordering $\succeq$. $\succeq$ is an ordering on the set $\mathcal{A}$ of acts. If f and g are acts in $\mathcal{A}$, we say that $f \succeq g$ if the agent weakly prefers act f to act g. The internal attitudes, on the other hand, are typically taken to be given by the agent's credences and her utilities. As mentioned above, her credences are defined on propositions in a σ-algebra $\mathcal{F}$ on the set of states $\mathcal{S}$. They measure how strongly she believes those propositions. And her utilities are defined on the outcomes in $\mathcal{X}$. They measure how strongly she desires or values those outcomes.[3] If you are a constructivist about the internal attitudes, then you will take only the external attitudes to be real: you will then take the business of decision theory to be the representation of the external attitudes by treating the agent *as if* she has internal attitudes and *as if* she combines those attitudes in a particular way to give her external attitudes. If, on the other hand, you are a realist about the internal attitudes, then you will take both sorts of attitudes to be real: you will then say that a rational agent's internal and external attitudes ought to relate in a particular way; indeed, they ought to relate *as if* she obtains her external attitudes by combining her internal attitudes in a particular way. We will have more to say about the business of decision theory later (cf. Section 5.2 below).

2.3. The EU rule of combination

Expected utility theory posits only two types of internal attitudes: these are given by the agent's credences and utilities. Her credences are given by a credence function $c : \mathcal{F} \to [0, 1]$, which we assume to be a probability function on $\mathcal{F}$. Her utilities are given by a utility function $u : \mathcal{X} \to \mathbb{R}$. As with most decision theories, expected utility theory posits one type of external attitude, namely, the agent's preference ordering. Expected utility theory then employs the following *rule of combination*, which states how her internal and external attitudes ought to relate:

EU Rule of Combination Suppose $f = \{E_1, x_1; \ldots; E_n, x_n\}$ is an act in $\mathcal{A}$ – that is, if E_i is true, the outcome of f is x_i. Then define

$$EU_{c,u}(f) := \sum_{i=1}^{n} c(E_i) u(x_i)$$

Then if the agent is rational, then

$$f \geq g \iff EU_{c,u}(f) \geq EU_{c,u}(g)$$

That is, an agent's preferences ought to order acts by their subjective expected utility.

A number of decision theorists wish to deny the EU Rule of Combination. Buchak is amongst them, but there are other so-called non-expected utility theorists (Allais 1953; Quiggin 1982; Schmeidler 1989). I disagree with them about the rule of combination; however, as we will see in the second half of this paper, I agree with them about the rationality of the preferences that they try to capture by reformulating the rule of combination. In Section 4, I try to effect a reconciliation between these two positions – the correctness of the EU Rule of Combination, on the one hand, and the rationality of risk-sensitive preferences, on the other. In this part of the paper, I wish to argue that we ought to combine our internal attitudes in exactly the way that expected utility theory suggests. That is, I want to argue for the EU Rule of Combination.

How can we tell between different rules of combination? It is commonly assumed that representation theorems help us to do this, but this is a mistake. A representation theorem *presupposes* a rule of combination. Relative to a particular rule of combination, it demonstrates that, for any agent whose preferences satisfy certain axioms, there are internal attitudes with certain properties (unique to some extent) such that these internal attitudes determine the preferences *in line with that rule of combination*. As many authors have emphasized, given a different rule of combination, there will often be different internal attitudes with different properties that determine the same preferences, but this time in line with this different rule of combination (Zynda 2000; Eriksson and Hájek 2007; Meacham and Weisberg 2011).

While both constructivists and realists must appeal to rules of combination, my argument for the EU Rule of Combination applies primarily to the realist. I attempt to show that, for an agent with a credence function of a certain sort and a utility function, they are irrational if they don't combine those two functions in a particular way and set their preferences in line with that way of combining them. It is directed at an agent whose credence function and utility function have a psychological reality beyond her being represented as having them. Thus, it does not apply to the constructivist, who thinks of the credence function and utility function as merely convenient mathematical ways of representing the preference ordering.

2.4. Estimates and the EU rule of combination

Finally, we come to state our argument in favour of the EU Rule of Combination. It draws on a mathematical result due to Bruno de Finetti, which we present as Theorem 1 below.

(EU1) A rational agent will weakly prefer one option to another if, and only if, her estimate of the utility of the first is at least her estimate of the utility of the second.
(EU2) A rational agent's estimate of a quantity will be her subjective expectation of it.
(3) Therefore,
(EUC) A rational agent's preference ordering $\succeq$ will be determined by the EU Rule of Combination.

The first premise (EU1) is supposed to be intuitively plausible. Suppose I desire only chocolate – obtaining as much of it as possible is my only goal. And suppose my estimate of the quantity of chocolate in the wrapper on my left is greater than my estimate of the quantity of chocolate in the wrapper on my right. And suppose that, nonetheless, I weakly prefer choosing the chocolate in the wrapper on my right. Then I would seem irrational. Likewise, if I desire only utility – surely an analytic truth if there are any – then I would seem irrational if my estimate of the utility of an act g were higher than my estimate of the utility another act f and yet I were to weakly prefer f to g. This is the argument for premise (EU1).

The second premise (EU2) is based on a mathematical argument together with a plausible claim about the goodness of estimates. Estimates, so the plausible claim goes, are better the closer they are to the true quantity they estimate. Indeed, we might take this to be an analytic truth. That is, we might take it to be a necessary condition on something being an estimate of a quantity that it is valued for its proximity to the actual value of that quantity. Thus, if I estimate that the amount of chocolate remaining in my cupboard is 73 g and my friend estimates that it is 79 g and in fact it is 80 g, then her estimate is better than mine. The mathematical argument is a generalization of a result due to de Finetti, which says, very roughly, that if an agent has estimates that are not expectations of the quantities that they estimate, there are alternative estimates of those quantities that are guaranteed to be closer to the true values of the quantities; so estimates that aren't expectations are irrational.

Let's make all of this precise. Suppose X is a quantity. Mathematically, we might understand this as a random variable, which is a function that takes a state of the world s and returns $X(s)$, which is the value that this quantity takes in this state of the world. Thus, if C is the quantity of chocolate in my cupboard in grams, and @ is the actual state of the world, where there is 80 g of chocolate in my cupboard, then $C(@) = 80$. Now, given what we said above about the goodness of estimates, we can measure the *badness* or *disvalue* of an estimate $e(X)$ of a quantity X given a state of the world s by the distance between $e(X)$ and $X(s)$. Now, I will focus on just one measure of distance here, for the sake of simplicity, but the result also holds of a wide range of distance measures that mathematicians call the *Bregman divergences*.[4] Having said that, in Section 2.5, I will offer a reason to prefer the measure of distance I use here to all other measures. The measure of distance between two numbers x and y that I will use here is the square of their difference $|x - y|^2$, which is itself a Bregman divergence. For obvious reasons, we call this the *quadratic distance measure* and we write it $q(x, y) := |x - y|^2$. Thus, relative to this measure of distance, the badness of an estimate $e(X)$ of a quantity X given a state of the world s is $q(e(X), X(s)) = |e(X) - X(s)|^2$.

Now, in the argument we wish to give for (EU2), we are interested in evaluating the goodness or badness not only of a single estimate of a single quantity, but also of a set of estimates of a set of quantities. So our next job is to say how we measure this. Suppose $\mathcal{X}$ is a set of quantities for which our agent has estimates. One of these quantities might be the quantity of chocolate in my cupboard, for instance; another might be the quantity of chocolate in my hand; another still might be the distance between my house and the nearest chocolate shop; and so on. And suppose that e is her *estimate function* – that is, e takes each quantity X in $\mathcal{X}$ and returns our agent's estimate $e(X)$ of that quantity. Then we will measure the badness of an estimate function at a state of the world by adding together the badness of each of the individual estimates that comprise it. Thus, the badness of e at the state of the world s is the sum of each $q(e(X), X(s))$ for each X in $\mathcal{X}$. So the badness of an estimate function e defined on the quantities in $\mathcal{X}$ at a state of the world s is

$$\mathfrak{I}(e, s) := \sum_{X \in \mathcal{X}} q(e(X), X(s)) = \sum_{X \in \mathcal{X}} |e(X) - X(s)|^2$$

With these notions defined, we have nearly defined everything that we need for our argument for (EU2). But there is one final observation to make. Consider our credences. It seems natural to say that my credence in a true proposition is better, epistemically speaking, the closer it is to the maximal credence, which is 1. And it seems natural to say that my credence in a false proposition is better, epistemically speaking, the closer it is to 0. That is, our credence in a proposition can be seen as an estimate of a particular quantity, namely, the quantity that takes value 1 if the proposition is true and value 0 if the proposition is false

(Jeffrey 1986; Joyce 1998). Given a proposition A, call this the *indicator quantity for A*: thus, $A(s) = 0$ if A is false at s; $A(s) = 1$ if A is true at s.

Now, suppose that our agent has credences in all propositions in a finite algebra $\mathcal{F}$. Let's say that her *credence function* is the function that assigns to each of these propositions her credence in it. Then the observation that a credence in a proposition is, or at least should be evaluated as if it is, an estimate of the indicator quantity for that proposition suggests that the badness of a credence function c at a state of the world s should be given by

$$\mathfrak{I}(c,s) := \sum_{A \in \mathcal{F}} q(c(A), A(s)) = \sum_{A \in \mathcal{F}} |c(A) - A(s)|^2$$

That is, it is the sum of the distance between each credence, $c(A)$, and the indicator quantity, A, corresponding to the proposition to which the credence is assigned.

Finally, we can say that an agent with a credence function c defined on the propositions in the finite algebra $\mathcal{F}$ and an estimate function e defined on a finite set of quantities $\mathcal{X}$ should be evaluated at a state of the world s as follows: her badness is given by

$$\mathfrak{I}(c,s) + \mathfrak{I}(e,s) = \sum_{A \in \mathcal{F}} q(c(A), A(s)) + \sum_{X \in \mathcal{X}} q(e(X), X(s))$$

That completes our account of how badly an agent is doing who has credences in propositions in $\mathcal{F}$ and certain estimates in quantities in $\mathcal{X}$.

Next, we turn to what we might show using this account. Let's say that our agent's credence function c defined on finite algebra $\mathcal{F}$ is *probabilistic* if

(i) (Range) $0 \leq c(A) \leq 1$ for all A in $\mathcal{F}$.
(ii) (Normalization) $c(\top) = 1$, where $\top$ is the tautologous proposition; that is, it is true at all states of the world.
(iii) (Additivity) $c(A \vee B) = c(A) + c(B)$ if A and B are mutually exclusive propositions; that is, A and B are not true together at any state of the world.

Now suppose that c is probabilistic. Then we say that the estimate function e defined on $\mathcal{X}$ is *expectational with respect to c* if

(iv) (Expectation) For each X in $\mathcal{X}$,

$$e(X) = \sum_{s \in S} c(s) X(s)$$

So an estimate function is expectational with respect to a probabilistic credence function if its estimate of each quantity is the weighted sum of the possible values of that quantity where the weights are given by the credence assigned to the relevant state of the world by the credence function. We say that a pair (c, e) is *probabilistic and expectational* if c is probabilistic and e is expectational with respect to c – that is, if they jointly satisfy (i)–(iv).

For instance, suppose there are just two states of the world, s_1 and s_2. And let C be the quantity of chocolate in my cupboard in grams. Let's suppose that, in state s_1, there is a meagre 80 g of chocolate in my cupboard (so $C(s_1) = 80$), whereas in state s_2, there is veritable bounty, namely, 1000 g (so $C(s_2) = 1000$). And suppose that, having resisted the temptation to indulge in wishful thinking, I have credence $c(s_1) = 0.9$ in state s_1 and $c(s_2) = 0.1$ in state s_2. Then my credences are probabilistic (since they sum to 1), and my estimate of C is expectational with respect to my credences just in case it is $e(C) = c(s_1)C(s_1) + c(s_2)C(s_2) = (0.9 \times 80) + (0.1 \times 1000) = 172$.

In order to establish (EU2), the second premise of the argument for the EU Rule of Combination, we need to show that it is a requirement of rationality that an agent have a probabilistic credence function and an estimate function that is expectational with respect to it. Our argument is based on the following mathematical theorem, which is due to de Finetti (1974, 136).

Theorem 1 (de Finetti) *Suppose c is a credence function on $\mathcal{F}$ and e is an estimate function on $\mathcal{X}$.*

(i) If (c, e) is not probabilistic and expectational, then there is another pair (c', e') that is probabilistic and expectational such that

for all states of the world s.

$$\mathfrak{I}(c', s) + \mathfrak{I}(e', s) < \mathfrak{I}(c, s) + \mathfrak{I}(e, s)$$

(ii) If (c, e) is probabilistic and expectational, then there is no other pair (c', e') such that

$$\mathfrak{I}(c', s) + \mathfrak{I}(e', s) \leq \mathfrak{I}(c, s) + \mathfrak{I}(e, s)$$

for all states of the world s.

Thus, if an agent either has a credence function that is not a probability function, or if her credence function is a probability function but her estimates of quantities are not all given by her expectations of those quantities relative to that credence function, then there are alternative credences and estimates that, taken together, will be less bad than her credences and estimates taken together; that is, the alternative credences and estimates will be closer to the quantities that they estimate however those quantities turn out to be. What's more, if her credence function is a probability function, and if her estimates are given by her expectations, then there are no alternative credences and estimates that are guaranteed to be better than hers; indeed, there are no alternative credences and estimates that are guaranteed to do at least as well as hers. I provide a proof of this result in the Appendix.

This gives us an argument for having credences that are probabilities and estimates that are expectations. If we fail to do this, the theorem says, there are alternative credences and estimates we might have had that are guaranteed to do better than our credences; and there is nothing that is guaranteed to do better than those alternatives; indeed, there is nothing else that is even guaranteed to do just as well as them. Compare: I am offered two gambles on a fair coin toss. On the first, if the coin lands heads, I receive £5; if it lands tails, I lose £6. On the second, if the coin lands heads, I receive £10; if it lands tails, I lose £3. Now suppose I choose the first gamble. You would charge me with irrationality. After all, the second is guaranteed to be better than the first; whether the coin comes up heads or tails, I'll end up with more money if I've taken the second gamble. We are using a similar piece of reasoning here to argue that an agent is irrational if she has credences that are not probabilities, or if she has credences that are probabilities, but her estimates are not expectations with respect to them. That is, we are appealing to the so-called *Dominance Principle*, which says that an option is irrational if there is an alternative that is guaranteed to be better than it, and if there is nothing that is guaranteed to be better than that alternative. This completes our justification of the second premise (EU2) of our argument for the EU Rule of Combination.

You might worry here that, in the preceding justification of (EU2), we appeal to one principle of rational choice in order to justify another: we are appealing to the Dominance Principle in order to establish the EU Rule of Combination. And of course we are. But that is permissible in this context. After all, the Dominance Principle is an uncontroversial principle of decision theory. It is agreed upon by all parties to the current debate. Buchak and all other non-expected utility theorists disagree with me and other expected utility theorists about how credences and utilities should combine to give preferences. But we all agree that if one option is guaranteed to be better than another, and there is nothing that is guaranteed to be better than the first, then the second is irrational. So the argument strategy is legitimate.

Having given our justification for (EU2), this completes our argument for the EU Rule of Combination. According to the first premise (EU1), our preference ordering over acts should match our estimates of the utility of those acts: that is, I should weakly prefer one act to another iff my estimate of the utility of the first is at least as great as my estimate of the utility of the second. According to the second premise (EU2), our estimate of a given quantity, whether it is the utility of an act or the mass of chocolate in my fridge, should be our expectation of that quantity; that is, it should be the weighted average of the possible values that that quantity might take where the weights are given by our credences in the relevant states of the world. Putting these together, we obtain the EU Rule of Combination.

2.5. Measuring the badness of estimates

Before we leave our argument for the EU Rule of Combination, it is worth noting two things about the distance measure q that we used to give the badness of an estimate of a given quantity at a given state of the world, and the function $\mathfrak{I}$ that we used to give the badness of a set of estimates in a set of quantities at a given world. First, as noted above, Theorem 1 holds for a wide range of alternative measures of distance; indeed, for any of the so-called Bregman divergences. However, second, it is also true that Theorem 1 fails for a wide range of alternative measures; indeed, it fails for the so-called *absolute value measure* $\mathfrak{a}$, which takes the distance between real numbers x and y to be the difference between them, that is, $\mathfrak{a}(x,y) := |x-y|$. Thus, this argument will be compelling to the extent that we can justify using the quadratic measure q, or some other Bregman divergence, instead of the absolute value measure $\mathfrak{a}$. Arguments have been given for this assumption in the case where we are measuring only the badness of credences (D'Agostino and Sinigaglia 2010; Leitgeb and Pettigrew 2010; Pettigrew ta 2016). In this context, it looks most promising to extend the argument of D'Agostino and Sinigaglia (2010). The arguments of Leitgeb and Pettigrew (2010) assume too much, and the argument of Pettigrew (ta) is too closely bound to the case of credences.

Above, we assumed that we begin with a measure $\mathfrak{d}$ of the distance between a single estimate $e(X)$ of a single quantity X and the true value $X(s)$ of X at a state of the world s; and then we measure the distance between an entire estimate function e defined on a set $\mathcal{X}$ of quantities, on the one hand, and the true values of those quantities at a state of the world s, on the other hand, by summing the distances, $\mathfrak{d}(e(X), X(s))$, between each $e(X)$ and $X(s)$ for X in $\mathcal{X}$. If we adapt the argument given by D'Agostino and Sinigaglia (2010), we do not make this assumption: instead, we justify it. That is, we assume that the badness of an estimate function e defined on $\mathcal{X}$ at a state of the world s is given by some function $\mathfrak{D}(e, s)$, and we lay down conditions on this function such that, if $\mathfrak{D}$ satisfies all of the conditions, then there is a continuous and strictly increasing function $H: \mathbb{R} \to \mathbb{R}$ such that

$$\mathfrak{D}(e, s) = H\left(\sum_{X \in \mathcal{X}} q(e(X), X(s))\right) = H\left(\sum_{X \in \mathcal{X}} |e(X) - X(s)|^2\right)$$

Since we appealed to the Dominance Principle in order to justify the EU Rule of Combination, and since the Dominance Principle pays attention only to the *ordering* of options at a world, rather than their *cardinal utilities* at that world, it does not matter whether we use the sum of the squared differences between the values or whether we use some strictly increasing transformation of that sum. Thus, this characterization of $\mathfrak{D}$ is sufficient for our purposes.

Here are the conditions that D'Agostino and Sinigaglia (2010) place on our measure $\mathfrak{D}$ of the badness of an estimate function.[5]

Extensionality Let us say that the *estimate profile* of e at s is the multiset of all pairs $(e(X), X(s))$ for X in $\mathcal{X}$ – that is, $\{\{(e(X), X(s)) : X \in \mathcal{X}\}\}$.[6] Then, if e has the same estimate profile at s as e' has at s', then $\mathfrak{D}(e, s) = \mathfrak{D}(e', s')$.

That is, the badness of your estimate function is a function only of its estimate profile. It does not depend on the particular quantities to which you assign estimates. If you and I assign estimates to very different quantities, but our estimate profiles match, then our estimates are exactly as bad as each other.

Accurate Extension Invariance If e is an estimate function on $\mathcal{X}$ and $\mathcal{X}' \subseteq \mathcal{X}$, then let $e|_{\mathcal{X}'}$ be the estimate function on $\mathcal{X}'$ that agrees with e on all quantities in $\mathcal{X}' - e|_{\mathcal{X}'}$ is sometimes called *the restriction of e to $\mathcal{X}'$*. Then, if the estimates that e assigns to quantities not in $\mathcal{X}'$ are equal to the true values of those quantities at s, then $\mathfrak{D}(e|_{\mathcal{X}'}, s) = \mathfrak{D}(e, s)$.

That is, adding perfectly accurate estimates to your estimate function does not affect its badness.

Difference Supervenience If e assigns an estimate to just one quantity X, then $\mathfrak{D}(e, s) = g(|e(X) - X(s)|)$ for some continuous and strictly increasing function $g : \mathbb{R} \to \mathbb{R}$.

That is, the badness of a single estimate is a continuous and strictly increasing function of the difference between that estimate and the true value of the quantity.

Separability If $\mathcal{X}' \subseteq \mathcal{X}$ and

(i) $\mathfrak{D}(e|_{\mathcal{X}'}, s) = \mathfrak{D}(e'|_{\mathcal{X}'}, s)$ and
(ii) $\mathfrak{D}(e|_{\mathcal{X}-\mathcal{X}'}, s) < \mathfrak{D}(e'|_{\mathcal{X}-\mathcal{X}'}, s)$,

then $\mathfrak{D}(e, s) < \mathfrak{D}(e', s)$.

That is, if two estimate functions are equally bad on some subset of the quantities to which they assign estimates, then one is worse than the other if it is worse on the remaining quantities.

Taken together, these four properties entail that there are continuous and strictly increasing functions $H : \mathbb{R} \to \mathbb{R}$ and $f : \mathbb{R} \to \mathbb{R}$ such that:

$$\mathfrak{D}(e, s) = H\left(\sum_{X \in \mathcal{X}} f(|e(X) - X(s)|)\right)$$

Indeed, these four conditions are equivalent to the existence of two such functions H and f. Thus, what we need for our conclusion is a further property that ensures that $f(x) = x^2$. That is the job of the final condition on $\mathfrak{D}$. To state it, we need the notion of an *order-reversing swap*. Suppose e is an estimate function defined on a set of quantities $\mathcal{X}$ and s is a state of the world. And suppose that the estimates that e assigns to quantities X and Y are ordered correctly at s. That is,

(i) $e(X) > e(Y)$ and $X(s) > Y(s)$ or
(ii) $e(X) < e(Y)$ and $X(s) < Y(s)$.

Then, if we define e_{XY} to be the estimate function that is obtained from e by swapping its estimates for X and Y – so $e_{XY}(X) = e(Y)$ and $e_{XY}(Y) = e(X)$ – then we say that e_{XY} is an *order-reversing swap of e*, since the estimates that e_{XY} assigns to quantities X and Y are ordered *incorrectly* at s. Our next condition says two things: first, it says that an order-reversing swap always increases the badness of the estimates; second, it says that if you compare two order-reversing swaps on the same estimate function and if (a) the two swaps involve swapping estimates that are themselves equally far apart and (b) the two swaps involve quantities whose true values are equally far apart, then the badness of the swaps is equal. The motivation for this condition is the following: The badness of a set of estimates is supposed to be determined by the extent to which they match the truth about the quantities that they estimate. As well as matching the *quantitative* facts about those quantities – such as their values – it also seems to be a good thing to match the *qualitative* facts about them – such as their ordering. Clearly e matches this qualitative fact for X and Y, whereas e_{XY} does not. Thus, other things being equal, e_{XY} is worse than e. And other things are equal, since all that has changed in the move from e to e_{XY} is that the quantities to which the estimates $e(X)$ and $e(Y)$ are assigned have been switched. Moreover, if we consider two possible order-reversing swaps on the same estimate function where (a) and (b) hold, then the effect of each swap on the badness of the estimate function should be the same, since there is nothing to tell between them.

The Badness of Order-Reversing Swaps Suppose e is defined on $\mathcal{X}$ and suppose X, Y, X', Y' are quantities in $\mathcal{X}$. And suppose $e(X), e(Y)$ are ordered as $X(s), Y(s)$ are; and $e(X'), e(Y')$ are ordered as $X'(s), Y'(s)$ are. And suppose $|e(X) - e(Y)| = |e(X') - e(Y')|$ and $|X(s) - Y(s)| = |X'(s) - Y'(s)|$. Then $\mathfrak{D}(e, s) < \mathfrak{D}(e_{XY}, s) = \mathfrak{D}(e_{X'Y'}, s)$.

We now have the following theorem:

Theorem 2 (D'Agostino & Dardanoni) *If $\mathfrak{D}$ satisfies Extensionality, Accurate Extension Invariance, Difference Supervenience, Separability and The Badness of Order-Reversing Swaps, then there is a continuous and strictly increasing functions $H: \mathbb{R} \to \mathbb{R}$ such that:*

$$\mathfrak{D}(e, s) = H\left(\sum_{X \in \mathcal{X}} |e(X) - X(s)|^2\right)$$

This gives us what we need.

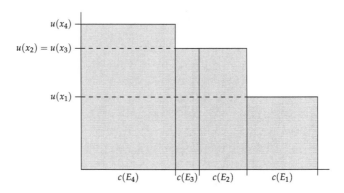

Figure 1. The expected utility $EU_{c,u}(h)$ of h is given by the grey area. Note: It is obtained by summing the areas of the four vertical rectangles: working from right to left, their areas are $c(E_1)u(x_1), \ldots, c(E_4)u(x_4)$.

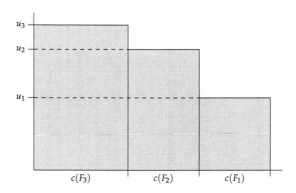

Figure 2. Again, the expected utility $EU_{c,u}(h)$ of h is given by the grey area. Note: It is obtained by summing the areas of the three vertical rectangles (the middle two vertical rectangles from Figure 1 have been merged): working from right to left, their areas are $c(F_1)u_1, \ldots, c(F_3)u_3$.

3. Expected utility and risk-weighted expected utility

In the previous section, we gave our defence of the EU Rule of Combination. In this section, we describe Lara Buchak's proposed alternative. To do this, we'll illustrate the difference between expected utility and risk-weighted expected utility using a particular act as an example. We'll first describe the expected utility of that act, and then we'll show how to define its risk-weighted expected utility. Our example is the following act: $h = \{E_1, x_1; \ldots; E_4, x_4\}$. The agent's probabilistic credences over the events $E_1, \ldots, E_4$ and her utilities for the outcomes $x_1, \ldots, x_4$ are given as follows:

	$(x_1, \overline{x_1})$	$(x_2, \overline{x_2})$	$(x_3, \overline{x_3})$	$(x_4, \overline{x_4})$
u^*	3	5	5	6

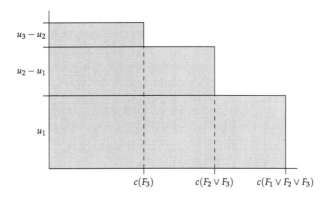

Figure 3. Once again, the expected utility $EU_{c,u}(h)$ of h is given by the grey area. Notes: It is obtained by summing the areas of the three *horizontal* rectangles. Working from bottom to top, their areas are $c(F_1 \vee F_2 \vee F_3)u_1 = u_y c(F_2 \vee F_3)(u_2 - u_1)$ and $c(F_3)(u_3 - u_2)$.

In Figure 1, we exploit a useful diagrammatic way of representing the expected utility of h, which is used by Quiggin (1993), Wakker (2010) and Buchak (2013).

Figure 1 suggests two ways in which we might reformulate $EU_{c,u}(f)$. These will be very useful in understanding how expected utility theory relates to Buchak's proposal.

- First, it is clear that $EU_{c,u}(f)$ depends only on the utilities of the outcomes to which the act f may give rise and the probabilities that f will produce outcomes with those utilities. Thus, given an act $f = \{E_1, x_1; \ldots ; E_n, x_n\}$ and a utility function u, we might redescribe f as $\{F_1, u_1; \ldots ; F_k, u_k\}$ where
- $u_1, \ldots, u_k$ are the utilities to which f might give rise ordered from least to greatest – that is, $u_1 < \ldots < u_k$. For instance, in our example act $h: u_1 = 3$, $u_2 = 5, u_3 = 6$.
- F_j is the proposition that f will give rise to u_j. Thus, $F_j = \{s \in S : u(h(s)) = u_j\}$. For instance, in our example act $h: F_1 \equiv E_1, F_2 \equiv E_2 \vee E_3, F_3 \equiv E_4$. We call this the *ordered utility-based description of f relative to u*. Then

$$EU_{c,u}(f) = \sum_{j=1}^{k} c(F_j)u_j$$

Figure 2 illustrates this reformulation of expected utility for our example act h.

- The second reformulation of $EU_{c,u}(f)$ builds on this first and is illustrated in Figure 3. Suppose $f = \{F_1, u_1; \ldots ; F_k, u_k\}$ is the ordered utility-based description of f relative to u. Then

$$EU_{c,u}(f) = u_1 + \sum_{j=2}^{k} c(F_j \vee \ldots \vee F_k)(u_j - u_{j-1})$$

Again, the expected utility of an act is given by a weighted sum: but this time the quantities to be weighted are the differences between one possible utility and the possible utility immediately below it; and the weight assigned to that difference is the probability that the act will give rise to at least that much utility.

With this in hand, we're ready to formulate Buchak's alternative to expected utility theory. Buchak is motivated by the apparent rationality of risk-sensitive behaviour. Notoriously, some seemingly rational risk-sensitive behaviour cannot be captured by expected utility theory at all: for instance, Allais described seemingly rational preferences that cannot be generated by any rational credence function and utility function in the way prescribed by expected utility theory (Allais 1953). Moreover, there are other seemingly rationally preferences that can be generated by a credence function and utility function in line with expected utility theory, but which seem to be rational even for agents who do not have credences and utilities that would generate them in this way. Thus, for instance, consider the two acts described in the introduction to this article: *Safe* = { Heads ∨ Tails, £50 }and *Risky* = { Heads, £100; Tails, £0} Suppose that our agent strictly prefers *Safe* to *Risky*: that is, *Safe* ≻ *Risky*. Can expected utility theory capture the rationality of this preference? Suppose that, since the coin is known to be fair, rationality requires that the agent assigns credences to the two states of the world as follows: $c(\text{Heads}) = 0.5 = c(\text{Tails})$. Then it is still possible to describe a utility function on the outcomes £0, £50, £100 that generates these preferences in the way expected utility theory requires. Let $u(£0) = 0$ and $u(£100) = £50 + £50) < u(£50) + u(£50)$. That is, suppose the agent treats money as a *dependent good*: how much utility it gives depends on how much of it she has already; so, money has diminishing marginal utility for this agent. Then, for an agent with this credence function and utility function, $EU_{c,u}(\textit{Safe}) > EU_{c,u}(\textit{Risky})$, as required. So expected utility theory can capture the rationality of these preferences. However, as Buchak rightly observes, those preferences – that is, *Safe* ≻ *Risky* – seem rational not only for an agent for whom money has diminishing marginal utility; they seem rational even for an agent whose utility is linear in money. And this is something that expected utility cannot capture. Thus, Buchak is interested not only in saving the Allais preferences, but also in saving other risk-sensitive behaviour without attributing the risk-sensitive behaviour to the shape of the utility function (Buchak 2013, Chapter 1).

How does Buchak hope to capture these risk-sensitive preferences? Where expected utility theory countenances only two types of internal attitude as relevant to preferences, Buchak countenances a third as well: this third component is supposed to capture the agent's attitude to risk, and it is given by a function $r:[0, 1] \to [0, 1]$, which Buchak assumes to be strictly increasing, continuous, and taking the following values, $r(0) = 0$ and $r(1) = 1$ (Buchak 2013, Section 2.2). Buchak's *risk-weighted expected utility theory* then employs the following

BELIEF, ACTION, AND RATIONALITY OVER TIME

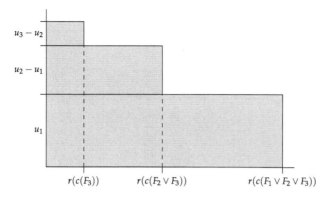

Figure 4. The risk-weighted expected utility $REU_{r_2,c,u}(h)$ of h is given by the grey area, where $r_2(x) := x^2$.

rule of combination, which states how an agent's internal and external attitudes ought to relate, where the agent has credence function c, utility function u and risk function r:

REU Rule of Combination (Buchak 2013, 53) Suppose $f = \{F_1, u_1; \ldots; F_k, u_k\}$ is the ordered utility-based description of act f relative to utility function u. Then let

$$REU_{r,c,u}(f) := u_1 + \sum_{j=2}^{k} r(c(F_j \vee \ldots \vee F_k))(u_j - u_{j-1})$$

Then if the agent is rational, then

$$f \geq g \iff REU_{r,c,u}(f) \geq REU_{r,c,u}(g)$$

In Figure 4, we illustrate the risk-weighted expected utility of our example act h when the agent has the risk function $r_2(x) := x^2$. Notice that the formulation of $REU_{r,c,u}(f)$ is exactly like the formulation of $EU_{c,u}(f)$ that we gave above except that each probability weight is transformed by the agent's risk function. Thus, if $r(x) < x$ (for all $0 < x < 1$), then, as Figure 4 illustrates, the lowest utility to which the act can give rise – namely, u_1 – contributes just as much to $REU_{r,c,u}(f)$ as it does to $EU_{c,u}(f)$ – it contributes u_1 to both. But further increases in utility – such as the increase from getting at least utility u_1 to getting at least u_2 – make less of a contribution since their probability – $c(F_2 \vee F_3)$ – is acted on by the risk function, and it is this reduced value – $r(c(F_2 \vee F_3))$ – that weights the possible increases in utility. Thus, such an agent displays risk-averse behaviour. r_2 is such a risk function.

Similarly, if $r(x) > x$ (for all $0 < x < 1$), then the lowest utility to which the act can give rise contributes just as much to $REU_{r,c,u}(f)$ as it does to $EU_{c,u}(f)$, but further increases in utility make more of a contribution since their probability is acted on by the risk function and it is this increased value that weights the

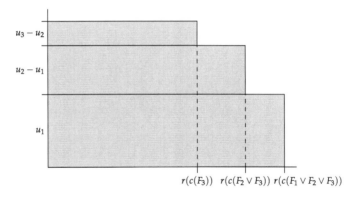

Figure 5. The risk-weighted expected utility $REU_{r_{0.5},c,u}(h)$ of h is given by the grey area, where $r_{0.5}(x) := \sqrt{x}$.

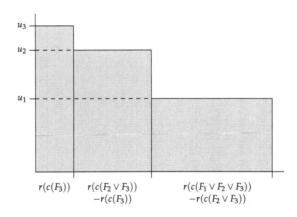

Figure 6. Again, the risk-weighted expected utility $REU_{r_2,c,u}(f)$ of f is given by the grey area, where $r_2(x) = x^2$.

possible increases in utility. This is illustrated in Figure 5. Such an agent displays risk-seeking behaviour. $r_{0.5}(x) := \sqrt{x}$ is such a risk function.

It's also easy to see that, if $r_1(x) := x$ (for $0 \leq x \leq 1$), then $REU_{r_1,c,u}(f) = EU_{c,u}(f)$. Thus, expected utility theory is the special case of risk-weighted expected utility theory given by a linear risk function. In such a situation, we say that the agent is *risk-neutral*. This means that Buchak's theory permits any preferences that expected utility theory permits. But it also permits a whole lot more. For instance, one can easily recover the Allais preferences or the preference *Safe* ≻ *Risky* described above by attributing to an agent a certain sort of risk function – in both cases, a risk-averse risk function.

This, then, is Buchak's proposal.

4. Redescribing the outcomes

Moving from expected utility theory to risk-weighted expected utility theory involves an agent evaluating an act in the way illustrated in Figure 3 to evaluating it in the way illustrated in Figure 4. In order to begin to see how we can redescribe the REU rule of combination as an instance of the EU rule of combination, we reformulate the REU rule in the way illustrated in Figure 6.[7] Thus, we can reformulate $REU_{r,c,u}(f)$ as follows:

$$REU_{r,c,u}(f) = \sum_{j=1}^{k-1}(r(c(F_j \vee \ldots \vee F_k)) - r(c(F_{j+1} \vee \ldots \vee F_k)))u_j + r(c(F_k))u_n$$

And we can reformulate this as follows:

$$REU_{r,c,u}(f) = \sum_{j=1}^{k-1} c(F_j) \frac{r(c(F_j \vee \ldots \vee F_k)) - r(c(F_{j+1} \vee \ldots \vee F_k))}{c(F_j \vee \ldots \vee F_k) - c(F_{j+1} \vee \ldots \vee F_k)} u_j + c(F_k)\frac{r(c(F_k))}{c(F_k)}u_n$$

since $c(F_j \vee \ldots \vee F_k) - c(F_{j+1} \vee \ldots \vee F_k) = c(F_j)$.

Now, suppose we let

$$s_j = \begin{cases} \frac{r(c(F_j \vee \ldots \vee F_k)) - r(c(F_{j+1} \vee \ldots \vee F_k))}{c(F_j \vee \ldots \vee F_k) - c(F_{j+1} \vee \ldots \vee F_k)} & \text{if } j = 1, \ldots, k-1 \\ \frac{r(c(F_j))}{c(F_j)} & \text{if } j = k \end{cases}$$

Then we have:

$$REU_{r,c,u}(f) = \sum_{j=1}^{k} c(F_j)s_j u_j$$

Reformulating Buchak's rule of combination in this way suggests two accounts of it. On the first, utilities attach ultimately to outcomes x_i, and they are weighted not by an agent's credences but rather by a function of those credences that encodes the agent's attitude to risk (given by a risk function). On this account, we group $c(F_j)s_j$ together to give this weighting. Thus, we assume that this weighting has a particular form: it is obtained from a credence function c and a risk function r to give $c(F_j)s_j$; this weighting then attaches to u_j to give $(c(F_j)s_j)u_j$. This is the account that Buchak favours.

On the second account, credences do provide the weightings for utility, as in the EU rule of combination, but utilities attach ultimately to outcome-act pairs (x_i, f). On this account, we group $s_j u_j$ together to give this utility; this utility is then weighted by $c(F_j)$ to give $c(F_j)(s_j u_j)$. That is, we say that an agent's utility function is defined on a new outcome space: it is not defined on a set of outcomes $\mathcal{X}$, but on a particular subset of $\mathcal{X} \times \mathcal{A}$, which we will call $\mathcal{X}^*$. $\mathcal{X}^*$ is the set of outcome-act pairs (x_i, f) such that x_i is a possible outcome of f: that is, $\mathcal{X}^* = \{(x, f) \in \mathcal{X} \times \mathcal{A} : \exists s \in S(f(s) = x)\}$. Now, just as the first account assumed that the weightings of the utilities have a certain form – namely, they are generated by a risk function and probability function in a certain way – so this account assumes something about the form of the new utility function u^* on $\mathcal{X}^*$: we assume that a certain relation holds between the utility that u^* assigns to outcome-act pairs in which the act is the constant act over the outcome and the utility u^* to outcome-act pairs in which this is not the case. We assume that the following holds:

$$u^*(x, f) = s_j u^*(x, \overline{x}) \tag{1}$$

If a utility function on $\mathcal{X}^*$ satisfies this property, we say that it *encodes attitudes to risk relative to risk function r*. Thus, on this account an agent evaluates an act as follows:

- She begins with a risk function r and a probability function c.
- She then assigns utilities to all constant outcome-act pairs $(x, \overline{x})$, defining u^* on $\overline{\mathcal{X}}^*$, where $\overline{\mathcal{X}}^* = \{(x, \overline{x}) : x \in \mathcal{X}\} \subseteq \mathcal{X}^*$.
- Finally, she extends u^* to cover all outcome-act pairs in $\mathcal{X}^*$ in the unique way required in order to make u^* a utility function that encodes attitudes to risk relative to r. That is, she obtains $u^*(x, f)$ by weighting $u^*(x, \overline{x})$ in a certain way that is determined by her probability function and her attitudes to risk.

Let's see this in action in our example act h; we'll consider h from the point of view of two risk functions, $r_2(x) = x^2$ and $r_{0.5}(x) = \sqrt{x}$. Recall: r_2 is a risk-averse risk function; $r_{0.5}$ is risk seeking. We begin by assigning utility to all constant outcome-act pairs $(x, \overline{x})$:

Then we do the same trick as above and amalgamate the outcome-act pairs with the same utility: thus, again, F_1 is the event in which the act gives outcome-act pair (x_1, h), F_2 is the event in which it gives (x_2, h) or (x_3, h), and F_3 the event in which it gives (x_4, h). Next, we assign utilities to (x_1, h), (x_2, h), (x_3, h) and (x_4, h) in such a way as to make u^* encode attitudes to risk relative to the risk function r.

Let's start by considering the utility of (x_1, h), the lowest outcome of h. Suppose our risk function is r_2; then

$$u^*(x_1, h) := \frac{r_2(c(F_1 \vee F_2 \vee F_3)) - r_2(c(F_2 \vee F_3))}{c(F_1 \vee F_2 \vee F_3) - c(F_2 \vee F_3)} u^*(x_1, \overline{x_1})$$

$$= \frac{r_2(1) - r_2(0.7)}{1 - 0.7} = 1.7 u^*(x_1, \overline{x_1})$$

And now suppose our risk function is $r_{0.5}$; then

$$u^*(x_1, h) := \frac{r_{0.5}(c(F_1 \vee F_2 \vee F_3)) - r_{0.5}(c(F_2 \vee F_3))}{c(F_1 \vee F_2 \vee F_3) - c(F_2 \vee F_3)} u^*(x_1, \overline{x_1})$$

$$= \frac{r_{0.5}(1) - r_{0.5}(0.7)}{1 - 0.7} \approx 0.54 u^*(x_1, \overline{x_1})$$

Thus, the risk-averse agent – that is, the agent with risk function r_2 – values this lowest outcome x_1 as the result of h more than she values the same outcome as the result of a certain gift of x_1, whereas the risk-seeking agent – with risk function $r_{0.5}$ – values it less. And this is true in general: if $r(x) < x$ for all x, the utility of the lowest outcome as a result of h will be more valuable than the same outcome as a result of the constant act on that outcome; if $r(x) < x$ it will be less valuable.

Next, let us consider the utility of (x_4, h), the highest outcome of h. Suppose her risk function is r_2; then

$$u^*(x_4, h) := \frac{r_2(c(F_3))}{c(F_3)} u^*(x_4, \overline{x_4}) = \frac{r_2(0.4)}{0.4} u^*(x_4, \overline{x_4}) = 0.4 u^*(x_4, \overline{x_4})$$

And now suppose her risk function is $r_{0.5}$; then

$$u^*(x_4, h) := \frac{r_{0.5}(c(F_3))}{c(F_3)} u^*(x_4, \overline{x_4}) = \frac{r_{0.5}(0.4)}{0.4} u^*(x_4, \overline{x_4}) = 2.5 u^*(x_4, \overline{x_4})$$

Thus, the risk-averse agent – that is, the agent with risk function r_2 – values this highest outcome x_4 as the result of h less than she values the same outcome as the result of a certain gift of x_4, whereas the risk-seeking agent – with risk function $r_{0.5}$ – values it more. And, again, this is true in general: if $r(x) < x$ for all x, the utility of the highest outcome as a result of h will be less valuable than the same outcome as a result of the constant act on that outcome; if $r(x) < x$ it will be more valuable.

This seems right. The risk-averse agent wants the highest utility, but also cares about how sure she was to obtain it. Thus, if she obtains x_1 from h, she knows she was guaranteed to obtain at least this much utility from h or from $\overline{x_1}$ (since x_1 is the lowest possible outcome of each act). But she also knows that h gave her some chance of getting more utility. So she values (x_1, h) more than $(x_1, \overline{x_1})$. But if she obtains x_4 from h, she knows she was pretty lucky to get this much utility, while she knows that she would have been guaranteed that much if she had obtained x_4 from $\overline{x_4}$. So she values (x_4, h) less than $(x_4, \overline{x_4})$. And similarly, but in reverse, for the risk-seeking agent.

Finally, let's consider the utilities of (x_2, h) and (x_3, h), the middle outcomes of h. They will have the same value, so we need only consider the utility of (x_2, h). Suppose her risk function is r_2; then

$$u^*(x_2, h) := \frac{r_2(c(F_2 \vee F_3)) - r_2(c(F_3))}{c(F_2 \vee F_3) - c(F_3)} u^*(x_2, \overline{x_2})$$

$$= \frac{r_2(0.7) - r_2(0.4)}{0.7 - 0.4} u^*(x_2, \overline{x_2}) = 1.1 u^*(x_2, \overline{x_2})$$

Thus, again, the agent with risk function r_2 assigns higher utility to obtaining x_2 as a result of h than to obtaining x_2 as the result of $\overline{x_2}$. But this is not generally true of risk-averse agents. Consider, for instance, a more risk-averse agent, who has a risk function $r_3(x) := x^3$. Then

$$u^*(x_2, h) := \frac{r_3(c(F_2 \vee F_3)) - r_3(c(F_3))}{c(F_2 \vee F_3) - c(F_3)} u^*(x_2, \overline{x_2})$$

$$= \frac{r_3(0.7) - r_3(0.4)}{0.7 - 0.4} u^*(x_2, \overline{x_2}) = 0.93 u^*(x_2, \overline{x_2})$$

Again, this seems right. As we said above, the risk-averse agent wants the highest utility, but she also cares about how sure she was to obtain it. The less risk-averse agent – whose risk function is r_2 – is sufficiently sure that h would obtain for her at least the utility of x_2 and possibly more that she assigns higher value to getting x_2 as a result of h than to getting it as a result of $\overline{x_2}$. For the more risk-averse agent – whose risk function is r_3 – she is not sufficiently sure. And reversed versions of these points can be made for risk-seeking agents with risk functions $r_{0.5}$ and $r_{0.333}$, for instance. Thus, we can see why it makes sense to demand of an agent that her utility function u^* on $\mathcal{X}^*$ encodes attitudes to risk relative to a risk function in the sense that was made precise above – see Equation 1.

Since what we have just provided is a genuine redescription of Buchak's REU Rule of Combination, we can see that Buchak's representation theorem is agnostic between a version of REU in which utilities attach to elements of $\mathcal{X}$, and a version of EU in which utilities attach to elements of $\mathcal{X}^*$.

Theorem 3 (Buchak) *If $\succeq$ satisfies the Buchak axioms, there is a unique probability function c, unique risk function, and unique-up-to-affine-transformation utility function u on $\mathcal{X}$ such that $\succeq$ is determined by r, c and u in line with the REU rule of combination.*

And we have the following straightforward corollary:

Theorem 4 *If $\succeq$ satisfies the Buchak axioms, there is a unique probability function c and unique-up-to-affine*-transformation utility function u^* on $\mathcal{X}^*$ that encodes attitudes to risk relative to a risk function such that $\succeq$ is determined by c and u^* in line with the EU rule of combination (where u^* is unique-up-to-affine*-transformation if $u^*|_{\overline{\mathcal{X}}}$ is unique-up-to-affine-transformation).*

Thus, by redescribing the set of outcomes to which our agent assigns utilities, we can see how her preferences in fact line up with her estimates of the utility of her acts, as required by the de Finetti-inspired argument for the EU Rule of Combination given in the previous section.

5. What's wrong with redescription?

Although Buchak does not address precisely this particular version of the redescription strategy, she does consider others nearby. Against those, she raises what amount to two objections (Buchak 2013, Chapter 4). (Buchak raises a further objection against versions of the redescription strategy that attempt to identify certain outcome-act pairs to give a more coarse-grained outcome space; but these do not affect my proposal.)

5.1. The problem of proliferation

One potential problem that arises when one moves from assigning utilities to $\mathcal{X}$ to assigning them to $\mathcal{X}^*$ is that an element in the new outcome space is never the outcome of more than one act: (x, f) is a possible outcome of act f but not of any act g other than f. Thus, this outcome never appears in the expected utility (or indeed risk-weighted expected utility) calculation of more than one act. The result is that very few constraints are placed on the utilities that must be assigned to these new outcomes and the probabilities that must be assigned to the propositions in order to recover a given preference ordering on the acts via the EU (or REU) rule of combination. Suppose $\succeq$ is a preference ordering on $\mathcal{A}$. Then, for each act f in $\mathcal{A}$, pick a real number r_f such that $f \succeq g$ iff $r_f \geq r_g$. Now there are many ways to do this, and they are not all affine transformations of one another – indeed, any strictly increasing $\tau : \mathbb{R} \to \mathbb{R}$ will take one such assignment to another. Now pick any probability function c on $\mathcal{F}$. Now, given an act $f = \{E_1, x_1; \ldots ; E_n, x_n\}$ the only constraint on the values $u^*(x_1, f), \ldots, u^*(x_n, f)$ is that $\sum_i c(E_i) u^*(x_i, f) = r_f$. And this of course permits many different values.[8] Buchak dubs this phenomenon *belief and desire proliferation* (Buchak 2013, 140).

Why is this a problem? There are a number of reasons to worry about belief and desire proliferation. There is the epistemological worry that, if utilities and probabilities are as loosely constrained as this, it is not possible to use an agent's observed behaviour to predict her unobserved behaviour. Divining her preferences between two acts will teach us nothing about the utilities she assigns to the outcomes of any other acts since those outcomes are unique to those acts. Also, those who wish to use representation theorems for the purpose of radical interpretation will be concerned by the complete failure of the uniqueness of the rationalization of preferences that such a decision theory provides.

Neither of these objections seems fatal to me. But in any case, the version of the redescription strategy presented here avoids them altogether. The reason is that I placed constraints on the sort of utility function u^* an agent can have over $\mathcal{X}^*$: I demanded that u^* encode attitudes to risk; that is, $u^*(x, f)$ is defined in terms of $u^*(x, \bar{x})$ in a particular way (given by Equation 1). And we saw in Theorem 4 above that, for any agent whose preferences satisfy the Buchak axioms, there is a unique probability function c and a unique utility function u^*

on $\mathcal{X}^*$ that encodes attitudes to risk relative to a unique risk function such that together c and u^* generate the agent's preferences in accordance with the EU Rule of Combination.

5.2. Ultimate ends and the locus of utility

Buchak's second objection initially seems more worrying (Buchak 2013, 137–138). A theme running through *Risk and Rationality* is that decision theory is the formalization of *instrumental* or *means-end reasoning*. One consequence of this is that an account of decision theory that analyses an agent as engaged in something other than means-end reasoning is thereby excluded.

Buchak objects to the redescription strategy on these grounds. According to Buchak, to understand an agent as engaged in means-end reasoning, one must carefully distinguish the means and the ends: in Buchak's framework, the means are the acts and the ends are the outcomes. One must then assign utilities to the ends only. Of course, in terms of these utilities and the agent's probabilities and possibly other representations of internal attitude such as the risk function, one can then assign value or utility to the means. But the important point is that this value or utility that attaches to the means is assigned on the basis of the assignment of utility to the ultimate ends. Thus, while there is a sense in which we assign a value or utility to means – i.e. acts – in expected utility theory, this assignment must depend ultimately on the utility we attach to ends – i.e. outcomes.

Thus, a first pass at Buchak's second complaint against the redescription strategy is this: the redescription strategy assigns utilities to something other than ends – it assigns utilities to outcome-act pairs, and these are fusions of means and ends. Thus, an agent analysed in accordance with the redescription strategy is not understood as engaged in means-end reasoning.

However, this seems problematic in two ways. Whether they constitute ultimate ends or not, there are at least two reasons why an agent *must* assign utilities to outcome-act pairs rather than outcomes on their own. That is, there are two reasons why at least this part of the redescription strategy – namely, the move from $\mathcal{X}$ to $\mathcal{X}^*$ – is necessary irrespective of the need to accommodate risk in expected utility theory.

Firstly, utilities must attach to the true outcomes of an act. But these true outcomes aren't the sort of thing we've been calling an outcome here. When I choose *Safe* over *Risky* and receive £50, the outcome of that act is not merely £50; it is £50 *as the result of Safe*. Thus, the true outcomes of an act are in fact the elements of $\mathcal{X}^*$ – they are what we have been calling the outcome-act pairs.

Of course, at this point, Buchak might accept that utilities attach to outcome-act pairs, but insist that it is nonetheless a requirement of rationality that an agent assign the same utility to two outcome-act pairs with the same act component; that is, $u^*(x, f) = u^*(x, g)$; that is, while utilities attach to fusions of means and ends, they must be a function only of the ends. But the second reason for attaching utilities to outcome-act pairs tells against this claim in general. The reason is this: As Bernard Williams urges, it is neither irrational nor even immoral to assign higher utility to a person's death as a result of something other than my agency than to that same person's death as a result of my agency (Williams and Smart 1973). This, one might hold, is what explains my hesitation in a Williams-style example in which I must choose whether or not to shoot a particular individual when I know that, if I don't shoot him, someone else will. I assign higher utility to the death of that person at the hands of someone else than to the death of that person at my hands. Thus, it is permissible in at least some situations to care about the act that gives rise to the outcome and let one's utility in an outcome-act pair be a function also of that act.

Nonetheless, this is not definitive. After all, Buchak could reply that this is peculiar to acts that have morally relevant consequences. Acts such as those in the Allais paradox do not have morally relevant consequences; but the redescription strategy still requires us to make utilities depend on acts as well as outcomes in those cases. Thus, for non-moral acts f and g, Buchak might say, it is a requirement of rationality that $u^*(x, f) = u^*(x, g)$, even if it is not such a requirement for moral cases. And this would be enough to scupper the redescription strategy.

However, it is not clear why the moral and non-moral cases should differ in this way. Consider again the Williams-style example from above: I must choose whether to shoot an individual or not; I know that, if I do not shoot him, someone else will. I strictly prefer not shooting him to shooting him. My reasoning might be reconstructed as follows: I begin by assigning a certain utility to this person's death as the result of something other than my agency – natural causes, for instance, or murder by a third party. Then, to give my utility for his death at my hand, I weight this original utility in a certain way, reducing it on the basis of the action that gave rise to the death. Thus, the badness of the outcome-act pair (*X's death, My agency*) is calculated by starting with the utility of another outcome-act pair with the same outcome component – namely, (*X's death, Not my agency*) – and then weighting that utility based on the act component. We might call (*X's death, Not my agency*) the *reference pair attached to the outcome X's death*. The idea is that the utility we assign to the reference pair attached to an outcome comes closest to what we might think of as the utility that attaches solely to the outcome; the reference pair attached to an outcome x is the outcome-act pair (x, f) for which the act f contributes least to the utility of the pair.

Now this is exactly analogous to what the redescription strategy proposes as an analysis of risk-sensitive behaviour. In that case, when you wish to calculate the utility of an outcome-act pair (x, f), you begin with the utility you attach to $(x, \overline{x})$. Then you weight that utility in a certain way that depends on the riskiness of the act. This gives the utility of (x, f). Thus, if we take $(x, \overline{x})$ to be the reference pair attached to the outcome x, then this is analogous to the moral case above.

In both cases, we can recover something close to the notion of utility for ultimate ends or pure outcomes (i.e. elements of $\mathcal{X}$): the utility of the pure outcome x – to the extent that such a utility can be meaningfully said to exist – is $u^*(x, \bar{x})$, the utility of the reference pair attached to x. That seems right. Strictly speaking, there is little sense to asking an agent for the utility they assign to a particular person's death; one must specify whether or not the death is the result of that agent's agency. But we often do give a utility to that sort of outcome; and when we do, I submit, we give the utility of the reference pair. Similarly, we often speak as if we assign a utility to receiving £50, even though the request makes little sense without specifying the act that gives rise to that pure outcome: again, when we do so, what we really do is give the utility of £50 *for sure*, that is, the utility of $(£50, \overline{£50})$.

Understood in this way, the analysis of a decision given by the redescription strategy still portrays the agent as engaged in means-end reasoning. Of course, there are no pure ultimate ends to which we assign utilities. But there is something that plays that role, namely, reference pairs. An agent's utility for an outcome-act pair (x, f) is calculated in terms of her utility for the relevant reference pair, namely, $(x, \bar{x})$; and the agent's value for an act f is calculated in terms of her utilities for each outcome-act pair (x, f) where x is a possible outcome of f. Thus, though the value of an act on this account is not ultimately grounded in the utilities of pure, ultimate outcomes of that act, it is grounded in the closest thing that makes sense, namely, the utilities of the reference pairs attached to the pure, ultimate outcomes of the act.

6. Conclusion

Buchak proposes a novel decision theory. It is formulated in terms of an agent's probability function on $\mathcal{F}$, utility function on $\mathcal{X}$ and risk function. It permits a great many more preference orderings than orthodox expected utility theory. On Buchak's theory, the utility that is assigned to an act is not the expectation of the utility of its outcome; rather it is the risk-weighted expectation. But the argument of Section 2 of this paper suggests that the value of an act for an agent should be her estimate of the utility of its outcome; and her estimate of a quantity should be her expectation of that quantity. And these, together, give the EU Rule of Combination. In this paper, we have tried to reconcile the preferences that Buchak endorses with the EU Rule of Combination. To do this, we redescribed the outcome space so that utilities were attached ultimately to outcome-act pairs rather than to outcomes themselves. This allowed us to capture precisely the preferences that Buchak permits, whilst letting the utility of an act be the expectation of the utility it will produce. The redescription strategy raises some questions: Does it prevent us from using decision theory for certain epistemological purposes? Does it fail to portray agents as engaged in means-end reasoning? In Section 5, we tried to answer these questions.

Notes

1. A finite set X of subsets of a set S is an algebra if (i) S is in X; (ii) if Z is in X, then its complement $S - Z$ is in X; (iii) if Z_1, Z_2 are in X, then their union $Z_1 \cup Z_2$ is in X.
2. The names should be considered labels only. I do not take them to imply that one sort of attitude can be observed directly, while the other sort is knowable only by inference.
3. As we will see below, one of Buchak's central contentions is that there is a third type of internal attitude with which decision theory deals, namely, attitudes to risk. In my alternative to Buchak's theory, I will incorporate such attitudes into the utilities on the outcomes. So, while these internal attitudes to risk will be present in my account, they will be a component of the utilities, not separate attitudes.
4. A technical note on the definition of Bregman divergences; what follows is not essential to the rest of the argument. Suppose C is a closed, convex subset of the real numbers. And suppose $\varphi: C \to \mathbb{R}$ is a continuously differentiable and strictly convex function. Then the Bregman divergence generated by φ is defined as follows: $\mathfrak{d}_\varphi(x,y) := \varphi(x) - \varphi(y) - \varphi'(y)(x-y)$. That is, $\mathfrak{d}_\varphi(x,y)$ is the difference between the value of φ at x and the value at x of the tangent to φ taken at y. q is the Bregman divergence generated by $\varphi(x) = x^2$.
5. See also (D'Agostino and Dardanoni 2009), where the original mathematical result is stated and proved.
6. Recall: like a set, a multiset is unordered, so that $\{\{1,2\}\} = \{\{2,1\}\}$. Unlike a set, it allows repetitions, so that $\{\{1,1,2\}\} \neq \{\{1,2,2\}\}$.
7. Note that Buchak (2013, Section 4.4) considers a redescription strategy that is very close to the one I describe in this section. However, she notes that it is ill-defined. The strategy that I describe here does not suffer from this problem.
8. In general, for $\alpha_1, \ldots, \alpha_n, r \in \mathbb{R}$, there are many sequences $0 \leq \lambda_1, \ldots, \lambda_n$ with $\sum_i \lambda_i = 1$ such that $\sum_i \lambda_i \alpha_i = r$, if there are any.
9. If C is a finite set of vectors in a vector space V over the real numbers, the *convex hull* of C is written C^+ and defined as follows: C^+ is the smallest convex set that includes C, where a set is convex if it contains every mixture of two vectors whenever it contains those vectors; alternatively,

$$C^+ := \left\{ \sum_{c \in C} \lambda_c c : 0 \leq \lambda \leq 1 \ \& \ \sum_{c \in C} \lambda_c = 1 \right\}$$

Funding

This work was supported by European Research Council (ERC) [grant number 308961-EUT].References

Allais, M. 1953. "Le comportement de l'homme rationnel devant le risque: critique des postulats et axiomes de l'école Américaine." *Econometrica* 21 (4): 503–546.

Buchak, L. 2013. *Risk and Rationality*. Oxford: Oxford University Press.

D'Agostino, M., and V. Dardanoni. 2009. "What's so Special about Euclidean Distance? A Characterization with Applications to Mobility and Spatial Voting." *Social Choice and Welfare* 33 (2): 211–233.

D'Agostino, M., and C. Sinigaglia. 2010. "Epistemic Accuracy and Subjective Probability." In *EPSA Epistemology and Methodology of Science: Launch of the European Philosophy of Science Association*, edited by M. Suárez, M. Dorato, and M. Rédei, 95–105. Dordrecht: Springer.

Eriksson, L., and A. Hájek. 2007. "What are Degrees of Belief?" *Studia Logica* 86 (2): 183–213.

de Finetti, B. 1974. *Theory of Probability*. vol. I. New York: Wiley.

Jeffrey, R. 1986. "Probabilism and Induction." *Topoi* 5: 51–58.

Joyce, J. M. 1998. "A Nonpragmatic Vindication of Probabilism." *Philosophy of Science* 65 (4): 575–603.

Leitgeb, H., and R. Pettigrew. 2010. "An Objective Justification of Bayesianism I: Measuring Inaccuracy." *Philosophy of Science* 77: 201–235.

Meacham, C. J. G., and J. Weisberg. 2011. "Representation Theorems and the Foundations of Decision Theory." *Australasian Journal of Philosophy* 89 (4): 641–63.

Pettigrew, R. (ta). 2016. *Accuracy and the Laws of Credence*. Oxford: Oxford University Press.

Quiggin, J. 1982. "A Theory of Anticipated Utility." *Journal of Economic Behavior and Organization* 3: 323–343.

Quiggin, J. 1993. *Generalized Expected Utility Theory: The Rank-Dependent Model*. Dordrecht: Kluwer Academic Publishers.

Schmeidler, D. 1989. "Subjective Probability and Expected Utility without Additivity." *Econometrica* 57 (3): 571–587.

Wakker, P. P. 2010. *Prospect Theory: For Risk and Ambiguity*. Cambridge: Cambridge University Press.

Williams, B., and J. J. C. Smart. 1973. *Utilitarianism: For and Against*. Cambridge: Cambridge University Press.

Zynda, L. 2000. "Representation Theorems and Realism about Degrees of Belief." *Philosophy of Science* 67 (1): 45–69.

Appendix 1

Proof of theorem 1

In this appendix, we prove Theorem 1. We begin by giving a geometric characterization of the pairs (c, e), where c is a credence function and e is an estimate function, such that c is probabilistic and e is expectational relative to c.

Lemma 5 *Suppose c is a credence function defined on $\mathcal{F}$ and e is an estimate function defined on $\mathcal{X}$. Then the following two propositions are equivalent:*

(i) c is probabilistic and e is expectational with respect to c.

(ii) For each state s, there is $0 \leq \lambda_s \leq 1$ such that $\sum_{s \in S} \lambda_s = 1$ and

(a) $c(A) = \sum_{s \in S} \lambda_s A(s)$, for each proposition A in $\mathcal{F}$;

(b) $e(X) = \sum_{s \in S} \lambda_s X(s)$, for each quantity X in $\mathcal{X}$.

Proof 1 First, we prove (ii) ⇒ (i). Suppose (ii). First, we show that c is probabilistic. Recall that there are three conditions on being probabilistic: Range, Normalization, Additivity. We take them each in turn.

- Range: Suppose A is in $\mathcal{F}$. Then, note that: (1) each λ_s lies between 0 and 1 inclusive; (2) all of the λ_ss summed together give 1; (3) $A(s) = 0$ or 1 for each s in S. Thus, it is certainly true that $\sum_{s \in S} \lambda_s A(s)$ lies between 0 and 1 inclusive.
- Normalization: Since T is true at all states of the world, $T(s) = 1$ for all s in S, so $c(T) = \sum_{s \in S} \lambda_s T(s) = \sum_{s \in S} \lambda_s = 1$.
- Additivity: If there are no states s at which both A and B are true, then $c(A \vee B) = \sum_{s \in S} \lambda_s (A \vee B)(s) = \sum_{s \in A \vee B} \lambda_s = \sum_{s \in A} \lambda_s + \sum_{s \in B} \lambda_s = \sum_{s \in S} \lambda_s A(s) + \sum_{s \in S} \lambda_s B(s) = c(A) + c(B)$.

Next, we show that e is expectational with respect to c. Suppose s' is a state of the world. Then note that $c(s) = \sum_{s \in S} \lambda_s s'(s)$. But of course, since the states of the world form a partition, $s'(s) = 0$ if $s' \neq s$ and $s'(s) = 1$ if $s = s'$. Thus, $c(s) = \lambda_s$. Thus, $e(X) = \sum_{s \in S} \lambda_s X(s) = \sum_{s \in S} c(s) X(s)$, as required. This gives Expectation.

Second, we prove (i) ⇒ (ii). Let $\lambda_s = c(s)$ and the result follows easily from Additivity and Expectation. □

The upshot of this result is the following: Suppose $\mathcal{F} = \{A_1, \ldots, A_m\}$ and $\mathcal{X} = \{X_1, \ldots, X_n\}$. And, if c is a credence function on $\mathcal{F}$ and e is an estimate function on $\mathcal{X}$, represent the pair (c, e) by the following vector in $\mathbb{R}^{m+n}$:

$$\vec{ce} := (c(A_1), \ldots, c(A_m), e(X_1), \ldots, e(X_n))$$

And represent a state of the world s by the following vector in $\mathbb{R}^{m+n}$:

$$\vec{s} := (A_1(s), \ldots, A_m(s), X_1(s), \ldots, X_n(s))$$

Then Lemma 5 says that (c, e) is probabilistic and expectational iff $\vec{ce}$ lies in the convex hull of the vectors $\vec{s}$ for s in S – that is, $\vec{ce} \in \{\vec{s} : s \in S\}^+$.[9]

The second lemma that we require to prove Theorem 1 is a geometric fact about the following measure of distance between two vectors in a real-valued vector space. If $\mathbf{x} = (x_1, \ldots, x_k)$ and $\mathbf{y} = (y_1, \ldots, y_k)$ are vectors in $\mathbb{k}^n$, then let

$$\mathfrak{Q}(\mathbf{x}, \mathbf{y}) = \sum_{i=1}^{k} |x_i - y_i|^2$$

Thus, clearly,

$$\mathfrak{I}(c, s) + \mathfrak{I}(e, s) = \mathfrak{Q}(\vec{ce}, \vec{s})$$

for any credence function c, estimate function e and state of the world s.

Lemma 6 Suppose $D \subseteq \mathbb{R}^k$. Then

(i) If $\mathbf{x} \notin D^+$, then there is $\mathbf{y} \in D^+$ such that $\mathfrak{Q}(\mathbf{d}, \mathbf{y}) < \mathfrak{Q}(\mathbf{d}, \mathbf{x})$, for all $\mathbf{d} \in D$.
(ii) If $\mathbf{x} \in D^+$, then there is no $\mathbf{x} \neq \mathbf{y} \in \mathbb{R}^k$ such that $\mathfrak{Q}(\mathbf{d}, \mathbf{y}) \leq \mathfrak{Q}(\mathbf{d}, \mathbf{x})$, for all $\mathbf{d} \in D$.

I won't provide a full proof of these geometric facts – proofs can be found in any geometry textbook. But here is a brief sketch. (i) is an easy consequence of the Hilbert Projection

Theorem, since $\mathfrak{D}$ is the square of the Euclidean metric. (ii) is a consequence of the fact that, if we measure distance between vectors using the Euclidean metric or its square, $\mathfrak{D}$, then, for any two vectors, the set of vectors that are closer to the first than to the second is a convex set.

Putting these two results together and, in Lemma 6, letting $D = \{\vec{s} : s \in S\}$, Theorem 1 follows.□

Costs of abandoning the Sure-Thing Principle

Rachael Briggs

Stanford University, Stanford, CA, USA

ABSTRACT
Risk-weighted expected utility theory (REU theory for short) permits preferences which violate the Sure-Thing Principle (STP for short). But preferences that violate the STP can lead to bad decisions in sequential choice problems. In particular, they can lead decision-makers to adopt a strategy that is dominated – i.e. a strategy such that some available alternative leads to a better outcome in every possible state of the world.

Lara Buchak's risk-weighted expected utility theory (REU theory, for short) is a flexible and well-motivated generalization of standard expected utility theory. But REU theory has a crucial cost: it permits preferences which violate the Sure-Thing Principle (STP). I will argue that violations of the STP come at significant cost, both to decision-makers and to the theorists who model them.

First, consider the decision-makers. A decision-maker whose preferences violate the STP may adopt a *dominated strategy* – i.e. a strategy such that some available alternative strategy leads to a better outcome in every possible state of the world.

In chapter 6, Buchak considers and rebuts a version of this objection which we might call
The Diachronic Challenge

(1) According to REU theory, it is sometimes permissible to choose a dominated strategy in an extended choice situation.
(2) Choosing a dominated strategy in an extended choice situation is irrational.

∴ REU theory fails to provide sufficient conditions for rationality.

Buchak challenges both premises. I'll respond to Buchak's arguments against each premise, and sketch out an alternative possible response to the Diachronic Challenge.

I'll also argue that REU theory's failure to accommodate the STP presents a pragmatic cost to decision theorists who aim to develop simple models of decision-makers. The STP, I claim, is a valuable tool that enables theorists to simplify so-called grand-world decisions into so-called small-world decisions. REU theory is missing this valuable tool.

1. The Sure-Thing principle

STP For all acts f and g, constant acts x and events E, $f_E x \succ g_E x$ iff $f_E \succ g_E$ (Buchak 2013, 107). A corollary of the STP is

Savage's STP For all acts f and g, constant acts x and y and events E, $f_E x \succ g_E x$ iff $f_E y \succ g_E y$ (Savage 1954, 23). Intuitively, the STP says that a person's preference between two acts should depend only on their outcomes in states where those outcomes differ. So (Savage's STP helps us elaborate) whatever your preference is between f if E and x otherwise and g if E and x otherwise, replacing x with y shouldn't affect that preference.

As an example of an application of the STP, suppose you are planning the route for your next bushwalk. You're choosing between two acts: you can either plan to take your favourite trail (which is reliably pleasant, but offers few surprises), or plan to take a new route (which will bring you stunning mountain views, if you can only manage the difficult hike to the summit). There is a small chance that it will rain, in which case both acts will yield the same outcome: you will cancel the bushwalk and sit indoors reading. The STP says that, when choosing which hike to prepare for, you should ignore the possibilities where it rains (since in that event, both decisions have the same outcome) and consider only what each hike will be like if it does not rain.

I will now give an example illustrating how REU theory violates the STP. Let Rhoda be an REU-maximizer for whom $r(p) = p^2$. At various points, I will find it useful to contrast Rhoda with Eulalie, an EU-maximizer for whom $r(p) = p$.

Let us consider how Rhoda and Eulalie would respond to the Allais Paradox (Allais 1953). In the Allais paradox, a ticket is drawn at random from a batch of 100 tickets numbered 1–100. Columns in the table correspond to states, which specify which ticket is drawn. Rows correspond to acts. Outcomes are labelled according to their utilities.

BELIEF, ACTION, AND RATIONALITY OVER TIME

	Ticket 1	Tickets 2-11	Tickets 12-100
L_1	1000	1000	1000
L_2	0	2000	1000
L_3	1000	1000	0
L_4	0	2000	0

Rhoda will prefer L_1 over L_2, and L_4 over L_3. Eulalie, on the other hand, will prefer L_2 over L_1 and L_4 over L_3.

Rhoda's pattern of preferences violates the STP. Where f is any act that yields 1000 utils if Tickets 1–11 are drawn, and g is any act that yields 0 utils if Ticket 1 is drawn and 2000 utils if Tickets 2–11 are drawn, and E is the proposition that one of Tickets 1–11 is drawn, we have

$$L_1 = f_E 1000$$
$$L_2 = g_E 1000$$
$$L_3 = f_E 0$$
$$L_4 = g_E 0$$

and so by Savage's STP, we have the requirement that $L_1 \succ L_2$ iff $L_3 \succ L_4$. Rhoda's preferences violate this biconditional, and hence Savage's STP, and hence STP.

2. Do REU-maximizers choose dominated options?

Buchak considers two arguments for Premise 1 of the Diachronic Challenge. (Recall, this is the premise that

1. According to REU theory, it is sometimes permissible to choose a dominated strategy in an extended choice situation.)

The first argument purports to show that agents who violate the STP will pay to go back on earlier decisions. The second purports to show that they will pay to avoid information. (Buchak also considers a third argument meant to establish that the REU-maximizer cannot stick to a plan, but this argument does not, strictly speaking, involve financial exploitation. I will omit discussion of this third argument; everything I have to say about it is covered in my discussion of Problem 1.)

Throughout my comments, I will focus on the special case of Rhoda. But what I say can be generalized to any REU-maximizer who violates the STP, as Buchak shows in the book.

Problem 1 Suppose Rhoda is offered the following sequence of choices. First, she may choose either L_1 or L_2+ (a version of L_2 that is sweetened by adding one util to each outcome). Next, a ticket is drawn. If Rhoda has chosen L_y and the ticket is numbered 1–11, then she is given the opportunity to switch to an unsweetened L_2. In extended form, the decision looks like this:

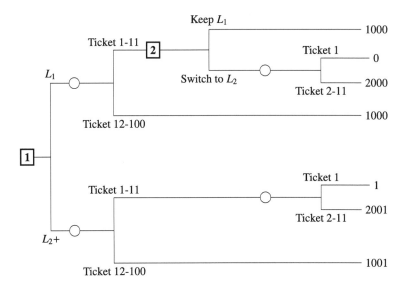

At node [1], Rhoda will choose L_1 over L_2+, since L_1 has a higher REU. But if she reaches node [2] and learns that one of tickets 1–11 has been drawn, she will switch to L_2, since L_2 will now have a higher REU than L_1 in the light of her new information. So Rhoda's strategy will be to choose L_1 at [1] and switch to L_2 at [2], if she gets there. But this strategy is dominated. The strategy of choosing L_2+ at node [1] results in a better outcome no matter which ticket is drawn.

Furthermore, the problem is essentially linked to the failure of the STP. At node [1], Rhoda strongly prefers choosing L_1 and sticking to L_1 (call this option 'stick') over choosing L_1 and sticking to L_2 (call this option 'switch'). But although

$$stick > switch,$$

where E is the proposition that a ticket from 1–11 is drawn, we also have both

$$switch_E > stick_E$$

and

$$switch_{\neg E} \gtrsim stick_{\neg E}$$

Rhoda strictly prefers sticking to switching, even though she weakly prefers switching to sticking conditional on both E and $\neg E$.

Problem 2 Suppose Rhoda will be offered a choice between L_1 and L_2. Beforehand, she has the opportunity to decide whether to make this choice in complete ignorance, or whether to make it with knowledge of whether the ticket drawn was numbered between 1–11 or between 12–100. Additionally, the knowledge comes with a sweetener: if she chooses knowledge, an extra util is added to each outcome.

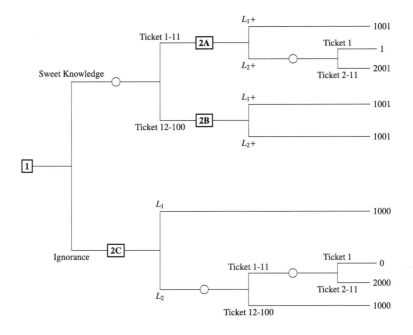

Rhoda can then reason as follows. If she gets to state [2A], she will choose L_2+ (since it will have a higher REU than L_1+); if she ends up in [2B], then she will end up with the same outcome no matter what she chooses. If she instead ends up at [2C], she will choose L_1. At state [1], she assigns higher REU to L_1 than to L_2+. So at state [1], she should choose ignorance (which will ensure that she ends up choosing L_1) over sweet knowledge (which may result in her choosing L_2+). But the strategy of choosing ignorance at [1], followed by L_1 at [2C], is dominated by the strategy of choosing sweet knowledge at [1], followed by choosing L_1+ at [2A] and at [2B].

Again, the problem is closely linked to the violation of the STP. We have all of the following:

$$L_1 > L_2+$$
$$L_2+_E > L_{1E}$$
$$L_2+_{\neg E} > L_{1\neg E}$$

Rhoda strictly prefers L_1 to L_2+, even though she strictly prefers L_2+ to L_1 conditional on both E and $\neg E$. From her L_1 perspective, she should avoid anything that will lead her to choose L_2+ over L_1 – which is precisely what knowledge whether E will do.

271

2.1. Preference and choice

I have argued that Rhoda will choose the dominated option in Problem 1, and that she will choose the dominated option in Problem 2. Buchak claims that both arguments are unsound.

She points out that both arguments rely on contentious assumptions about the relationship between preference and choice. In fact, Buchak notes, the assumptions needed to prove that Rhoda will choose a dominated strategy in Problem 1 contradict the assumptions needed to prove that Rhoda will choose a dominated strategy in Problem 2, so it cannot be that both arguments are sound. To unpack these assumptions, it will be helpful to discuss Rhoda's preferences in each of the problems in more detail.

First, consider Problem 1. The following table gives Rhoda's preference ranking over all the strategies at each node, as determined by REU theory. (The left-hand column lists the node at which the preferences are held; the right-hand column lists the strategies from most-preferred at the top, to least-preferred at the bottom. All preferences are strict.)

Node 1	[1] L_1, [2] Stay
	[1] L_2+
	[1] L_1, [2] Switch
Node 2	[1] L_2+
	[1] L_1, [2] Switch
	[1] L_1 [2] Stay

Next, consider Problem 2. Rhoda does not care (at any node) what she chooses at [2B] – if two strategies differ only with respect to what she chooses at [2B], then she is always indifferent between them. I will therefore consider her preferences among coarse-grained strategies, which do not specify what she chooses at [2B]. Her preference ranking is as follows at each node.

Node 1	[1] Sweet Knowledge [2A] L_1+
	[1] Ignorance [2C] L_1
	[1] Sweet Knowledge [2A] L_2+
	[1] Ignorance [2C] L_2
Node 2A	[1] Sweet Knowledge [2A] L_2+
	[1] Ignorance [2C] L_2,
	[1] Sweet Knowledge [2A] L_1+
	[1] Ignorance [2C] L_1
Node 2C	[1] Sweet Knowledge [2A] L_1+
	[1] Ignorance [2C] L_1
	[1] Sweet Knowledge [2A] L_2+
	[1] Ignorance [2C] L_2

There are three possible ways to derive choices from preferences in extended-form decision problems. All three coincide in the above problems for Eulalie, but they come apart for Rhoda.

Naive Choice At each node, choose the action that belongs to the best strategy (according to your current preferences) available at that node.

Sophisticated Choice Assume that if you reach a final choice node n, you will choose the action with the best outcome (according to your preferences at n). Assume that no other outcome is possible once you reach node n. Work backward through the tree until you reach the first choice node (Hammond 1988).

Resolute Choice Choose the best strategy at the first node (according to your preferences at the first node) and adhere to it at all other nodes, regardless of your later preferences (McClennen 1990). In Problem 1, naive Rhoda will adopt the dominated strategy of choosing L_1 at [1] and switching at [2]. But neither the sophisticated nor the resolute chooser will take up a dominated plan. Sophisticated Rhoda will pick L_2+ at [1] to avoid switching at [2]. And resolute Rhoda will pick L_1 and stick to it.

In Problem 2, it is sophisticated Rhoda who will adopt the dominated strategy of choosing Ignorance at [1] (to stave off the possibility of choosing L_2+ at [2A]), followed by L_1 at [2C]. Naive and resolute Rhoda will pick Sweet Knowledge at [1]. (Naive Rhoda will follow up with L_2+, should she reach [2A], while resolute Rhoda will follow up with L_1+.)

Buchak does not think that sophisticated Rhoda will choose a dominated option in Problem 2. She offers the following rebuttal. (I have altered Buchak's notation to match my own.)

> If [objectors like Machina (1989) and McClennen (1990)] are correct that sophisticated choosers can end up with a dominated option, then sophisticated choosers are in trouble. However, the sophisticated chooser can respond to this argument by pointing out that although she ends up with L_y, L_1+ is not actually an available option for the agent at [1], since at [1] the agent knows she will not choose L_1+ at [2C]. The view of agency which makes sophisticated choice attractive in the first place is one on which once our future preferences are fixed, certain logically possible future options are not within our grasp. Granted, the fact that the option is unavailable to the agent at [1] because of her own future choices might reveal that she has diachronically inconsistent preferences, a possibility which I will examine in the following section; but her plan does yield, for each given time-slice, the best consequence available to that time-slice [189].

The objection is that by the sophisticated chooser's lights, Rhoda's options are *acts*. But there is no time at which L_1 is the result of any act that is available to sophisticated Rhoda. It is not available at [1], because if she gets to node [2A], she will choose L_2+ and not L_1+. It is not available at node [2A], because, being the kind of person who will choose sweet ignorance at [1], she will never reach [2A]. And it is not available at [2C], because L_1+ is no longer available at [2C].

Nonetheless, there is a sequence of actions, each of which Rhoda can perform, that will guarantee that she ends up with L_1+. (All she has to do is choose sweet knowledge at [1], and choose L_1+ at [2A], should she get there.) In other words, there is a strategy that is available to Rhoda that results in her ending up with L_1+. Buchak holds that on the view that motivates sophisticated choice, we are not entitled to evaluate entire strategies, since there is no time at which strategies are the object of choice. But the objector should press the point that a strategy can be available, even if there is no one time at which it is available.

The upshot is that if Rhoda is either naive or sophisticated, she will choose a dominated strategy in one of the above examples. If Rhoda is resolute, she will never choose a dominated strategy – not in the above problems, and not in any other extended decision problem.[1] Unless the REU theorist is prepared to accept that resolute choice is the right approach to extended decision problems, she is compelled to accept Premise 1.

3. Is choosing a dominated strategy a sign of irrationality?

The Diachronic Challenge against REU theory has not yet succeeded. Buchak also presents arguments against Premise 2, which states:

> 2. Choosing a dominated strategy in an extended choice situation is irrational.

The first part of Buchak's argument is negative: she points out that several apparently tempting diagnoses of the irrationality fail. For instance, it is *not* true that Rhoda is incapable of picking a strategy and sticking to it. If Rhoda is sophisticated or resolute, she will stick to the strategy she chooses at the first node of the decision tree.

Nor, Buchak argues, can Rhoda be accused of having inconsistent preferences across time. Her preferences over outcomes remain constant throughout Problem 1 and Problem 2. True, her preferences over lotteries change, but so do Eulalie's preferences over lotteries: Eulalie strictly prefers L_2 over L_1+, but will reverse this preference if she learns that E.

The objector might make the following complaint: REU theory allows preferences to change in a predictable direction, while the more restrictive EU theory does not. If an EU-maximizer is prepared to revise her assessment of a lottery *upward* on learning E, she must also be prepared to revise it *downward* on learning $\neg E$. Not so for the REU-maximizer Rhoda, who revises her opinion of L_2 upward whether she learns E, or $\neg E$.

In addition to her negative account of what is *not* wrong with choosing a dominated option in REU theory, Buchak has a positive explanation of why REU-maximizers are willing to pay to avoid information. The positive account is aimed not just at *explaining* the choices of sophisticated REU-maximizers, but at *vindicating* them – showing that they are not inconsistent. The positive diagnosis is as follows.

Because REU theory allows for foreseeable preference reversals, Buchak argues, it counts new information about E as bad, from Rhoda's initial perspective. This information will foreseeably reverse Rhoda's preferences, causing her to make a decision whose potential costs (when appropriately weighted according to their probabilities, by her own lights) outweigh its potential benefits. So,

Rhoda has a pragmatic reason to avoid this information, even if she has to pay to avoid it (as in Problem 2).

The trouble (from Rhoda's initial perspective) is that the information may be misleading – and the prospect of being misled is both bad enough and likely enough to make the information bad overall. There are some states of the world where Rhoda learns E, and accepts L_2 on the basis of that information, even though L_2 in fact leads to a very bad outcome in those states. (The relevant state in the example is that Ticket 1 is drawn.) Furthermore, because Rhoda is risk-averse, the possibility of being misled has a stronger negative impact on the overall value of the information than it would for Eulalie.

From Rhoda's later perspective, however, the information is good on balance. While it still has a chance of being misleading, the outcome in which she is misled is not bad enough and likely enough to make the information bad overall. Instead, the information is either good (if she learns E) or neutral (if she learns $\neg E$). From her later perspective, she should act on this overall good information, even if it means going back on an earlier, less-informed decision (as in Problem 1).

But is the information good overall, or bad overall? There is no answer to this question, says Buchak. The information is bad from the earlier perspective and good from the later perspective – there is no neutral perspective from which to reconcile them. While it is true that Rhoda's later views about the value of information are guaranteed to diverge from her earlier views, there is no requirement that her earlier and later views agree. Thus, it is perfectly consistent for Rhoda's views about the value of information to change in a predictable way.

So the disagreement between Buchak and her objector can be recast as a disagreement about whether there must always be a neutral perspective from which to evaluate new information: the objector thinks there must be, and Buchak thinks there needn't be. Both views are internally consistent. To mount a good argument against the REU theorist, the objector needs to either find a compelling internal argument that REU theory is inconsistent, or find a compelling external reason that the REU theorist's assumptions about rationality are implausible.

I think there is another line of argument available to the objector here. There is a simpler story available about why choosers who settle on dominated strategies are practically irrational. Being disposed to settle on a dominated strategy is not *indicative* of some rational flaw such as inconsistency. Rather, it already *constitutes* practical irrationality.

This argument has both an internal and an external version. According to the internal version, choosing dominated strategies is also irrational by the REU-maximizer's own lights. Notice that REU lets us evaluate both acts and strategies. On any continuous r function with a minimum of 0 and a maximum of 1, L_1+ has a strictly higher REU than L_1, and L_2+ has a strictly higher REU than L_2. So dominated strategies are worse than the strategies that dominate them by the REU-maximizer's own lights. By their own lights, both the sophisticated and the naive REU-maximizer will sometimes choose a worse strategy when a better one is available.

According to the external version of the argument, the aim of decision theory is to enable us to choose options with the best consequences. To choose a dominated option (whether 'option' is understood as 'act' or 'strategy') frustrates this aim, in a way that is foreseeable *a priori*. The following is an independently compelling claim about rationality: if it is knowable *a priori* that strategy *a* yields a better result than strategy *b*, then it is pragmatically irrational to choose strategy *b* when strategy *a* is available.

3.1. Where things stand so far

So far, I have raised arguments against Buchak's response to the Diachronic Argument. I have argued in favour of Premise 1, which says that every REU-maximizer who violates the STP will sometimes choose a dominated strategy. Adopting a resolute account of rational choice solves the problem, but naive and sophisticated choice do not. Therefore, I claim REU theorists can deny Premise 1 only at the cost of embracing resolute choice.

And I have argued in favour of Premise 2, which says that if an REU-maximizer is disposed to choose a dominated strategy, then that REU-maximizer is irrational. I claim that being disposed to choose a dominated strategy is constitutive of irrationality, whether or not it is also the sign of some deeper inconsistency.

I would like to briefly suggest a third way out: why not require that the REU-maximizer's *r* functions change in response to new information? In both Problem 1 and Problem 2, I assumed that $r(p) = p^2$ both before and after Rhoda learned *E*. And in both problems, the exploitation of Rhoda turned on foreseeable preference reversals: there were some node (*n*) partition $\mathcal{E} = \{E_1, E_2, \ldots E_m\}$ and gambles *f* and *g* such that

- At node *n*, Rhoda would learn which member of $\mathcal{E}$ was true.
- Rhoda preferred *f* to *g*.
- For every member of $\mathcal{E}$, if Rhoda were to learn *E*, Rhoda would prefer *g* to *f*.

To get around the problem, an REU theorist would need to claim that Rhoda's preferences were not just *permitted* to change, but *required* to change in the light of new information. A fully fleshed out version of this argument would include rules about how to change *r* in the light of new evidence, but I propose it as a promising avenue of future research.

4. A lesson about simplifying lotteries

I think there is another lesson to be drawn from Rhoda's preference reversals – one that brings out a hidden cost of REU theory. Buchak has already pointed out that for Rhoda, information lacks a stable value. I suggest an underlying reason for this: for Rhoda, sub-acts lack stable utility values.

In claiming that sub-acts lack stable values, I don't aim to say only that the utilities of sub-acts can change in the light of new information. Rhoda and Eulalie agree that L_2+_E loses value in the light of the information that Ticket 1 was drawn, because this information rules out some of the states in E – it tells us something about which states obtain if E is true. But for Rhoda, even propositions entailed by E – that is, even propositions that give no information about which states obtain if E is true – will affect the value of sub-acts on E.

To see why sub-acts lack stable values for Rhoda, consider L_2+_E, which yields 1 util if Ticket 1 is drawn, and 2001 utils if one of tickets 2–11 is drawn. What, we might ask, is the utility of L_2+_E?

If Rhoda is at [2A] in Problem 2, where she is certain of E (the proposition that a ticket numbered 1–11 is drawn), then we can calculate the utility of L_2+_E as the utility of the outcome o such that she would be indifferent between L_E+_2 and an assured prize of o:

$$u(o) = REU(L_2+_E) = 1 + \left(\frac{10}{11}\right)^2 \times (2001 - 1) = \frac{500,121}{121} = 991.1$$

If Rhoda is at node [1] in Problem 2, then we can calculate the utility of L_2+_E as the utility of the outcome o such that she would be indifferent between L_2+ and $o_E L_2+$ (the act that yields o in the event that E and the same outcome as L_2+ in the event that $\neg E$. Since L_2+ yields 1001 utils in all $\neg E$ states, I will also write this act as $o_E 1001$).

$$REU(L_2+) = REU(o_E L_2+)$$
$$990.1 = REU(o_E 1001)$$

Since $REU(o_E 1001) < 1000$, we know that $u(o) < 1001$. Thus:

$$990.1 = u(o) + \left(\frac{11}{100}\right)^2 1001$$
$$u(o) = 979$$

So the same sub-act L_2+_E is worth 991.1 utils at node [1] and 979 utils at node [2]. And this despite the fact that Rhoda's credences conditional on E are the same at the two nodes.

This instability in the values of sub-acts explains why information has no fixed value. Learning which member of a partition $\{E_1, E_2, \ldots, E_n\}$ is true is good insofar as it might lead the agent to choose a better sub-act on each of the E_is in the partition, and bad insofar as it might lead her to choose a worse sub-act. If there are no stable facts about the values of these sub-acts, then there are no stable facts about the value of information.

BELIEF, ACTION, AND RATIONALITY OVER TIME

Another consequence of this instability is that REU theorists lose a key strategy for simplifying 'grand world' decisions by recasting them as 'small world' decisions. This consequence, too, is best illustrated by an example.

Suppose I am deciding whether to buy a frogurt, which looks delicious, but which I fear may be cursed. I'm also not sure whether the frogurt comes with a free topping (that's good), or whether the free topping contains potassium benzoate, also known as E212 (that's bad, since E212 may mildly irritate my skin, eyes, and mucous membranes). The following matrix depicts the possible states of the world, with their probabilities noted (columns), the acts available to me (rows) and the utilities of the outcomes in each act-state pair (cells).

	cursed topping E212 ($p = 0.12$)	cursed topping no E212 ($p = 0.12$)	cursed no topping ($p = 0.36$)	not cursed topping E212 ($p = 0.08$)	not cursed topping no E212 ($p = 0.08$)	not cursed no topping ($p = 0.24$)
buy	−50	−30	−45	10	30	15
don't buy	0	0	0	0	0	0

This is a complicated decision problem, with six different states to keep track of. (In fact, a truly accurate portrayal of the decision problem would be vastly more complicated: my mucous membranes might or might react to the E212; the free topping might be delicious chocolate fudge or boring old caramel sauce; my astrologer might help me evade the curse, or fate may catch up with me no matter what I do, and then there are many possible ways to be cursed…) I'd like to reduce the complicated decision problem to a simpler, more coarse-grained decision problem with the following form:

	cursed $p = ???$	not cursed $p = ???$
buy	???	???
don't buy	???	???

But how can I fill in the blank spots in the smaller table? Given a probability function p over fine-grained states, and a utility function u over fine-grained outcomes, how do I generate a probability function p^* over coarse-grained states, and a utility function u^* over coarse-grained outcomes.

The probability function is easy enough. Each s^* in the coarse-grained space of states corresponds to an event $E(s^*)$ in the fine-grained space of states. For instance, the state cursed in the coarse-grained space corresponds to the event {⟨cursed, topping, E212⟩, ⟨cursed, topping, no E212⟩, ⟨cursed, no topping⟩} in the fine-grained space. In general, the probability of a coarse-grained state can be obtained by adding up the probabilities of the fine-grained states that make it up:

$$p^*(s^*) = p(E(s^*))$$

For EU-maximizers, deriving u^* is also simple: The utility of a coarse-grained outcome of act A in state s^* is the expected utility of the sub-act $A_{E(s^*)}$. Furthermore, this expected utility depends only on how things stand within $E(s^*)$: it is a function of the probabilities of states in $E(s^*)$, and the utilities of outcomes that result from A in these states. In the frogurt example, to calculate the utility of buying a cursed frogurt, we take an average of the values of the more fine-grained outcomes that might result from buying a cursed frogurt, weighted by the conditional probabilities of the states that give rise to the outcomes, given that the frogurt is cursed.

$$u^*(\text{buy} \wedge \text{cursed}) = u_{\text{cursed}}(\text{buy})(-50 \times 0.4) + (-30 \times 0.4) + (-45 \times 0.6) = -43$$

In general, where A is an act, s^* is a coarse-grained state, E is the set of fine-grained states corresponding to s^*, p and u are probabilities over the fine-grained space, and p^* and u^* are probabilities and utilites over the coarse-grained space:

$$u^*(A \wedge s^*) = \sum_{s \in E^*} p(s|E)u(E)$$

Applying this idea to the frogurt example gives us the following table:

	cursed $p = 0.6$	not cursed $p = 0.4$
buy	−43	17
don't buy	0	0

Our REU-maximizer can find ways of filling in the cells in of the small-world problem, assigning $u^*(\text{buy} \wedge \text{cursed})$ and $u^*(\text{buy} \wedge \neg \text{cursed})$ so that

$$REU(\text{buy}) = (0.6)^2[u^*(\text{buy} \wedge \text{cursed}) - u^*(\text{buy} \wedge \neg \text{cursed})]$$

However, these values will not be a function of the probabilities and utilities of states in which the frogurt is cursed. They will also depend on both the probabilities and utilities of the states in which the frogurt is not cursed.

Thus, REU theory makes it more difficult to simplify grand world problems into small world problems. In chapter 6, Buchak gives us an extensive discussion of one way in which this complexity plays out: bets turn out not to have stable values independent of background patterns of risk. I have pointed out another way in which the complexity plays out: sub-acts turn out not to have stable values independent of the larger acts in which they are embedded.

5. Conclusion

Where does this leave the STP? I have argued that all the key premises in the Diachronic Argument are appealing: both naive and sophisticated REU-maximizers will sometimes choose dominated strategies, and that being disposed to choose dominated strategies is constitutive of irrationality. REU theorists can get out of the argument by endorsing a resolute view of choice, but this amounts to a substantive commitments, with some drawbacks (in particular, at some nodes, resolute choosers will choose acts they disprefer over acts they prefer, simply because of their past preferences). Another avenue for REU theorists to explore is to prescribe changing one's r values in the light of new information.

For REU theorists, sub-acts, like bets, lack context-independent values. Just as the values of bets depend on background distributions of risk, the values of sub-acts depend on the larger acts in which sub-acts are embedded. This means that lotteries cannot be treated like constant acts, for the purpose of simplifying decision problems.

Neither of these points is a knock-down objection to REU theory. In response to the first point, REU theorists can adopt a resolute account of choice, or prescribe changing r values. And in response to the second point, REU theory is a global theory, so in some sense it is no surprise that it should stymie our attempts to break complex decisions down into simple parts. But each point highlights a cost. The real question, then, is whether the costs are worth paying.

Notes

1. More precisely, as long as Strategy 1 weakly dominates Strategy 2, and the set of states in which Strategy 1 yields a strictly better outcome than Strategy 2 is greater than 0, the REU of Strategy 1 will be strictly greater than the REU of strategy 2 at the first node of the decision tree.

Funding

This work was supported by the Stanford University.

References

Allais, Maurice. 1953. "Le comportement de l'homme rationnel devant le risque: critique des postulats et axiomes de l'ècole amèricaine." *Econometrica* 21 (4): 503–546.
Buchak, Lara. 2013. *Risk and Rationality*. Oxford: OUP.
Hammond, Peter J. 1988. "Consequentialist Foundations for Expected Utility." *Theory and Decision* 25 (1): 25–78.
Machina, Mark. 1989. "Dynamic Consistency and Non-expected Utility Models of Choice Under Uncertainty." *Journal of Economic Literature* 27 (4): 1622–1668.
McClennen, Edward F. 1990. *Rationality and Dynamic Choice: Foundational Explorations*. Cambridge: Cambridge University Press.
Savage, Leonard J. 1954. *The Foundations of Statistics*. New York: Wiley Publications in Statistics.

Revisiting Risk and Rationality: a reply to Pettigrew and Briggs

Lara Buchak

Department of Philosophy, UC Berkeley, Berkeley, CA, USA

ABSTRACT
I have claimed that risk-weighted expected utility (REU) maximizers are rational, and that their preferences cannot be captured by expected utility (EU) theory. Richard Pettigrew and Rachael Briggs have recently challenged these claims. Both authors argue that only EU-maximizers are rational. In addition, Pettigrew argues that the preferences of REU-maximizers can indeed be captured by EU theory, and Briggs argues that REU-maximizers lose a valuable tool for simplifying their decision problems. I hold that their arguments do not succeed and that my original claims still stand. However, their arguments do highlight some costs of REU theory.

1. Introduction

In *Risk and Rationality*, I argued against what we might call the expected utility (*EU*) *thesis*: the claim that individuals are rational if and only if they maximize EU. I made a case for two claims. The first is that there are preferences that seem reasonable but cannot be described as cases of EU maximization, or even *re-described* as such by individuating outcomes more finely. The second is that the standard arguments for the EU thesis are not in fact strong enough to support that thesis. I proposed that we jettison the EU thesis and adopt the weaker risk-weighted expected utility (*REU*) *thesis*: individuals are rational if and only if they maximize REU.

A key difference between the EU thesis and the REU thesis is that while the former holds that there are only two internal attitudes that are combined in preferences – utilities and credences – the latter holds that there are three: utilities, credences, and risk attitudes.[1] Roughly, utilities measure how much an individual values a particular outcome, credences measure how likely an individual takes a given state to be, and risk-attitudes measure how much an individual takes into account what happens in worse states of an act as opposed to better states. For example, individuals who are risk-avoidant REU-maximizers give more weight to what happens in the worst-case scenario than the best, even when these scenarios are equally likely. This contrasts with EU-maximization, according to which individuals give equal weight to scenarios that have equal probability. Whereas in EU theory, the value contribution of a particular outcome to the total value of the act is that outcome's utility times that outcome's probability, in REU theory, the value contribution of a particular outcome to the total value of the act is that outcome's utility times a factor which depends on both the outcome's probability and its position in the act's ordering.[2]

Richard Pettigrew (2015) and Rachael Briggs (2015) advance new considerations in favor of EU theory. Pettigrew advances a novel argument for the EU thesis, namely that an individual whose preferences conform to EU maximization will be better at estimating the utility values of the acts she is choosing among. He also proposes that those with REU-maximizing preferences can be redescribed as EU-maximizers. Specifically, he proposes a way of combining risk attitudes and utilities so that there are ultimately only two fundamental internal states. Consequently, he concludes that while the EU thesis holds, we can agree about which actual preferences are rational, since REU-maximization is merely a special case of EU-maximization.

Briggs has two main criticisms of REU theory. The first is a rejoinder to one of my arguments against the EU thesis. I argued that REU-maximizers are diachronically rational, and Briggs challenges this claim: in particular, while I claimed that both sophisticated and resolute choice can vindicate the diachronic choice behavior of REU-maximizers, she argues that sophisticated choice cannot in fact vindicate their diachronic choice behavior. Briggs's other criticism stems from the fact that for REU-maximizers, sub-acts lack stable utility values. Because sub-acts lack stable utility values, she claims, REU-maximizers lose a valuable tool for simplifying decision problems. This isn't an argument for the EU-thesis per se, but it foregrounds a practical cost of REU theory: REU-maximizers face more difficulties actually making ordinary decisions than EU-maximizers do.

Each of these arguments is insightful, original, and challenging. In this article, I outline responses on behalf of REU theory. In addition to allowing us to continue to deny the EU thesis, these responses will illuminate why positing three factors in preference is different from positing two potentially more complex factors; how we ought to think about the aim of decision theory; and what are the genuine costs of accepting REU theory.

Following Briggs, it will be helpful to anchor the discussion using two individuals: Eulalie, who maximizes EU, and Rhoda, who maximizes REU with $r(p) = p^2$. My claims will be that Rhoda cannot be redescribed as an EU-maximizer, that she is both synchronically and diachronically rational, and that she is able to simplify her decision problems in natural ways.

2. Pettigrew's first challenge: re-description

Let us begin with Pettigrew's argument that Rhoda cannot be redescribed as an EU-maximizer. Redescription involves making the outcomes (the original bearers of utility) more fine-grained, and then assigning values to these fine-grained outcomes, which we can call utility* values. The upshot will be that even though there is no utility assignment to coarse-grained outcomes according to which the individual maximizes EU, there is a utility* assignment to the fine-grained outcomes according to which she maximizes EU*. Thus, Rhoda *is* an EU- maximizer, merely one with a utility function that ranges over fine-grained outcomes.

The dilemma I presented for redescription of REU-maximizers is this: there is no strategy for fine-graining outcomes and assigning utility* to fine-grained outcomes that both generates a consistent utility* function and survives what I call the proliferation problems (Buchak 2013, Ch. 4). The proliferation problems occur when the EU theorist fine-grains in such a way that too much is up for grabs: for example, if outcomes are maximally fine-grained and there are no extra-theoretical constraints on how we assign utility* to them, then we can attribute to the agent one of any number of utility functions, and any probability function whatsoever. But the only other alternative, I claimed, is to leave too little up for grabs: if outcomes are coarse-grained enough or if there are enough extra-theoretical constraints on utility* to avoid the proliferation problems, then we cannot consistently assign expectational utility* values at all.

One redescription that avoids the proliferation problems but suffers from the inconsistency problem is what I called the 'comonotonic individuation' (Buchak 2013, 141). Recall that in EU theory, the value contribution of a particular outcome is that outcome's utility times that outcome's probability, and in REU theory, the value contribution of a particular outcome is that outcome's utility times a factor which depends on both the outcome's probability and its position in the act's ordering. The comonotonic individuation first redescribes outcomes as <outcome, act> pairs. Letting 'utility' refer to an outcome's utility according to REU theory and 'utility*' refer to an <outcome, act> pair's utility according to EU theory, the comonotonic individuation assigns utility* to each pair as follows. It first sets the *utility* contribution* of the <outcome, act> pair equal to the utility contribution of the outcome to the utility of the act, and it then sets the *utility** of the pair equal to the utility* contribution divided by the probability of the outcome according to the act.

More formally, where events in act h are ordered (1 to *n*) from worst to best and x_i stands for the outcome that results from event E_i, the comonotonic individuation sets $u^*(x_i, h) = t_i u^*(x_i)$, where t_i is the marginal difference in r that $p(E_i)$ makes, divided by $p(E_i)$:

$$t_i = \begin{cases} \dfrac{r(p(E_i \cup \ldots \cup E_n)) - r(p(E_{i+1} \cup \ldots \cup E_n))}{p(E_i \cup \ldots \cup E_n) - p(E_{i+1} \cup \ldots \cup E_n)} & \text{if } i = 1, \ldots, n-1 \\ \dfrac{r(p(E_i))}{p(E_i)} & \text{if } i = n \end{cases}$$

(Pettigrew uses c to stand for the agent's credence (subjective probability) function, but I use p to match my earlier terminology.) Notice that t_i is defined almost identically to Pettigrew's s_i: the key difference is that t_i is defined as the coefficient of the difference that the utility of *outcome* x_i makes, while s_i is defined as the coefficient of the difference that *utility* u_i makes. These two values are different because there can be multiple outcomes with the same utility. The comonotonic individuation treats outcomes with the same utility separately – it takes as a starting point the value contribution that each distinct outcome makes – but Pettigrew's individuation treats them together: it takes as a starting point the value contribution that all of the outcomes with a particular utility make together. We will see that this difference is crucial.

So, for example, let us consider the three-outcome act $g = \{E_1, x_1; E_2, x_2; E_4, x_4\}$, where the ordered utilities and the probabilities are given by:

	x_1	x_2	x_4
u	3	5	6
p	E_1	E_2	E_4
	0.3	0.3	0.4

(We are examining an example that bears some similarity to Pettigrew's, so we can see clearly what problem his individuation solves.) The REU of this act for Rhoda (who has $r(p) = p^2$) is 4.14.[3]

According to the comonotonic individuation, Rhoda's utility* values are:
$u^*(x_1, g) = 1.7(3) = 5.1$
$u^*(x_2, g) = 1.1(5) = 5.5$
$u^*(x_4, g) = 0.4(6) = 2.4$

Therefore, the 'new' EU of the act agrees with the 'old' REU: the EU is $(0.3)(5.1) + (0.3)(5.5) + (0.4)(2.4) = 4.14$.

So far, so good. But this strategy doesn't work in general, because some acts can be ordered in more than one way: when an act contains two events that yield outcomes of the same utility, either event can come first in the 'ordered' act. And the comonotonic individuation, applied to these two orderings, won't yield a consistent utility* assignment to the outcomes in those acts. To see this, let us consider Pettigrew's example, the four-outcome act $h = \{E_1, x_1; E_2, x_2; E_3, x_3; E_4, x_4\}$, whose ordered utilities and probabilities are given by:

	x_1	x_2	x_3	x_4
u	3	5	5	6
p	E_1	E_2	E_3	E_4
	0.3	0.2	0.1	0.4

Applying the comonotonic individuation to this ordered act, Rhoda's utility* values are:

$u^*(x_1, h) = 1.7(3)$ $u^*(x_2, h) = 1.2(5)$ $u^*(x_3, h) = 0.9(5)$ $u^*(x_4, h) = 0.4(6)$

However, the following is an *equivalent* description of the act, *also* ordered from worst to best:

	x_1	x_3	x_2	x_4
u	3	5	5	6
	E_1	E_3	E_2	E_4
p	0.3	0.1	0.2	0.4

And applying the comonotonic individuation to this (equivalent) ordered act, Rhoda's utility* values are:

$u^*(x_1, h) = 1.7(3)$ $u^*(x_2, h) = 1(5)$ $u^*(x_3, h) = 1.3(5)$ $u^*(x_4, h) = 0.4(6)$

These two assignments are incompatible. As we can see, the comonotonic individuation is not well-defined: it does not yield a consistent assignment of utility* values to outcomes. That is because, as I pointed out (p. 143), 'the quantity that is well-defined is the total contribution that *all outcomes of a particular utility value* make to the REU of an act.'

Because an outcome can occupy more than one position in an act's ordering, I was pessimistic about whether any re-description that defined utility* in terms of an outcome's position in the act's ordering could work. However, Pettigrew ingeniously uses the quoted fact to define a different kind of redescription than the ones I considered. Specifically, he first amalgamates all outcomes with the same utility value. He then looks at how much *these outcomes together* contribute to the overall value of an act. Next, he assigns this value to these outcomes together as their utility* contribution. Finally, the utility* of the <outcome, act> pair for each of the outcomes will again be their utility* contribution divided by their total probability according to the act. This *will* give a consistent assignment. Thus, Pettigrew has successfully answered an objection I had to the redescription strategy, namely that there is no way of redescribing that will be consistent and avoid the proliferation problem.

Pettigrew's individuation manages to avoid the proliferation problem while remaining well-defined, because it directly incorporates the quantity that is well-defined. However, Pettigrew's strategy faces another problem.

To see this, let us first look at the utility* assignment we get in Pettigrew's example.

	x_1	x_2	x_3	x_4
u	3	5	5	6
u*	5.1	5.5	5.5	2.4

Notice that the worst outcome and the middle outcomes are all ranked *higher* than the best outcome, according to utility*. Since u* is supposed to characterize the agent's preferences, this means that the agent prefers <x_1, h>, <x_2, h>, and <x_3, h>, each to <x_4, h>. And this is true even though she'd rather have a guaranteed x_4 than a guaranteed x_1.

Perhaps this is not too devastating a worry, and the relative value of a fine-grained outcome just doesn't reflect which outcome one would prefer to have for certain. A fine-grained outcome is, after all, a coarse-grained outcome with a particular probability, in addition to one with a particular position in an act. However, there is a more serious worry: *two utility* assignments that represent the same preference ordering will not in general order the fine-grained outcomes in the same way.*

To see this, first notice that Pettigrew's Theorem 4 (the re-interpretation of the REU Representation Theorem) includes the clause 'unique up to affine* transformation.' A utility* function is unique up to affine* transformation if the utility function from which it is defined is unique up to affine transformation. Thus, if we apply an affine transformation to u and then calculate $u*$ of the result, $u*$ will represent the original preference ordering, in Pettigrew's sense of 'represent.' With this in mind, here are the $u*$ values that result from our original u shifted down by three units, and down by five units, respectively:

	x_1	x_2	x_3	x_4
u	0	2	2	3
$u*$	0	2.2	2.2	1.2
u	−2	0	0	1
$u*$	−3.4	0	0	0.4

All three utility* assignments represent the exact same preference ordering. However, the $u*$'s order the fine-grained outcomes differently. This means that for a particular family of $u*$'s that purport to represent the same preferences, even the *ordering* of outcomes according to $u*$ isn't preserved. This is because $u*$ is defined as the product of two factors, u and a function of both r and p, and applying an affine transformation to just the first factor means that we will not in general replicate the same ordering for each u in a family.

The extent to which one thinks that this feature is a serious problem for EU theory will depend on how one interprets the utility* function. Although some decision theorists – realists – hold that utility values exist independently of preferences, it is more typical to hold that they are constructed from preferences, and thus that cardinal comparisons of utility are meaningless in themselves. However, we only need to be *ordinal* realists about utility* for the feature under discussion to be a problem. If there is a fact of the matter about how Rhoda *ranks* fine-grained outcomes, then utility* as Pettigrew defines it cannot track this fact. Furthermore, even constructivists about ordinal preferences will have to admit that Theorem 4 doesn't yield a value function that corresponds to any recognizable feature of preferences.

This highlights a more general difference between the REU Representation Theorem and Theorem 4. On the REU Theorem, the role of each of the three internal attitudes is clear (Buchak 2013, Ch. 3). Even if we are not realists about these attitudes, there are three clearly distinct and recognizable features of preferences. Utilities determine, or are determined by, which pairs of outcomes constitute 'equal tradeoffs' in acts that order events in the same way.[4] Whether one assigns higher probability to one event than to another determines, or is determined by, whether one would rather bet on that event than on the other. The risk function determines, or is determined by, how much what happens in an event with a particular probability matters to the evaluation of an act, when that event is the best event: how much compensation in the rest of the act is required to make up for what happens in that event. So we have a nice story about the role each entity plays in preferences, which fits (at least somewhat) our pre-theoretical intuitions about what the role of such an entity would be. But we don't have this on Pettigrew's story: utility* is a muddle of two of these entities. Forcing two distinct attitudes to count as a single hybrid attitude results both in the hybrid attitude not being a readily recognizable contributor to preferences and in our being unable to make sense of the values we assign to it.

3. Pettigrew's second challenge: estimates

Let us now turn to Pettigrew's other challenge. Pettigrew provides a novel argument for the EU thesis: for Rhoda (as for any non-EU-maximizer), there will be some EU assignment of values to acts that *dominates* her assignment of values to acts, in the following sense. In every state, the EU assignment is closer to the true value of the act than Rhoda's assignment is.

We need to be clear about what this argument says, and in particular two things it does not say. First, it does not say that Rhoda will select a dominated *act*, an act such that there is an alternative act she prefers no matter how the world turns out. The object that is dominated here is an *estimate of act values*, not an act itself. It is dominated in the sense that there is an alternative assignment that is a better estimate no matter how the world turns out. Second, the argument does not say that any *one* act's estimate is dominated in all worlds in this sense; rather, the estimate of all the acts, taken as a whole, is dominated in the sense that the *sum* of the errors for each act is higher than it could be in each world. Let me illustrate with a simple example.

Suppose we have two states and three acts, with the following payoffs (in utility):

	HEADS	TAILS
Bet on heads	100	0
Bet on tails	0	100
Don't bet	50	50

Then Eulalie (our EU-maximizer) and Rhoda give the following assignments of act values and truth values:

	Eulalie	Rhoda
Value of act 'Bet on Heads'	50	25
Value of act 'Bet on Tails'	50	25
Value of act 'Don't Bet'	50	50
Truth value of 'Coin lands Heads'	0.5	0.5
Truth value of 'Coin lands Tails'	0.5	0.5

We now ask about the distance of each assignment from the true value of each entity in each state. Following Pettigrew, we calculate this distance using the quadratic distance measure:

Distance of Eulalie's assignments in each state

	Distance from truth, in HEADS	Distance from truth, in TAILS
Value of act 'Bet on Heads'	$(50 - 100)^2 = 2500$	$(50 - 0)^2 = 2500$
Value of act 'Bet on Tails'	$(50 - 0)^2 = 2500$	$(50 - 100)^2 = 2500$
Value of act 'Don't Bet'	$(50 - 50)^2 = 0$	$(50 - 50)^2 = 0$
Truth value of 'Coin lands Heads'	$(1 - 0.5)^2 = 0.25$	$(0 - 0.5)^2 = 0.25$
Truth value of 'Coin lands Tails'	$(0 - 0.5)^2 = 0.25$	$(1 - 0.5)^2 = 0.25$

Distance of Rhoda's assignments in each state

ACT	Distance from truth, in HEADS	Distance from truth, in TAILS
Value of act 'Bet on Heads'	$(25 - 100)^2 = 5625$	$(25 - 0)^2 = 625$
Value of act 'Bet on Tails'	$(25 - 0)^2 = 625$	$(25 - 100)^2 = 5625$
Value of act 'Don't Bet'	$(50 - 50)^2 = 0$	$(50 - 50)^2 = 0$
Truth value of 'Coin lands Heads'	$(1 - 0.5)^2 = 0.25$	$(0 - 0.5)^2 = 0.25$
Truth value of 'Coin lands Tails'	$(0 - 0.5)^2 = 0.25$	$(1 - 0.5)^2 = 0.25$

To find out the total distance from truth of the set of estimates at each world, we *sum* the distance from truth of each estimate:

	Total distance from truth in HEADS	Total distance from truth in TAILS
Eulalie's assignments	2500 + 2500 + 0 + 0.25 + 0.25 = 5000.5	2500 + 2500 + 0 + 0.25 + 0.25 = 5000.5
Rhoda's assignments	5625 + 625 + 0 + 0.25 + 0.25 = 6250.5	625 + 5625 + 0 + 0.25 + 0.25 = 6250.5

This illustrates Theorem 1's conclusion that Rhoda's assignments are further from the truth in both the HEADS state and the TAILS state than Eulalie's are. Rhoda's assignment is dominated in the sense that Pettigrew notes. It is dominated because although Rhoda's assignment is closer than Eulalie's by 25 utils to the value of 'Bet on Heads' in TAILS and 'Bet on Tails' in HEADS (true value: 0; Rhoda: 25; Eulalie: 50) and further than Eulalie's by 25 utils from the value of 'Bet on Heads' in HEADS and 'Bet on Tails' in TAILS (true value: 100; Rhoda: 25; Eulalie: 50), the distance measure implies that it is worse to be further from the truth, the further you already are. Being 75 rather than 50 utils from the true value is worse than being 50 rather than 25 utils from the true value.

Again, the conclusion is not that Rhoda will select a dominated act: she will select 'Don't Bet,' which is not dominated. It is also not that any particular estimate will be dominated by Eulalie's estimate in every state: while Rhoda's estimate of 'Bet on Heads' does worse in the HEADS state, it does better in the TAILS state. Incidentally, it is also worth noting that although in this particular example, there is a dominating assignment that has the same probabilities as Rhoda's assignment, this won't always hold. In particular, if all of the acts are comonotonic and if Rhoda and Eulalie agree about the probabilities, then Rhoda's assignment will be closer to the truth in the worst state than Eulalie's is. So although there will be a dominating assignment (a fact which we know to be true by Theorem 1), it won't preserve Rhoda's *beliefs*. Others have raised and responded to related concerns about dominance arguments (see Easwaran and Fitelson 2012; Pettigrew 2013), so I will leave it to the reader to decide whether this is a problem for the argument.

This consideration aside, should Rhoda care about the kind of dominance she is subject to? Let us start by observing that it is not a kind of dominance that captures what she *does* care about. Why? For her, not all error is created equal. Recall that when Rhoda evaluates a bet on TAILS, the possibility of ending up with 0 utils is weighted more heavily than the possibility of ending up with 100 utils. This is to say, when she evaluates an act, she considers being 25 rather than 50 utils away from the true value when that value is 0 to be *better* than being 50 rather than 75 away from the true value when that value is 100. Is it not just distance from the true value that matters, but how good that value is: roughly speaking, it is more important to correctly estimate worse values than better ones. Rhoda will object to the method Theorem 1 employs for determining the total distance from the true value in a particular state: she will object to simply summing the errors of each estimate. No score that treats the error in worse states within an act the same as the error in better states within that act will capture what she cares about. Rhoda does not care about all errors equally.

We have just established that Rhoda doesn't care about the kind of dominance mentioned in the argument. *Should* she? I claim that she need not. Decision theory is a theory of instrumental rationality, and what we want from decision theory is a *ranking* of acts (and perhaps an assessment of their relative instrumental value) rather than an *estimate* of the actual value of an act. The instrumental value of an act – its EU or REU – is not an estimate of how valuable that act will in fact turn out to be, but an assessment of its value in potentially realizing some of one's aims, relative to other possible acts. Being close to an act's actual value (the success condition for an estimate) is only helpful for decision-making insofar as the ranking of act-estimates corresponds to which acts turn out to be best at potentially realizing some of one's aims. But the disagreement is precisely about which acts turn out to be best in this way. Therefore, to assume a distance measure that treats all estimation error the same is to prejudge the answer to this question. However, Pettigrew's argument does reveal a cost of REU theory: if we accept REU theory, we cannot see the agent as trying to accurately estimate the values of acts, where accuracy is defined without reference to a quantity's relative position.

4. Briggs's first challenge: choice over time

Like Pettigrew, Briggs claims that Rhoda will forgo something that dominates what she actually does – but where Pettigrew claimed that she would forgo a dominant estimate of act values, Briggs claims that she will forgo a dominant *strategy*, where a strategy is a series of acts over time.

To understand Briggs's argument, we must recall three methods of choice over time: naïve choice, sophisticated choice, and resolute choice. Choosing naively means choosing at each time the act that is part of your preferred strategy going forward, with no regard to what your past or future selves *do* or *prefer*. Choosing sophisticatedly means choosing at each time as if your future act is determined by your future selves' preferences, using backward induction to eliminate options that you know your future self will not choose.[5] Choosing resolutely means picking a strategy and sticking to it – the strategy could be determined by your earliest preferences, or it could represent some compromise between the preferences of all your time-slices.[6]

Keeping these methods in mind, let us examine the dialectic. Briggs interprets me as having challenged both premises in the following argument:

(1) According to REU theory, it is sometimes permissible for an agent to choose a strategy in an extended choice situation, where that strategy is dominated by some option available to the agent.

(2) Choosing a strategy that is dominated by some available option in an extended choice situation is irrational.

I've altered her statement of the first premise to make clear that the dominance must be by some strategy that is available to the agent. For example, buying baseball tickets with a dollar-off coupon dominates buying them without the coupon – it is preferable whether I sit in the cheap seats or the expensive seats – but if the option of using the coupon is not available to me, then I do nothing wrong by paying full price. (I will later consider a slightly different interpretation of Briggs's argument, one that recasts the first premise in a different way.)

I challenged the first premise, Briggs points out, by claiming that only naïve choosers pick strategies that are dominated by other strategies available to them, and that both resolute and sophisticated choosers do not do so: resolute choosers because although all of the relevant options are available to them, they do not select a dominated one; and sophisticated choosers because the only options that dominate their selected option are not available to them. Briggs objects to my challenge by arguing that the strategy that dominates the sophisticated chooser's selection is in fact available to her. She leaves unchallenged the claim that resolute choosers do not pick dominated options. So, according to Briggs, only proponents of resolute choice can deny the first premise – proponents of sophisticated choice must accept it.

According to Briggs, I also challenged the second premise by claiming that choosing a dominated strategy in an extended choice situation can be rational, on the grounds that we can explain and vindicate why an agent would make these choices. And her response is to argue that choosing a dominant strategy *constitutes* irrationality. I prefer to put things slightly differently. I agree with premise (2) that choosing a strategy dominated by an available option in an extended choice situation is irrational; therefore, I agree with Briggs that naïve Rhoda is irrational, and that if sophisticated Rhoda really does choose an option dominated by an available option, then sophisticated Rhoda is also irrational. However, I think that having preferences of a certain form – preferences that necessitate sophisticated or resolute choice – is rational. That was the intended force of my arguments that Briggs mentions in her Section 3. (These preferences *would* lead one to choose a dominated strategy *if* one chose naively, so the misinterpretation is understandable.) Still, we can recast Briggs's argument against choosing dominated options as instead against having these preferences: she can argue that *having preferences that necessitate sophisticated or resolute choice* constitutes practical irrationality.

Let us begin with the question of whether sophisticated Rhoda indeed chooses a strategy that is dominated by a strategy available to her: Briggs claims she does, I claim she does not. Our locus of disagreement is the choice problem that Briggs labels Problem 2, in which Rhoda faces a choice between two acts, L_1 and L_2 (from Allais [1953] 1979). Rhoda prefers L_1 to L_2. But before making her choice, she first must choose whether to accept more information about the true state of the world along with a sweetener – a sweetener which is not sweet enough to make sweetened L_2 preferable to unsweetened L_1. The information will reveal which of two events obtains, and for both events, Rhoda will prefer the sub-act of sweetened L_2 under that event to that of unsweetened L_1 under that event. Since Rhoda is a sophisticated chooser, she knows she will choose according to her preferences after obtaining the information, and will therefore end up with an act logically equivalent to sweetened L_2 if she does receive the information. As a sophisticated chooser, she therefore sees her initial choice as between receiving the information and ending up with sweetened L_2, or forgoing the information and ending up with unsweetened L_1. Since she prefers L_1, she will forgo the information. However, there was a series of choices she could have made – namely, accepting the information and the sweetener, and choosing (the logical equivalent of) L_1 – which would have resulted in sweetened L_1. Since sweetened L_1 strictly dominates what she ends up with (unsweetened L_1), she chooses a dominated option.

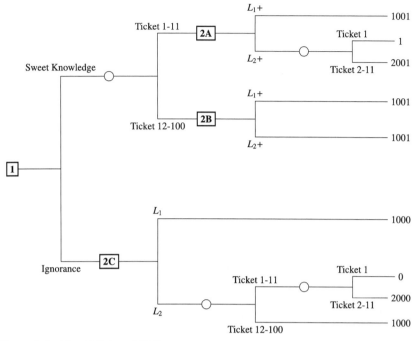

Figure 1. Problem 2 (Briggs, 2015).

What I said in *Risk and Rationality* is that sweetened L_1 is not available to sophisticated Rhoda. Sophisticated choice only makes sense if we operate with a restricted notion of an agent's options: an agent's options are her options at a particular time. And there is no time at which the acts that constitute choosing sweetened L_1 are available to Rhoda. However, Briggs challenges this point (note that 'L_{1+}' stands for sweetened L_1):

> Nonetheless, there is a sequence of actions, each of which Rhoda can perform, that will guarantee she ends up with L_{1+}. (All she has to do is choose sweet knowledge at [1], and choose L_{1+} at [2A], should she get there.) In other words, there is a strategy available to Rhoda that results in her ending up with L_{1+}. Buchak holds that on the view that motivates sophisticated choice, we are not entitled to evaluate entire strategies, since there is no time at which strategies are the object of choice. But the objector should press the point that *a strategy can be available, even if there is no one time at which it is available*. (p. [8], italics mine)

The argument says, look, Rhoda can have sweetened L_1 – it's available to her! All she has to do is select, at each time, the acts that constitute it. There is a difference between saying that an option is available to Rhoda and saying that there is a single time at which it is available to her, and sweetened L_1 is available to Rhoda in this former sense.

I want to press my point that the reasons you might have for accepting sophisticated choice are also reasons to think that availability is just availability at a time. Recall that there are two views one might have of what an agent is. One is the time-slice view, which sees a rational agent as a series of time-slices that each forms preferences and makes decisions in isolation of what other time-slices prefer. On this view, one's choices are fully determined by what each of one's time-slices prefers, and furthermore, one stands in a similar relationship to one's other time-slices as one does to other people. I can influence others' actions indirectly – by incentivizing them in various ways (changing their payoffs) or by limiting what they can do (changing their options) or by convincing them to care about what I care about (indirectly changing their preferences) – but I cannot choose for them. So too can I influence the actions of my future self only indirectly: I can set up rewards and penalties, I can remove future options, I can cultivate a desire to honor past wishes, but I cannot now choose what to do later in a way that will bind me to that choice. An individual at a time has influence over the actions of her time-slices taken together to the same extent and in the same way (though perhaps by a different mechanism) that an individual has influence over the actions of a group of which she is a part. Carrying out a strategy is the result of several 'selves' trying to get what they most prefer, given the behavior they can expect from the other selves. As I put it in *Risk and Rationality*, there is no agent to whom temporally extended acts are available: there is only a temporal extension of time-slices to whom acts-at-a-time are available.[7]

The time-slice view provides a natural home for sophisticated choice: sophisticated choice enjoins me to see my future selves' choices as fixed, and to treat them as I would treat the choices of other individuals. Sophisticated choice looks less natural on a holistic view of agency. On this view, the primary locus of action is the temporally extended agent. And the primary entities over which such an agent has control are temporally extended acts. Given these assumptions, sophisticated choice is a puzzling strategy. Why should I treat my future actions as determined, while deliberating about my present actions? I should instead deliberate about strategies over time, and choose once for all. This is why resolute choice finds a natural home in this picture.

I won't adjudicate the debate between the time-slice view of agency, with sophisticated choice, and the holistic view of agency, with resolute choice. What I continue to claim is that we don't have a reason to accept both sophisticated choice *and* the claim that the dominating option is available. The proponent of EU theory will have to supply a picture on which this combination of commitments makes sense. Indeed, what Briggs highlights is that if we accept sophisticated choice, then the debate between REU theory and EU theory hinges on what counts as an option.

Before moving on to a different version of Briggs's argument, let us briefly return to her second point. Recall that she reads me as denying that choosing dominated strategies is irrational, on the grounds that we can explain and vindicate these choices. Her point as stated is that choosing dominated strategies is *constitutive* of irrationality, because doing so is both 'internally' irrational – it amounts to choosing something that is worse by Rhoda's own lights – and 'externally' irrational – it frustrates the aim of choosing the act with the best consequences. I agree with this point, and this is a good way of explaining what's wrong with choosing dominated strategies. However, recall that what I actually deny is that having preferences that in some situations require sophisticated or resolute choice is irrational. So, let us look at an amended version of Briggs's argument for the claim that having these preferences is constitutive of irrationality. This argument would say that having such preferences is irrational because having them amounts to preferring something that is worse by Rhoda's own lights, or that having such preferences is irrational because having them frustrates the aim of preferring the act with the best consequences. But these claims only hold if preferences over strategies are determined *both* by the consequences of those strategies *and* by what one would do if one were naïve – and there is no reason to think this second clause holds. Therefore, the amended version of the argument has not yet revealed that Rhoda is irrational.

We can further explore the question of whether anything is wrong with sophisticated Rhoda by considering the interpersonal analogue of Problem 2. Assume that choices are made by two different agents with different knowledge states, rather than by two time-slices of the same agent before and after receiving information. These agents, Rhoda$_1$ (who doesn't know whether E) and Rhoda$_2$ (who does know whether E), have Rhoda's preferences about outcomes and lotteries. Rhoda$_1$ will choose Sweet Knowledge or Ignorance at the initial decision node, and if she chooses Ignorance she will also choose at 2C; and Rhoda$_2$ will choose at 2A (we will ignore the choice at 2B, as Briggs does, because both Rhoda's are indifferent between the two options at that node). We can represent this choice using a game matrix, where Rhoda$_1$ is the 'row' player, Rhoda$_2$ is the 'column' player, and the payoffs to each player are the lotteries that they will receive.

	2A: L_{1+}	2A: L_{2+}
Sweet knowledge	$L_{1+}, (L_{1+E}$ or $L_{1+(-E)})$	$L_{2+}, (L_{2+}E$ or $L_{2+(-}E_)})$
Ignorance; 2C: L_1	$L_{1'}, (L_1 E$ or $L_{1(-}E_))$	$L_{1'}, (L_1 E$ or $L_{1(-}E_))$
Ignorance; 2C: L_2	$L_{2'}, (L_{2E}$ or $L_{2(-E)})$	$L_{2'}, (L_2 E$ or $L_{2(-}E_))$

The two highlighted acts constitute the *sub-game perfect equilibrium*, the result of backward induction: Rhoda$_2$ will choose L_{2+} at 2A; so the payoff of Sweet Knowledge for Rhoda$_1$ will be L_{2+}; so Rhoda$_1$ chooses Ignorance and L_1.

What of the original claim that Rhoda employs a strategy that is diachronically dominated? Translating into the interpersonal framework, it is the claim that Rhoda$_1$ and Rhoda$_2$ choose an act pair that is *strictly sub-optimal*: there is an alternative act pair whose outcome is strictly preferred by both Rhoda$_1$ and Rhoda$_2$ to the selected outcome: namely, (Sweet Knowledge, L_{1+}).[8] Thus, the notion of diachronic dominance in the intrapersonal framework translates into the notion of sub-optimality in the intrapersonal framework; and the strategy selected by sophisticated choice translates into the sub-game perfect equilibrium. The interpersonal framework also has a concept of *dominance*: an individual player's act is dominated if there is some alternative act which leads to a preferred outcome given any choice made by the other player. Dominance in this sense is a property of an individual's act, not of an act pair. Translation in hand, we can restate my claim that the (intrapersonal) strategy that selects L_1 is not dominated by any other available option: for the acts chosen by each Rhoda-at-a-time, there is no alternative act that is preferable no matter what the other Rhoda's-at-a-time choose.

If we take seriously the correspondence between the intrapersonal problem and the interpersonal problem – as it seems the time-slice view must – then what is bad about Rhoda's strategy is the bad of an act pair's being sub-optimal. Given this, we can construct the following version of Briggs's argument:[9]

(1') According to REU theory, it is permissible for the sophisticated chooser to choose a strategy (a pair of acts-over-time) in an extended choice situation, where that strategy is intrapersonally sub-optimal.

(2') Choosing a strategy that intrapersonally sub-optimal is irrational for the sophisticated chooser.

This argument correctly isolates what is available to an agent on the time-slice picture, so premise (1') is true. But is premise (2') true? We must consider what norms an agent is subject to, on the time-slice picture.

Let us examine the corresponding interpersonal question: is it *irrational* for two players to select a sub-optimal act pair? The standard view is that choosing a sub-optimal act pair is not irrational because there is no one for whom it is irrational. Being in a problem in which the equilibria are sub-optimal is unfortunate, but the result is not a failure of rationality on the part of any actors, since both are doing the best they can given what the other chooses. Analogously, if rational norms concern the agent at a time,[10] then choosing a sub-optimal act pair is not irrational because there is no *one time-slice* for whom it is irrational. It is unfortunate that the agent over time suffers, but each time-slice is acting rationally, and one is only answerable for what one does at a time.

There is a minority view according to which selecting a sub-optimal strategy pair in the interpersonal situation is in fact irrational. However, those who accept this view typically accept the analogue of resolute choice *for groups*, that separate individuals can jointly decide on an act pair and each do their part.[11] Thus, on this view, selecting a sub-optimal strategy pair is irrational because *both* players are acting irrationally. Analogously, a proponent of the time-slice picture could hold that both time-slices ought to choose resolutely – resolute Rhoda would be irrational to pick a sub-optimal act pair, but she won't do so. If we accept the time-slice picture, then either the time-slices ought to choose resolutely, in which case Rhoda won't end up with the sub-optimal strategy, or they ought not to, in which case Rhoda won't be violating any norms in ending up with the sub-optimal strategy.

What Briggs and I agree on is that decision theorists face a choice. If a theorist wants to accept sophisticated choice *and* the idea that diachronic dominance by a strategy only available to the agent-over-time is irrational, she must reject REU theory. I do not think this is worrisome for REU theory, because sophisticated choice and this idea do not fit together well. In any case, the REU theorist still has many theoretical options open to her: she can be a proponent of sophisticated choice and hold that this kind of diachronic dominance is not bad. Or she can be a proponent of resolute choice, holding that Rhoda will not be subject to diachronic dominance. Insofar as one is convinced that the intrapersonal problem is not like the interpersonal problem – that there is a unity among time-slices that does not hold among people – this latter option may be the best.

5. Briggs's second challenge: simplifying choices

Briggs's other criticism of REU theory is that for Rhoda, sub-acts lack stable utility values: the contribution of a particular sub-act to an act's value can depend on what happens in the rest of the act. Put another way, the certainty equivalent of each sub-act – the sure-thing amount we can substitute for that sub-act while preserving the value of the act – can depend on what happens in the rest of the act. This follows from the fact that preferences about 'sure-thing' sub-acts are fixed – if an agent prefers a sure-thing x to a sure-thing y, she will always rather include x as a sub-act than include y as a sub-act – but preferences about 'gamble' sub-acts depend on which other sub-acts they are paired with. Since there is a stable ordering of sure-thing sub-acts, but not of gamble sub-acts, certainty equivalents for gamble sub-acts cannot stay fixed.

Is the fact that sub-acts lack stable values bad? One possible way to argue in the affirmative, though Briggs herself does not make this argument, is to claim that not being able to assign stable values to sub-acts is in itself bad. One could claim that the individual who does not stably value sub-acts has inconsistent values. But the REU response is to point out that since the instrumental value of an act depends on its global properties, the contribution of any sub-act will depend on which global properties it helps instantiate, which depends on which sub-acts it is paired with. In short, REU theory holds that while there is a fixed fact of the matter about the value of an outcome, and about the instrumental value of an entire act, there is no fixed fact of the matter about the instrumental value of a sub-act, apart from the act in which it is embedded. As I said in *Risk and Rationality*, what instrumental value is like generally – including whether sub-acts with the same instrumental value are interchangeable – is not a pre-theoretical question. So this argument would straightforwardly beg the question against REU-maximization.

The argument Briggs actually makes is that because sub-acts lack fixed values, REU-maximizers lose a key strategy for simplifying 'grand world' decisions by recasting them as 'small world' decisions. This isn't necessarily to say that Rhoda is irrational, but she will have a more difficult time actually making decisions. REU theory is unwieldy and impractical.

Briggs's example involves a decision between buying a frogurt and not buying a frogurt, where one does not know whether the frogurt is cursed, whether it comes with a free topping, and if so whether the topping contains E212. The decision matrix is as follows:

	Cursed Topping E212	Cursed Topping No E212	Cursed No topping	Not cursed Topping E212	Not cursed Topping No E212	Not cursed No topping
Buy	−50	−30	−45	10	30	15
Don't buy	0	0	0	0	0	0

Briggs points out that Eulalie can easily simplify the problem by 'collapsing' the values under 'cursed' and 'not cursed' into the expected values in those events. However, claims Briggs, while Rhoda can impute values to these events, the value of the event in which the frogurt is cursed 'will not be a function of the probabilities and utilities of states in which the frogurt is cursed,' but instead 'will also depend on both the probabilities and utilities of the states in which the frogurt is not cursed'([13]); and similarly for the value of the event in which the frogurt is not cursed. More generally, while Eulalie will be able to coarse-grain her problem by collapsing some states into a single event with a fixed utility value, Rhoda cannot coarse-grain her decision problems in this way.

As it turns out, only a weakened version of Briggs's claim is true. To see this, let us first consider an abstract example in which there are four states. Let $u(S)$ stand for the utility of ACT in state S, and let $u(A) \leq u(B) \leq u(C) \leq u(D)$:

	A	B	C	D
ACT	$u(A)$	$u(B)$	$u(C)$	$u(D)$

The REU of ACT is:

$$\text{REU}(ACT) = u(A) + r(p(B \vee C \vee D))(u(B) - u(A)) + r(p(C \vee D))(u(C) - u(B)) + r(p(D))(u(D) - u(C))$$

Which can be rewritten as:

$$\text{REU}(ACT) = u(A)(1 - r(p(\neg A))) + u(B)(r(p(A)) - r(p(\neg(A \vee B))) + u(C)(r(p(C \vee D)) - r(p(D))) + u(D)(r(p(D)))$$

Notice that the terms on the first line are a function only of the probabilities and utilities of states A and B, and the terms on the second line are a function only of the probabilities and utilities of the states C and D. So we can, indeed, divide the REU of ACT into two parts, an 'A or B' part and a 'C or D' part. But notice that we cannot divide the REU of ACT into an 'A or C' part and a 'B or D' part: we cannot separate terms that involve only probabilities and utilities of A and C from those that involve only probabilities and utilities of B and D.

We can separate ACT in one way and not the other because the successful separation involves a division into events that are *contiguous*. Define a contiguous event (set of states) for a given act as follows: E is contiguous iff E contains all states S such that $\min_{T \in E} u(T) < u(S) < \max_{T \in E} u(T)$. And we can note that if the states of an act are divided into two contiguous events, then the value contribution of each event to the act will depend only on the probabilities and utilities of the states in the event.[12] For the sub-act over each contiguous event, its value will be stable and will depend only on the probabilities and utilities of the states *within* that event.

It is worth noting two caveats in support of Briggs's objection, as well as an additional fact in support of Rhoda's ability to simplify decisions. First, even with a contiguous division, there will be no natural way to divide the value of each event into a 'probability' and 'utility' component, as there is for EU theory. Second, the claim that the value of each event only depends on the probabilities of the states in that event only holds true for a coarse-graining into *more than* two events if the probabilities of all the coarse events are fixed. However, in support of REU theory, the sub-acts of any contiguous division (including those into more than two events) do have stable certainty equivalents. We know this because preferences about sub-acts are stable for acts that are comonotonic, and substituting a certainty equivalent for a sub-act on a contiguous event preserves comonotonicity (because the certainty equivalent will always be between the minimum and maximum value of the sub-act).

To return to the frogurt problem: in this problem, all of the cursed states have lower utility than all of the non-cursed states. If we coarse-grain the problem into the event in which the frogurt is cursed and that in which the frogurt is not cursed, we can separately determine the value of the act in the 'cursed' states and in the 'non-cursed' states – where 'value' here means the value contributed to the REU by these states – and these two values will depend only on the probabilities and utilities within those states. This also means that the value of act in the cursed states will be stable across changes to probabilities and utilities in the non-cursed states. For example, here are some possible changes: the value of a not-cursed frogurt with no topping might change; or the agent might come to realize that this value depends on a further unknown (whether it is possible to swirl two flavors or whether one has to choose only one); or the probability that a non-cursed frogurt comes with a topping might change, holding fixed the probability that the frogurt is cursed. As long as these changes do not disrupt the contiguity of the division into cursed and non-cursed states or the probability of these two events, then these changes will only alter the value of the non-cursed event – the value of the cursed event will stay the same. So we *can* simplify the decision problem by separately considering how good the cursed event is and how good the non-cursed event is.

However, if we coarse-grain the problem into the event in which the frogurt comes with a free topping and the event in which is does not, we cannot separately consider how good each event is. So we cannot simplify the decision problem by separately considering how good the free-topping event is and how good the no-free-topping event is.

To sum up: for some coarse-grainings of the problem – coarse-grainings into contiguous sets – Rhoda can assign stable values to coarse-grained events, and these values will depend only on what happens within those events. For other coarse-grainings, this will not be possible. Coarse-graining will be an effective way of simplifying a decision problem only if it involves a division into two contiguous events (or into two or more contiguous events where probabilities of events are fixed or the value of an is allowed to depend on the probability of the other events). But this may not be very bad for REU theory. Indeed, it explains why some ways of thinking about a decision problem strike us as productive and others as unproductive. In the frogurt problem, the consideration that ought to loom largest in our minds is whether or not the frogurt is cursed, not whether or not the frogurt comes with a free topping. It is true that Rhoda has a more difficult time simplifying her decision problems than Eulalie does: only certain simplifications will do. But perhaps this just means that Rhoda is appropriately discerning in how she thinks about decision problems.

6. Conclusion

Pettigrew and Briggs both raise important challenges for REU theory. Pettigrew's first challenge tried to show that REU theory is superfluous, since Rhoda can in fact be recast as an EU-maximizer. However, his way of incorporating her risk-attitudes into the utility value assignment did not generate a stable ordering of outcomes. Pettigrew's second challenge tried to show that Rhoda's utility and probability assignments are dominated in the sense that there is an alternative set of assignments that are closer to the truth in every world. However, there are reasons to think that she will reject the measure of closeness according to which this is true. Furthermore, one could hold that what decision theory is concerned with is not estimating truth values, but with comparing acts – on this view, dominance according to this measure need not be irrational. Briggs's first challenge concerned a different kind of dominance: diachronic dominance. However, depending on our picture of agency and norms, we must either hold that Rhoda will not choose the dominated option or that choosing the "dominated" option is not irrational. Still, Briggs brings out a cost of accepting REU theory: one cannot also accept both sophisticated choice and the claim that norms of rationality apply non-derivatively to the agent over time. Finally, Briggs's second challenge pointed out that Rhoda lacks a way to simplify her decisions, a way that Eulalie possesses. Importantly, this claim is only true in a limited sense: Rhoda can simplify her decisions in some ways but not others, and this distinction plausibly tracks ways of simplifying decisions that seem natural to us.

These challenges help us see more clearly what REU theory is committed to, as well as some of the costs of rejecting the EU thesis. For my part, I continue to hold that it is rational to take risk into account in a way that cannot be subsumed under EU-maximization, and that rational preferences involve three internal attitudes: utilities, credences, and risk-attitudes.

Notes

1. Throughout, except where it is an explicit topic of discussion, I remain neutral on whether the relevant attitudes exist independently of preferences or are constructed from them.
2. More precisely, the REU of an act $f = \{E_1, x_1; \ldots; E_n, x_n\}$, where $u(x_1) \leq \ldots \leq u(x_n)$, is $u(x_1) + r(\sum_{i=2}^{n} p(E_i))(u(x_2) - u(x_1)) + r(\sum_{i=3}^{n} p(E_i))(u(x_3) - u(x_2)) + \ldots + r(p(E_n))(u(x_n) - u(x_{n-1}))$. In other words, REU$(f) = \sum_{j=1}^{n} r(\sum_{i=j}^{n} p(E_i))(u(x_j) - u(x_{j-1}))$ This is equivalent to REU$(f) = \sum_{j=1}^{n} (r(\sum_{i=j}^{n} p(E_i)) - r(\sum_{i=j+1}^{n} p(E_i)))u(x_j)$. We can see REU as a generalization of Quiggin's (1982) anticipated utility to subjective rather than objective probabilities; or as a restriction of Gilboa's (1987) (and, recast, Schmeidler's 1989) Choquet EU to weightings that are a function of probabilistic credences; or as a similar generalization of objective cumulative prospect theory or restriction of subjective cumulative prospect theory (see Kahneman and Tversky 1979; Tversky and Kahneman 1992), with the additional stipulation that gains and losses are not treated differently. See (Buchak 2013, Ch. 1 and 2) for a discussion of the relationship of REU theory to other non-EU theories.
3. REU $= u(x_1) + r(p(E_2) + p(E_4))(u(x_2) - u(x_1)) + r(p(E_4))(u(x_4) - u(x_2)) = 3 + (0.3 + 0.4)^2(5 - 3) + 0.4^2(6 - 5) = 4.14$.
4. More precisely, since the only real facts about utility functions are difference ratios, the utility difference between two pairs of outcomes is the same if these two pairs constitute equal tradeoffs in acts with the same structure.
5. See Strotz (1955), Hammond (1988), and McClennen (1990).
6. See Strotz (1955), McClennen (1990, 1997), and Gauthier (1997).
7. This coheres with a view recently put forth by Hedden (2015), a proponent of the time-slice picture, of what an option is: 'your options are all and only the *decisions* you are presently able to make' (95).
8. The usual game-theoretic terminology is 'strategy' for an individual's choice and 'strategy pair' for the pair of strategies chosen by the two agents. However, since I follow Briggs in using 'strategy' to refer to the pair of acts chosen by the agent at the earlier time and at the later time, the interpersonal analogue of which is the pair of acts chosen by the two agents, I will instead use 'act' and 'act pair.'
9. This isn't quite the right way to interpret Briggs herself, because the argument of mine that Briggs cites against premise (1) would actually concern premise (2'). Nonetheless, this argument is at least strongly suggested by her discussion.
10. A recent proponent of this view is Hedden (2015), who argues for 'time-slice rationality,' according to which 'how you rationally ought to be at a time directly depends only on your mental states at that time, not on how you (or time-slices psychologically continuous with you) were in the past or will be in the future' (7). Moss (2015) argues for a similar view in epistemology, which she dubs 'time-slice epistemology.'

11. See, for example, McClennen (1997), who explicitly makes the connection between intrapersonal decisions and the interpersonal decisions, and argues that resolute choice can resolve problems within both. Gauthier (1997) denies that the two types of decisions are analogous: other people's concerns always ought to be taken seriously but my past concerns can cease to matter when I no longer embrace them. Furthermore, he holds that sophisticated choice rather than resolute choice ought to be employed in typical intrapersonal situations; however, when sophisticated choice would be sub-optimal, resolute choice ought to be employed. Thus, insofar as he holds that landing on a sub-optimal strategy pair is irrational, he holds that resolute choice is appropriate.
12. Notice that if there are two states with the same utility, then a contiguous event with this utility as the minimum or maximum value can include one state, the other state, or both. This won't pose the same kind of problem as it does for the comonotonic individuation (discussed in Section 2), since we are not trying to come up with a utility contribution for an event independent of the ordering under consideration (i.e. independent of the particular coarse-graining we consider).

References

Allais, Maurice. ([1953] 1979). "The Foundations of a Positive Theory of Choice Involving Risk and a Criticism of the Postulates and Axioms of the American School." In *Expected Utility Hypothesis and the Allais Paradox*, edited by Maurice Allais and Ole Hagen (1979), 27–145. Dordrecht: Reidel. English Translation of "Fondements d'une Théorie Positive des Choix Comportant un Risque et Critique des Postulats et Axiomes de L'Ecole Americaine," Econometrie (1953): 257–332.

Briggs, Rachael. 2015. "Costs of Abandoning the Sure-thing Principle." *Canadian Journal of Philosophy* (forthcoming).

Buchak, Lara. 2013. *Risk and Rationality*. Oxford: Oxford University Press.

Easwaran, Kenny, and Branden Fitelson. 2012. "An 'Evidentialist' Worry About Joyce's Argument for Probabilism." *Dialectica* 66 (3): 425–433.

Gauthier, David. 1997. "Resolute Choice and Rational Deliberation: A Critique and a Defense." *Noûs* 31 (1): 1–25.

Gilboa, Itzhak. 1987. "Expected Utility with Purely Subjective Non-additive Probabilities." *Journal of Mathematical Economics* 16: 65–88.

Hammond, Peter. 1988. "Consequentialist Foundations for Expected Utility." *Theory and Decision* 25: 25–78.

Hedden, Brian. 2015. *Reasons Without Persons: Rationality, Identity, and Time*. Oxford: Oxford University Press.

Kahneman, Daniel, and Amos Tversky. 1979. "Prospect Theory: An Analysis of Decision under Risk." *Econometrica* 47: 263–291.

McClennen, Edward F. 1990. *Rationality and Dynamic Choice: Foundational Explorations.* Cambridge: Cambridge University Press.

McClennen, Edward F. 1997. "Pragmatic Rationality and Rules." *Philosophy and Public Affairs* 26 (3): 210–258.

Moss, Sarah. 2015. "Credal Dilemmas." *Noûs* 49 (4): 665–683.

Pettigrew, Richard. 2013. "Accuracy and Evidence." *Dialectica* 67 (4): 579–596.

Pettigrew, Richard. 2015. "Risk, Rationality, and Expected Utility Theory." *Canadian Journal of Philosophy* (forthcoming).

Quiggin, John. 1982. "A theory of anticipated utility." *Journal of Economic Behavior and Organization* 3: 323–343.

Schmeidler, David. 1989. "Subjective Probability and Expected Utility Without Additivity." *Econometrica* 57 (3): 571–587.

Strotz, R. H. 1955. "Myopia and Inconsistency in Dynamic Utility Maximization." *The Review of Economic Studies* 23 (3): 165–180.

Tversky, Amos, and Daniel Kahneman. 1992. "Advances in Prospect Theory: Cumulative Representation of Uncertainty." *Journal of Risk and Uncertainty* 5: 297–323.

Index

Note: Page numbers in **bold** type refer to figures and those followed by 'n' refer to notes

a posteriori 145; knowledge 145
a priori 144, 160–4, 166–70, 174–7, 180n16
abduction 171
absolute value measure 247
access internalism 161, 187, 204n6
accessibility 222
accident 174
accuracy 196; expected 198, 201; gradational 199; maximizing expected 199, 201
accuracy dominance avoidance 199
accuracy-centered epistemology 197
accurate extension invariance 248
action 87; at a distance 175–6; influencing 293; reasons for 101
action theory 115, 175
activities 92
acts 73, 273; dominated 287, 288; evaluating 255; instrumental value of 296; ordering 284, 285; outcomes of 251, 260; permissible 195; ranking 289; set of 239; value assignments of 287
additive aggregation 39
advantage 4
advice 129n22
again 34
agency 87, 261, 293; ideal 129n26
agents 56, 59, 64; deliberating 119; ideal 192; ideal rational 202; rational 52, 129n22, 293; risk-averse 257, 258; risk-neutral 254; risk-seeking 257; scrambled 188; temporally extended 293; wise 134–5
agony 23, 25, 45n10
akrasia 88
algebra 226n3
alienation 91, 92, 93, 100–4

Allais, M. 268
Alston, W. 88
alternatives 5; permissible 77
analysis: fallacy of 65n1
Andreou, C. 2–15
answer 49, 60; concurrent 210, 211, 213; learning 201; posterior 210, 211, 223
antecedents 78
anti-additive-aggregationist approach 31, 32
appearances 52
appraisals: categorical 6–9; categories 7–10; relational 6–9; responses 7; subjective 7, 8
architecture question 112, 121, 123, 126
Aristotle 57
arithmetic: Wittgensteinian 50–3
arm 50, 51, 60
Armstrong, D. 167
Arntzenius, F. 137, 139
asking 66n8
aspect 57
assertion 107n8
assessment 102
assumptions 101, 200; background 222
Astros 151
asymmetry 124, 125
atoms 22–3, 45n8
attitudes 71, 79, 133; conclusion 74; constant 121; contents of 76; earlier 113; external 240, 253; fixed 112; hybrid 287; internal 240, 253, 281, 282; judgment-sensitive 120; lining up 111; multiple 114; network of 87; new 85; premise 74; relations between 240, 253; to risk 252, 255, 263n3, 281; wise 134
authority 103

INDEX

availability 292
awareness 61, 62

bachelors 162
bad life 27
badness 33, 34, 247–50; total 28
Barnett, D.J. 146
baseball 110, 114, 121, 122, 124, 290
Bayesian norms 214
Bayesian rationality 184
Bayesianism 185–6
before 34
behavior 259
beings 65n1; miserable 24; rational 73; sentient 20, 23, 40n2
belief: based on beliefs 83; changing 157, 159, 178n2, 190, 191, 204n9; coherence of 172; consequences of 194; contradictory 71; degrees of 158, 239; inducing 204n13; justified 160; losing 191; management 117; norms about 157; proliferation of 259; reasons for 157; right 214; stability of 172; state 186
belief-forming rules 161
believer: passive 128n19
believing 85, 89–93
benefits 31
Bernecker, S. 150
best system account 168
best worlds 219, 221, 222
best-off 38
bets 280, 288
better 246
better than 13n7
bias: involuntary 195
birth 34
Boolean algebra 226n3
boundaries: fuzzy 8, 9
bounty 245
Bratman, M.E. 65n3, 115, 116
Bregman divergence 243, 247, 263n4
Briggs, R. 267–80, 282, 290–9
bringing about 51–2
Broome, J. 70–86, 129n26, 230n27
Buchak, L. 250–62, 267, 269, 273–4, 281–302
burdens: distributing 31
Burge, T. 144
bushwalk 268

camera 138
canonical language 181n21
capital punishment 189
capped model 34–6

caring 72, 74, 85, 289
Carnap, R. 162
Carr, J.R. 184–206
Cartesian skepticism 171
cases: multiple evidence 213
categorical responses 6–9
category: abstract 57
causal connection 79
causal process 122, 129n26
causality 49, 51–2, 53
causation 79; instantaneous 227n13
certainties 184
chains 60
chance 73, 214
change 223; concurrent 227n12; global 227n12; predictable 274; required 276
character trait 126
charity 165
chess 214
children 143, 152n3
chocolate 7, 8, 242, 243, 245
choice 274–6, 282, 291; about credences 226n1; future 293; over time 290–6; and preferences 272–4; problem 291; rationally-governed 10, 11; series of 6; simplifying 296–9
choosing 270
Christensen, D. 198, 229n18
circularity 160, 166, 174
civilizations 19, 21, 22, 34, 42n5
cleverness 12n6
cloudy sky 171, 173
Coady, C.A.J. 143
coarse-grained outcomes 283
coarse-grained states 278, 279
coarse-grained strategies 272
cognitive architecture 112, 121, 123
cognitive bias 189
cognitive capabilities 212
cognitive capacity 121, 143
cognitive error 91
cognitive illusion 99
cognitive limitations 194
cognitive malfunction 96
cognitive skill 107n15
coherence 184
coin toss 140, 141, 191, 200–2, 226n2, 239–40, 246
color experience 6
coloring 51
combination 240–6
comfort 3
commitments 148
comonotonic individuation 283, 284
completion 58, 63

INDEX

complexity 63
complication 4–5
concept 55
conclusion attitude 74
conclusions 75; consequences of 122; reasons for 101
conditional 220
conditional content 78
conditional norms 220
conditional proposition 75
conditionalization 103, 111, 137, 158, 159
conference 95
confidence 94, 95, 101, 104, 191, 208
conflict: problem of 231n38
conjunction 228n15
conscious states 40n3
consciousness 43n6, 45n9
consequences 14n14, 122, 276, 294; of beliefs 194; morally relevant 261
consequent 78, 220; affirming 74
consequentialism 18, 41n3
conservatism 153n5, 203
consideration 149
consistency: internal 10
consolidate additional benefits view 31
constancy 112, 121
constraints 195, 208, 210, 221
constructivism 240, 241
contradictions 71, 184, 188
contraposed instrumental requirement 84–5
contraposed *modus ponens* permission 81
contraposition 78, 81
control: voluntary 192
conversion scale 44n7
convex set 263n9
correctness 74–5, 82–3
corruption 93
creature construction 130n30
credence 133, 185–6, 190, 207; adopting new 210; constraints 221; defining 208; degrees of 239; downloader 198, 201; estimating 244, 245, 246; functions 200, 241, 244; imprecise 178n2; maintaining 216–17; normative constraints on 208, 210; posterior 221; prior 221; rational agents' 203n1; and utilities 255, 281, 282
credibility 152n3
crutch 101
cumulative prospect theory 300n2
curse 278, 297, 299

D'Agostino, M. 248
daydream 53

days 33
de Finetti, B. de 242
death 34, 35, 261
decision-makers 267
decisions 88, 148, 300n7; going back on 269; grand world 268, 297; interpersonal 301n11; past 4; problems 239–40, 272; rules 199; simplifying 297, 298, 299; small world 268, 297; wise 134
decompositional approach 49, 52, 63
deductive closure 184
deductive logic 162
deductive-nomological model 174
default authority 103
defeasibility 161; clause 141
delay 46n11
deliberating 90, 98, 103, 119, 293
delusions 195
demand 211
density 210
deontic logic 219–20, 230n24
deontic theory 188, 193–4
dependence 133
descendants 42n5
description 55, 56; form of 59–62
determining 159
diachronic challenge 267, 269
diachronic choice behavior 282
diachronic coherence 184
diachronic dominance 296, 299
diachronic evidentialism 186, 202
diachronic rationality 185
diachronicity 188–9
dialetheist 71
difference supervenience 248
disadvantage 163
disappointment 35
disbelief 186
discarding 189–90, 195
discretion 88
disperse additional burdens view 31
distance 18, 243, 288; measure 247
distortion 93, 106n7
distribution 19, 28, 31, 36, 39
distributive principles 32
disutility 32
doing 63
dominance 26, **29**; arguments 289; principle 246, 247
dominated strategy 267, 272, 274–6, 290, 291
doubt 143, 144, 147
doxastic deliberation 90, 103
doxastic downloader 198, 200

305

INDEX

doxastic self-control 99
drugs 96
duplicates: perfect 168
duration 58
Dutch book argument 159, 163
dying out 22

echolocation 122, 124
Eddington, Sir A. 122–3
effects: long-term 15
efficacy 61
electric current 3
emeralds 162–3, 173, 178n8, 180n20
emotions 96
empiricism 167
emptiness 36
empty 44n7, 45n9
endpoints 13n13
ends 60, 61, 64, 71, 72, 260; intending 81; ultimate 260–2
energy 95
English 225
epistemic ideality 193–4
epistemic misfortune 191
epistemic states 100
epistemic utility theory 188, 197, 199–200
equilibrium 294
error theory 239
errors 91, 102, 287, 289
estimates 241–6, 262, 287–9; badness of 247–50; expectational 244, 245, 246; important 289
estimation error 289
evaluations 118
events 287, 298, 299
everyone 28
evidence 89, 90, 93, 207; acquiring 133; assessing 94, 102; constant 112; continuous 217, 219; credence-dependent 217, 218–19; cumulative 103, 216, 229n16; forgotten 152; initial 150; insignificant 151; judging 113, 114; and knowledge 133, 134; misleading 147, 151; new 101, 105; partition 218, 229n19; perceptual 133; principle 227n8; receiving 210; testimonial 96; time of 210–15, 223; transmission of 136, 137; uncertain 209
evidential probability 142
evidential standards 156; *a posteriori* 159; privileged 170
evidential support 177n1; relations 162–3, 164, 166

evidentialism 114, 133–5, 149; diachronic 202
examples 30, 62–4
executive virtue 126
existing again 34
expectations 242, 246, 262
experiences 34, 35
experiment 201
experimentation 3
explanation 61, 111
explanationism 171–7
explanatoriness 117
explanatory goodness 175
explanatory priority 134
explanatory standards 174–7
exploitation: financial 269
exploration 16–17
expressivism 175
extended choice situation 290
extended-form decision problems 272
extensional adequacy 123, 125, 130n33
extensionality 248
extentional adequacy 116
external attitudes 240
external world 170–1, 172, 188
externalism 152, 203
extinction 34
extremes 159
eyes-on asymmetry 124, 125

factors: formal 162; objective 159
facts: *a priori* 160; about evidential support 177n1; about naturalness 166; empirical 166; external world 188; fundamental 160; internal 185; non-historical 127n5, 127n6; non-relative 156; past 187; precise 157; qualitative 249; quantitative 249; stable 277
fallacy 65n1
fantastic results 7, 9, 10
fear 34, 35
Fermat's Little Theorem 144
Ferrero, L. 119
Fields, H. 160
filling 43n6
final value theory 188
finality 34
fine-grained outcomes 278, 283, 286
first person 63; perspective 91, 93, 97–100
flip-flops 124, 130n29
flu 83
Foley, R. 98
following 76

INDEX

forever 34
forgetting 103, 105, 119–20, 146–7, 151, 189, 191
form 55, 162
formal category 55
formal epistemology 194
formal factors 162
freedom 44n7
friend 218
frogurt 278, 297, 298, 299
fundamental rational requirements 230n28
future 18, 19, 42n5, 97, 290, 293

galaxies 19–20
gambles 246, 296
gaps 43n5
generative theory 136
genus 66n9
global accounts 115, 128n15, 128n20
global approaches 117
global theory 280
God 24
Goldbach Conjecture 83
good: dependent 252; future 18; of life 35; total 28
good life 27
Goodman, N. 162–4, 173, 177
goodness 33; limited 37; of outcomes 38
grounding 127n5
groups 36, 295
grue paradox 162–4, 173, 177, 180n19
guarantee 246
gullibility 136

habits 76
happenings 58, 59; mere 50
Harman, G. 147
head 43n6
headache 145
Hedden, B. 156–83, 300n10
Hell 25, 46n11
here 18
hereafter 18
hike 268
Holton, R. 148
hopes 42n5
how 60, 61
human beings 40n2
Humean skepticism 171
hybrid theory 18
hypothesis 157

ice cream 44n7
ideal performance norms 214, 227n11

ideal rational agent 202
ideal system 169
ideality: epistemic 193–4
ideals 42n5
identity 47n13, 115–16, 128n14
ignorance 270, 271, **292**, 294
illusions 93, 99
immodesty 161, 166
imperative 76
imperfection 194
impersonal neutralist view 27–8
imprecision 178n2
incentivizing 293
inconsistency 213, 275
indefeasibility 181n23
independence 168
indicator quantity 244
indirect theory 142–5
induction 171; backward 290, 294; enumerative 172, 174
inductive logic 162, 163
inductive methods 161, 166
inductive virtue 175, 176
inertia 102
inevitability 50
inference 160, 171, 172, 174
infinity 19, 24, 25, 30
influences: non-evidential 94
informal epistemology 193
information 12n3; accepting 291; avoiding 269; chance 190; gaining 197–9; gatherer 197, 205n17; good 275; lifelong retention of 193; losing 195; loss 196, 197–202; on memory 143; misleading 275; new 72; sensory 218; value of 277
informational tradeoff 198–9, 200–2
inner mental states 54
inquiry 148, 149
insecurity 95
insignificance 35
instrumental permission 83
instrumental rationality 289
instrumental reasoning 260
instrumental requirements 72, 74, 78, 84–5
intelligence 53
intention 76, 77, 115
interests 17
interior state 53
internal attitudes 240
internalism 102, 103, 152, 185, 187, 189, 203; access 161; mentalist 161; time-slice 187
interpersonal problem 295, 296

interruption 58
interval conditionalization 219, 220, 225, 226
interval updating 204n7, 215–19
intervals: arbitrary 216
intransitivity 12n5
intrapersonal problem 295, 296
intrapersonal situations 301n11
intuitions 17, 83
investigations: external 123
irrational states 70
irrationality 91, 111, 134, 146, 157, 189–90, 194, 274–6; external 294; internal 293

Jeffrey Conditionalization 209, 217–19, 229n19
Jenkins, C. 165
judgments 30, 53; corruption of 93, 95; future 98; of outcomes 32; past 92, 93, 98, 100
justifications 160; default 160, 161

Kagan, S. 45n9
Kamm, F. 34
Kelly, T. 127n5
kinesis 55, 57, 58
knowing 52
knowledge: background 174; of beliefs 90; losing 191; practical 54, 62; sweet 271, **292**, 294
Kolodny, N. 231n38
Korsgaard, C.M. 115
Kratzer, A. 230n24
Kripke, S. 76

language dependence 160–4, 166
Lasonen-Aarnio, M. 135, 151
laundering 145–50
Lavin, D. 49–69
lawlike statement 174
learning 152n3
Lewis, D. 133, 165, 168
liberal norm 202
life 22; agonizing 23; bad 27; conscious 45n10; entry into 46n11; eternal 35; good 27; goods of 35; high-quality 36, 38; quality of 20, 21, 23, 31; shape of 30
lifespan 34
light 79
limbo man 34–6
limits 37
linguistics 230n24
litter 115, 120

local problems 115, 117, 128n15, 128n20
location 18, 40n1
logical consequences 162
logical form 208, 225, 226
London 78, 79, 80
lotteries 274, 276–7, 280
luminosity 106n4

MacIntosh, D. 13n9
McMahan, J. 42n5
maintaining 102
mammals 73, 79
marked contents 77
Marmite 140
mass 170
masses 32
matchbox 50, 51
mathematical argument 242
maximizing epistemology 195
me 18
Meacham, C. 204, 207–37
meanings 71, 72
means 60, 61, 71, 72, 260; intending 81–2
measurement 199, 243, 247–50, 288
medical device 3
memory 64, 97, 99, 102, 107n15, 107n16; loss 119, 120
men 162
mental architecture 121
mental processes 70
mental state theorist 40n3
mental states 54, 70, 121, 127n5, 187
mentalist internalism 161, 187
mere happening 50
mere movements 50–1
metaphysics 19, 227n13
methodological constraint 55
methodological principles 181n23
mind 52–3, 54; and action 52–3; fallible 91; making up 114, 127n11
mind-changing 110, 118, 124, 149
minimal supervenience base 167–8, 180n1
misery 23, 24
misfortune 191
misleading 147, 151, 275
mistakes 146, 147
mnemonic knowledge 145, 151
mnemonic processes 151
mnemonic seemings 139, 146
modal base 232n43, 232n44
modal logic 219
moderation 159

INDEX

modus ponens: requirement 72, 73, 75; rule 77
money 252
money pump argument 12n3
moral ideals 37–9
moral reasons 163
moral relevance 261
mosquito bites 32
Moss, S. 119
mountains 138, 140
movements 50–1, 54, 64; temporality of 56–9
multiple evidence cases 213
multiset 263n6

Nagel, T. 46n11
naive choice 273, 276, 290
narrow scope norms 220–5, 230n28
natural preferences 3
naturalness 164–71, 179n11
nature: laws of 168–9
nearness 18
necessity operators 219–20
network 87
neutralist theory 17
new evil demon problem 152
Newton, I. 175
no dilemmas principle 148
nonsense 165
normative constraints 208, 210
normative force 163–4
normative theories 188–9
normativity: problem of 231n38
norms 119, 220–5, 230n28, 230n30, 231n38; Bayesian 214; conditional 220; ideal performance 214, 227n11; narrow scope 220–5, 230n28, 230n30, 231n38; synchronic 196; wide scope 220–5, 230n28, 230n30, 231n38
noun phrases 66n11
nouns 66n11
now 18

object 55
objective factors 159
objective perspectives 46n11
objective value 196–7
objectivism 178n5
objects 43n6
obligation operators 219–20, 229
obligations 222
oblique cognition 108n19
observation 56, 63, 173, 180n20, 259
omniscience 195

options 10, 300n7; dominated 272; ordering 247; swapping 8
order 61
order-reversing swap 248, 249
ordinal realism 286
ought implies can 191–3, 211, 212, 222
oughts: trivial 222–3
outcome-act pairs 255, 256, 260, 283
outcomes 239; better 39; coarse-grained 283; desiring 240; distinct 284; fine-grained 278, 283, 286; goodness of 38; judging 32; probability of 282; ranking 285; true 260, 262; and utilities 251, 255; valuing 39, 240, 257; worse 39
outer worldly happenings 54
over-riding 150–1
overall value theory 188, 194–6

pain 3
Paineau, D. 6–7
Parfit, D. 17–18
particular 63
passive reasoning 73
passivity 87, 92
past 19, 57, 100; beliefs about 92; honoring 293; immutable 223; perspectives 96, 102
path 138
Paul, S.K. 87–109
Peano's Axioms 83
penalties 293
perceptions 170
perfect tournament chess play 214
perfective thought 67n12
performance 214, 227n11
permanence 34
permission operators 219–20
permissions 80–2, 83, 195, 276
permissiveness 128n12
permissivism 118, 123, 157, 178n3; and uniqueness 158–9
person-affecting views 33, 47n16
personal dominance principle 26
perspectives: neutral 275; past 96, 102
Pettigrew, R. 238–66, 282, 283–9
phases 59, 63
PhD 106
phenomenology 133
phlogiston theory 180n17
physical properties 167
physics 41n3, 167, 168
planes 150
plans 72
platypuses 73, 79
pleasure 44n7

pluralism 164
point of view 56
poison 60
policies 105
politics 104
population increase 22
possibility 34, 89, 227n13, 244; operators 219–20
potential 34
predicates 57; special 179n10
preferences 291; and choice 272–4; and combination 241; inconsistent 274; ordering 241, 262, 286; ranking 272; reversals 274; risk-sensitive 241; strategy 294; and values 286
premise 75; attitudes 74
prescriptions 118, 125; inconsistent 213; symmetric 221, 224
present 18, 19, 57, 97, 146; reportative 66n12
present-aim theory 17
preservation 150
primitivism 112, 164
principal principle 214, 224
principle of total evidence 227n8
principles: ought-implies-can 191–3
prior probability function 158
probabilism 186, 208
probability 246, 287; axioms 126n2; functions 178n2, 180n18, 184
problems 279; local 115
procedural rational requirements 214
processes 85; mental 70; mnemonic 151; reasoning 75, 84, 122, 130n33; reliabilism 203; subpersonal 73
production 19
progress 42n5, 58
prohibition 77–80
proliferation 259–60, 283, 285
properties: global 296; mutually independent 168; natural 164–71, 179n11, 180n11, 180n16; physical 167; ranking 195; scientific theoretical 170; special 179n10
propositions: confidence in 208; inevitable 222; justifying 160; obligatory 222; *a priori* 160; strongest 211; weaker 232n45
protons 179
pump 60
pure theory 17
purpose 61

quadratic distance measure 243, 288
qualifications 17

quality: life 31
quantity 243; expectations of 262
quarks 170
questions 49, 55, 111; closed 186; deliberating 90, 92; deliberative 98; learning answers to 201; truth 97

Raffman, D. 13n13
rain 75, 173, 268
raise 50
rational: ideally 190
rational agent 52; manual 129n22
rational belief requirements 214
rational breakdown 91
rational dilemma 148, 149
rational imperfection 194
rational pressures 113, 114
rational requirements 214, 220, 221, 230n28
rationality 193–4, 281; Bayesian 184, 207; constraints 186; diachronic 185, 187–8; ideal 193–4; instrumental 289; permission of 82; time-slice 189–97, 300n10
Rawls, J. 37
Raz, J. 89
re-description 283–7
real life case 147
realism 240, 241, 286
reality 168
reasonableness 135
reasoning: *a priori* 144; implicit 143; instrumental 160; means-end 260, 262
reasoning processes 75, 84, 122, 130n33
reasons 102, 129n24; for beliefs 92, 157; for conclusions 101; later 119, 120, 125; moral 163; self-sufficient 136; small 116; sufficient 41n3; theory of 112; weaker 89
reconsideration 116, 119, 124, 148
redeliberation 95, 101
redescription strategy 259–62
reference 165; magnetism 179n11; pairs 262
reflective equilibrium 37
regions 43n6
relational responses 3, 6–9
relations 9, 52
relativity 41n4, 122
relativizing 17, 18
reliability 136, 142, 143, 144, 147
religions 35
renormalizing 209
report 139

representation theorems 241, 259
repugnant conclusion 32, 37
requirements 71, 84, 214, 220, 230n28, 276
resolute choice 273, 276, 282, 290, 295
responses 110; appraisal 7; categorical 6–9; relational 6–9, 10
results 7, 9, 10
rewards 293
risk-sensitive behavior 252
risk-sensitive preferences 241
risk-weighted expected utility theory 239, 250–62, **253**, **254**
robot 205n17
rule-utilitarian theories 128n16

sacrifices 20, 22
San Francisco 116
satisficing epistemology 195
sceptic 148
scepticism 142
Scheffler, S. 42n5
Schwarz, W. 197
science 114, 167, 168, 175
scientific understanding 42n4
sea 138
second guessing 148
seemings 146
self 290, 293; current 98; earlier 145; future 290, 293; past 98
self-conception 97
self-consciousness 56, 61
self-governance 115–16
self-interest theory 18, 26
self-knowledge 106n5
self-manipulation 93, 95
self-sufficiency 136
sense perception 145
sensory information 218
sentences 162; form 162
sentient beings 23, 40n2
sentient life 22
separability 248
sequence 111; infinite 30
sequential conditionalization 219, 220, 224, 226
sequential updating 204n7, 215–19
series 8, 9; nested 60
sets: contiguous 299
settlement 121
Shah, N. 90
Shangri La case 137–42, **138**, **141**, 203n3
shape 30
shooting 261

Sidgwick, H. 18, 41n3
simplicity 169, 175, 176, 178n2, 181n21
simultaneity 23
Sinigaglia, C. 248
skill 107n15
sleep deprivation 96
snow 75
soccer cones 120, 125
sophisticated choice 273, 276, 282, 290, 293, 296
sorites case 13n13
source 52
space 19–26, 40n1
spatial dominance principle 26, **29**
species 66n9
spectrum 9, 12n5, 158
speeding ticket 192
stage setting 17–18
stakes 101
standpoints 63, 64, 105
states 92, 100, 121, 127n5, 157, 158; best 282; changing 178n2; collapsing 297; duration of 121; interior 53; internal 282; mental 70; occurrent 146; probabilities of 297; set of 239; time of 187; wise 134
steps: series of 8, 9
sticking 270, 290
stopping point 4, 6
strategy 300n8; preferences about 294; reasonable 4; sticking to 290
strategy pair 300n8
structure 51, 58
sub-acts 277, 280, 282, 296
sub-game perfect equilibrium 294, 295
sub-optimality 294
subject 57
subject-verb statements 52
subjective appraisals 7, 8
subjective factors 156
subjective perspective 46n11
subjective value 196–7
subjectivism 159
substantive factors 162
substantive rational requirements 214
suffering 45n10
sum: weighted 252
surfaces 6
suspended animation 25
swap 8, 248, 249
sweetener 270, 291
switching 270

INDEX

sychronic demands 126
symmetrical prescriptions 221
synchronic coherence 184
synchronic constraints 195
synchronic norms 158, 196
syntactic factors 162

taking 107n13
taste 7
tea puzzle 5
telic processes 67n16
Temkin, L. 14n17, 16–48
temporal dominance principle 26, **29**
temporally extended theory 132, 137, 142, 149, 152
temporally local theories 132, 137, 139, 142, 144
tense 57
terrible results 7, 9, 10
terror 35
testimony 96, 98, 135–7, 145, 152n1, 152n2
theoretical perspective 91
theoretical rationality 123
theory: hybrid 18; pure 17
there 18
third-person perspective 91, 100
Thoma, J. 43n6, 43n7
thoughts 43n6, 53
ticket 76
time 81, 95, 184; choice over 290–6
time intervals 215–19, 217, 226n6
Time of Obligation question 229n23
time-slice internalism 189
time-slice rationality 189–97
time-slice view 100, 113, 118, 178n5, 290, 293, 295
Titelbaum, M. 110–31, 159, 163, 179n10, 179n11
toast 140
topping 298, 299
torture 25, 32
toxin puzzle 148
tradeoffs 287
traffic laws 192
tragedy 22
train 79, 80
trampoline 227n12
transaction costs 12n3
transformation 52, 286
transmission 136, 137
transmissive theory 145
transmissivism 152
transparency 89–93, 105, 106n4
trust 142, 161

truth 88, 90–2; analytic 242; approximated 197; bearing relation to 107n12; and belief 90; distance from 199, 288; perceptions of 94; progressive 58; questions about 97; regulating for 99; standpoint on 105

underdetermination 88
unification 175, 176
unified account 117
uniqueness 108n23, 113–14, 118, 135, 157–9, 177, 191
universals 167
universe 19–26
update strategy 199–200
updating 197, 215–19; instant 228n13; rational 214–15; rules 204n7; as soon as possible 212–13
utilitarianism 17, 18, 19, 28, 40
utility 26, 240, 251, 282; assignment 283, 286; and credences 255, 281, 282; distributing 31; estimating 242; functions 241, 300n4; locus of 260–2; and outcomes 255; values 283, 286, 296

value: fixed 277; instrumental 289; objective epistemic 196–7; of outcomes 39; subjective epistemic 196–7; theories of 188, 194–6; of well-being 37
values: collapsing 297; and preferences 286; stable 277; true 288; utility 283, 286, 296
variable: random 243
Vegemite 7, 140
Venice 76, 77
verbs 51, 65n2
virtue: executive 126
visiting 77
visual experience 6–7

water: poisoned 60
Weatherson, B. 132–55, 165
Weisberg, J. 42n5
well-being 20, 28, 37, 38, 39; distribution of 39; total 31
White, R. 173
White Sox 132, 133, 147, 150
why 54–62
wide scope norms 220–5, 230n28
will 52, 87, 89–93
Williams, B. 91, 261
Williamson, T. 133, 134
willpower 104

INDEX

window 218
wisdom 134
wish 53
Wittgensteinian arithmetic 50–3
wood bed 148
world: external 171, 172, 188

worlds: best 219, 221, 222; possible 239, 240
worst-case scenario 282

yeast extract 7, 140
you 18, 63